P9-CIU-043

*the
gutenberg
galaxy*

the Gutenberg galaxy

**the
making
of
typographic
man**

by Marshall McLuhan

University of Toronto Press

Contents

The Gutenberg Galaxy develops a mosaic or field approach to its problems. Such a mosaic image of numerous data and quotations in evidence offers the only practical means of revealing causal operations in history.

The alternative procedure would be to offer a series of views of fixed relationships in pictorial space. Thus the galaxy or constellation of events upon which the present study concentrates is itself a mosaic of perpetually interacting forms that have undergone kaleidoscopic transformation— particularly in our own time.

With reference to the current transformation, the reader may find the end of the book, "The Galaxy Reconfigured," the best prologue.

Prologue

❋ The present volume is in many respects complementary to *The Singer of Tales* by Albert B. Lord. Professor Lord has continued the work of Milman Parry, whose Homeric studies had led him to consider how oral and written poetry naturally followed diverse patterns and functions. Convinced that the poems of Homer were oral compositions, Parry "set himself the task of proving incontrovertibly if it were possible, the oral character of the poems, and to that end he turned to the study of the Yugoslav epics." His study of these modern epics was, he explained, "to fix with exactness the *form* of oral story poetry. . . . Its method was to observe singers working in a thriving tradition of unlettered song and see how the form of their songs hangs upon their having to learn and practice their art without reading and writing."[1]

Professor Lord's book, like the studies of Milman Parry, is quite natural and appropriate to our electric age, as *The Gutenberg Galaxy* may help to explain. We are today as far into the electric age as the Elizabethans had advanced into the typographical and mechanical age. And we are experiencing the same confusions and indecisions which they had felt when living simultaneously in two contrasted forms of society and experience. Whereas the Elizabethans were poised between medieval corporate experience and modern individualism, we reverse their pattern by confronting an electric technology which would seem to render individualism obsolete and the corporate interdependence mandatory.

Patrick Cruttwell had devoted an entire study (*The Shakespearean Moment*) to the artistic strategies born of the Elizabethan experience of living in a divided world that was dissolving and resolving at the same time. We, too, live at such a moment of interplay of contrasted cultures, and *The Gutenberg Galaxy* is intended to trace the ways in which the *forms* of experience and of mental outlook and expression have been modified, first by the phonetic alphabet and then by printing. The enterprise which Milman Parry undertook with reference to the contrasted *forms* of oral and written poetry is here extended to the *forms* of thought and the organization of experience in society and politics. That such a study of the divergent nature of oral and written social organization has not been carried out by historians long ago is rather hard to explain. Perhaps the reason for the omission is simply that the job could only be done when the two conflicting forms of written and oral experience were once again co-existent as they are today. Professor Harry Levin indicates as much in his preface to Professor Lord's *The Singer of Tales* (p. xiii):

[1]Quoted in *The Singer of Tales*, p. 3.

1

The term "literature," presupposing the use of letters, assumes that verbal works of imagination are transmitted by means of writing and reading. The expression "oral literature" is obviously a contradiction in terms. Yet we live at a time when literacy itself has become so diluted that it can scarcely be invoked as an esthetic criterion. The Word as spoken or sung, together with a visual image of the speaker or singer, has meanwhile been regaining its hold through electrical engineering. A culture based upon the printed book, which has prevailed from the Renaissance until lately, has bequeathed to us—along with its immeasurable riches—snobberies which ought to be cast aside. We ought to take a fresh look at tradition, considered not as the inert acceptance of a fossilized corpus of themes and conventions, but as an organic habit of re-creating what has been received and is handed on.

The omission of historians to study the revolution in the *forms* of thought and social organization resulting from the phonetic alphabet has a parallel in socio-economic history. As early as 1864–67 Karl Rodbertus elaborated his theory of "Economic Life in Classical Antiquity." In *Trade and Market in the Early Empires* (p. 5), Harry Pearson describes his innovation as follows:

This remarkably modern view of the social function of money has not been sufficiently appreciated. Rodbertus realized that the transition from a "natural economy" to a "money economy" was not simply a technical matter, which resulted from a substitution of money purchase for barter. He insisted instead that a monetarized economy involved a social structure entirely different from that which went with an economy in kind. It was this change in the social structure accompanying the use of money rather than the technical fact of its use which ought to be emphasized, he thought. Had this point been expanded to include the varying social structures accompanying trading activity in the ancient world the controversy might have been resolved before it began.

In other words, had Rodbertus further explained that different forms of money and exchange structured societies in varying ways, generations of confused controversy might have been avoided. The matter was finally explained when Karl Bucher approached the classical world not from our conventional mode of historical retrospect but from the primitive side. By starting with non-literate societies and moving toward the classical world, "he suggested that ancient economic life might better be understood if viewed from the perspective of primitive rather than modern society."[2]

Such a reverse perspective of the literate Western world is the one afforded to the reader of Albert Lord's *Singer of Tales*. But we also live in an electric or post-literate time when the jazz musician uses all the techniques of oral poetry. Empathic identification with all the oral modes is not difficult in our century.

[2]*Trade and Market in the Early Empires*, p. 5.

In the electronic age which succeeds the typographic and mechanical era of the past five hundred years, we encounter new shapes and structures of human interdependence and of expression which are "oral" in form even when the components of the situation may be non-verbal. This question is raised more fully in the concluding section of *The Gutenberg Galaxy*. It is not a difficult matter in itself, but it does call for some reorganization of imaginative life. Such a change of modes of awareness is always delayed by the persistence of older patterns of perception. The Elizabethans appear to our gaze as very medieval. Medieval man thought of himself as classical, just as we consider ourselves to be modern men. To our successors, however, we shall appear as utterly Renaissance in character, and quite unconscious of the major new factors which we have set in motion during the past one hundred and fifty years.

Far from being deterministic, however, the present study will, it is hoped, elucidate a principal factor in social change which may lead to a genuine increase of human autonomy. Peter Drucker writing on "The Technological Revolution" of our time in *Technology and Culture* (vol. II, no. 4, 1961, p. 348) states: "There is only one thing we do not know about the Technological Revolution—but it is essential: What happened to bring about the basic change in attitudes, beliefs, and values which released it? 'Scientific progress', I have tried to show, had little to do with it. But how responsible was the great change in world outlook which, a century earlier, had brought about the great Scientific Revolution?" *The Gutenberg Galaxy* at least attempts to supply the "one thing we do not know." But even so, there may well prove to be some other things!

The method employed throughout this study is directly related to what Claude Bernard presented in his classic introduction to *The Study of Experimental Medicine*. Observation, Bernard explains (pp. 8–9), consists in noting phenomena without disturbing them, but: "Experiment, according to the same physiologists, implies, on the contrary, the idea of a variation or disturbance that an investigator brings into the conditions of natural phenomena. . . . To do this, we suppress an organ in the living subject, by a section or ablation; and from the disturbance produced in the whole organism or in a special function, we deduce the function of the missing organ."

The work of Milman Parry and Professor Albert Lord was directed to observing the entire poetic process under oral conditions, and in contrasting that result with the poetic process which we under written conditions, assume as "normal." Parry and Lord, that is, studied the poetic organism when the auditory function was suppressed by literacy. They might also have considered the effect on the organism when the visual function of language was given extraordinary extension and power by literacy. And this is a factor in the experimental method which may have been overlooked just because it was inconvenient to manage. But given intense and exaggerated action, "the disturbance produced in the whole organism or in a special function" is equally observable.

Man the tool-making animal, whether in speech or in writing or in radio, has long been engaged in extending one or another of his sense organs in such a manner as to disturb all of his other senses and faculties. But having made these experiments, men have consistently omitted to follow them with observations.

J. Z. Young, writing on *Doubt and Certainty in Science*, notes (pp. 67–8):

The effect of stimulations, external or internal, is to break up the unison of action of some part or the whole of the brain. A speculative suggestion is that the disturbance in some way breaks the unity of the actual pattern that has been previously built up in the brain. The brain then selects those features from the input that tend to repair the model and to return the cells to their regular synchronous beating. I cannot pretend to be able to develop this idea of models in our brain in detail, but it has great possibilities in showing how we tend to fit ourselves to the world and the world to ourselves. In some way the brain initiates sequences of actions that tend to return it to its rhythmic pattern, this return being the act of consummation, or completion. If the first action performed fails to do this, fails that is to stop the original disturbance, then other sequences may be tried. The brain runs through its rules one after another, matching the input with its various models until somehow unison is achieved. This may perhaps only be after strenuous, varied, and prolonged searching. During this random activity further connexions and action patterns are formed and they in turn will determine future sequences.

The inevitable drive for "closure," "completion," or equilibrium occurs both with the suppression and the extension of human sense or function. Since *The Gutenberg Galaxy* is a series of historical observations of the new cultural completions ensuing upon the "disturbances," first of literacy, and then of printing, the statement of an anthropologist may assist the reader at this point:

Today man has developed extensions for practically everything he used to do with his body. The evolution of weapons begins with the teeth and the fist and ends with the atom bomb. Clothes and houses are extensions of man's biological temperature-control mechanisms. Furniture takes the place of squatting and sitting on the ground. Power tools, glasses, TV, telephones, and books which carry the voice across both time and space are examples of material extensions. Money is a way of extending and storing labor. Our transportation networks now do what we used to do with our feet and backs. In fact, all man-made material things can be treated as extensions of what man once did with his body or some specialized part of his body.[3]

[3]Edward T. Hall, *The Silent Language*, p. 79.

That outering or uttering of sense which is language and speech is a tool which "made it possible for man to accumulate experience and knowledge in a form that made easy transmission and maximum use possible."[4]

Language is metaphor in the sense that it not only stores but translates experience from one mode into another. Money is metaphor in the sense that it stores skill and labour and also translates one skill into another. But the principle of exchange and translation, or metaphor, is in our rational power to translate all of our senses into one another. This we do every instant of our lives. But the price we pay for special technological tools, whether the wheel or the alphabet or radio, is that these massive *extensions* of sense constitute *closed* systems. Our private senses are not closed systems but are endlessly translated into each other in that experience which we call con-sciousness. Our extended senses, tools, technologies, through the ages, have been closed systems incapable of interplay or collective awareness. Now, in the electric age, the very instantaneous nature of co-existence among our technological instruments has created a crisis quite new in human history. Our extended faculties and senses now constitute a single field of experience which demands that they become collectively conscious. Our technologies, like our private senses, now demand an interplay and ratio that makes *rational* co-existence possible. As long as our technologies were as slow as the wheel or the alphabet or money, the fact that they were separate, closed systems was socially and psychically supportable. This is not true now when sight and sound and movement are simultaneous and global in extent. A ratio of interplay among these extensions of our human functions is now as necessary collectively as it has always been for our private and personal rationality in terms of our private senses or "wits," as they were once called.

Hitherto historians of culture have tended to isolate technological events much in the way that classical physics dealt with physical events. Louis de Broglie, describing *The Revolution in Physics*, makes much of this limitation of the Cartesian and Newtonian procedures which are so near those of the historians using an individual "point of view" (p. 14):

Faithful to the Cartesian ideal, classical physics showed us the universe as being analogous to an immense mechanism which was capable of being described with complete precision by the localization of its parts in space and by their change in the course of time. . . . But such a conception rested on several implicit hypotheses which were admitted almost without our being aware of them. One of these hypotheses was that the framework of space and time in which we seek almost instinctively to localize all of our sensations is a perfectly rigid and fixed framework where each physical event can, in principle, be rigorously localized independently of all the dynamic processes which are going on around it.

[4]Leslie A. White, *The Science of Culture*, p. 240.

5

We shall see how not only Cartesian but Euclidean perceptions are constituted by the phonetic alphabet. And the revolution that de Broglie describes is a derivative not of the alphabet but of the telegraph and of radio. J. Ż. Young, a biologist, makes the same point as de Broglie. Having explained that electricity is not a thing that "flows" but is "the condition we observe when there are certain spatial relations between things," he explains (p. 111):

Something similar has happened as physicists have devised ways of measuring very small distances. It has been found no longer possible to use the old model of supposing that what was being done was to divide up something called matter into a series of bits, each with definite properties called size, weight, or position. Physicists do not now say that matter 'is made' of bodies called atoms, protons, electrons, and so on. What they have done is to give up the materialist method of describing their observations in terms of something made as by a human process of manufacture, like a cake. The word atom or electron is not used as the name of a piece. It is used as part of the description of the observations of physicists. It has no meaning except as used by people who know the experiments by which it is revealed.

And, he adds, "it is important to realize that great changes in ways of *ordinary* human speaking and acting are bound up with the adoption of new instruments."

Had we meditated on such a basic fact as that long ago, we might easily have mastered the nature and effects of all our technologies, instead of being pushed around by them. At any rate, *The Gutenberg Galaxy* is a prolonged meditation on that theme of J. Z. Young.

Nobody has been more conscious of the futility of our closed systems of historical writing than Abbot Payson Usher. His classic, *A History of Mechanical Inventions*, is an explanation of why such closed systems cannot make contact with the facts of historical change: "The cultures of antiquity do not fit the patterns of the linear sequences of social and economic evolution developed by the German Historical Schools. . . . If linear concepts of development are abandoned and the development of civilization is viewed frankly as a multilinear process much can be done toward the understanding of the history of Western culture as a progressive integration of many separate elements." (pp. 30–1)

A historical "point of view" is a kind of closed system that is closely related to typography, and flourishes where the unconscious effects of literacy flourish without countervailing cultural forces. Alexis de Tocqueville, whose literacy was much modified by his oral culture, seems to us now to have had a kind of clairvoyance concerning the patterns of change in the France and America of his time. He did not have a point of view, a fixed position from which he filled in a visual perspective of events. Rather he sought the operative dynamic in his data:

But if I go further and seek among these characteristics the principal one, which includes almost all the rest, I discover that in most of the operations of the mind each American appeals only to the individual effort of his own understanding.

America is therefore one of the countries where the precepts of Descartes are least studied and are best applied. . . . Everyone shuts himself tightly up within himself and insists upon judging the world from there.[5]

His skill in creating interplay between the written and oral modes of perceptual structure enabled de Tocqueville to achieve "scientific" insights into psychology and politics. By this interplay of two modes of perception he achieved prophetic understanding while other observers were merely expressing their private viewpoints. De Tocqueville knew well that typographic literacy had not only produced the Cartesian outlook but also the special traits of American psychology and politics. By his method of interplay among divergent perceptual modes, de Tocqueville was able to react to his world, not in sections but as a whole, and as to an open *field*. And such is the method which A. P. Usher notes has been absent from the study of cultural history and change. De Tocqueville had employed a procedure such as J. Z. Young describes (p. 77): "It may be that a great part of the secret of the brain's powers is the enormous opportunity provided for interaction between the effects of stimulating each part of the receiving fields. It is this provision of interacting-places or mixing-places that allows us to react to the world *as a whole* to much greater degree than other animals can do." But our technologies are by no means uniformly favourable to this organic function of interplay and of interdependence. To investigate this question with respect to alphabetic and typographic culture is the task of the present book. And it is today a quest which cannot but be undertaken in the light of new technologies which deeply affect the traditional operation and achieved values of alphabetic literacy and typographic culture.

There is a recent work that seems to me to release me from the onus of mere eccentricity and novelty in the present study. It is *The Open Society and Its Enemies* by Karl R. Popper, a work devoted to the study of aspects of detribalization in the ancient world and of retribalization in the modern world. For the "open society" was effected by phonetic literacy, as will shortly appear, and is now threatened with eradication by electric media, as will be discussed in the conclusion of this study. Needless to say, the "is," rather than the "ought," of all these developments, is alone being discussed. Diagnosis and description must precede valuation and therapy. To substitute moral valuation for diagnosis is a natural and common enough procedure, but not necessarily a fruitful one.

Karl Popper devotes the first part of his large study to the detribalization

[5]*Democracy in America*, part II, book I, chap. I.

7

of ancient Greece and the reaction to it. But neither in Greece nor in the modern world does he give any consideration to the dynamics of our technologically extended senses as factors either in the opening or closing of societies. His descriptions and analyses follow an economic and political point of view. The passage below is especially relevant to *The Gutenberg Galaxy* because it begins with the interplay of cultures *via* commerce and ends with the dissolution of the tribal state, even as it is dramatized by Shakespeare in *King Lear*.

It is Popper's view that tribal or closed societies have a biological unity and that "our modern open societies function largely by way of abstract relations, such as exchange or co-operation." That the abstracting or opening of closed societies is the work of the phonetic alphabet, and not of any other form of writing or technology, is one theme of *The Gutenberg Galaxy*. On the other hand, that closed societies are the product of speech, drum, and ear technologies, brings us at the opening of the electronic age to the sealing of the entire human family into a single global tribe. And this electronic revolution is only less confusing for men of the open societies than the revolution of phonetic literacy which stripped and streamlined the old tribal or closed societies. Popper offers no analysis of the causes of such change, but he does give (p. 172) a description of the situation that is very relevant to *The Gutenberg Galaxy*:

By the sixth century B.C., this development had led to the partial dissolution of the old ways of life, and even to a series of political revolutions and reactions. And it had led not only to attempts to retain and to arrest tribalism by force, as in Sparta, but also to that great spiritual revolution, the invention of critical discussion, and in consequence of thought that was free from magical obsessions. At the same time we find the first symptoms of a new uneasiness. *The strain of civilization was beginning to be felt.*

This strain, this uneasiness, is a consequence of the breakdown of the closed society. It is still felt even in our day, especially in times of social change. It is the strain created by the effort which life in an open and partially abstract society continually demands from us—by the endeavor to be rational, to forego at least some of our emotional social needs, to look after ourselves, and to accept responsibilities. We must, I believe, bear this strain as the price to be paid for every increase in knowledge, in reasonableness, in co-operation and in mutual help, and consequently in our chances of survival, and in the size of the population. It is the price we have to pay for being human.

The strain is most closely related to the problem of the tension between the classes which is raised for the first time by the breakdown of the closed society. The closed society itself does not know this problem. At least to its ruling members, slavery, caste, and class rule are 'natural' in the sense of being unquestionable. But with the breakdown of the closed society, this certainty disappears, and with it all feeling of security. The tribal community (and later the 'city') is the place of security for the member of the tribe. Surrounded by enemies and by dangerous or even hostile magical forces, he experiences the tribal community as a child experiences his family and his home, in which he plays his definite part; a part he knows well, and plays well. The breakdown of the closed society, raising as it does the problem of class and other problems of social status, must have had the same effect upon the citizens as a serious family quarrel and the breaking up of the family home is liable to have on children. Of course, this kind of strain was felt by the privileged classes, now that they were threatened, more strongly than by those who had formerly been suppressed; but even the latter felt uneasy. They also were frightened by the breakdown of their 'natural' world. And though they continued to fight their struggle, they were often reluctant to exploit their victories over their class enemies who were supported by tradition, the *status quo*, a higher level of education, and a feeling of natural authority.

These observations lead us straight on to a consideration of *King Lear* and the great family quarrel in which the sixteenth century found itself involved early in the Gutenberg Era.

The Gutenberg Galaxy

✻ When King Lear proposes "our darker purpose" as the subdivision of his kingdom, he is expressing a politically daring and *avant-garde* intent for the early seventeenth century:

> Only we still retain
> The name, and all th' additions to a king. The sway,
> Revenue, execution of the rest,
> Beloved sons, be yours; which to confirm,
> This coronet part betwixt you.[1]

Lear is proposing an extremely modern idea of delegation of authority from centre to margins. His "darker purpose" would have been recognized at once as left-wing Machiavellianism by an Elizabethan audience. The new patterns of power and organization which had been discussed during the preceding century were now, in the early seventeenth century, being felt at all levels of social and private life. *King Lear* is a presentation of the new strategy of culture and power as it affects the state, the family, and the individual psyche:

> Meantime we shall express our darker purpose.
> Give me the map there. Know we have divided
> In three our kingdom;

The map was also a novelty in the sixteenth century, age of Mercator's projection, and was key to the new vision of peripheries of power and wealth. Columbus had been a cartographer before he was a navigator; and the discovery that it was possible to continue in a straight-line course, as if space were uniform and continuous, was a major shift in human awareness in the Renaissance. More important, the map brings forward at once a principal theme of King Lear, namely the isolation of the visual sense as a kind of blindness.

It is in the first scene of the play that Lear expresses his "darker purpose," using the Machiavellian cant term. Earlier in the first scene the darkness of Nature, as it were, is shown in the boasting of Gloucester about the illegitimacy of his handsome love-child Edmund: "But I have, sir, a son by order of law, some year older than this, who is yet no dearer in my account." The gaiety with which Gloucester alludes to the begetting of Edmund is later alluded to by Edgar:

---

[1] *The Complete Works of Shakespeare*, ed. G. L. Kittredge. All quotations from *King Lear*, unless otherwise noted, are from Act I, scene i. Kittredge's edition is cited throughout.

> The dark and vicious place where thee he got
> Cost him his eyes. (V, iii)

Edmund, the love-child, opens the second scene of the play with:

> Thou, Nature, art my goddess; to thy law
> My services are bound. Wherefore should I
> Stand in the plague of custom, and permit
> The curiosity of nations to deprive me,
> For that I am some twelve or fourteen moonshines
> Lag of a brother?

Edmund has *l'esprit de quantité* so essential to tactile measurement and to the impersonality of the empirical mind. Edmund is presented as a force of nature, eccentric to mere human experience and "the curiosity of nations." He is a prime agent in the fragmentation of human institutions. But the great fragmenter is Lear himself, with his inspired idea of setting up a constitutional monarchy by means of delegating by authority. His plan for himself is that he become a specialist:

> Only we still retain
> The name, and all th' additions to a King.

Following his specialist cue, Goneril and Regan leap into the act of filial devotion with specialist and competitive intensity. It is Lear who fragments them by insisting on a divisive eulogistic competition:

> Tell me, my daughters
> (Since now we will divest us, both of rule,
> Interest of territory, cares of state),
> Which of you shall we say doth love us most?
> That we our largest bounty may extend
> Where nature doth with merit challenge. Goneril
> Our eldest-born, speak first.

Competitive individualism had become the scandal of a society long invested with corporate and collective values. The role played by print in instituting new patterns of culture is not unfamiliar. But one natural consequence of the specializing action of the new forms of knowledge was that all kinds of power took on a strongly centralist character. Whereas the role of the feudal monarch had been inclusive, the king actually including in himself all his subjects, the Renaissance prince tended to become an exclusive power centre surrounded by his individual subjects. And the result of such centralism, itself dependent on many new developments in roads and commerce, was the habit of delegation of powers and the specializing of many functions in separate areas and individuals. In *King Lear*, as in other plays, Shakespeare shows an utter clairvoyance concerning the social and personal consequences of denudation and stripping of attributes and functions for the sake of speed, precision, and increased power. His insights appear so richly in his lines that it is very difficult to select among them. But with the very opening words of Goneril's aria we are deep in them:

> I love you more than words can wield the matter;
> Dearer than eyesight, space, and liberty:

The stripping of the very human senses themselves will be one of the themes of this play. The separation of sight from the other senses has already been stressed in Lear's expression of his "darker purpose" and his resort to the mere visual map. But whereas Goneril is ready to strip off sight as an expression of devotion, Regan rallies to her challenge with:

> . . . I profess
> Myself an enemy to all other joys
> Which the most precious square of sense professes, . . .

Regan will strip off all the human senses so long as she possesses Lear's love.

The allusion to "the most precious square of sense" shows Shakespeare doing an almost scholastic demonstration of the need for a ratio and interplay among the senses as the very constitution of rationality. His theme in Lear is that of John Donne in *An Anatomy of the World*:

> 'Tis all in pieces, all coherence gone;
> All just supply, and all Relation:
> Prince, subject, Father, Son, are things forgot,
> For every man alone things he hath got
> To be a Phoenix . . .

The breaking of "the most precious square of sense" means the isolation of one sense from another by separate intensities with the ensuing irrationality and clash among wits and persons and functions. This breaking of the ratios among wits (or senses) and persons and functions is the theme of the later Shakespeare.

As Cordelia observes the flash agility of those specialists in filial piety, Goneril and Regan, she says:

> . . . I am sure my love's
> More richer than my tongue.

Her rational fulness is as nothing to the specialism of her sisters. She has no fixed point of view from which she can launch bolts of eloquence. Her sisters are cued for particular occasions, streamlined by fragmentation of sense and motive for exact calculation. They are like Lear, *avant-garde* Machiavels, able to deal explicitly and scientifically with occasions. They are resolute and consciously liberated not only from the square of sense but from its moral analogate, "conscience." For that ratio among motives "does make cowards of us all." And Cordelia is a coward hindered from specialist action by the complexities of her conscience, her reason, and her role.

13

King Lear is a working model of the process of denudation by which men translated themselves from a world of roles to a world of jobs.

✳ *King Lear* is a kind of elaborate case history of people translating themselves out of a world of roles into the new world of jobs. This is a process of stripping and denudation which does not occur instantly except in artistic vision. But Shakespeare saw that it had happened in his time. He was not talking about the future. However, the older world of roles had lingered on as a ghost just as after a century of electricity the West still feels the presence of the older values of literacy and privacy and separateness.

Kent, Edgar, and Cordelia are "out of phase" in the language of W. B. Yeats. They are "feudal" in their total loyalty which they consider merely natural to their *roles*. In role they exercise no delegated authority or powers. They are autonomous centres. As Georges Poulet in his *Studies in Human Time* points out (p. 7): "For the man of the Middle Ages, then, there was not one duration only. There were *durations*, ranked one above another, and not only in the universality of the exterior world but within himself, in his own nature, in his own human existence." The easy habit of configuration which had lasted through several centuries yields with the Renaissance to continuous, lineal, and uniform sequences for time and space and personal relationships alike. And the analogous world of roles and ratios is suddenly succeeded by a new lineal world, as in *Troilus and Cressida* (III, iii):

> Take the instant way;
> For honour travels in a strait so narrow
> Where one but goes abreast. Keep then the path,
> For emulation hath a thousand sons
> That one by one pursue. If you give way,
> Or hedge aside from the direct forthright,
> Like to an ent'red tide, they all rush by,
> And leave you hindmost;

The idea of homogeneous segmentation of persons and relations and functions could only appear to the sixteenth century as the dissolution of all bonds of sense and reason. *King Lear* offers a complete demonstration of how it felt to live through the change from medieval to Renaissance time and space, from an inclusive to an exclusive sense of the world. His changed attitude to

Cordelia exactly reflects the idea of the Reformers concerning fallen nature. Poulet says (p. 10):

For them, too, both man and nature were divinely animated. For them also there had been a time when nature and man had participated in the creative power.... But that time existed for them no longer. The time when nature was divine was now succeeded by the time of fallen nature; fallen by its own fault, by the free act in consequence of which it had separated itself from its origin, cut itself off from its source, denied God. And from that moment on, God had withdrawn from nature and from man.

Lear is quite explicit in designating Cordelia as a Puritan:

> Let pride, which she calls plainness, marry her.

The Reformers in their stress on individual function and independence naturally saw no point in all the formalities that belong to quite impersonal roles in society. It is clear to the audience, however, that it is rather Cordelia's dedication to her traditional role that makes her so helpless in the presence of the new individualism both of Lear and her sisters:

> I love your Majesty
> According to my bond; no more nor less.

She well knows that her devoted *role* adds up to "nothing" in terms of the new shrill and expansive individualism. Poulet describes (p. 9) this new world as "no longer anything more than an immense organism, a gigantic network of interchanges and reciprocal influences which was animated, which was guided interiorly in its cyclical development by a force everywhere the same and perpetually diversified, that could be called indiscriminately God, or Nature, or the Soul of the World, or Love."

The anguish of the third dimension is given its first verbal manifestation in poetic history in *King Lear*.

✱ Shakespeare seems to have missed due recognition for having in *King Lear* made the first, and so far as I know, the only piece of verbal three-dimensional perspective in any literature. It is not again until Milton's *Paradise Lost* (II, ll. 1-5) that a fixed visual point of view is deliberately provided for the reader:

15

> High on a Throne of Royal State, which far
> Outshon the wealth of *Ormus* and of *Ind*,
> Or where the gorgeous East with richest hand
> Showrs on her Kings *Barbaric* Pearl and Gold,
> Satan exalted sat, . . .

The arbitrary selection of a single static position creates a pictorial space with vanishing point. This space can be filled in bit by bit, and is quite different from non-pictorial space in which each thing simply resonates or modulates its own space in visually two-dimensional form.

Now the unique piece of three-dimensional verbal art which appears in King Lear is in Act IV, scene vi. Edgar is at pains to persuade the blinded Gloucester to believe the illusion that they are at the edge of a steep cliff:

> *Edgar.* . . . Hark, do you hear the sea?
> *Gloucester.*   No, truly.
> *Edgar.* Why then, your other senses grow imperfect
>   By your eyes' anguish. . . .
>   Come on, sir; here's the place. Stand still. How fearful
>   And dizzy 'tis to cast one's eyes so low!

The illusion of the third dimension is discussed at length in E. H. Gombrich's *Art and Illusion.* Far from being a normal mode of human vision, three-dimensional perspective is a conventionally acquired mode of seeing, as much acquired as is the means of recognizing the letters of the alphabet, or of following chronological narrative. That it was an acquired illusion Shakespeare helps us to see by his comments on the other senses in relation to sight. Gloucester is ripe for illusion because he has suddenly lost his sight. His power of visualization is now quite separate from his other senses. And it is the sense of sight in deliberate isolation from the other senses that confers on man the illusion of the third dimension, as Shakespeare makes explicit here. There is also the need to fix the gaze:

> Come on, sir; here's the place. Stand still. How fearful
> And dizzy 'tis to cast one's eyes so low!
> The crows and choughs that wing the midway air
> Show scarce so gross as beetles. Halfway down
> Hangs one that gathers sampire—dreadful trade!
> Methinks he seems no bigger than his head.
> The fishermen that walk upon the beach,
> Appear like mice; and yond tall anchoring bark,
> Diminish'd to her cock; her cock, a buoy
> Almost too small for sight. The murmuring surge,
> That on th' unnumb'red idle pebbles chafes,
> Cannot be heard so high. I'll look no more,
> Lest my brain turn, and the deficient sight
> Topple down headlong.

What Shakespeare does here is to place five flat panels of two-dimensions, one behind the other. By giving these flat panels a diagonal twist they succeed each other, as it were, in a perspective from the "stand still" point. He is utterly aware that the disposition to this kind of illusionism results from the separation of the senses. Milton learned to make the same kind of visual illusion after his blindness. And by 1709 Bishop Berkeley in his *New Theory of Vision* was denouncing the absurdity of Newtonian visual space as a mere abstract illusion severed from the sense of touch. The stripping of the senses and the interruption of their interplay in tactile synesthesia may well have been one of the effects of the Gutenberg technology. This process of separation and reduction of functions had certainly reached a critical point by the early seventeenth century when *King Lear* appeared. But to determine how far such a revolution in the human sense life could have proceeded from Gutenberg technology calls for a somewhat different approach from merely sampling the sensibility of a great play of the critical period.

King Lear is a kind of medieval sermon-exemplum or inductive reasoning to display the madness and misery of the new Renaissance life of action. Shakespeare explains minutely that the very principle of *action* is the splitting up of social operations and of the private sense life into specialized segments. The resulting frenzy to discover a new over-all interplay of forces ensures a furious activation of all components and persons affected by the new stress.

Cervantes had a similar awareness, and his *Don Quixote* is galvanized by the new form of the book as much as Machiavelli had been hypnotized by the special segment of experience that he had chosen to step up to the highest intensity of awareness. Machiavelli's abstraction of the entity of personal power from the social matrix was comparable to the much earlier abstraction of *wheel* from animal form. Such abstraction ensures a great deal more movement. But the Shakespeare-Cervantes vision is of the futility of such movement and of action deliberately framed on a fragmentary or specialist bias.

W. B. Yeats has an epigram which puts the themes of *King Lear* and *Don Quixote* in cryptic form:

> Locke sank into a swoon
> The garden died
> God took the spinning jenny
> Out of his side.

The Lockean swoon was the hypnotic trance induced by stepping up the visual component in experience until it filled the field of attention. Psychologists define hypnosis as the filling of the field of attention by one sense only. At such a moment "the garden" dies. That is, the garden indicates the interplay of all the senses in haptic harmony. With the instressed concern with one sense only, the mechanical principle of abstraction and repetition emerges

17

into explicit form. Technology is explicitness, as Lyman Bryson said. And explicitness means the spelling out of one thing at a time, one sense at a time, one mental or physical operation at a time. Since the object of the present book is to discern the origins and modes of the Gutenberg configuration of events, it will be well to consider the effects of the alphabet on native populations today. For as they *are* in relation to the phonetic alphabet, so we once *were*.

The interiorization of the technology of the phonetic alphabet translates man from the magical world of the ear to the neutral visual world.

✱ J. C. Carothers, writing in *Psychiatry* (November, 1959) on "Culture, Psychiatry and the Written Word," set forth a number of observations contrasting non-literate natives with literate natives, and the non-literate man with the Western man generally. He starts (p. 308) with the familiar fact that

by reason of the type of educational influences that impinge upon Africans in infancy and early childhood, and indeed throughout their lives, a man comes to regard himself as a rather insignificant part of a much larger organism—the family and the clan—and not as an independent, self-reliant unit; personal initiative and ambition are permitted little outlet; and a meaningful integration of a man's experience on individual, personal lines is not achieved. By contrast to the constriction at the intellectual level, great freedom is allowed for at the temperamental level, and a man is expected to live very much in the 'here and now,' to be highly extraverted, and to give very free expression to his feelings.

In a word, our notions of the "uninhibited" native ignore the utter inhibition and suppression of his mental and personal life which is unavoidable in a non-literate world:

Whereas the Western child is early introduced to building blocks, keys in locks, water taps, and a multiplicity of items and events which constrain him to think in terms of spatiotemporal relations and mechanical causation, the African child receives instead an education which depends much more exclusively on the spoken word and which is relatively highly charged with drama and emotion. (p. 308)

That is, a child in any Western milieu is surrounded by an abstract explicit visual technology of uniform time and uniform continuous space in which "cause" is efficient and sequential, and things move and happen on single planes and in successive order. But the African child lives in the implicit, magical world of the resonant oral word. He encounters not efficient causes but formal causes of configurational field such as any non-literate society cultivates. Carothers repeats again and again that "rural Africans live largely in a world of sound—a world loaded with direct personal significance for the hearer—whereas the Western European lives much more in a visual world which is on the whole indifferent to him." Since the ear world is a hot hyperesthetic world and the eye world is relatively a cool, neutral world, the Westerner appears to people of ear culture to be a very cold fish indeed.[2]

Carothers reviews the familiar non-literate idea of the "power" of words where thought and behaviour depend upon the magical resonance in words and their power to impose their assumptions relentlessly. He cites Kenyatta concerning love magic among the Kikuyu:

It is very important to acquire the correct use of magical words and their
proper intonations, for the progress in applying magic effectively depends
on uttering these words in their ritual order. . . . In performing these acts
of love magic the performer has to recite a magical formula. . . . After this
recitation he calls the name of the girl loudly and starts to address her
as though she were listening. (p. 309)

It is a matter of "rite words in rote order," as Joyce put it. But once more any Western child today grows up in this kind of magical repetitive world as he hears advertisements on radio and TV.

Carothers next asks (p. 310) how literacy in a society might operate to effect the change from the notion of words as resonant, live, active, natural forces to the notion of words as "meaning" or "significance" for minds:

I suggest that it was only when the written, and still more the printed, word
appeared on the scene that the stage was set for words to lose their magic
powers and vulnerabilities. Why so?
I developed the theme in an earlier article with reference to Africa, that
the nonliterate rural population lives largely in a world of sound, in contrast
to western Europeans who live largely in a world of vision. Sounds are in a
sense dynamic things, or at least are always indicators of dynamic things—
of movements, events, activities, for which man, when largely unprotected
from the hazards of life in the bush or the veldt, must be ever on the
alert. . . . Sounds lose much of this significance in western Europe, where
man often develops, and must develop, a remarkable ability to disregard
them. Whereas for Europeans, in general, "seeing is believing," for rural
Africans reality seems to reside far more in what is heard and what is said.

[2]See chapter on "Acoustic Space" by E. Carpenter and H. M. McLuhan in *Explorations in Communication*, pp. 65–70.

19

. . . Indeed, one is constrained to believe that the eye is regarded by many Africans less as a receiving organ than as an instrument of the will, the ear being the main receiving organ.

Carothers reiterates that the Westerner depends on a high degree of visual shaping of spatio-temporal relations without which it is impossible to have the mechanistic sense of causal relations so necessary to the order of our lives. But the quite different assumptions of native perceptual life have led him to ask (p. 311) what has been the possible role of written words in shifting habits of perception from the auditory to visual stress:

When words are written, they become, of course, a part of the visual world. Like most of the elements of the visual world, they become static things and lose, as such, the dynamism which is so characteristic of the auditory world in general, and of the spoken word in particular. They lose much of the personal element, in the sense that the heard word is most commonly directed at oneself, whereas the seen word most commonly is not, and can be read or not as whim dictates. They lose those emotional overtones and emphases which have been described, for instance, by Monrad-Krohn. . . Thus, in general, words, by becoming visible, join a world of relative indifference to the viewer—a world from which the magic 'power' of the word has been abstracted.

Carothers continues his observations into the area of "free ideation" permitted to literate societies and quite out of the question for oral, non-literate communities:

The concept that verbal thought is separable from action, and is, or can be, ineffective and contained within the man . . . has important sociocultural implications, for it is only in societies which recognize that verbal thoughts can be so contained, and do not of their nature emerge on wings of power, that social constraints can, in theory at least, afford to ignore ideation. (p. 311)

Thus, in a society still so profoundly oral as Russia, where spying is done by ear and not by eye, at the memorable "purge" trials of the 1930's Westerners expressed bafflement that many confessed total guilt not because of what they had done but what they had thought. In a highly literate society, then, visual and behavioural conformity frees the individual for inner deviation. Not so in an oral society where inner verbalization is effective social action:

In these circumstances it is implicit that behavioural constraints *must* include constraint of thought. Since all behaviour in such societies is governed and conceived on highly social lines, and since directed thinking can hardly be other than personal and unique for each individual, it is furthermore implicit in the attitude of these societies that the very possibility of such thinking is hardly to be recognized. Therefore, if and when such thinking does occur, at other than strictly practical and utilitarian levels, it is apt to be seen as deriving from the devil or from other external evil influences, and as something to be feared and shunned as much in oneself as in others. (p. 312)

It is, perhaps, a little unexpected to hear the compulsive and rigid patterns of a deeply oral-aural community referred to as "governed and conceived on highly social lines." For nothing can exceed the automatism and rigidity of an oral, non-literate community in its non-personal collectivity. As Western literate communities encounter the various "primitive" or auditory communities still remaining in the world, great confusion occurs. Areas like China and India are still audile-tactile in the main. Such phonetic literacy as has penetrated there has altered very little. Even Russia is still profoundly oral in bias. Only gradually does literacy alter substructures of language and sensibility.

Alexander Inkeles in his book on *Public Opinion in Russia* (p. 137) gives a useful account of how the ordinary and unconscious bias, even of the Russian literate groups, has a direction quite counter to anything a long-literate community would consider "natural." The Russian attitude, like that of any oral society, reverses our stress:

In the United States and England it is the freedom of expression, the right itself in the abstract, that is valued. . . . In the Soviet Union, on the other hand, the *results* of exercising freedom are in the forefront of attention, and the preoccupation with the freedom itself is secondary. It is for this reason that the discussions between Soviet and Anglo-American representatives characteristically reach absolutely no agreement on specific proposals, although both sides assert that there should be freedom of the press. The American is usually talking about freedom of *expression*, the right to say or not to say certain things, a right which he claims exists in the United States and not in the Soviet Union. The Soviet representative is usually talking about *access* to the *means* of expression, not to the right to say things at all, and this access he maintains is denied to most in the United States and exists for most in the Soviet Union.

Soviet concern with media *results* is natural to any oral society where interdependence is the result of instant interplay of cause and effect in the total structure. Such is the character of a village, or, since electric media, such is also the character of global village. And it is the advertising and PR community that is most aware of this basic new dimension of global interdependence. Like the Soviet Union, they are concerned about *access* to the media and about *results*. They have no concern whatever about self-expression and would be shocked by any attempt to take over, say, a public advertisement for oil or coke as a vehicle of private opinion or personal feeling. In the same way the literate bureaucrats of the Soviet Union cannot imagine anybody wanting to use public media in a private way. And this attitude has just nothing to do with Marx, Lenin, or Communism. It is a normal tribal attitude of any oral society. The Soviet press is their equivalent of our Madison Avenue in shaping production and social processes.

21

Schizophrenia may be a necessary consequence of literacy.

✱ Carothers stresses that until phonetic writing split apart thought and action, there was no alternative but to hold all men responsible for their thoughts as much as their actions. His great contribution has been to point to the breaking apart of the magical world of the ear and the neutral world of the eye, and to the emergence of the detribalized individual from this split. It follows, of course, that literate man, when we meet him in the Greek world, is a split man, a schizophrenic, as all literate men have been since the invention of the phonetic alphabet. Mere writing, however, has not the peculiar power of the phonetic technology to detribalize man. Given the phonetic alphabet with its abstraction of meaning from sound and the translation of sound into a visual code, and men were at grips with an experience that transformed them. No pictographic or ideogrammic or hieroglyphic mode of writing has the detribalizing power of the phonetic alphabet. No other kind of writing save the phonetic has ever translated man out of the possessive world of total interdependence and interrelation that is the auditory network. From that magical resonating world of simultaneous relations that is the oral and acoustic space there is only one route to the freedom and independence of detribalized man. That route is *via* the phonetic alphabet, which lands men at once in varying degrees of dualistic schizophrenia. Here is how Bertrand Russell describes (in his *History of Western Philosophy*, p. 39) this condition of the Greek world in the early throes of dichotomy and the trauma of literacy:

Not all of the Greeks, but a large proportion of them, were passionate, unhappy, at war with themselves, driven along one road by the intellect and along another by the passions, with the imagination to conceive heaven and the wilful self-assertion that creates hell. They had a maxim "nothing too much", but they were in fact excessive in everything—in pure thought, in poetry, in religion, and in sin. It was the combination of passion and intellect that made them great, while they were great. . . . There were, in fact, two tendencies in Greece, one passionate, religious, mystical, other worldly, the other cheerful, empirical, rationalistic, and interested in acquiring knowledge of a diversity of facts.

The division of faculties which results from the technological dilation or externalization of one or another sense is so pervasive a feature of the past century that today we have become conscious, for the first time in history, of how these mutations of culture are initiated. Those who experience the first onset of a new technology, whether it be alphabet or radio, respond most emphatically because the new sense ratios set up at once by the technological dilation of eye or ear, present men with a surprising new world, which evokes a vigorous new "closure," or novel pattern of interplay, among all of the senses together. But the initial shock gradually dissipates as the entire community absorbs the new habit of perception into all of its areas of work and association. But the real revolution is in this later and prolonged phase of "adjustment" of all personal and social life to the new model of perception set up by the new technology.

The Romans carried out the alphabetic translation of culture into visual terms. The Greeks, whether ancient or Byzantine, clung to much of the older oral culture with its distrust of action and applied knowledge. For applied knowledge, whether in military structure or industrial organization, depends upon uniformity and homogenization of populations. "It is certain," wrote the symbolist Edgar Allan Poe, "that the mere act of inditing tends in a great degree to the logicalization of thought." Lineal, alphabetic inditing made possible the sudden invention of "grammars" of thought and science by the Greeks. These grammars or explicit spellings out of personal and social processes were visualizations of non-visual functions and relations. The functions and processes were not new. But the means of arrested visual analysis, namely the phonetic alphabet, was as new to the Greeks as the movie camera in our century.

We can ask ourselves later why the fanatic specialism of the Phoenicians, which hacked the alphabet out of the hieroglyphic culture, did not release any further intellectual or artistic activity in them. Meantime, it is relevant to note that Cicero, the encyclopedic synthesizer of the Roman world, when surveying the Greek world, reproves Socrates for having been the first to make a split between mind and heart. The pre Socratics were still mainly in a non-literate culture. Socrates stood on the border between that oral world and the visual and literate culture. But he wrote nothing. The Middle Ages regarded Plato as the mere scribe or amanuensis of Socrates. And Aquinas considered that neither Socrates nor Our Lord committed their teaching to writing because the kind of interplay of minds that is in teaching is not possible by means of writing.[3]

[3]Utrum Christus debuerit doctrinam Suam Scripto tradere. *Summa Theologica*, part III, q. 42, art. 4.

Does the interiorization of media such as letters alter the ratio among our senses and change mental processes?

✱ What concerned Cicero, the practical Roman, was that the Greeks had put difficulties in the way of his own program for the *doctus orator*. In chapters xv–xxiii of the third book of the *De oratore*, he offers a history of philosophy from the beginning to his own time, trying to explain how it came about that the professional philosophers had made a breach between eloquence and wisdom, between practical knowledge and knowledge which these men professed to follow for its own sake. Before Socrates learning had been the preceptress of living rightly and speaking well. But with Socrates came the division between the tongue and the heart. That the eloquent Socrates should have been of all people the one to initiate a division between thinking wisely and speaking well was inexplicable: ". . . quorum princeps Socrates fuit, is, qui omnium eruditorum testimonio totiusque judicio Graeciae cum prudentia et acumine et venustate et subtilitate, tum vero eloquentia, varietate, copia, quam se cumque in partem dedisset omnium fuit facile princeps . . ."

But after Socrates things became much worse in Cicero's opinion. The Stoics despite a refusal to cultivate eloquence, have alone of all the philosophers declared eloquence to be a virtue and wisdom. For Cicero, wisdom is eloquence because only by eloquence can knowledge be applied to the minds and hearts of men. It is applied knowledge that obsesses the mind of Cicero the Roman as it did the mind of Francis Bacon. And for Cicero, as for Bacon, the technique of application depends upon the Roman brick procedure of uniform repeatability and homogeneous segments of knowledge.

If a technology is introduced either from within or from without a culture, and if it gives new stress or ascendancy to one or another of our senses, the ratio among all of our senses is altered. We no longer feel the same, nor do our eyes and ears and other senses remain the same. The interplay among our senses is perpetual save in conditions of anesthesia. But any sense when stepped up to high intensity can act as an anesthetic for other senses. The dentist can now use "audiac"—induced noise—to remove tactility. Hypnosis depends on the same principle of isolating one sense in order to anesthetize the others. The result is a break in the ratio among the senses, a kind of loss of identity. Tribal, non-literate man, living under the intense stress on auditory organization of all experience, is, as it were, entranced.

Plato, however, the scribe of Socrates as he seemed to the Middle Ages, could in the act of writing[4] look back to the non-literate world and say:

It would take a long time to repeat all that Thamus said to Theuth in praise or blame of the various arts. But when they came to letters, This, said Theuth, will make the Egyptians wiser and give them better memories; it is a specific both for the memory and for the wit. Thamus replied: O most ingenious Theuth, the parent or inventor of an art is not always the best judge of the utility or inutility of his own inventions to the users of them. And in this instance, you who are the father of letters, from a paternal love of your own children have been led to attribute to them a quality which they cannot have; for this discovery of yours will create forgetfulness in the learners' souls, because they will not use their memories; they will trust to the external written characters and not remember of themselves. The specific which you have discovered is an aid not to memory, but to reminiscence, and you give your disciples not truth, but only the semblance of truth; they will be hearers of many things and will have learned nothing; they will appear to be omniscient and will generally know nothing; they will be tiresome company, having the show of wisdom without the reality.

Plato shows no awareness here or elsewhere of how the phonetic alphabet had altered the sensibility of the Greeks; nor did anybody else in his time or later. Before his time, the myth-makers, poised on the frontiers between the old oral world of the tribe and the new technologies of specialism and individualism, had foreseen all and said all in a few words. The myth of Cadmus states how this King who had introduced the Phoenician script, or the phonetic alphabet to Greece, had sown the dragon's teeth and they had sprung up armed men. This, as with all myth, is a succinct statement of a complex social process that had occurred over a period of centuries. But it was only in recent years that the work of Harold Innis opened up the Cadmus myth fully. (See, for example, *The Bias of Communication* and *Empire and Communications*.) The myth, like the aphorism and maxim, is characteristic of oral culture. For, until literacy deprives language of his multi-dimensional resonance, every word is a poetic world unto itself, a "momentary deity" or revelation, as it seemed to non-literate men. Ernst Cassirer's *Language and Myth* presents this aspect of non-literate human awareness, surveying the wide range of current study of language origins and development. Towards the end of the nineteenth century numerous students of non-literate societies had begun to have doubts about the *a priori* character of logical categories. Today, when the role of phonetic literacy in the creating of the techniques of enunciation of propositions ("formal logic") is well known, it is still supposed, even by some anthropologists, that Euclidean space and three-dimensional visual perception is a universal datum of mankind. The absence of

[4]*Phaedrus*, trans. B. Jowett, 274–5. All quotations from Plato are from Jowett's translation.

such space in native art is considered by such scholars to be owing to lack of artistic skill. Cassirer, reporting on the notion of words as myth (the etymology of *mythos* indicates that it means "word") says (p. 62):

According to Usener, the lowest level to which we can trace back the origin of religious concepts is that of "momentary gods", as he calls those images which are born from the need or the specific feeling of a critical moment . . . and still bearing the mark of all its pristine volatility and freedom. But it appears that the new findings which ethnology and comparative religion have put at our disposal during the three decades since the publication of Usener's work enable us to go back one step further yet.

Civilization gives the barbarian or tribal man an eye for an ear and is now at odds with the electronic world.

✱ This step takes to a more generalized sense of the manifestations of divine potency, away from particular, individualized "archetypes" and epiphanies of "momentary deities." It must often have puzzled the scholars and physicists of our time that just in the degree to which we penetrate the lowest layers of non-literate awareness we encounter the most advanced and sophisticated ideas of twentieth-century art and science. To explain that paradox will be an aspect of the present book. It is a theme around which much emotion and controversy are daily engendered as our world shifts from a visual to an auditory orientation in its electric technology. The controversy, of course, ignores the cause of the process altogether and clings to the "content." Setting aside the effects of the alphabet in creating Euclidean space for the Greek sensibility, as well as the simultaneous discovery of perspective and chronological narrative, it will be necessary to return briefly to the native world with J. C. Carothers. For it is in the non-literate world that it is easiest to discern the operation of phonetic letters in shaping our Western world.

That the Greeks were able to do more with the written word than other communities such as the Babylonian and Egyptian was, according to H. A. L. Fisher (*A History of Europe*, p. 19) that they were not under "the paralysing control of organized priestcraft." But even so, they had only a brief period of exploration and discovery before settling into a *clichéd* pattern of repetitive thought. Carothers feels that the early Greek intelligentsia not only had the stimulus of sudden access to the acquired wisdom of other peoples, but, having none of its own, there were no vested interests in acquired knowledge to frustrate the immediate acceptance and development of the new. It is this very situation which today puts the Western world at such a disadvantage, as against the "backward" countries. It is our enormous backlog of literate and mechanistic technology that renders us so helpless and inept in handling the new electric technology. The new physics is an auditory domain and long-literate society is not at home in the new physics, nor will it ever be.

This, of course, is to overlook the utter discrepancy between the phonetic alphabet and any other kind of writing whatever. Only the phonetic alphabet makes a break between eye and ear, between semantic meaning and visual code; and thus only phonetic writing has the power to translate man from the tribal to the civilized sphere, to give him an eye for an ear. The Chinese culture is considerably more refined and perceptive than the Western world has ever been. But the Chinese are tribal, people of the ear. "Civilization" must now be used technically to mean detribalized man for whom the visual values have priority in the organization of thought and action. Nor is this to give any new meaning or value to "civilization" but rather to specify its character. It is quite obvious that most civilized people are crude and numb in their perceptions, compared with the hyperesthesia of oral and auditory cultures. For the eye has none of the delicacy of the ear. Carothers goes on (p. 313) to observe that:

So far as Plato's thinking can be considered representative of the thinking of the Greeks, it is very clear that the word, whether thought or written, still retained, for them, and from our point of view, vast powers in the 'real' world. Although at last it was seen as nonbehavioural itself, it now came to be regarded as the fount and origin not only of behaviour but of all discovery: it was the only key to knowledge, and thought alone—in words or figures—could unlock all doors for understanding the world. In a sense, indeed, the power of words or other visual symbols became greater than before . . . now verbal and mathematical thought became the only truth, and the whole sensory world came to be regarded as illusory, except insofar as thoughts were heard or seen.

In his dialogue of the *Cratylus*, named for his teacher of language and grammar, Plato has Socrates say (438):

But if these things are only to be known through names, how can we suppose that the givers of names had knowledge, or were legislators before there were names at all, and therefore before they could have known them?
   Cratylus: I believe, Socrates, the true account of the matter to be, that a power more than human gave things their first names, and that the names which were thus given are necessarily their true names.

This view of Cratylus was the basis of most language study until the Renaissance. It is rooted in the old oral "magic" of the "momentary deity" kind such as is favoured again today for various reasons. That it is most alien to merely literary and visual culture is easily found in the remarks of incredulity which Jowett supplies as his contribution to the dialogue.

Carothers turns to David Riesman's *The Lonely Crowd* (p. 9) for further orientation in his queries concerning the effects of writing on non-literate communities. Riesman had characterized our own Western world as developing in its "typical members a social character whose conformity is insured by their tendency to acquire early in life an internalized set of goals." Riesman made no effort to discover why the manuscript culture of the ancient and medieval worlds should not have conferred inner direction, nor why a print culture should inevitably confer inner direction. That is part of the business of the present book. But it can be said at once that "inner direction" depends upon a "fixed point of view." A stable, consistent character is one with an unwavering outlook, an almost hypnotized visual stance, as it were. Manuscripts were altogether too slow and uneven a matter to provide either a fixed point of view or the habit of gliding steadily on single planes of thought and information. As we shall see, manuscript culture is intensely audile-tactile compared to print culture; and that means that detached habits of observation are quite uncongenial to manuscript cultures, whether ancient Egyptian, Greek, or Chinese or medieval. In place of cool visual detachment the manuscript world puts empathy and participation of all the senses. But non-literate cultures experience such an overwhelming tyranny of the ear over the eye that any balanced interplay among the senses is unknown at the auditory extreme, just as balanced interplay of the senses became extremely difficult after print stepped up the visual component in Western experience to extreme intensity.

The modern physicist is at home with oriental field theory.

✳ Carothers finds Riesman's classification of "tradition-directed" peoples as corresponding "quite closely to those areas occupied by societies which are non-literate or in which the great majority of the population has been untouched by literacy" (p. 315). It should be understood that to be "touched" by literacy is not a very sudden affair, nor is it a total matter at any time or in any place. That should become very clear as we move through the sixteenth and later centuries. But today, as electricity creates conditions of extreme interdependence on a global scale, we move swiftly again into an auditory world of simultaneous events and over-all awareness. Yet the habits of literacy persist in our speech, our sensibilities, and in our arrangement of the spaces and times of our daily lives. Short of some catastrophe, literacy and visual bias could bear up for a long time against electricity and "unified field" awareness. And the same is true the other way around. Germans and the Japanese, while far-advanced in literate and analytic technology, retained the core of auditory tribal unity and total togetherness. The advent of radio, and electricity generally, was not only for them but for all tribal cultures a most intense experience. Long-literate cultures have naturally more resistance to the auditory dynamic of the total electric field culture of our time.

Riesman, referring to tradition-directed people, says (p. 26):

Since the type of social order we have been discussing is relatively unchanging, the conformity of the individual tends to be dictated to a very large degree by power relations among the various age and sex groups, the clans, castes, professions, and so forth—relations which have endured for centuries and are modified but slightly, if at all, by successive generations. The culture controls behavior minutely, and, . . . careful and rigid etiquette governs the fundamentally influential sphere of kin relationships. . . . Little energy is directed toward finding new solutions of the age-old problems . . .

Riesman points out that to meet even the rigid demands of complex religious ritual and etiquette "individuality of character need not be highly developed." He speaks as a highly literate man for whom "development" means having a private point of view. High development as it might appear to a native would not be accessible to our visual mode of awareness. We can get some idea of the attitude of a member of a tradition-directed society to technological improvements from a story related by Werner Heisenberg in *The Physicist's Conception of Nature*. A modern physicist with his habit of "field" perception, and his sophisticated separation from our conventional habits of Newtonian space, easily finds in the pre-literate world a congenial kind of wisdom.

Heisenberg is discussing "science as a part of the interplay between man and Nature" (p. 20):

In this connection it has often been said that the far-reaching changes in our environment and in our way of life wrought by this technical age have also changed dangerously our ways of thinking, and that here lie the roots of the crises which have shaken our times and which, for instance, are also expressed in modern art. True, this objection is much older than modern technology and science, the use of implements going back to man's earliest beginnings. Thus, two and a half thousand years ago, the Chinese sage Chuang-Tzu spoke of the danger of the machine when he said:
'As Tzu-Gung was travelling through the regions north of the river Han, he saw an old man working in his vegetable garden. He had dug an irrigation ditch. The man would descend into the well, fetch up a vessel of water in his

29

arms and pour it out into the ditch. While his efforts were tremendous the results appeared to be very meagre.

'Tzu-Gung said, "There is a way whereby you can irrigate a hundred ditches in one day, and whereby you can do much with little effort. Would you not like to hear of it?" Then the gardener stood up, looked at him and said, "And what would that be?"

'Tzu-Gung replied, "You take a wooden lever, weighted at the back and light in front. In this way you can bring up water so quickly that it just gushes out. This is called a draw-well."

'Then anger rose up in the old man's face, and he said, "I have heard my teacher say that whoever uses machines does all his work like a machine. He who does his work like a machine grows a heart like a machine, and he who carries the heart of a machine in his breast loses his simplicity. He who has lost his simplicity becomes unsure in the strivings of his soul. Uncertainty in the strivings of the soul is something which does not agree with honest sense. It is not that I do not know of such things; I am ashamed to use them." '

Clearly this ancient tale contains a great deal of wisdom, for "uncertainty in the strivings of the soul" is perhaps one of the aptest descriptions of man's condition in our modern crisis; technology, the machine, has spread through the world to a degree that our Chinese sage could not even have suspected.

The sort of "simplicity" envisaged by the sage is a more complex and subtle product than anything that occurs in a society with specialized technology and sense life. But perhaps the real point of the anecdote is that it appealed to Heisenberg. It would not have interested Newton. Not only does modern physics abandon the specialized visual space of Descartes and Newton, it re-enters the subtle auditory space of the non-literate world. And in the most primitive society, as in the present age, such auditory space is a total field of simultaneous relations in which "change" has as little meaning and appeal as it had for the mind of Shakespeare or the heart of Cervantes. All values apart, we must learn today that our electric technology has consequences for our most ordinary perceptions and habits of action which are quickly recreating in us the mental processes of the most primitive men. These consequences occur, not in our thoughts or opinions, where we are trained to be critical, but in our most ordinary sense life, which creates the vortices and the matrices of thought and action. This book will try to explain why print culture confers on man a language of thought which leaves him quite unready to face the language of his own electro-magnetic technology. The strategy any culture must resort to in a period like this was indicated by Wilhelm von Humboldt:

Man lives with his objects chiefly—in fact, since his feeling and acting depends on his perceptions, one may say exclusively—as language presents them to him. By the same process whereby he spins language out of his own being, he ensnares himself in it; and each language draws a magic circle round the people to which it belongs, a circle from which there is no escape save by stepping out of it into another.[5]

Such awareness as this has generated in our time the technique of the suspended judgment by which we can transcend the limitations of our own assumptions by a critique of them. We can now live, not just amphibiously in divided and distinguished worlds, but pluralistically in many worlds and cultures simultaneously. We are no more committed to one culture—to a single ratio among the human senses—any more than to one book or to one language or to one technology. Our need today is, culturally, the same as the scientist's who seeks to become aware of the bias of the instruments of research in order to correct that bias. Compartmentalizing of human potential by single cultures will soon be as absurd as specialism in subject or discipline has become. It is not likely that our age is more obsessional than any other, but it has become sensitively aware of the conditions and fact of obsession beyond any other age. However, our fascination with all phases of the unconscious, personal and collective, as with all modes of primitive awareness, began in the eighteenth century with the first violent revulsion against print culture and mechanical industry. What began as a "Romantic reaction" towards organic wholeness may or may not have hastened the discovery of electromagnetic waves. But certainly the electro-magnetic discoveries have recreated the simultaneous "field" in all human affairs so that the human family now exists under conditions of a "global village." We live in a single constricted space resonant with tribal drums. So that concern with the "primitive" today is as banal as nineteenth-century concern with "progress," and as irrelevant to our problems.

The new electronic interdependence recreates the world in the image of a global village.

✱ It would be surprising, indeed, if Riesman's description of tradition-directed people did not correspond to Carothers' knowledge of African tribal societies. It would be equally startling were the ordinary reader about native societies not able to vibrate with a deep sense of affinity for the same,

[5]Quoted by Cassirer in *Language and Myth*, p. 9.

31

since our new electric culture provides our lives again with a tribal base. There is available the lyrical testimony of a very Romantic biologist, Pierre Teilhard de Chardin, in his *Phenomenon of Man* (p.240):

Now, to the degree that—under the effect of this pressure and thanks to their psychic permeability—the human elements infiltrated more and more into each other, their minds (mysterious coincidence) were mutually stimulated by proximity. And as though dilated upon themselves, they each extended little by little the radius of their influence upon this earth which, by the same token, shrank steadily. What, in fact, do we see happening in the modern paroxysm? It has been stated over and over again. Through the discovery yesterday of the railway, the motor car and the aeroplane, the physical influence of each man, formerly restricted to a few miles, now extends to hundreds of leagues or more. Better still: thanks to the prodigious biological event represented by the discovery of electro-magnetic waves, each individual finds himself henceforth (actively and passively) simultaneously present, over land and sea, in every corner of the earth.

People of literary and critical bias find the shrill vehemence of de Chardin as disconcerting as his uncritical enthusiasm for the cosmic membrane that has been snapped round the globe by the electric dilation of our various senses. This externalization of our senses creates what de Chardin calls the "noosphere" or a technological brain for the world. Instead of tending towards a vast Alexandrian library the world has become a computer, an electronic brain, exactly as in an infantile piece of science fiction. And as our senses have gone outside us, Big Brother goes inside. So, unless aware of this dynamic, we shall at once move into a phase of panic terrors, exactly befitting a small world of tribal drums, total interdependence, and super-imposed co-existence. It is easy to perceive signs of such panic in Jacques Barzun who manifests himself as a fearless and ferocious Luddite in his *The House of the Intellect*. Sensing that all he holds dear stems from the operation of the alphabet on and through our minds, he proposes the abolition of all modern art, science, and philanthropy. This trio extirpated, he feels we can slap down the lid on Pandora's box. At least Barzun localizes his problem even if he has no clue as to the kind of agency exerted by these forms. Terror is the normal state of any oral society, for in it everything affects everything all the time.

Reverting to the earlier theme of conformity, Carothers continues (pp. 315–16): "Thought and behavior are not seen as separate; they are both seen as behavioral. Evil-willing is, after all the most fearful type of "behavior" known in many of these societies, and a dormant or awakening fear of it lies ever in the minds of all their members." In our long striving to recover for the Western world a unity of sensibility and of thought and feeling we have no more been prepared to accept the tribal consequences of such unity than we were ready for the fragmentation of the human psyche by print culture.

Literacy affects the physiology as well as the psychic life of the African.

✱ Carothers concludes his discussion of the effects of phonetic writing on Africans with an excerpt (pp. 317–18) from an article that appeared in a Kenya daily newspaper, the *East African Standard*. The author, a missionary doctor, headed his article "How Civilization Has Affected the African."

The purpose of this article is to show that through a very little education a remarkably rapid and far-reaching change has taken place in African boys and girls, so much so that in a generation, human characteristics and reactions have altered to a degree which one would have expected to have taken centuries.

The high qualities of the African untouched by missions or education impress nearly everyone. Those of this district are good workers, cheerful, uncomplaining, unaffected by monotony or discomforts, honest and usually remarkably truthful. But it is not uncommon to hear uncomplimentary comparisons made between those Africans and those born of Christian parents or those who started school at an early age. A writer, however, who visited schools in Madagascar says that these untouched children are naturally lethargic. They sit still too long: the impulse to play seems to be dormant. They are impervious to monotony and their mental lethargy enables them to perform, for children, prodigious acts of endurance. These children naturally develop into the uneducated African, who is incapable of filling any skilled post. At the most he can be trained to carry out work that requires no reasoning. That is the penalty paid for his good qualities.

The African will remain in permanent servitude if only to ignorance unless there is willingness to risk the destruction of those qualities in the changes education brings and a desire to face building up his character again but with a totally different mentality. This different mentality may show itself in a shirking of work, trouble over food or in a desire to have his wife living with him however difficult for the employer. The reasons are clear; the African's whole capacity for interest, pleasure and pain are immensely increased through even a little education.

For the educated African (using this term for even the comparatively low standard achieved by the average African schoolboy) the sense of interest has been aroused through the new variety of life and monotony has become a trial to him as it is to the normal European. It takes greater will-power for him to be faithful to uninteresting work, and lack of interest brings fatigue.

The author next turned to the changed attitudes to taste and sex and pain resulting from literacy:

I suggest also that the nervous system of the untouched African is so lethargic that he needs little sleep. Many of our workmen walk some miles to their jobs, work well all day and then return home and spend most of the night sitting up guarding their gardens against the depredations of wild pigs. For weeks on end they sleep only two or three hours a night.

The important moral inference from all this is that the African of the old generation with whom we have nearly all worked, will never be seen again. The new generation is completely different, capable of rising to greater heights and of descending to greater depths. They deserve a more sympathetic knowledge of their difficulties and their far greater temptations. African parents need to be taught this before it is too late so that they may realize that they are dealing with finer bits of mechanism than they themselves were.

Carothers stresses the fact that it is indeed a very little literacy that produces these effects, "some familiarity with written symbols—in reading, writing and arithmetic."

Finally (p. 318), Carothers turns for a moment to China, where printing had been invented in the seventh or eighth century and yet "seems to have had little effect in emancipating thought." He calls in the testimony of Kenneth Scott Latourette, who writes in *The Chinese, Their History and Culture* (p. 310):

The hypothetical visitor from Mars might well have expected the Industrial Revolution and the modern scientific approach to have made their first appearance in China rather than the Occident. The Chinese are so industrious, and have shown such ingenuity in invention and by empirical processes have forestalled the West in arriving at so much useful agricultural and medical lore that they, rather than the nations of the West, might have been looked to as the forerunners and leaders in what is termed the scientific approach towards the understanding and mastery of man's natural environment. It is little short of amazing that a people who pioneered in the invention of paper, printing, gunpowder, and the compass—to speak only of some of their best known innovations—did not also take precedence in devising the power loom, the steam engine, and the other revolutionary machines of the eighteenth and nineteenth centuries.

The purpose of printing among the Chinese was not the creation of uniform repeatable products for a market and a price system. Print was an alternative to their prayer-wheels and was a visual means of multiplying incantatory spells, much like advertising in our age.

But we can learn much about print from the Chinese attitude towards it. For the most obvious character of print is repetition, just as the obvious effect of repetition is hypnosis or obsession. Moreover, printing ideograms is totally different from typography based on the phonetic alphabet. For the ideograph even more than the hieroglyph is a complex *Gestalt* involving all of the senses at once. The ideogram affords none of the separation and specialization of sense, none of the breaking apart of sight and sound and meaning which is the key to the phonetic alphabet. So that the numerous specializations and separations of function inherent in industry and applied knowledge simply were not accessible to the Chinese. Today they appear to be proceeding along the lines of the phonetics alphabet. This ensures that they will liquidate their present and traditional culture *in toto*. They will then proceed by the paths of schizophrenia and multiply dichotomies in the direction of physical power and aggressive organization, on a centre-margin or Roman pattern.

The quite irrelevant ground that Carothers assigns to explaining the earlier Chinese indifference to industrialism is that Chinese writing—or printing—requires much erudition for its understanding. The same is true in varying degrees of all non-alphabetic forms of writing. The comment of Latourette on this point will help here as well as later:

The greater part of the voluminous literature in Chinese has been written in the classical style . . . The Chinese classical language presents difficulties. It is highly artificial. It is often replete with allusions and quotations and to appreciate and even to understand much of it the reader has to bring to it a vast store of knowledge of existing literature . . . It is only by going through a prodigious amount of literature and especially by memorising quantities of it that the scholar obtains a kind of sixth sense which enables him to divine which of several readings is correct. Even the perusal of the classical language, therefore, requires long preparation. Composition is still more of a task. Few Occidentals have achieved an acceptable style and many a modern Chinese who is the finished product of the present-day curriculum is far from adept.

The concluding observation of Carothers is that genetic studies of human groups offer no certainty and very small data, indeed, compared to cultural and environmental approaches. My suggestion is that cultural ecology has a reasonably stable base in the human sensorium, and that any extension of the sensorium by technological dilation has a quite appreciable effect in setting up new ratios or proportions among all the senses. Languages being that form of technology constituted by dilation or uttering (outering) of all of our senses at once, are themselves immediately subject to the impact or intrusion of any mechanically extended sense. That is, writing affects speech directly, not only its accidence and syntax but also its enunciation and social uses.[6]

[6]H. M. McLuhan, "The Effect of the Printed Book on Language in the Sixteenth Century," in *Explorations in Communication*, pp. 125–35.

Why non-literate societies cannot see films or photos without much training.

✱ Since the present object is to elucidate the effective causality of phonetic writing in setting up new kinds of perception, let us turn to a paper[7] by Professor John Wilson of the African Institute of London University. For literate societies it is not easy to grasp why non-literates cannot see in three dimensions or perspective. We assume that this is normal vision and that no training is needed to view photos or films. Wilson's experiences arose from trying to use film in teaching natives to read:

The next bit of evidence was very, very interesting. This man—the sanitary inspector—made a moving picture, in very slow time, very slow technique, of what would be required of the ordinary household in a primitive African village in getting rid of standing water—draining pools, picking up all empty tins and putting them away, and so forth. We showed this film to an audience and asked them what they had seen, and they said they had seen a chicken, a fowl, and we didn't know that there was a fowl in it! So we very carefully scanned the frames one by one for this fowl, and, sure enough, for about a second, a fowl went over the corner of the frame. Someone had frightened the fowl and it had taken flight, through the righthand, bottom segment of the frame. This was all that had been seen. The other things he had hoped they would pick up from the film they had not picked up at all, and they had picked up something which we didn't know was in the film until we inspected it minutely. Why? We developed all sorts of theories. Perhaps it was the sudden movement of the chicken. Everything else was done in slow technique— people going forward slowly picking up the tin, demonstrating and all the rest of it, and the bird was apparently the one bit of reality for them. For them there was another theory that the fowl had religious significance, which we rather dismissed.

Question: Could you describe in more detail the scene in the film?

Wilson: Yes, there was very slow movement of a sanitary laborer coming along and seeing a tin with water in it, picking the tin up and very carefully pouring the water out and then rubbing it into the ground so no mosquito could breed and very carefully putting this tin in a basket on the back of a donkey. This was to show how you disposed of rubbish. It was like the man in the park with a spiked stick, picking up the bits of paper and putting them in the sack. All this was done very slowly to show how important it was to pick up those things because of mosquitoes breeding in standing water. The cans were all very carefully taken away and disposed of in the ground and

[7]"Film Literacy in Africa," *Canadian Communications*, vol. I, no. 4, summer, 1961, pp. 7–14.

covered up so there would be no more standing water. The film was about five minutes long. The chicken appeared for a second in this kind of setting.

Question: Do you literally mean that when you talked with the audience you came to believe that they had not *seen* anything else but the chicken?

Wilson: We simply asked them: What did you see in this film?

Question: Not what did you *think*?

Wilson: No, what did you *see*?

Question: How many people were in the viewing audience of whom you asked this question?

Wilson: 30-odd.

Question: No one gave you a response other than "We saw the chicken"?

Wilson: No, this was the first quick response—"We saw a chicken."

Question: They did see a man, too?

Wilson: Well, when we questioned them further they had seen a man, but what was really interesting was they hadn't made a whole story out of it, and in point of fact, we discovered afterwards that they hadn't seen a whole frame—they had inspected the frame for details. Then we found out from the artist and an eye specialist that a sophisticated audience, an audience that is accustomed to the film, focuses a little way in front of the flat screen so that you take in the whole frame. In this sense, again, a picture is a convention. You've got to look at the picture as a whole first, and these people did not do that, not being accustomed to pictures. When presented with the picture they began to inspect it, rather as the scanner of a television camera, and go over it very rapidly. Apparently, that is what the eye unaccustomed to pictures does—scans the picture—and they hadn't scanned one picture before it moved on, *in spite* of the slow technique of the film.

The key facts are at the end of the passage. Literacy gives people the power to focus a little way in front of an image so that we take in the whole image or picture at a glance. Non-literate people have no such acquired habit and do not look at objects in our way. Rather they scan objects and images as we do the printed page, segment by segment. Thus they have no detached point of view. They are wholly *with* the object. They go empathically into it. The eye is used, not in perspective but tactually, as it were. Euclidean spaces depending on much separation of sight from touch and sound are not known to them.

Further difficulties which these natives had with film will help us to see how many of the conventions of literacy are built into even non-verbal forms like film:

My point is that I think we've got to be very wary of pictures; they can be interpreted in the light of your experience. Now, next we thought that if we are going to use these films we've got to have some sort of process of education and we've got to have some research. We found also some fascinating things in this research process. We found that the film is, as produced in the West, a very highly conventionalized piece of symbolism although it looks very real. For instance, we found that if you were telling a story about two men to an African audience and one had finished his business and he went off the edge of the screen, the audience wanted to know what had happened to him; they didn't accept that this was just the end of him and that he was of no more interest in the story. They wanted to know what happened to this fellow, and we had to write stories that way, putting in a lot of material that wasn't to us necessary. We had to follow him along the street until he took a natural turn—he mustn't walk off the side of the screen, but must walk down the street and make a natural turn. It was quite understandable that he could disappear around the turn. The action had to follow a natural course of events.

Panning shots were very confusing because the audience didn't realize what was happening. They thought the items and details inside the picture were literally moving. You see, the convention was not accepted. Nor was the idea of a person sitting still while the camera was brought in to a close-up; this was a strange thing, this picture growing bigger in your presence. You know the common way of starting a film: show the city, narrow it down to a street, narrow it down to one house, take your camera in through the window, etc. This was literally interpreted as *you* walking forward and doing all those things until you were finally taken in through the window.

All of this meant that to use the film as a really effective medium we had to begin a process of education in useful conventions and make those films which would educate people to one convention, to the idea, for example, of a man walking off the side of the screen. We had to show that there was a street corner and have the man walk around the street corner and then in the next part of the film show him walking away, and then cut the scene.

African audiences cannot accept our passive consumer role in the presence of film.

✳ A basic aspect of any literate audience is its profound acceptance of a passive consumer role in the presence of book or film. But an African audience had had no training in the private and silent following of a narrative process.

This is an important matter. An African audience does not sit silently without participating. They like to participate, so the person who shows the films and makes the live commentary must be flexible, stimulating, and get responses. If there is a situation where a character sings a song, the song is sung and the audience is invited to join in. This audience participation had to be thought of as the film was made and opportunities provided for it. Live commentators who presented the films had to be trained to the last degree in what the film meant and in their interpretation of the film for different audiences. They were Africans taken out of the teaching profession and trained for this business.

But even when trained to follow film the native of Ghana cannot accept a film about Nigerians. He cannot generalize his experience from film to film, such is the depth of involvement in particular experiences. This empathic involvement, natural to the oral society and the audile-tactile man, is cracked by the phonetic alphabet which abstracts the visual component from the sensory complex. This leads to one further point of Wilson's. He explained the relevance of Chaplin technique in making films for native audiences. The story was in the gestures, and the gestures were complex and precise. Wilson noted the inability of Africans to follow complex narratives but also their subtlety in dramatization:

One thing we were ignorant of at this time, and something we ought to have known a lot more about is that those African audiences are very good at role-playing. Part of a child's education in a pre-literate society is role-playing; he's got to learn to play the role of elders in certain given situations. One thing fortunately we did discover was that the cartoon went down very well. This puzzled us until we found out that puppetry is quite a common pastime.

But there is more to this point than Wilson supposes. Had TV been available he would have been amazed to discover how much more readily the Africans took to it than they did to film. For with film you are the camera and the non-literate man cannot use his eyes like a camera. But with TV you are the screen. And TV is two-dimensional and sculptural in its tactile contours. TV is not a narrative medium, is not so much visual as audile-tactile. That is why it is empathic, and why the optimal mode of TV image is the cartoon. For the cartoon appeals to natives as it does to our children, because it is a world in which the visual component is so small that the viewer has as much to do as in a crossword puzzle.[8]

More important still, with the bounding line of a cartoon, as with a cave painting, we tend to be in an area of the interplay of the senses, and hence of strongly haptic or tactile character. That is to say, the art of the draughtsman and the *celator* alike is a strongly tactile and tangible art. And even Euclidean geometry is by modern standards very tactile.

This is a matter discussed by William Ivins, Jr., in *Art and Geometry: A Study in Space Intuitions*. He explains the unverbalized assumptions of Greek space awareness: "The Greeks never mentioned among the axioms and postulates of their geometry their basic assumption of congruence, and yet

[8]For more data on the new space orientation in TV-viewing, see H. M. McLuhan, "Inside the Five Sense Sensorium," *Canadian Architect*, June, 1961, vol. 6, no. 6, pp. 49–54.

. . . it is among the most fundamental things in Greek geometry, and plays a determining role in its form, its power, and its limitations." (p. x) Congruence was a new and exciting visual dimension, unknown to audile-tactile cultures. As Ivins says in this regard, "Unlike the eye, the unaided hand is unable to discover whether three or more objects are on a line." (p. 7) It is very obvious why Plato might have insisted that "no one destitute of geometry enter" his academy. A similar motive leads the Viennese musician Carl Orff to forbid children to study music in his school if they have already learned to read and write. The visual bias so attained he feels makes it quite hopeless to develop their audile-tactile powers in music. Ivins goes on to explain why we have the illusion of space as a kind of independent container, whereas in fact space is "a quality or relationship of things and has no existence without them." (p. 8) Yet in comparison with later centuries, "the Greeks were tactile minded and . . . whenever they were given the choice between a tactile or a visual way of thought they instinctively chose the tactile one." (pp. 9–10) Such remained the case until well after Gutenberg in Western experience. Considering the history of Greek geometry, Ivins observes: ". . . again and again during a period of six or seven centuries they went right up to the door of modern geometry, but that, inhibited by their tactile-muscular, metrical ideas, they were never able to open that door and pass out into the great open spaces of modern thought." (p. 58)

When technology extends one of our senses, a new translation of culture occurs as swiftly as the new technology is interiorized.

✳ Although the main theme of this book is the Gutenberg Galaxy or a configuration of events, which lies far ahead of the world of alphabet and of scribal culture, it needs to be known why, without alphabet, there would have been no Gutenberg. And, therefore, we must get some insight into the conditions of culture and perception that make first, writing, and then, perhaps, alphabet possible at all.[9]

[9]The Koreans by 1403 were making cast-metal type by means of punches and matrices (*The Invention of Printing in China and its Spread Westward* by T. F. Carter). Carter had no concern with the alphabet relation to print and was probably unaware that the Koreans are reputed to have a phonetic alphabet.

Wilson's account of the years of perceptual training needed to enable adult Africans to be able to see movies has its exact analogue in the difficulties which Western adults have with "abstract" art. In 1925 Bertrand Russell wrote his *ABC of Relativity*, pointing out on the first page that:

Many of the new ideas can be expressed in non-mathematical language, but they are none the less difficult on that account. What is demanded is a change in our imaginative picture of the world. . . . The same sort of change was demanded by Copernicus, when he taught that the earth is not stationary . . . To us now there is no difficulty in this idea, because we learned it before our mental habits had become fixed. Einstein's ideas, similarly, will seem easier to generations which grow up with them; but for us a certain effort of imaginative reconstruction is unavoidable.

It is simpler to say that if a new technology extends one or more of our senses outside us into the social world, then new ratios among all of our senses will occur in that particular culture. It is comparable to what happens when a new note is added to a melody. And when the sense ratios alter in any culture then what had appeared lucid before may suddenly be opaque, and what had been vague or opaque will become translucent. As Heinrich Wolfflin stated the matter in 1915, in his revolutionary *Principles of Art History* (p. 62) "the effect is the thing that counts, not the sensuous facts." Wolfflin began working from the discoveries of the sculptor Adolf von Hildebrand, whose *Problem of Form in the Figurative Arts* had first clearly explained the disorder in ordinary human sense perception, and the role of art in clarifying this confusion. Hildebrand had shown how tactility was a kind of synesthesia or interplay among the senses, and as such, was the core of the richest art *effects*. For the low definition imagery of the tactile mode compels the viewer into an active participant role. When Africans watch movies as if they were low definition forms for active participation, we are amused by the incongruity. Working from effect rather than from cause, which we have already seen as native to the Russian, was for us a novel mode of procedure in the later nineteenth century, and will come in for fuller discussion later in this book.

A recent work by Georg von Bekesy, *Experiments in Hearing,* offers an exactly reverse answer to the problem of space to the one which Carothers and Wilson have just given us. Whereas they are trying to talk about the perception of non-literate people in terms of literate experience, Professor von Bekesy chooses to begin his discussion of acoustical space on its own terms. As one proficient in auditory spaces, he is keenly aware of the difficulty of talking about the space of hearing, for the acoustical is necessarily a world in "depth."[10] It is of the utmost interest that in trying to elucidate the nature of hearing and of acoustic space, Professor von Bekesy should

[10]See "Acoustic Space."

41

deliberately avoid viewpoint and perspective in favour of mosaic field. And to this end he resorts to two-dimensional painting as a means of revealing the resonant depth of acoustic space. Here are his own words (p. 4):

It is possible to distinguish two forms of approach to a problem. One, which may be called the theoretical approach, is to formulate the problem in relation to what is already known, to make additions or extensions on the basis of accepted principles, and then to proceed to test these hypotheses experimentally. Another, which may be called the mosaic approach, takes each problem for itself with little reference to the field in which it lies, and seeks to discover relations and principles that hold within the circumscribed area.

Von Bekesy then proceeds to introduce his two paintings:

A close analogy to these two approaches may be found in the field of art. In the period between the eleventh and seventeenth centuries the Arabs and the Persians developed a high mastery of the arts of description. . . . Later, during the Renaissance, a new form of representation was developed in which the attempt was made to give unity and perspective to the picture and to represent the atmosphere. . . .
    When in the field of science a great deal of progress has been made and most of the pertinent variables are known, a new problem may most readily be handled by trying to fit it into the existing framework. When, however, the framework is uncertain and the number of variables is large the mosaic approach is much the easier.

The mosaic approach is not only "much the easier" in the study of the simultaneous which is the auditory field; it is the only relevant approach. For the "two-dimensional" mosaic or painting is the mode in which there is muting of the visual as such, in order that there may be maximal interplay among all of the senses. Such was the painterly strategy "since Cézanne," to paint as if you held, rather than as if you saw, objects.

A *theory of cultural change is impossible without knowledge of the changing sense ratios effected by various externalizations of our senses.*

✱ It is very much worth dwelling on this matter, since we shall see that from the invention of the alphabet there has been a continuous drive in the

Western world toward the separation of the senses, of functions, of operations, of states emotional and political, as well as of tasks—a fragmentation which terminated, thought Durkheim, in the *anomie* of the nineteenth century. The paradox presented by Professor von Bekesy is that the two-dimensional mosaic is, in fact, a multidimensional world of interstructural resonance. It is the three-dimensional world of pictorial space that is, indeed, an abstract illusion built on the intense separation of the visual from the other senses.

There is here no question of values or preferences. It is necessary, however, for any other kind of understanding to know why "primitive" drawing is two-dimensional, whereas the drawing and painting of literate man tends towards perspective. Without this knowledge we cannot grasp why men ever ceased to be "primitive" or audile-tactile in their sense bias. Nor could we ever understand why men have "since Cézanne" abandoned the visual in favour of the audile-tactile modes of awareness and of organization of experience. This matter clarified, we can much more easily approach the role of alphabet and of printing in giving a dominant role to the visual sense in language and art and in the entire range of social and of political life. For until men have up-graded the visual component communities know only a tribal structure. The detribalizing of the individual has, in the past at least, depended on an intense visual life fostered by literacy, and by literacy of the alphabetic kind alone. For alphabetic writing is not only unique but late. There had been much writing before it. In fact, any people that ceases to be nomadic and pursues sedentary modes of work is ready to invent writing. No merely nomadic people ever had writing any more than they ever developed architecture or "enclosed space." For writing is a visual enclosure of non-visual spaces and senses. It is, therefore, an abstraction of the visual from the ordinary sense interplay. And whereas speech is an outering (utterance) of all of our senses at once, writing abstracts from speech.

At the present time it is easier to grasp this specific technology of writing. The new institutes for teaching speeded-up reading habits work on the separation of eye-movements from inner verbalization. It will be indicated later that all reading in the ancient and medieval worlds was reading aloud. With print the eye speeded up and the voice quieted down. But inner verbalizing was taken for granted as inseparable from the horizontal following of the words on the page. Today we know that the divorce of reading and verbalizing can be made by vertical reading. This, of course, pushes the alphabetic technology of the separation of the senses to an extreme of inanity, but it is relevant to an understanding of how writing of any sort gets started.

In a paper entitled "A History of the Theory of Information," read to the Royal Society in 1951, E. Colin Cherry of the University of London, observed that "Early invention was greatly hampered by an inability to dissociate mechanical structure from animal form. The invention of the wheel was one outstanding early effort of such dissociation. The great spurt in invention which began in the sixteenth century rested on the gradual dissociation of the machine from animal form." Printing was the first mechanization of an ancient handicraft and led easily to the further mechanization of all handicrafts. The modern phases of this process are the theme of *Mechanization Takes Command* by Siegfried Giedion.

However, Giedion is concerned with a minute tracing of the stages by which in the past century we have used mechanism to recover organic form:

> In his celebrated studies of the 'seventies on the motions of men and animals, Edward Muybridge set up a series of thirty cameras at twelve-inch intervals, releasing their shutters electromagnetically as soon as the moving object passed before the plate. . . . Each picture showed the object in an isolated phase as arrested by each camera. (p. 107)

That is to say, the object is translated out of organic or simultaneous form into a static or pictorial mode. By revolving a sequence of such static or pictorial spaces at a sufficient speed, the illusion of organic wholeness, or interplay of spaces, is created. Thus, the wheel finally becomes the means of moving our culture away from the machine. But it was by means of electricity applied to the wheel that the wheel merges once more with animal form. In fact, the wheel is now an obsolete form in the electric-missile age. But hypertrophy is the mark of obsolescence, as we shall see again and again. Just because wheel is now returning to organic form in the twentieth century it is quite easy for us to understand how primitive man "invented" it. Any creature in motion is a wheel in that repetition of movement has a cyclic and circular principle in it. Thus the melodies of literate societies are repeatable cycles. But the music of non-literate people has no such repetitive cyclic and abstract form as melody. Invention, in a word, is translation of one kind of space into another.

Giedion devotes some time to the work of the French physiologist, Etienne Jules Morey (1830–1904), who devised the myograph for recording the movements of muscles: "Morey quite consciously looks back to Descartes, but instead of graphically representing sections he translates organic movement into graphic form." (p. 19)

The twentieth century encounter between alphabetic and electronic faces of culture confers on the printed word a crucial role in staying the return to the Africa within.

✱ The invention of the alphabet, like the invention of the wheel, was the translation or reduction of a complex, organic interplay of spaces into a single space. The phonetic alphabet reduced the use of all the senses at once, which is oral speech, to a merely visual code. Today, such translation can be effected back and forth through a variety of spatial forms which we call the "media of communication." But each of these spaces has unique properties and impinges upon our other senses or spaces in unique ways.

Today, then, it is easy to understand the invention of the alphabet because, as A. N. Whitehead pointed out in *Science and the Modern World* (p. 141) the great discovery of the nineteenth century was the discovery of the method of discovery:

The greatest invention of the nineteenth century was the invention of the method of invention. A new method entered into life. In order to understand our epoch, we can neglect all the details of change, such as railways, telegraphs, radios, spinning machines, synthetic dyes. We must concentrate on the method in itself; that is the real novelty which has broken up the foundations of the old civilization. . . . One element in the new method is just the discovery of how to set about bridging the gap between the scientific ideas, and the ultimate product. It is a process of disciplined attack upon one difficulty after another.

The method of invention, as Edgar Poe demonstrated in his "Philosophy of Composition," is simply to begin with the solution of the problem or with the effect intended. Then one backtracks, step by step, to the point from which one must begin in order to reach the solution or effect. Such is the method of the detective story, of the symbolist poem, and of modern science. It is, however, the twentieth century step beyond this method of invention which is needed for understanding the origin and the action of such forms as the wheel or the alphabet. And that step is not the backtracking from *product* to starting point, but the following of *process* in isolation from product. To follow the contours of process as in psychoanalysis provides the only means of avoiding the product of process, namely neurosis or psychosis.

It is the purpose of the present book to study primarily the print phase of alphabetic culture. The print phase, however, has encountered today the new organic and biological modes of the electronic world. That is, it is now interpenetrated at its extreme development of mechanism by the electro-biological, as de Chardin has explained. And it is this reversal of character which makes our age "connatural," as it were, with non-literate cultures. We have no more difficulty in understanding the native or non-literate experience, simply because we have recreated it electronically within our own culture. (Yet post-literacy is a quite different mode of interdependence from pre-literacy.) So my dwelling upon the earlier phases of alphabetic technology is not irrelevant to an understanding of the Gutenberg era.

Colin Cherry had this to say about early writing:

A detailed history of spoken and written languages would be irrelevant to our present subject, but nevertheless there are certain matters of interest which may be taken as a starting-point. The early writings of Mediterranean civilizations were in picture, or "logographic" script: simple pictures were used to represent objects and also, by association, ideas, actions, names, and so on. Also, what is much more important, phonetic writing was developed, in which sounds were given symbols. With the passage of time, the pictures were reduced to more formal symbols as determined by the difficulty of using a chisel, or a reed brush, while the phonetic writing simplified into a set of two or three dozen alphabetic letters, divided into consonants and vowels.

In Egyptian hieroglyphics we have a supreme example of what is now called *redundancy* in languages and code; one of the difficulties in deciphering the Rosetta stone lay in the fact that a polysyllabic word might give each syllable not one symbol but a number of different ones in common use, in order that the word should be thoroughly understood. (The effect when literally transcribed into English is one of stuttering.) On the other hand the Semitic languages show an early recognition of redundancy. Ancient Hebrew script had no vowels: modern Hebrew has none, too, except in children's books. Many other ancient scripts have no vowels. Slavonic Russian went a step further in condensation: in religious texts, commonly used words were abbreviated to a few letters, in a manner similar to our present-day use of the ampersand, abbreviations such as lb and the increasing use of initials, e.g., U.S.A., Unesco, O.K.

It is not the avoidance of redundancy that is the key to the phonetic alphabet and its effects on person and society. "Redundancy" is a "content" concept, itself a legacy of alphabetic technology. That is, any phonetic writing is a visual code for speech. Speech is the "content" of phonetic writing. But it is not the content of any other kind of writing. Pictographic and ideographic varieties of writing are *Gestalts* or snapshots of various situations, personal or social. In fact, we can get a good idea of non-alphabetic forms of writing from modern mathematical equations like $E = MC^2$ or from the ancient Greek and Roman "figures of rhetoric." Such equations or figures have no content but are structures like an individual melody which evoke their own world. The figures of rhetoric are postures of the mind, as hyperbole, or irony, or litotes, or simile, or paranomasia. Picture writing of all kinds is a ballet of such postures which delights our modern bias towards synesthesia and audile-tactile richness of experience, far more than does the bare, abstract alphabetic form. It would be well today if children were taught a good many Chinese ideograms and Egyptian hieroglyphs as a means of enhancing their appreciation of our alphabet.

Colin Cherry, then, misses the point about the unique character of our alphabet, namely that it dissociates or abstracts, not only sight and sound, but separates all meaning from the sound of the letters, save so far as the meaningless letters relate to the meaningless sounds. So long as any other meaning is vested in sight or sound, the divorce between the visual and the other senses remains incomplete, as is the case in all forms of writing save the phonetic alphabet.

Current concern with reading and spelling reform steers away from visual to auditory stress.

✻ It is interesting that today there is a growing unrest about our alphabetic dissociation of the senses. On page 49 there is a sample of a recent attempt at a new alphabet that would restore more phonic character to our script. The most notable thing about the sample is that it has the highly textural and tactile quality of an ancient manuscript page. In our desire to restore some unity of interplay among our senses we grope towards ancient manuscript forms which must be read aloud to be read at all. Side by side with this extreme development is that of the new institutes for speeded-up reading. There they are taught how to use the eye on the page so as to avoid all verbalization and all incipient movements of the throat which accompany our cinematic chase from left to right, in order to create the mental sound movie which we call reading.

The most definitive work we have on the phonetic letters is *The Alphabet* by David Diringer. He begins his story as follows (p. 37):

> The alphabet is the last, the most highly developed, the most convenient and the most easily adaptable system of writing. Alphabetic writing is now universally employed by civilized peoples; its use is acquired in childhood with ease. There is an enormous advantage, obviously, in the use of letters

which represent single sounds rather than ideas or syllables; no sinologist knows all the 80,000 or so Chinese symbols, but it is also far from easy to master the 9,000 or so symbols actually employed by Chinese scholars. How far simpler is it to use 22 or 24 or 26 signs only! The alphabet may also be passed from one language to another without great difficulty; the same alphabet is used now for English, French, Italian, German, Spanish, Turkish, Polish, Dutch, Czech, Croatian, Welsh, Finnish, Hungarian and others, and has derived from the alphabet once used by the ancient Hebrews, Phoenicians, Aramaeans, Greeks, Etruscans and Romans.

Thanks to the simplicity of the alphabet, writing has become very common; it is no longer a more or less exclusive domain of the priestly or other privileged classes, as it was in Egypt, or Mesopotamia, or China. Education has become largely a matter of reading and writing, and is possible for all. The fact that alphabetic writing has survived with relatively little change for three and a half millennia, notwithstanding the introduction of printing and the typewriter, and the extensive use of shorthand-writing, is the best evidence for its suitability to serve the needs of the whole modern world. It is this simplicity, adaptability and suitability which have secured the triumph of the alphabet over the other systems of writing.

Alphabetic writing and its origin constitute a story in themselves; they offer a new field for research which American scholars are beginning to call "alphabetology." No other system of writing has had so extensive, so intricate and so interesting a history.

Diringer's observation that the alphabet is "now universally employed by civilized peoples" is a bit tautological since it is by alphabet alone that men have detribalized or individualized themselves into "civilization." Cultures can rise far above civilization artistically but without the phonetic alphabet they remain tribal, as do the Chinese and the Japanese. It is necessary to stress that my concern is with the process of separation of sense by which the detribalizing of men is achieved. Whether such personal abstraction and social detribalization be a "good thing" is not for any individual to determine. But a recognition of the process may disembarrass the matter of the miasmal moral fogs that now invest it.

The alphabet is an aggressive and militant absorber and transformer of cultures, as Harold Innis was the first to show.

✱ Another observation of Diringer's that deserves comment is the acceptability among all peoples of a technology that uses letters to "represent single

> helpiŋ the bliend man
>
> loŋ agœ thær livd a
> bliend man. hee livd whær
> trees and flouers grω; but
> the bliend man cωd not see
> the trees or flouers.
>
> the pωr man had tω feel
> the wæ to gœ with his stick.
> tap-tap-tap went his stick on
> the rœd. hee waukt slœly.

The New York Times

NEW 43-UNIT ALPHABET: This is a page from a work called "Jesus the Helper," printed in the experimental augmented Roman alphabet in Britain. The alphabet, based largely on phonetics, contains the conventional alphabet with letters "q" and "x" discarded and nineteen new letters added. There are no capital letters. Under the system, the letter "o" is unchanged in the sound of "long," but "ago" is spelled "agoe" with the "o" and "e" joined. Another new letter is an inverted "z,' for sounds like "trees." The conventional "s" is used in words like "see." Other new letters include "i" and "e" joined by a cross-bar for words like "blind;" "o" and "u" joined for words like "flowers," and two "o's" that are joined together. In September, about 1,000 British children will start to learn to read with this phonetic, experimental alphabet.

Figure 1, from the *New York Times*, July 20, 1961.

49

sounds rather than ideas or syllables." Another way of putting this is to say that any society possessing the alphabet can translate any adjacent cultures into its alphabetic mode. But this is a one-way process. No non-alphabetic culture can take over an alphabetic one; because the alphabet cannot be assimilated; it can only liquidate or reduce. However, in the electronic age we may have discovered the limits of the alphabet technology. It need no longer seem strange that peoples like the Greeks and Romans, who had experienced the alphabet, should also have been driven in the direction of conquest and organization-at-a-distance. Harold Innis, in *Empire and Communications*, was the first to pursue this theme and to explain in detail the simple truth of the Cadmus myth. The Greek King Cadmus, who introduced the phonetic alphabet to Greece, was said to have sown the dragon's teeth and that they sprang up armed men. (The dragon's teeth may allude to the old hieroglyphic forms.) Innis also explained why print causes nationalism and not tribalism; and why print causes price systems and markets such as cannot exist without print. In short, Harold Innis was the first person to hit upon the *process* of change as implicit in the *forms* of media technology. The present book is a footnote of explanation to his work.

Diringer is emphatic about only one thing concerning the alphabet. No matter how or when it was achieved:

At any rate, it must be said that the great achievement of the invention was not the creation of the *signs*. It lies in the adoption of a purely alphabetic system, which, moreover, denoted each sound by one sign only. For this achievement, simple as it now seems to us, the inventor, or the inventors are to be ranked among the greatest benefactors of mankind. No other people in the world has been able to develop a true alphabetic writing. The more or less civilized peoples of Egypt, Mesopotamia, Crete, Asia Minor, Indus Valley, China, Central America, reached an advanced stage in the history of writing, but could not get beyond the transitional stage. A few peoples (the ancient Cypriotes, the Japanese and others), developed a syllabary. But only the Syro-Palestinian Semites produced a genius who created the alphabetic writing, from which have descended all past and present alphabets.

Each important civilization modifies its script and time may make its relation to some of its near relatives quite unrecognizable. Thus, the Brahmi, the great mother-script of India, the Korean alphabet, the Mongolian scripts are derived from the same source as the Greek, the Latin, the Runic, the Hebrew, the Arabic, the Russian alphabet, although it is practically impossible for a layman to see a real resemblance between them. (pp. 216–17)

By the meaningless sign linked to the meaningless sound we have built the shape and meaning of Western man. Our next concern will be to trace somewhat sketchily the effects of the alphabet in manuscript culture in the ancient and medieval world. After that, we shall look much more closely at the transformation of alphabetic culture by the printing press.

The Homeric hero becomes a split-man as he assumes an individual ego.

✷ In his *Art and Illusion*, E. H. Gombrich writes (p. 116):

If I had to reduce the last chapter to a brief formula it would be "making
comes before matching." Before the artist ever wanted to match the sights
of the visible world he wanted to create things in their own right. . . . The
very violence with which Plato denounces this trickery reminds us of the
momentous fact that at the time he wrote, mimesis was a recent invention.
There are many critics now who share his distaste, for one reason or
another, but even they would admit there are few more exciting spectacles
in the whole history of art than the great awakening of Greek sculpture
and painting between the sixth century and the time of Plato's youth toward
the end of the fifth century B.C.

Etienne Gilson makes much of the distinction between making and matching in his *Painting and Reality*. And whereas till Giotto a painting was a
thing, from Giotto till Cézanne painting became the representation of things.
See his chapter VIII on "Imitation and Creation."

There was, of course, the same development towards representation and
direct lineal narrative in poetry and prose, as we shall see. What is essential
for understanding this process, however, is that *mimesis* in Plato's (not
Aristotle's) sense is the necessary effect of separating out the visual mode
from the ordinary enmeshment with the audile-tactile interplay of senses. It
is this process, brought about by the experience of phonetic literacy, that
hoicks societies of the world of "sacred" or cosmic space and time into the
detribalized or "profane" space and time of civilized and pragmatic man.
Such is the theme of *The Sacred and The Profane: The Nature of Religion* by
Mircea Eliade.

In *The Greeks and the Irrational*, E. R. Dodds discusses the emotional
instability and manias of the Homeric heroes: "And we may also ask ourselves why a people so civilised, clear-headed, and rational as the Ionians
did not eliminate from their national epics these links with Borneo and the
primitive past, just as they eliminated the fear of the dead . . ." (p. 13)
But it is his next page that is especially helpful:

"His own behaviour . . . has become alien to him. He cannot understand it.
It is for him no part of his Ego." This is a perfectly true observation, and
its relevance to some of the phenomena we have been considering cannot,
I think, be doubted. Nilsson is also, I believe, right in holding that experiences
of this sort played a part—along with other elements, such as the Minoan
tradition of protecting goddesses—in building up that machinery of *physical*

51

intervention to which Homer resorts so constantly and, to our thinking, often so superfluously. We find it superfluous because the divine machinery seems to us in many cases to do no more than duplicate a natural psychological causation. But ought we not perhaps to say rather that the divine machinery "duplicates" a psychic intervention—that is, presents it in a concrete pictorial form? This was not superfluous; for only in this way could it be made vivid to the imagination of the hearers. The Homeric poets were without the refinements of language which would have been needed to "put across" adequately a purely psychological miracle. What more natural than that they should first supplement, and later replace, an old unexciting threadbare formula like μένος ἔμβαλε θυμῷ by making the god appear as a physical presence and exhort his favourite with the spoken word? How much more vivid than a mere inward monition is the famous scene in *Iliad* I where Athena plucks Achilles by the hair and warns him not to strike Agamemnon! But she is visible to Achilles alone: "none of the others saw her." That is a plain hint that she is projection, the pictorial expression, of an inward monition—a monition which Achilles might have described by such a vague phrase as ἐνέπνευσε φρεσὶ δαίμων. And I suggest that in general the inward monition, or the sudden unaccountable feeling of power, or the sudden unaccountable loss of judgement, is the germ out of which the divine machinery developed.

The hero has become a split man as he moves towards the possession of an individual ego. And the "split" is manifest as pictorialized models or "machinery" of complex situations such as tribal, auditory man had made no effort to visualize. That is to say, detribalization, individualization, and pictorialization are all one. The magical mode disappears in proportion as interior events are made visually manifest. But such manifestation is also reduction and distortion of complex relations which are more fully sensed when there is full interplay of all the senses at once.

Mimesis to Plato had appeared, quite understandably, as varieties of representation, especially visual. In his *Poetics* 4, Aristotle made mimesis central to his entire cognitive and epistemological world, not limiting it to any one sense. But the first onset of literacy, and, therefore, of visuality as abstracted from the other senses, seemed to Plato a diminution of ontological awareness, or an impoverishment of Being. Bergson somewhere asks, how should we be able to know if some agent could double the speed of *all* events in the world? Quite simply, he answered. We would discern a great loss of richness in experience. Such seems to have been Plato's attitude towards literacy and visual mimesis.

Gombrich begins his tenth chapter of *Art and Illusion* with further observations on visual mimesis:

The last chapter has led this inquiry back to the old truth that the discovery of appearances was not due so much to a careful observation of nature as to the invention of pictorial effects. I believe indeed that the ancient writers who were still filled with a sense of wonder at man's capacity to fool the eye came closer to an understanding of this achievement than many later critics . . . but if we discard Berkeley's theory of vision, according to which we "see" a flat field but "construct" a tactile space, we can perhaps rid art history of its obsession with space and bring other achievements into focus, the suggestion of light and of texture, for instance, or the mastery of physiognomic expression.

Berkeley's *New Theory of Vision* (1709) is now favoured by psychologists of our sense lives. But Berkeley was concerned to refute Descartes and Newton, who had wholly abstracted the visual sense from the interaction of the other senses. On the other hand, the suppression of the visual sense in favour of the audile-tactile complex, produces the distortions of tribal society, and of the configuration of jazz and primitive art imitations which broke upon us with radio, but not just "because" of radio.[11]

Gombrich not only has all the most relevant information about the rise of the pictorial mode; he has all the right difficulties. He ends his *Art and Illusion* by commenting (pp. 117–18):

There is finally the history of Greek painting as we can follow it in painted pottery, which tells of the discovery of foreshortening and the conquest of space early in the fifth century and of light in the fourth. . . . Emanuel Loewy at the turn of the century first developed his theories about the rendering of nature in Greek art that stressed the priority of conceptual modes and their gradual adjustment to natural appearances. . . . But in itself it explains very little. For why was it that this process started comparatively so late in the history of mankind? In this respect our perspective has very much changed. To the Greeks the archaic period represented the dawn of history, and classical scholarship has not always shaken off this inheritance. From this point of view it appeared quite natural that the awakening of art from primitive modes should have coincided with the rise of all those other activities, that, for the humanist, belong to civilization: the development of philosophy, of science, and of dramatic poetry.

[11]Georg von Bekesy's article on "Similarities between Hearing and Skin Sensations" (*Psychological Review*, Jan., 1959, pp. 1–22) provides a means of understanding why no sense can function in isolation nor can be unmodified by the operation and diet of the other senses.

The world of the Greeks illustrates why visual appearances cannot interest a people before the interiorization of alphabetic technology.

✱ The discovery that the representation of "natural appearances" is quite abnormal and also quite unperceptible as such to non-literate peoples, has created some disturbance of mind nowadays. For the same distortions of reality that we associate with our conventions of abstractly visual perception also invaded mathematics, science and the verbal arts of logic and poetry. In the past century of non-Euclidean geometries, symbolic logics, and symbolist poetry, the same discovery has been repeated. That is to say, single-plane lineal, visual, and sequential codification of experience is quite conventional and limited. It is in danger of being brushed aside today in every area of Western experience. We have long been accustomed to praising the Greeks for the invention of visual order in sculpture, painting, science, as well as in philosophy, literature, and politics. But today, having learned how to play with each of the senses in isolation, scholars look askance at the Greeks for their pusillanimity: "Whatever else the story, as I have pieced it together, may tell, it brings out the fact that Greek art and Greek geometry were based on the same tactile-muscular sensuous intuitions, that in many ways their developments went along similar lines, and that their limitations were implicit in those intuitions." [12]

From the point of view of recent intense awareness of the visual components of experience, then, the Greek world looks timid and tentative. But there was nothing in the manuscript phase of alphabetic technology that was intense enough to split the visual from the tactile entirely. Not even Roman script had the power to do that. It was not until the experience of mass production of exactly uniform and repeatable type, that the fission of the senses occurred, and the visual dimension broke away from the other senses.

Oswald Spengler noted in *The Decline of the West* (p. 89) the liquidation of the visual, Western awareness in our new physics, greeting the return to the unseen with a tribal cheer:

Once the space-element or point had lost its last persistent relic of visualness and, instead of being represented to the eye as a cut in

[12]Ivins, *Art and Geometry*, p. 59.

co-ordinate lines, was defined as a group of three independent numbers, there was no longer any inherent objection to replacing the number *3* by the general number *n*. The notion of dimension was radically changed. It was no longer a matter of treating the properties of a point metrically with reference to its position in a visible system, but of representing the entirely abstract properties of a number-group . . .

"Entirely abstract" means the non-visual resonating interplay of the audile-tactile by which electricity and radio especially were to regenerate what Conrad called "the Africa within" the Western experience.

It would seem that the extension of one or another of our senses by mechanical means, such as the phonetic script, can act as a sort of twist for the kaleidoscope of the entire sensorium. A new combination or ratio of the existing components occurs, and a new mosaic of possible forms presents itself. That such switch of sense ratios should occur with every instance of external technology is easy to see today. Why has it been unnoticed before? Perhaps because the shifts have in the past occurred somewhat gradually. Now we experience such a series of new technologies even in our own world and, besides, have means of observing so many other cultures that only great inattention could now conceal the role of new media of information in altering the posture and relations of our senses.

Merely for the purpose of finding our bearings it may be helpful to compare and contrast a few instances of literature and art in the newly literate Greek world, on one hand, and the non-literate world, on the other.

It is significant, however, that the Romans did go beyond the Greeks in the awareness of visual properties:

Lucretius is neither speaking of, nor interested in, the problems of representation. His description of the purely optical phenomena does, however, go considerably beyond the cautious observations of Euclid. It is a complete description, not of the expanding visual cone, but of the apparent cone of contraction, or diminution, which is its counterpart. The ideas which Lucretius expresses a quarter of a century before the writing of "De Architectura" are the optical equivalent of the perspective system whichVitruvius describes.[13]

Likewise, the Romans exceeded the Greeks in their bias towards the life of action, of applied knowledge, and the lineal organization of many levels of living. In art this bias appears in the setting of flat planes, one behind the other, in order that action may appear by an oblique or diagonal shift in the planes. But there is one observation of John White's (*The Birth and Rebirth of Pictorial Space*, p. 237) which is especially valuable in illuminating the most striking feature of Greek narrative: "All the forms lie in a single plane. All the movement is in one direction." In a work devoted entirely to the

[13]John White, *The Birth and Rebirth of Pictorial Space*, p. 257.

55

victory of the visual over the other senses, White examines spatial design in antiquity and later. "The simple spatial patterns which appear for the first time upon the delicate, curved surfaces of antique vases seem to echo no elaborate theoretical construction. In themselves they call for no inquiry as to the nature of perspective systems which, if they existed, find no echo in surviving work." (p. 270)

The Greek *point of view* in both art and chronology has little in common with ours but was much like that of the Middle Ages.

✷ White's view is that although some attributes of perspective occur in antiquity, there was not much interest in them as such. In the Renaissance it became recognized technique that perspective called for a *fixed* point of view. Such a stress on private stance, while common to a print culture, simply did not concern a manuscript culture. The dynamics of individualism and nationalism were merely latent in the scribal mode. For in the highly tactile product of the scribe the reader found no means for splitting off the visual from the audile-tactile complex, such as the sixteenth and seventeenth century reader did. A great deal of what is said by Bernard van Groningen in his study of the Greek time sense, *In the Grip of the Past*, is useful in understanding the effects of visual bias as they concern the time sense. As might be expected, the new Greek sense of chronological order and a one-way movement of events was an overlay on the older mythical and cosmic idea of simultaneous time, which is common to all non-literate communities. Van Groningen observes (p. 17): "The Greeks often refer to the past and by doing so, they bind the matter in question to a chronological conception. But as soon as we inquire after the real meaning, it becomes obvious that the idea is not temporal but is used in general sense."

This is, in respect to time, like having foreshortening without a fixed point of view or vanishing point. And that, indeed, was the Greek stage of visual abstraction. Somewhat in the same way, van Groningen argues, Herodotus having "freed himself from myth and mythical speculations," made a gesture "to use the past as an explanation of the present, or at any rate, of a later phase in the development." (p. 26) This visualizing of chronological sequences is unknown to oral societies, as it is now irrelevant in the electric age of information movement. The "narrative line" in a literature is immediately revealing in the same way as the painterly or sculptural line. It tells exactly how far the dissociation of the visual from the other senses has proceeded. Erich Auerbach[14] confirms in literature all aspects of the Greek development as it has appeared thus far in the other arts. Thus Homer's Achilles and Odysseus are presented in flat vertical planes by "fully externalized description, uniform illumination, uninterrupted connection, free expression, all events in the foreground, displaying unmistakable meanings, few elements of historical development and of psychological perspective . . ."

The visual makes for the explicit, the uniform, and the sequential in painting, in poetry, in logic, history. The non-literate modes are implicit, simultaneous, and discontinuous, whether in the primitive past or the electronic present, which Joyce called "eins within a space."

Van Groningen relates the new visual and sequential idea of chronology with "the awakening of the scientific sense in Greece," which, it is true, tries to observe the facts with accuracy, but wishes even more to know the explanation and looks for it in preceding causes. This visual notion of "causality" found its extreme expression in Newtonian physics. Sir Edmund Whittaker writes in *Space and Spirit* (p. 86):

Newtonianism, like Aristotelianism, attempts to understand the world by tracing the connection of events with one another; and this is effected by ordering our experiences according to the category of cause and effect, discovering for every phenomenon its determining agents or antecedents. The affirmation that this connection is all-embracing, that no event happens without a cause, is the *postulate* of *causality*.

The extreme visual bias of this notion of cause obtrudes very incongruously in an electric and simultaneous world. Sir Edmund adds (p. 87), by way of contrast:

Thus, the notion of force tended to become replaced by the notions of *interaction* and of the *energy* possessed by the aggregate of a set of particles; and instead of considering single bodies under the influence of forces, the mathematical physicists developed theories such as that of Lagrange in dynamics, in which mathematical equations are obtained capable of predicting the future of a whole system of bodies simultaneously, without bringing in the ideas of "force" or "cause" at all. . . .

The pre-Socratic or pre-literate philosophers like the post-literate scientists of our day have only to listen to the inner resonance of a problem in order to derive it and the universe from water or fire or some single "world-function." That is, the speculators of our time can as easily fall unawares into the auditory bias of "field" theory as the Greeks leapt into the flatland

[14]*Mimesis: The Representation of Reality in Western Literature.* This book is devoted to a stylistic analysis of the narrative lines in Western letters from Homer to the present.

of abstract visuality and one-way lineality. The Greeks, says van Groningen (pp. 36–7), eagerly sought the past:

Odysseus is nowhere the adventurer who, drawn by the unknown, likes to go farther and farther, who is charmed by the coming events, and urged on by the mysteries of the future to ever receding regions. Quite the contrary. He only wants to go back; the past fascinates him; he wants restoration of the things of the past, he travels by compulsion, driven along by Poseidon's wrath, Poseidon the god of the strange and unknown land which attracts the adventurers but terrifies Odysseus. This endless wandering to him means adversity and misfortune; the return, happiness and peace. The mysterious future strikes agony into his heart; he has to steel himself against it; but he feels safe with the past, with the known.

The idea of the past, discovered by means of the new visual chronology as an area of peace in a distant perspective was, indeed, a novelty. It would have been impossible save by phonetic literacy, and it is a vision which is quite difficult for us to imagine today as ever being accessible again. Van Groningen's analysis of the reasons for the Greek obsession with the past, as scientific and as psychological security, helps to explain the natural literary bias of all humanist ages in favour of ruins. For nowhere does the past speak so eloquently to the solitary musings of the scholar as from the midst of ruins. There is another feature of the time which bridges from the Greek present into the past: "The time discussed is clearly homogeneous. It bears the character of an uninterrupted sequence of occurrences in which everything is in its right place." (p. 95)

The Greeks invented both their artistic and scientific novelties after the interiorization of the alphabet.

✱ Homogeneity, uniformity, repeatability, these are basic component notes of a visual world newly emergent from an audile-tactile matrix. Such components the Greeks used as a bridge from present to past, but not from present to future. Van Groningen writes (p. 95): "The Greek knows and the oriental knows not, how uncertain the future is; an undisturbed past and a prosperous present are in no way a guarantee of a happy future. So we can only value a human life . . . when it has become a complete past, at man's death, as with Tellus the Athenian."

The analysis of William Ivins strongly supports van Groningen when the latter writes: "The conception which they have of the future is, of course, only an expected, dreaded or desired parallel to the past." But the visual element in the Greek sensibility was still much embedded in the audile-tactile complex, giving to their fifth century, as to the Elizabethan Age, the character of a relatively balanced sensibility.[15] That the same limitation of mere visual parallelism affected Greek geometry Ivins points out in his *Art and Geometry* (pp. 57–8):

When Pappus had finished, the situation was that the late Greek geometers knew two focal ratios, three directrix-focus ratios, and the visual transformation of a circle into an ellipse. They also knew, and these I shall come back to, not only particular cases of the invariance of anharmonic ratios but Euclid's "porism", the latter of which was as close a miss as possible for Desargues' Theorem. But they regarded these things as isolated propositions having no relation to each other. Had the late Greeks only added to them the one further idea that parallel lines meet at infinity, they would have had in their hands at least logical equivalents of the basic ideas for geometrical continuity and for perspective and perspective geometry. That is to say that again and again during a period of six or seven centuries they went right up to the door of modern geometry, but that, inhibited by their tactile-muscular, metrical ideas, they were never able to open that door and pass out into the great open spaces of modern thought.

The story of uniformity, continuity, and homogeneity was the new mode in Greek logic as it was in geometry. Jan Lukasieqicz, in *Aristotle's Syllogistic* stresses: "Syllogistic as conceived by Aristotle requires terms to be homogeneous with respect to their possible positions as subjects and predicates. This seems to be the true reason why singular terms were omitted by Aristotle." (p. 7) And: "This is the greatest defect of the Aristotelian logic, that singular terms and propositions have no place in it. What was the cause?" (p. 6) The cause was the same as in all the Greek seeking of the novelties of visual order and lineal homogeneity. But our analyst has a further note (p. 15) on the inseparable nature of "logic" and the abstract visual faculty: "Modern formal logic strives to attain the greatest possible exactness. This aim can be reached only by means of a precise language built up of stable, visually perceptible signs. Such a language is indispensable for any science." But such a language is made by excluding all but the visual sense even of words.

The only concern here is to spot the degree of effect which the alphabet had on its first users. Lineality and homogeneity of parts were "discoveries," or rather changes in the sense life of the Greeks under the new regime of phonetic writing. The Greeks expressed these new modes of visual perception

[15]See the expansion of this theme in *The Shakespearean Moment* by Patrick Cruttwell.

in the arts. The Romans extended lineality and homogeneity into the civic and military spheres, and into the world of the arch and of enclosed or visual space. They did not so much extend the Greek "discoveries" as undergo the same process of detribalization and visualization. They extended lineality into an Empire and homogenization into the mass-processing of citizens, statuary, and books. Today the Roman would be quite at home in the U.S.A. and the Greek by comparison would prefer the "backward" and oral cultures of our world, such as Ireland or the Old South.

The kind and degree of literate experience of the Greek was not intense enough to enable him to translate his audile-tactile heritage into the "enclosed" or "pictorial" space that was only widely available to human sensibility after printing. Between the extreme visuality of perspective and the flat planes of Greek and medieval art there is a further degree of abstraction or dissociation of our sense lives which we quite naturally feel to be the difference between the ancient-medieval and the modern worlds. Since new, empathic methods of art and cultural analysis give us easy access to all modalities of human sensibility we are no longer limited to a perspective of past societies. We recreate them.

There is entire consistency in the effects of the emergent visual component in every sector of the ancient world. The steady increase of stress on retinal impression from the Greek into the Roman time has been noted by John Hollander in *The Untuning of the Sky* (p. 7):

But with the exception of oral, pre-literary poetry, added complications to the consideration of poetry as sound arise in the existence and use of written languages. If a poem is to be treated as a highly complex utterance in a spoken language, its written form becomes a simple coding of it, word by word, onto a page. The poem will thus be defined in terms of patterns of sound classes. But starting as early as the first Latin use of Greek meters, literary analysis has been confronted with poems whose written versions, or codings, contain significant individual and conventional elements which do not appear in the original, or aural, versions, and vice versa. To state that both music and poetry are composed of sound, without specifying the degree to which this is true, therefore, becomes misleadingly inadequate. The difficulties of such a reduction have resulted not only in categorical esthetic confusions, but in those which produced the unnecessary conflicts among traditional European prosodic theories since Hellenistic times. The *locus classicus* of these confusions for our literary history occurred in the equation of what was actually a musical system (Greek meter) to a more graphic prosodic one (Latin quantitative scansion). It seems to be generally true that borrowed foreign literary conventions, as well as revivals and adaptations of past traditions, invade the linguistic structure of poetry at the written level. Any thorough formalistic analysis of the structure of poetry, and of its relation to the language in which it is written, must deal with the written language as a system in itself, as well as with the spoken one.

Albert Einstein, in his *Short History of Music* (p. 20), offers a further vista of these changes towards the visual organization of musical structures in the Middle Ages:

The music being purely vocal, the notation dispensed with indications of rhythm; but it possessed an immediate intelligibility that was lacking in the Greek system, since it actually gave a visual representation of the rise and fall of melody. It became the sure foundation on which modern notation was to be built; . . .

Einstein extends his vista into the Gutenberg area itself (p. 45):

This international influence was made possible by the invention of music-printing about 1500. This produced as great a revolution in the history of music as book-printing had done in the history of general European culture. A quarter of a century after Gutenberg's first attempts, German and Italian printers produced printed missals. The decisive step—the printing of the notation of measured music from type—was taken by Ottaviano dei Petrucci of Fossombrone . . . at Venice. . . . Venice . . . remained the principal centre for the printing and publishing of polyphonic music.

The continuity of Greek and medieval art was assured by the bond between caelatura or engraving and illumination.

✳ In his *Approach to Greek Art* (p. 43) Charles Seltman writes:

. The Greeks had no paper: papyrus was expensive, reserved for documents and unsuitable for drawing. Wax tablets had no permanence. In fact, the surface of the vase was the drawing-paper of the artist. . . . It is significant that from 650 B.C. onwards Athenian potters had already established a big export trade and were sending their products overseas to Aegina, Italy, and the East.

Seltman in this passage indicates why the Greeks made so much less of literacy than the Romans with their high organization of paper in production and the book trade. The decline of the papyrus supplies in the later Roman Empire is a regularly assigned cause for the "collapse" of that Empire and its road system. For the Roman road was a paper route in every sense.[16]

[16]There is much on this subject in *Empire and Communications* by Harold Innis, as well as in his *The Bias of Communication*. In the chapter on "The Problem of Space" in the latter book (pp. 92–131) he has much to say on the power of the written word to reduce the oral and magical dimensions of acoustic space: "The oral tradition

The principal theme of Seltman's *Approach to Greek Art* is that the major mode of Greek expression was not that of the sculptor but the *celator* or engraver (p. 12):

> For more than four centuries men have been instructed that the very best things which the Greeks ever made were of marble, and that is why you may read in a book on Greek art written little more than a score of years ago that "sculpture was in many ways the most characteristic art of Greece; . . . it achieved the highest attainments". Such has been the usual approach to Greek art. The prize must go to sculpture in stone, with which large works cast in bronze were often associated; next came painting, which is now represented mainly by drawings made on the surfaces of ancient vases; third came the so-called "minor arts", under which label were grouped with condescension and convenience the work of die-cutters, gem-engravers, jewellers, and celators (or metalchasers). But does such "classing" in any way correspond with the ideas which the Greeks themselves held about artists and art?
> It is certain that they had very different views.
> Even in the distant age of bronze the inhabitants of Greece and the islands held the skilled worker in metal in very high regard. His art was both a mystery and a delight, and he was thought to owe his gifts to supernatural beings around whom many legends grew. There were creatures called Dactyls, smelters of bronze; Curetes and Corybantes, armourers; Cabeiroi, who were skilful smiths; Telchines, gifted workers in gold, silver and bronze who made weapons for gods and the earliest statues; and lastly the mighty Cyclopes forging the bolts of Zeus. All these are vague giants, goblins and godlings— patron saints of the workshop and the forge whom you might do well to appease and some of whose names just meant "Fingers", "Hammer", "Tongs", and "Anvil". Then, by the time that the Homeric epic began to take form, one of these beings seems to have grown in stature until he attained Olympian rank.

Embossing, and chasing, and engraving "on gold, silver, bronze, ivory or gems" was the art called in Latin *caelatura*. It is significant that in our time we should find it natural to observe many ancient productions in Seltman's way:

> Exciting as are the marbles of the Parthenon and certain sensitive tombstones of Attic work, it is not among such things that the finest art of the fifth century is to be sought. The most admired artists among the Greeks them-

---

of the Druids reported by Caesar as designed to train the memory and to keep learning from becoming generally accessible had been wiped out." And: "The development of the Empire and Roman law reflected the need for institutions to meet the rise of individualism and cosmopolitanism which followed the breakdown of the polis and the city state." (p. 13) For if paper and roads broke up the city states and set individualism in place of Aristotle's "political animal," "Decline in the use of papyrus particularly after the spread of Mohammedanism necessitated the use of parchment." (p. 17) On the role of papyrus in the book trade and Empire alike see also *From Papyrus to Print* by George Herbert Bushnell and especially *Ancilla to Classical Learning* by Moses Hadas.

selves were not the masons, nor even the modellers, casters and finishers of fine bronzes—but the celators. (p. 72)

The work of the *celator* and engraver is much more tactile than visual and corresponds to the new bias of our electric age. But as regards the present book, the argument of Seltman is most relevant, for he traces the art of the *celator* all the way through Greek and Roman times and through the medieval world in the art of illumination (p. 115):

Painting in this same age was also able to display its excellence especially in the making of miniatures upon glass set against a gold-leaf background. A certain Greek named Bounneris signed one of these (Plate 102a) with portraits of a mother and two children, and another similar work, unsigned (Plate 102g), shows an agreeable male likeness. This is a fine aristocratic art which was to give rise later to the art of illumination on vellum; and it is an art contemporary with the philosopher Plotinus, a man more sensitive to fine art than ever Plato or Aristotle had been.

The increase of visual stress among the Greeks alienated them from the primitive art that the electronic age now reinvents after interiorizing the unified field of electric all-at-onceness.

❋ The prevalence of the art of the *celator*, in a word, is a cue and a key to the tactile mode of sensibility as it is interwoven with an incipient stage of literacy, whether in Greece, Rome, or in the flat illumination of the Middle Ages.

Seltman, like most of his contemporaries, approaches Greek art, not in a perspective, but as a configuration or a mosaic of items in a field. Co-existence and interplay among the figures in the flat field create a multi-levelled and multi-sensuous awareness. This mode of approach tends to partake of the character of auditory, inclusive, and unenclosed space, as Georg von Bekesy has shown in his *Experiments in Hearing*. But it was the method used everywhere, even by Percy Wyndham Lewis, the critical analyst of the return of auditory space to the twentieth century, in his *Time and Western Man*. And so, Seltman pursues an acoustic field approach, even to the story of the origins of perspective (p. 31):

. . . Homer cannot be described as more childish than Aeschylus, but as a different kind of poet; Plato is not called a riper stylist than Thucydides, but a different kind of writer with a different theme; St. Paul's letters are not more decadent than Cicero's, merely different. For the literature of the ancient world this Growth and Decay Formula will not work. Are we justified in applying it to Fine Art?

"Well," you may say, "why worry if people have this harmless illusion about Growth and Decay?" But it happens not to be so harmless, because it implies another doctrine. Implicit in the formula is the dogma that earlier Greek artists must have been striving all the while to attain a naturalism, to achieve a life-like imitation that was beyond their powers. Yet, reverting to literary comparison, it is not generally claimed that in dramatic presentation, Aeschylus, to take an example, was struggling to be as true to life as Menander; or Shakespeare as true to life as Shaw. It is even conceivable—rather probable—that Aeschylus would have disapproved of the New Comedy, and Shakespeare of Shaw.

Seltman keeps the whole range of Greek interests in simultaneous play, as it were, waiting for the intrusion of a new theme or pressure in the complex configuration. He watches the reduction of the resonant poetic modes to the simple visual lines of prose, and cites the Parthenon sculptures as "the most perfect art-prose work of the Greeks." These representational forms of sculpture he notes (p. 66) as prose because of their "descriptive realism":

The fact, however, remains that prose literature and art-prose began to appear among the Greeks at about the same time, and that before the fifth century was out each had produced its masterpiece; the history of Thucydides, and the sculptures of the Parthenon.

What cause or causes led to the adoption of descriptive realism in art to the near exclusion of poetic formalism? It is of no use to talk of development or growth, for the Parthenon no more grew out of Olympia than the history of Thucydides out of the dramas of Aeschylus. Rather, it seems that the fifth-century Greeks, having experimented in realistic art, began to find it more to their taste than formal art because they acquired a liking for verisimilitude.

A nomadic society cannot experience enclosed space.

✳ Instead of using Seltman's unique observations about Greek celature as a take-off strip for the medieval manuscript culture, I am going to enlarge the present mosaic of exhibits a little more. Before approaching the five centuries of the Gutenberg galaxy, it will be well to note how profoundly indifferent are non-literate men to visual values in the organization of perception and experience. This indifference is shared by the artist "since Cézanne." A great art historian like Siegfried Giedion has extrapolated the new art approaches to space "since Cézanne" to include "popular culture" and "anonymous history." Art is for him as inclusive an idea as "mimesis" is for Aristotle. He is currently completing a massive work on *The Beginnings of Art* as a companion to his artistic analysis of all the abstract modes of twentieth-century mechanization. It is necessary to understand the close interrelation between the world and art of the cave man, and the intensely organic interdependence of men in the electric age. Of course, it could be argued that a lyric disposition to applaud the audile-tactile gropings of child and cave art betokens a naive and uncritical obsession with the unconscious modes of an electric or simultaneous culture. But it was a great thrill for many late Romantics to break through suddenly into an "understanding" of primitive art. As Emile Durkheim had insisted, men could not take much more of the fragmentation of work and experience by visual specialization. For the real "abstract" art is that of realism and naturalism based on a separation of the visual faculty from the interplay of the other senses. So-called abstract art is, in fact, the result of much sense interplay with varying dominance of ear and touch. I would suggest that "touch" is not so much a separate sense as the very interplay of the senses. That is why it recedes in significance as the visual faculty is given separate and abstract intensity.

In a very interesting section from his forthcoming book on the beginnings of art printed in *Explorations in Communication* (pp. 71–89), Giedion explains the space awareness of the cave painters:

No traces of human dwellings have been found in the interior of the caverns. These were holy places in which, with the aid of magically potent pictures, the sacred rituals could be performed.

These caverns possess no space in our meaning of this word, for in them perpetual darkness reigns. The caverns are, spatially speaking, empty. This is well appreciated by anyone who has tried alone to find his way out from one of them. The weak beam of light from his light torch is swallowed up by the absolute darkness around him, while rocky tunnels and crumbling slopes repeat themselves in every direction and re-echo his question: where is the outlet from this labyrinth?

Light and the Art of the Caverns

Nothing is more destructive of the true values of primeval art than the glare of electric light in this realm of eternal night. Flares or small stone lamps burning animal fat, of which examples have been found, permit one to obtain only fragmentary glimpses of the colors and lines of the objects depicted. In such a soft, flickering light these take on an almost magical

65

movement. The engraved lines, and even the colored surfaces, lose their intensity under a strong light and sometimes disappear altogether. Only in this way can the fine veining of the drawings be seen unsmothered by their rough background.

Maybe enough has now been said to show that prehistoric man did not associate the caverns with architecture. In his view the caverns simply provided him with places that he could use for his magic arts. He selected these places with the utmost care.

A hole in the ground is not enclosed space because, like a triangle or a tepee, it merely exhibits the lines of force. A square does not exhibit the lines of force, but is a translation of such tactile space into visual terms. No such translation occurs before writing. And anyone who takes the trouble to read Emile Durkheim's *The Division of Labour* can find the reasons why. For until sedentary life permits some specialization of human tasks, there is no specialization of the sense life such as leads to the stepping up of visual intensity. Anthropologists have suggested to me that any kind of carving or sculpture is already an indication of some stress in the visual area. It would seem reasonable, therefore, that nomadic people having very little specialization of tasks or of sense life would never develop rectangular spaces. But by the time they showed some sculpture they would be readying themselves for the further degree of visualization that is carving and writing and square enclosures. Sculpture, now as ever, is the frontier between the spaces of sight and sound. For sculpture is not enclosed space. It modulates space, as does sound. And architecture, too, has this mysterious dimension of the frontier between two worlds of space. Le Corbusier argues that it is best felt at night. It is only partly in the visual mode.

E. S. Carpenter's book *Eskimo* is concerned with the space concepts of the Eskimo, revealing his quite "irrational" or non-visual attitude to spatial forms and orientations:

I know of no example of an Aivilik describing space primarily in visual terms. They don't regard space as static, and therefore measurable; hence they have no formal units of spatial measurement, just as they have no uniform divisions of time. The carver is indifferent to the demands of the optical eye, he lets each piece fill its own space, create its own world, without reference to background or anything external to it. . . . In the oral tradition, the myth-teller speaks as many-to-many, not as person-to-person. Speech and song are addressed to all. . . . As poet, myth-teller, carver, the Eskimo conveys anonymous tradition to all. . . . The work of art can be seen or heard equally well from any direction.

The multidirectional space orientation, which is acoustic or auditory, causes the Eskimo to be much amused at squirming efforts of visitors to look at pictures "right-side up." Pages from magazines when stuck on igloo ceilings to prevent dripping, often tempt the white visitor to crane his neck to see them. In the same way the Eskimo may start a drawing or carving on one side of a board and continue right over. There is no word for art in their language yet: "Every Aivilik adult is an accomplished ivory carver: carving is a normal, essential requirement, just as writing is with us."

Giedion pursues the same spatial themes in *Explorations in Communication* (p. 84): "As is universally the case in primeval art, the eye of the Ice Age hunter discovers images of the animals he seeks in the structure of the rocks. The French describe this recognition of natural formations as "epouser les contours". A few lines, a little carving, or some color are enough to bring the animal into view." Our rediscovery of a passion for contours is inseparable from the recognition of precise interdependence and function, and of all forms as organic, which is thrust upon us by the electro-magnetic wave technology. That is, the recovery of primitive organic values in art and architecture is the central technological pressure of our time. Yet there are some anthropologists even today who vaguely suppose that non-literate men have Euclidean space perceptions.[17] And many more report their primitive data in terms of Euclidean models of organization. So it is scarcely surprising that a J. C. Carothers should be a rare figure. As a psychologist who crossed functional lines into the anthropological area, he was quite unprepared for what he found. What he found is still known to very few people, indeed. If the effects of the written word, in substituting visual for auditory dimensions of experience, were known to Mircea Eliade, for example, would he continue to express the same zeal for the "resacralizing" of human life?

Primitivism has become the vulgar cliché of much modern art and speculation.

✳ It is possible that the entire group influenced by Marinetti and Moholy-Nagy has been beguiled by a misunderstanding of the origins and causes of the profane configuration of life, on one hand, as of the "sacral" configuration, on the other. On the contrary, it is possible that even admitting the merely mechanical operation of technology in "sacralizing" and "desacralizing" human life, that the entire group of "irrationalists" in our century would still elect the "sacral" or auditory mode of organization of experience. For one thing, it is the emergent mode of the electro-magnetic or electronic, as

[17]E. S. Carpenter suggests that Vladimir G. Bogaaz (1860–1936) may have been the first anthropologist to state that non-literate man had non-Euclidean space conceptions. He states these themes in an article, "Ideas of Space and Time in the Concept of Primitive Religion," *American Anthropologist*, vol. 27, no. 2, April, 1925, pp. 205–66.

de Chardin stresses. And for many the new, as such, is a mandate from outer space, even when it is a plunge back into non-literate patterns of awareness. Though we see no inherent religious relevance or importance, either in the "sacred" or "profane" as presented by Eliade or any other "irrational" mystic of our time, we would not belittle the merely cultural power of the non-literate and the literate forms of life to shape the perceptions and biases of the entire human community. The miseries of conflict between the Eastern and Roman churches, for example, are a merely obvious instance of the type of opposition between the oral and the visual cultures, having nothing to do with the Faith.

I would ask, however, whether it is not time that we put these "childish things" under some sort of measured restraint so that their perpetual brain-washings of the human community be subjected to some degree of predictable operation. It has been said that the inevitable war is one whose causes have not been discerned. Since there can be no greater contradiction or clash in human cultures than that between those representing the eye and the ear, it is not strange that our metamorphosis into the eye mode of Western man should be only less agonizing than our present shift into the auditory mode of electronic man. But there is enough inner trauma in such change without the auditory cultures and the optical cultures flinging themselves at each other in outer manifestations of sadistic self-righteousness.

Mircea Eliade begins his introduction to *The Sacred and the Profane* as a manifesto announcing the long-delayed recognition of "the Sacred" or of auditory space in our century. He hails (pp. 8–9) Rudolf Otto's *Das Heilige* (*The Sacred*) of 1917: "Passing over the rational and speculative side of religion, he concentrated chiefly on its irrational aspect. For Otto had read Luther and had understood what the "living God" meant to a believer. It was not the God of the philosophers—of Erasmus, for example; it was not an idea, an abstract notion, a mere moral allegory. It was a terrible *power*, manifested in the divine wrath." Eliade then explains his project: "The aim of the following pages is to illustrate and define this opposition between sacred and profane." Sensing that "the modern Occidental experiences a certain uneasiness before many manifestations of the sacred," as when, "for many human beings, the sacred can be manifested in stones or trees," he proposes to show why man "of the archaic societies tends to live as much as possible *in* the sacred or in close proximity to consecrated objects":

Our chief concern in the following pages will be to elucidate this subject—
to show in what ways religious man attempts to remain as long as possible
in a sacred universe, and hence what his total experience of life proves to
be in comparison with the experience of the man without religious feeling,
of the man who lives, or wishes to live, in a desacralized world. It should
be said at once that the completely profane world, the wholly desacralized

cosmos, is a recent discovery in the history of the human spirit. It does not devolve upon us to show by what historical processes and as the result of what changes in spiritual attitudes and behavior modern man has desacralized his world and assumed a profane existence. For our purpose it is enough to observe that desacralization pervades the entire experience of the nonreligious man of modern societies and that, in consequence, he finds it increasingly difficult to rediscover the existential dimensions of religious man in the archaic societies. (p. 13)

Eliade is under a gross illusion in supposing that modern man "finds it increasingly difficult to rediscover the existential dimensions of religious man in the archaic societies." Modern man, since the electro-magnetic discoveries of more than a century ago, is investing himself with all the dimensions of archaic man *plus*. The art and scholarship of the past century and more have become a monotonous crescendo of archaic primitivism. Eliade's own work is an extreme popularization of such art and scholarship. But that is not to say that he is factually wrong. Certainly he is right in saying that "the wholly desacralized cosmos is a recent discovery in the history of the human spirit." In fact, the discovery results from the phonetic alphabet and the acceptance of its consequences, especially since Gutenberg. But I question the quality of insight that causes a human voice to quaver and resonate with hebdomadal vehemence when citing the "history of the human spirit."

The Gutenberg Galaxy is concerned to show why alphabetic man was disposed to desacralize his mode of being.

✽ The later section of this book will accept the role declined by Eliade when he says: "It does not devolve upon us to show by what historical processes . . . modern man has desacralized his world and assumed a profane existence." To show by exactly what historical process this was done is the theme of *The Gutenberg Galaxy*. And having shown the process, we can at least make a conscious and responsible choice concerning whether we elect once more the tribal mode which has such attraction for Eliade:

The abyss that divides the two modalities of experience—sacred and profane—will be apparent when we come to describe sacred space and the ritual building of the human habitation, or the varieties of the religious experience of time, or the relations of religious man to nature and the world of tools, or the consecration of human life itself, the sacrality with which man's vital functions (food, sex, work and so on) can be charged. Simply calling to mind what the city or the house, nature, tools, or work have become for modern and nonreligious man will show with the utmost vividness all that distinguishes such a man from a man belonging to any archaic society, or even from a peasant of Christian Europe. For modern consciousness, a physiological act—eating, sex and so on—is in some only an organic phenomenon, ... But for the primitive, such an act is never simply physiological; it is, or can become, a sacrament, that is, a communion with the sacred.

The reader will very soon realize that *sacred* and *profane* are two modes of being in the world, two existential situations assumed by man in the course of his history. These modes of being in the world are not of concern only to the history of religions or to sociology; they are not the object only of historical, sociological, or ethnological study. In the last analysis, the *sacred* and *profane* modes of being depend upon the different positions that man has conquered in the cosmos; hence they are of concern both to the philosopher and to anyone seeking to discover the possible dimensions of human existence. (pp. 14–15)

Any oral man is preferred by Eliade to the desacralized or literate man; even "a peasant of Christian Europe" retains some of the old auditory resonance and aura of sacral man, as the Romantics insisted more than two hundred years ago. So long as a culture is non-literate, it has for Eliade the indispensable sacral ingredients (p. 17):

It is obvious, for example, that the symbolisms and cults of Mother Earth, of human and agricultural fertility, of the sacrality of woman, and the like, could not develop and constitute a complex religious system except through the discovery of agriculture; it is equally obvious that a preagricultural society, devoted to hunting, could not feel the sacrality of Mother Earth in the same way or with the same intensity. Hence there are differences in religious experience explained by differences in economy, culture, and social organization—in short, by history. Nevertheless, between the nomadic hunters and the sedentary cultivators there is a similarity in behavior that seems to us infinitely more important than their differences: *both live in a sacralized cosmos*, both share in a cosmic sacrality manifested equally in the animal world and in the vegetable world. We need only compare their existential situations with that of a man of the modern societies *living in a desacralized cosmos*, and we shall immediately be aware of all that separates him from them.

We have already seen that sedentary or specialized man, as opposed to nomadic man, is on the way to discovery of the visual mode of human experience. But as long as *homo sedens* avoids the more potent kinds of optical conditioning, as found in literacy, the mere shades of sacral life, as between nomadic and sedentary man, do not faze Eliade. That Eliade chooses to call the oral man "religious" is, of course, as fanciful and arbitrary as calling blondes bestial. But it is not in the least confusing to those who understand that the "religious" for Eliade is, as he insists from the start, the irrational. He is in that very large company of literacy victims who have acquiesced in supposing that the "rational" is the explicitly lineal, sequential, visual. That is, he prefers to appear as an eighteenth-century mind in rebellion against the dominant visual mode which then was new. Such was Blake and a host of others. Today Blake would be violently anti-Blake, because the Blake reaction against the abstract visual is now the dominant *cliché* and claque of the big battalions, as they move in regimented grooves of sensibility.

"For religious man, space is not homogeneous; he experiences interruptions, breaks in it." (p. 20) Likewise in time. For the modern physicist, as also for the non-literate, space is not homogeneous, nor is time. By contrast, the geometrical space invented in antiquity, far from being diverse, unique, pluralistic, sacral, "can be cut and delimited in any direction; but no qualitative differentiation and, hence, no orientation are given by virtue of its inherent structure." (p. 22) The next statement applies entirely to the relative interplay of the optical and the auditory modes in the shaping of human sensibility:

It must be added at once that such a profane existence is never found in the pure state. To whatever degree he may have desacralized the world, the man who has made his choice in favor of a profane life never succeeds in completely doing away with religious behavior. This will become clearer as we proceed; it will appear that even the most desacralized existence still preserves traces of a religious valorization of the world. (p. 23)

The method of the twentieth century is to use not single but multiple models for experimental exploration–the technique of the suspended judgment.

✱ William Ivins, Jr., in *Prints and Visual Communications*, stresses (p. 63) how natural it is in the world of the written word to move towards a merely nominalist position such as no non-literate man could dream of:

... Plato's Ideas and Aristotle's forms, essences, and definitions, are specimens of this transference of reality from the object to the exactly repeatable and therefore seemingly permanent verbal formula. An essence, in fact, is not part of the object but part of its definition. Also, I believe, the well-known notions of substance and attributable qualities can be derived from this operational dependence upon exactly repeatable verbal descriptions and definitions—for the very linear order in which words have to be used results in a syntactical time order analysis of qualities that actually are simultaneous and so intermingled and interrelated that no quality can be removed from one of the bundles of qualities we call objects without changing both it and all the other qualities. After all, a quality is only a quality of a group of other qualities, and if you change anyone of the group they all necessarily change. Whatever the situation may be from the point of view of a verbalist analysis, from the point of view of visual awarenesses of the kind that have to be used in an art museum the object is a unity that cannot be broken down into separate qualities without becoming merely a collection of abstractions that have only conceptual existence and no actuality. In a funny way words and their necessary linear syntactical order forbid us to describe objects and compel us to use very poor and inadequate lists of theoretical ingredients in the manner exemplified more concretely by the ordinary cook book recipes.

Any phonetic alphabet culture can easily slip into the habit of putting one thing under or in another; since there is constant pressure from the subliminal fact that the written code carries for the reader the experience of the "content" which is speech. But there is nothing subliminal in non-literate cultures. The reason we find myths difficult to grasp is just this fact, that they do not exclude any facet of experience as literate cultures do. All the levels of meaning are simultaneous. Thus natives, when asked Freudian questions about the symbolism of their thoughts or dreams, insist that all the meanings are right there in the verbal statement. The work of Jung and Freud is a laborious translation of non-literate awareness into literary terms, and like any translation distorts and omits. The main advantage in translation is the creative effort it fosters, as Ezra Pound spent his life in telling and illustrating. And culture that is engaged in translating itself from one radical mode such as the auditory, into another mode like the visual, is bound to be in a creative ferment, as was classical Greece or the Renaissance. But our own time is an even more massive instance of such ferment, and just because of such "translation."

As our age translates itself back into the oral and auditory modes because of the electronic pressure of simultaneity, we become sharply aware of the uncritical acceptance of visual metaphors and models by many past centuries. The linguistic analysis now followed by Gilbert Ryle at Oxford is an unremitting critique of visual models in philosophy:

We should begin by dismissing a model which in one form or another dominates many speculations about perception. The beloved but spurious question, 'How can a person get beyond his sensations to apprehension of external realities?' is often posed as if the situation were like this. There is immured in a windowless cell a prisoner, who has lived there in solitary confinement since birth. All that comes to him from the outside world is flickers of light thrown upon his cell-walls and tappings heard through the stones; yet from these observed flashes and tappings he becomes, or seems to become, apprised of unobserved football-matches, flower-gardens and eclipses of the sun. How then does he learn the ciphers in which his signals are arranged, or even find out that there are such things as ciphers? How can he interpret the messages which he somehow deciphers, given that the vocabularies of those messages are the vocabularies of football and astronomy and not those of flickers and tappings?

This model is of course the familiar picture of the mind as a ghost in a machine, about the general defects of which nothing more need be said. But certain particular defects do need to be noticed. The use of this sort of model involves the explicit or implicit assumption that, much as the prisoner can see flickers and hear tappings, but cannot, unfortunately, see or hear football matches, so we can observe our visual and other sensations, but cannot, unfortunately, observe robins.[18]

We become extremely conscious of cultural models and bias when moving from one dominant form of awareness to another, as between Greek and Latin or English and French. So we are no longer amazed that the oriental world has no concept of "substance" or of "substantial form," since they experience no visual pressure to break up experience into such packages. And we have seen how his training in the world of prints enabled William Ivins to translate the meaning of typography as nobody else has done. In his *Prints and Visual Communication* (p. 54) he offers a general principle:

Thus the more closely we can confine our data for reasoning about things to data that come to us through one and the same sense channel the more apt we are to be correct in our reasoning, even though it be much more restricted in its scope. One of the most interesting things in our modern scientific practice has been the invention and perfection of methods by which the scientists can acquire much of their basic data through one and the same sensuous channel of awareness. I understand that in physics, for example, the scientists are happiest when they can get their data with the aid of some dial or other device which can be read by vision. Thus heat, weight, lengths, and many other things that in ordinary life are apprehended through senses other than vision have become for science matters of visual awareness of the positions of mechanical pointers.

Does this not imply that if we can devise a consistent means of translating *all* aspects of our world into the language of *one* sense only, we shall then have a distortion that is scientific because consistent and coherent? Blake thought this had actually occurred in the eighteenth century when he sought liberation "from single vision and Newton's sleep." For the dominance of one sense is the formula for hypnosis. And a culture can be locked in the sleep of any one sense. The sleeper awakes when challenged in any other sense.

[18]Ryle, *The Concept of Mind*, pp. 223–4.

Only a fraction of the history of literacy has been typographic.

✱ Till now we have been concerned mostly with the written word as it transfers or translates the audile-tactile space of "sacral" non-literate man into the visual space of civilized or literate or "profane" man. Once this transfer or metamorphosis occurs we are soon in the world of books, scribal or typographic. The rest of our concern will be with books written and printed and the results for learning and society. From the fifth century B.C. to the fifteenth century A.D. the book was a scribal product. Only one third of the history of the book in the Western world has been typographic. It is not incongruous, therefore, to say as G. S. Brett does in *Psychology Ancient and Modern* (pp. 36–7):

> The idea that knowledge is essentially book learning seems to be a very modern view, probably derived from the mediaeval distinctions between clerk and layman, with additional emphasis provided by the literary character of the rather fantastic humanism of the sixteenth century. The original and natural idea of knowledge is that of "cunning" or the possession of wits. Odysseus is the original type of thinker, a man of many ideas who could overcome the Cyclops and achieve a significant triumph of mind over matter. Knowledge is thus a capacity for overcoming the difficulties of life and achieving success in this world.

Brett here specifies the natural dichotomy which the book brings into any society, in addition to the split within the individual of that society. The work of James Joyce exhibits a complex clairvoyance in these matters. His Leopold Bloom of *Ulysses*, a man of many ideas and many devices, is a free-lance ad salesman. Joyce saw the parallels, on one hand, between the modern frontier of the verbal and the pictorial and, on the other, between the Homeric world poised between the old sacral culture and the new profane or literate sensibility. Bloom, the newly detribalized Jew, is presented in modern Dublin, a slightly detribalized Irish world. Such a frontier is the modern world of the advertisement, congenial, therefore, to the transitional culture of Bloom. In the seventeenth or Ithaca episode of *Ulysses* we read: "What were habitually his final meditations? Of some one sole unique advertisement to cause passers to stop in wonder, a poster novelty, with all extraneous accretions excluded, reduced to its simplest and most efficient terms not exceeding the span of casual vision and congruous with the velocity of modern life."

In the *Books at the Wake*, James S. Atherton points out (pp. 67–8):

Amongst other things *Finnegans Wake* is a history of writing. We begin with writing on 'A bone, a pebble, a ramskin . . . leave them to cook in the mutthering pot: and Gutenmorg with his cromagnon charter, tintingfats and great prime must once for omniboss stepp rubrickredd out of the wordpress' (20.5). The 'mutthering pot' is an allusion to Alchemy, but there is some other significance connected with writing, for the next time the word appears it is again in a context concerning improvement in systems of communication. The passage is: 'All the airish signics of her dipandump helpabit from an Father Hogam till the Mutther Masons , . .' (223.3). 'Dipandump helpabit' combine the deaf and dumb alphabet's signs in the air—or airish signs—with the ups and downs of the ordinary ABC and the more pronounced ups and downs of Irish Ogham writing. The Mason, following this, must be the man of that name who invented steel pen nibs. But all I can suggest for 'mutther' is the muttering of Freemasons which does not fit the context, although they, of course, also make signs in the air.

"Gutenmorg with his cromagnon charter" expounds by mythic gloss the fact that writing meant the emergence of the caveman or sacral man from the audile world of simultaneous resonance into the profane world of daylight. The reference to the masons is to the world of the bricklayer as a type of speech itself. On the second page of the *Wake*, Joyce is making a mosaic, an Achilles shield, as it were, of all the themes and modes of human speech and communication: "Bygmeister Finnegan, of the Stuttering Hand, freemen's maurer, lived in the broadest way immarginable in his ruchlit toofarback for messuages before joshuan judges had given us numbers . . ." Joyce is, in the *Wake*, making his own Altamira cave drawings of the entire history of the human mind, in terms of its basic gestures and postures during all phases of human culture and technology. As his title indicates, he saw that the wake of human progress can disappear again into the night of sacral or auditory man. The Finn cycle of tribal institutions can return in the electric age, but if again, then let's make it a wake or awake or both. Joyce could see no advantage in our remaining locked up in each cultural cycle as in a trance or dream. He discovered the means of living simultaneously in all cultural modes while quite conscious. The means he cites for such self-awareness and correction of cultural bias is his "collideorscope." This term indicates the interplay in colloidal mixture of all components of human technology as they extend our senses and shift their ratios in the social kaleidoscope of cultural clash: "deor," savage, the oral or sacral; "scope" the visual or profane and civilized.

Until now a culture has been a mechanical fate for societies, the automatic interiorization of their own technologies.

✱ Hitherto most people have accepted their cultures as a fate, like climate or vernacular; but our empathic awareness of the exact modes of many cultures is itself a liberation from them as prisons. Hence Joyce's title is also a manifesto. In a most competent survey, *Man: His First Million Years*, Ashley Montagu comments (pp. 193–4) on aspects of non-literacy in a way that relates to these themes:

> Nonliterate man casts the net of thought over the whole world. Mythology and religion may be closely related, but where one grows out of man's everyday life, the other grows out of his concern with the supernatural. And so it is with his view of the world, which will be compounded of secular, religious, mythological, magical, and experiential elements all rolled into one.
>
> Most nonliterate peoples are extreme realists. They are bent on bringing the world under control, and many of their practices are devised to insure that reality will perform according to their bidding. In the conviction that the spirits are on his side, a man may then make all the necessary preparations for the success of an expedition. Coercing reality to do one's bidding by manipulating it in the prescribed manner is, for the nonliterate, a part of reality.
>
> It is necessary to understand that nonliterate peoples identify themselves very much more closely with the world in which they live than do the literate peoples of the world. The more "literate" people become, the more they tend to become detached from the world in which they live.
>
> What happens *is* reality to the nonliterate. If ceremonies calculated to increase the birth of animals and the yield of plants are followed by such increases, then the ceremonies are not only connected with them but are part of them; for without the ceremonies the increase of animals and plants would not have occurred—so the nonliterate reasons. It is not that the nonliterate is characterized by an illogical mind; his mind is perfectly logical, and he uses it very well, indeed. An educated white man finding himself suddenly deposited in the Central Australian desert would be unlikely to last very long. Yet the Australian aboriginal manages very well. The aboriginals of all lands have made adjustments to their environments which indicate beyond any doubt that their intelligence is of high order. The trouble with the nonliterate is not that he isn't logical, but that he applies logic too often, many times on the basis of insufficient premises.

He generally assumes that events which are associated together are causally connected. But this is a fallacy which the majority of civilized people commit most of the time, and it has been known to happen among trained scientists! Nonliterates tend to adhere too rigidly to the rule of association as causation, but most of the time it works, and by the pragmatic rule what works is taken to be true.

Nothing could be further from the truth than the idea that nonliterates are utterly credulous, superstition- and fear-ridden creatures, without any capacity or opportunity for independent and original thought. In addition to good horse sense, the nonliterate usually displays much practical sense based on an appreciation of the hard realities of life. . . .

What Montagu opens up here concerning the intense practicality of the non-literate applies perfectly as gloss to Joyce's Bloom or Odysseus, the resourceful man. What could be more practical for a man caught between the Scylla of a literary culture and the Charybdis of post-literate technology to make himself a raft of ad copy? He is behaving like Poe's sailor in the *Maelstrom* who studied the action of the whirlpool and survives. May not it be our job in the new electronic age to study the action of the new vortex on the body of the older cultures?

The techniques of uniformity and repeatability were introduced by the Romans and the Middle Ages.

✱ *Prints and Visual Communication* by William Ivins is a major resource for any student of the role of books in shaping human knowledge and society. The fact that Ivins stood a bit aside from the central literary aspect of the book seems to have given him an advantage over literary men. The student of literature and philosophy is prone to be concerned with book "content" and to ignore its form. This failure is peculiar to phonetic literacy in which the visual code always has the "content" that is the speech recreated by the person engaged in reading. No Chinese scribe or reader could make the mistake of ignoring the form of writing itself, because his written character does not separate speech and visual code in our way. But in a world of phonetic literacy this compulsion to split form and content is universal, and affects non-literary people as much as the scholar. Thus the Bell Telephone Laboratories spend millions on research but have never even noticed the peculiar form that is the telephone and what it does to speech and to personal relations. As an expert in prints Ivins became aware of their difference from the printed books in which they appeared. This in turn made him aware of the great difference between printed and manuscript books. At the outset (pp. 2–3) he draws attention to the dimension of repeatability built into the phonetic written characters, in order to stress the same dimensions of repeatability as it is found in pre-Gutenberg block printing of pictures from woodcuts:

Although every history of European civilization makes much of the invention in the mid-fifteenth century of ways to print words from movable types, it is customary in those histories to ignore the slightly earlier discovery of ways to print pictures and diagrams. A book, so far as it contains a text, is a container of exactly repeatable word symbols arranged in an exactly repeatable order. Men have been using such containers for at least five thousand years. Because of this it can be argued that the printing of books was no more than a way of making very old and familiar things more cheaply. It may even be said that for a while type printing was little more than a way to do with a much smaller number of proof readings. Prior to 1501 few books were printed in editions larger than that handwritten one of a thousand copies to which Pliny the Younger referred in the second century of our era. The printing of pictures, however, unlike the printing of words from movable types, brought a completely new thing into existence— it made possible for the first time pictorial statements of a kind that could be exactly repeated during the effective life of the printing surface. This exact repetition of pictorial statements has had incalculable effects upon knowledge and thought, upon science and technology, of every kind. It is hardly too much to say that since the invention of writing there has been no more important invention than that of the exactly repeatable pictorial statement.

The too obvious character of exact repeatability that is inherent in typography misses the literary man. He attaches little significance to this merely technological feature and concentrates on the "content," as if he were listening to the author. As an artist aware of formal structures as complex statements in themselves, Ivins brought to prints and typography and manuscript alike, a rare mode of attention. He saw (p. 3) how technological forms can shape the sciences as much as the arts:

For our great grandfathers, and for their fathers back to the Renaissance, prints were no more and no less than the only exactly repeatable pictorial statements.... Until a century ago, prints made in the old techniques filled all the functions that are now filled by our line cuts and half tones, by our photographs and blueprints, by our various colour processes, and by our political cartoons and pictorial advertisements. If we define prints from the functional point of view so indicated, rather than by any restriction of process or aesthetic value, it becomes obvious that without prints we should have very few of our modern sciences, technologies, archaeologies, or ethnologies—for all of these are dependent, first or last, upon information conveyed by exactly repeatable visual or pictorial statements.

This means that, far from being merely minor works of art, prints are among the most important and powerful tools of modern life and thought. Certainly we cannot hope to realize their actual role unless we get away from the snobbery of modern print collecting notions and definitions and begin to think of them as exactly repeatable pictorial statements or communications, without regard to the accident of rarity or what for the moment we may regard as aesthetic merit. We must look at them from the point of view of general ideas and particular functions, and, especially, we must think about the limitations which their techniques have imposed on them as conveyors of information and on us as receivers of that information.

The technology of exact repeatability was a stress that the Romans introduced into the Greek visual analysis. This stress on the continuous, uniform line with its indifference to the oral values of pluralistic organization was, in the view of Ivins (pp. 4–5) effectively transmitted to and by the Dark Ages:

Historians until very recent times have been literary men and philologues. As students of the past they have rarely found anything they were not looking for. They have been so full of wonder at what the Greeks said, that they have paid little attention to what the Greeks did not do or know. They have been so full of horror at what the Dark Ages did not say, that they have paid no attention to what they did do and know. Modern research, by men who are aware of low subjects like economics and technology, is rapidly changing our ideas about these matters. In the Dark Ages to use their traditional name, there was little assured leisure for pursuit of the niceties of literature, art, philosophy, and theoretical science, but many people, nevertheless addressed their perfectly good minds to social, agricultural, and mechanical problems. Moreover, all through those academically debased centuries, so far from there having been any falling off in mechanical ability, there was an unbroken series of discoveries and inventions that gave the Dark Ages, and after them the Middle Ages, a technology, and, therefore, a logic, that in many most important respects far surpassed anything that had been known to the Greeks or to the Romans of the Western Empire.

His theme is that "the Dark and Middle Ages in their poverty and necessity produced the first great crop of Yankee ingenuity." Perhaps Ivins overdoes this emphasis on the Dark and Middle Ages as "a culture of techniques and technologies," but it is a kind of approach which makes scholasticism understandable, and that prepares us for the great medieval invention of typography that was the "take-off" moment into the new spaces of the modern world.[19]

[19]Ivins cites the article of Lynn White on "Technology and Invention in the Middle Ages" in *Speculum*, vol. XV, April, 1940, pp. 141–59.

The word modern was a term of reproach used by the patristic humanists against the medieval schoolmen who developed the new logic and physics.

✱ Since then many books on medieval science have appeared which confirm the Ivins view. *The Science of Mechanics in the Middle Ages* by Marshall Clagett is an example from which I will select a few themes that illustrate the continuous development of the visual stress which we have seen emerge in the Greek world as an effect of phonetic literacy. Thus: "It will be evident from the material I have presented in the first two chapters that medieval statics, like the other aspects of medieval mechanics, depends greatly on the mechanical concepts and their analysis given by Greek mechanicians: the Aristotelian author of the *Mechanica*, Archimedes, Hero, and others." (p. xxiii)

In the same way "the achievements of medieval kinematics were very much more an integral part of the scholastic discussions of Aristotelian statements regarding force and motion . . . Particularly important was the development of a concept of instantaneous velocity and consequently of an analysis of various kinds of acceleration." (p. xxv)

More than a century before printing, scientists at Merton College, Oxford, developed a theorem of "a uniform acceleration and a movement uniform at the speed possessed by the uniformly accelerating body at the middle instant of the time of acceleration." With the invention of uniform repeatable and movable types we enter further into this medieval world of measurable quantities. What Clagett does is to establish the lines of continuity between Greek visual analysis and medieval science, and to show how much further the scholastic mind pushed the Greek concepts.

The Merton kinematics spread to Italy and France. This was an idea for translating motion into visual terms:

The basic idea of the system is simple. Geometric figures, particularly areas, can be used to represent the quantity of a quality. Extension of the quality in a subject is to be represented by a horizontal line, while the qualitative intensities at different points in the subject are to be represented by perpendiculars erected on the extension or subject line. In the case of motion, the line of extension represents time, and the line of intensity, velocity. (p. 33)

Clagett presents the treatise of Nicholas of Oresme "On the Configurations of Qualities" in which Oresme says: "Every measurable thing except numbers is conceived in the manner of continuous quantity." This recalls us to the Greek world in which as Tobias D. Dantzig points out in his *Number: The Language of Science* (pp. 141–2):

The attempt to apply rational arithmetic to a problem in geometry resulted in the first crisis in the history of mathematics. The two relatively simple problems, the determination of the diagonal of a square and that of the circumference of a circle, revealed the existence of new mathematical beings for which no place could be found within the rational domain . . .

A further analysis showed that the procedures of algebra were generally just as inadequate. So it became apparent that an extension of the number field was unavoidable. . . . And since the old concept failed on the terrain of geometry, we must seek in geometry a model for the new. The continuous indefinite straight line seems ideally adapted for such a model.

Number is the dimension of tactility, as Ivins explained in *Art and Geometry* (p. 7): "In any continuous pattern the hand needs simple and static forms and it likes repeated ones. It knows objects separately, one after another, and unlike the eye it has no way of getting a practically simultaneous view or acquaintance with a group of objects as a single awareness. Unlike the eye, the unaided hand is unable to discover whether three or more objects are on a line."

But what concerns us about the first crisis in mathematics is the evident fictions which must be resorted to in order to translate the visual into the tactile. But the greater fictions lay ahead in the infinitesimal calculus.

As we shall see, with regard to the sixteenth century, number and visuality, or tactility and retinal experience, split quite asunder and went their divergent ways to set up the rival empires of Art and Science. This divergence, so strikingly initiated in the Greek world, was held in relative abeyance until the Gutenberg take-off. Throughout the centuries of manuscript culture it will appear that the visual did not become quite dissociated from tactility, even though it diminished the auditory empire drastically. This matter will get separate discussion apropos of medieval reading habits. The relation of tactility to the visual, so necessary to an understanding of the fortunes of the phonetic alphabet, only became starkly defined after Cézanne. Thus Gombrich makes tactility a central theme of *Art and Illusion*, as does Heinrich Wölfflin in his *Principles of Art History*. And the reason for this new stress was that in an age of photography the divorce of the visual from the interplay of the other senses was pushed all the way into reaction. Gombrich records the stages of nineteenth-century discussion and analysis of "sense data" leading to the Helmholtz case for "unconscious inference" or mental action even in the most basic sense experience. "Tactility" or interplay among all the senses was felt to be the very mode of this "inference" and led at once to the disintegration of the idea of the "imitation of nature" as a visual affair. Gombrich writes (p. 16):

Two German thinkers are prominent in this story. One is the critic Konrad Fiedler, who insisted, in opposition to the impressionists, that "even the simplest sense impression that looks like merely the raw material for the operations of the mind is already a mental fact, and what we call the external world is really the result of a complex psychological process."

But it was Fiedler's friend, the neoclassical sculptor Adolf von Hildebrand, who set out to analyze this process in a little book called *The Problem of Form in the Figurative Arts*, which came out in 1893 and gained the ear of a whole generation. Hildebrand, too, challenged the ideals of scientific naturalism by an appeal to the psychology of perception: if we attempt to analyze our mental images to discover their primary constituents, we will find them composed of sense data derived from vision and from memories of touch and movement. A sphere, for instance, appears to the eye as a flat disk; it is touch which informs us of the properties of space and form. Any attempt on the part of the artist to eliminate this knowledge is futile, for without it he would not perceive the world at all. His task is, on the contrary, to compensate for the absence of movement in his work by clarifying his image and thus conveying not only visual sensations but also those memories of touch which enable us to reconstitute the three-dimensional form in our minds.

It is hardly an accident that the period when these ideas were so eagerly debated was also the period when the history of art emancipated itself from antiquarianism, biography, and aesthetics. Issues which had been taken for granted so long suddenly looked problematic and required reassessment. When Bernard Berenson wrote his brilliant essay on the Florentine painters, which came out in 1896, he formulated his aesthetic creed in terms of Hildebrand's analysis. With his gift for the pregnant phrase, he summed up almost the whole of the sculptor's somewhat turgid book in the sentence "The painter can accomplish his task only by giving tactile value to retinal impressions." For Berenson, Giotto's or Pollaiuolo's claim on our attention is that they had done precisely this . . .

In antiquity and the Middle Ages reading was necessarily reading aloud.

✱ "It is not too much to say that with Aristotle the Greek world passed from oral instruction to the habit of reading," writes Frederic G. Kenyon in *Books and Readers in Ancient Greece and Rome* (p. 25). But for centuries to come "reading" meant reading aloud. In fact, it is only today that the decree *nisi* has been handed down by the speed-reading institutes to divorce eye and speech in the act of reading. The recognition that in reading from left to right we make incipient word formations with our throat muscles was discovered to be the principal cause of "slow" reading. But the hushing up of the reader has been a gradual process, and even the printed word did not succeed in silencing all readers. But we have tended to associate lip movements and mutterings from a reader with semi-literacy, a fact which has contributed to the American stress on a merely visual approach to reading in elementary learning. Yet Gerard Manley Hopkins was crusading for tactile stress in word use and for vigorous oral poetry exactly at the time that Cézanne was giving tactile values to the retinal impression. Referring to his poem "Spelt from Sibyl's Leaves," Hopkins wrote:

Of this long sonnet above all remember what applies to all my verse, that it is, as living art should be, made for performance and that its performance is not reading with the eye but loud, leisurely, poetical (not rhetorical) recitation, with long rests, long dwells on the rhyme and other marked syllables, and so on. This sonnet should be sung: it is most carefully timed in *tempo rubato*.[20]

Again he writes: "Take breath and read it with the ears, as I always wish to be read, and my verse comes all right." And Joyce never tired of explaining how in *Finnegans Wake* "the words the reader sees are not the words that he will hear." As with Hopkins, the language of Joyce only comes alive when read aloud, creating a synesthesia or interplay of the senses.

But if reading aloud favours synesthesia and tactility, so did the ancient and medieval manuscript. We have already seen an example of a recent attempt to create an oral typography for modern English readers. Naturally, such a script presents the highly textural and tactile mode of an old manuscript. "Textura," the name for Gothic lettering in its own time, meant "tapestry." But the Romans had developed a much less textural and more highly visual lettering which is called "Roman" and which is the lettering we find in ordinary print, as on this page. But the early printers avoided Roman letters except to create the illusion of the fake antique, of the old Roman letters beloved of the Renaissance humanists.

It is strange that modern readers have been so slow to recognize that the prose of Gertrude Stein with its lack of punctuation and other visual aids, is a carefully devised strategy to get the passive visual reader into participant, oral action. So with E. E. Cummings, or Pound, or Eliot. *Vers libre* is for the ear as much as for the eye. And in *Finnegans Wake* when Joyce wants to create "thunder," the "shout in the street" indicating a major phase of collective action, he sets up the word exactly like an ancient manuscript word: "The fall (bababadalgharaghtakamminarronnkonnbronntonnerronn-tuonnthunntrovarrhounawnskawntoohoohooardenenthurnuk!) of a once

[20]John Pick, ed., *A Gerard Manley Hopkins Reader*, p. xxii.

wallstrait oldparr is retaled early in bed and later on life down through all christian minstrelsy . . ." (p. 1)

In the absence of visual aids the reader will find himself doing exactly what ancient and medieval readers did, namely reading aloud. Readers continued to read aloud after the beginning of word separation in the later Middle Ages, and even after the coming of print in the Renaissance. But all these developments fostered speed and visual stress. Today, scholars using manuscripts read them silently for the most part, and the study of reading habits in the ancient and medieval world remains to be done. The comments of Kenyon (in his *Books and Readers in Ancient Greece and Rome*, p. 65) are helpful: "The lack of assistance to readers, or of aids to facilitate reference, in ancient books is very remarkable. The separation of words is practically unknown, except very rarely when an inverted comma or dot is used to mark a separation where some ambiguity might exist. Punctuation is often wholly absent, and is never full and systematic." "Full and systematic" would be for the eye, whereas punctuation even in the sixteenth and seventeenth centuries continued to be for the ear and not the eye.[21]

Manuscript culture is conversational if only because the writer and his audience are physically related by the form of publication as performance.

✳ There is no lack of indication that "reading" throughout ancient and medieval times meant reading aloud, or even a kind of incantation. But nobody has ever gathered adequate data on this question. I can at least give a few samples from various periods of the sort of evidence that is readily available. Thus in his *Poetics* (26) Aristotle points out: "That Tragedy may produce its effect even without movement or action in just the same way as Epic poetry; for from the mere reading of a play its quality may be seen." Sidelights on the above aspect of reading as recitation are available from the Roman practice of public recitation as a principal form of book publication. Such it remained until printing. Kenyon (*Books and Readers*, pp. 83–4) reports on the Roman practice:

[21]See references on this subject in my article on "The Effect of the Printed Book on Language in the Sixteenth Century," *Explorations in Communications*, pp. 125–35.

Tacitus describes how an author would be compelled to hire a house and chairs, and collect an audience by personal entreaty; and Juvenal complains that a rich man would lend his disused house, and send his freedmen and poor clients to form an audience, but would not bear the cost of the chairs. The whole practice finds its analogy in the modern musical world, where a singer is compelled to hire a hall and do his best to collect an audience, in order that his voice may be heard; or a patron desiring to assist him may lend his drawing-room for the purpose, and use his influence to get his friends to attend. It was not a healthy phase for literature, since it encouraged compositions which lent themselves to rhetorical declamation; and one may doubt whether it did any service to the circulation of books.

Moses Hadas in his *Ancilla to Classical Reading* goes into the question of oral publication more thoroughly than Kenyon (p. 50):

The concept of literature as something to be listened to in public rather than scanned silently in private in itself makes the notion of literary property more difficult to grasp. We ourselves are more conscious of an author's contribution when we read his book than we are of a composer's when we hear his work performed. Among the Greeks the regular method of publication was by public recitation, at first, significantly, by the author himself, and then by professional readers or actors, and public recitation continued to be the regular method of publication even after books and the art of reading had become common. How this affected the poet's livelihood we shall see in another connection; here we may pause to notice the effect of oral presentation on the character of the literature.

Just as music written for a small group of instruments has a different tone and tempo from music designed for large halls, so with books. Printing has enlarged the "hall" for the author's performance until all aspects of style have been altered. Hadas is most relevant here:

All classic literature, it may be said, is conceived of as conversation with, or an address to, an audience. Ancient drama is significantly different from modern because plays acted in bright sunlight before 40,000 spectators cannot be like plays acted before 400 in a darkened room. Similarly, a piece intended for declamation at a festival cannot be like a piece intended for the perusal of a cloistered student. Poetry in particular shows that all its varieties were intended for oral presentation. Even epigrams represent a vocal address to the passer-by ("Go, stranger," or the like) and sometimes, as in some of the epigrams of Callimachus and of his imitators, the stone is thought of as carrying on a brief dialogue with the passer-by. Homeric epic was of course designed for public reading, and long after private reading became common, rhapsodes made a profession of reciting epic. Pisistratus, who had something (we do not know how much) to do with regularizing the text of Homer, also instituted the public reading of his poems at the Panathenaic festival. From Diogenes Laertius (1.2.57) we learn that 'Solon provided that the public recitations of Homer shall follow a fixed order; thus the second reciter must begin from the place where the first left off.'

85

Prose no less than poetry was presented orally, as we know from reports concerning Herodotus and others, and the practice of oral presentation affected the nature of prose as it did of poetry. The elaborate attention to sound which characterizes Gorgias' pioneer productions would have been meaningless unless his pieces were intended for recitation. It was the artfulness which Gorgias gave it that enabled Isocrates to maintain that prose was the legitimate successor of poetry and must replace it. Later critics like Dionysius of Halicarnassus judge historians by the same gauge as oratory and make comparisons between their works with no allowances for what we should consider necessary differences in genera. (pp. 50–1)

Hadas then turns (pp. 51–2) to the well-known passage in St. Augustine's *Confessions*:

Throughout antiquity and long thereafter even private readers regularly pronounced the words of their text aloud, in prose as well as poetry. Silent reading was such an anomaly that St. Augustine (*Confessions* 5, 3) finds Ambrose's habit a very remarkable thing: "But when he was reading his eye glided over the pages and his heart searched out the sense, but his voice and tongue were at rest." Visitors came to watch this prodigy, and Augustine conjectures explanations:
'Perchance he dreaded lest if the author he read should deliver anything obscurely, some attentive or perplexed hearer should desire him to expound it, or to discuss some of the harder questions; so that his time being thus spent, he could not turn over so many volumes as he desired; although the preserving of his voice (which a very little speaking would weaken) might be the truer reason for his reading to himself. But with what intent soever he did it, certainly in such a man it was good.'

The manuscript shaped medieval literary conventions at all levels.

✱ Hadas pursues this theme elsewhere in his excellent work. And it is taken up again for the medieval period by H. J. Chaytor in *From Script to Print*, a book to which the present one owes a good deal of its reason for being written.

No one is likely to contest the statement that the invention of printing and the development of that art mark a turning-point in the history of civilisation. Not so readily appreciated is the fact that association with printed matter has changed our views of literary art and style, has introduced ideas concerning originality and literary property of which the age of manuscript knew little or nothing, and has modified the psychological processes by which we use words for the communication of thought. The breadth of the gulf which separates the age of manuscript from the age of print is not always, nor fully, realised by those who begin to read and criticise medieval literature. When we take up a printed edition of a medieval text, provided with an introduction, a critical apparatus of variant readings, notes and glossary, we bring unconsciously to its perusal those prejudices and prepossessions which years of association with printed matter have made habitual. We are liable to forget that we are dealing with the literature of an age when orthographical standards varied and grammatical accuracy was not highly esteemed, when language was fluid and was not necessarily regarded as a mark of nationality, when style meant the observance of fixed and complicated rules of rhetoric. To copy and circulate another man's book might be regarded as a meritorious action in the age of manuscript; in the age of print, such action results in law suits and damages. Writers who wish to derive profit by amusing a public now write for the most part in prose; until the middle of the thirteenth century, only verse could obtain a hearing. Hence, if a fair judgment is to be passed upon literary works belonging to the centuries before printing was invented, some effort must be made to realise the extent of the prejudices under which we have grown up, and to resist the involuntary demand that medieval literature must conform to our standards of taste or be regarded as of interest purely antiquarian. In the words of Renan, 'l'essence de la critique est de savoir comprendre des états très différents de celui où nous vivons'. (p. 1)

It was learning from Chaytor how literary conventions are affected by the oral, written, or the printed forms, that suggested to me the need for *The Gutenberg Galaxy*. Medieval language and literature were somewhat in the state of the present movie or the TV show in that, in Chaytor's words, it

produced little formal criticism in our sense of the term. If an author wished to know whether his work was good or bad, he tried it on an audience; if it was approved, he was soon followed by imitators. But authors were not constrained by models or systems . . . the audience wanted a story with plenty of action and movement, the story, as a rule, showed no great command of character drawing; this was left to the reciter for portrayal by change of voice and gesture. (p. 3)

The twelfth century audience took these recitals in instalments but "we can sit and read it at our leisure and turn back to previous pages at our will. In short, the history of the progress from script to print is a history of the gradual substitution of visual for auditory methods of communicating and receiving ideas." (p. 4) Chaytor quotes (p. 7) a passage from *Our Spoken Language* by A. Lloyd James (p. 29) which comes to grips with the alteration of our sense lives by way of literacy:

"Sound and sight, speech and print, eye and ear have nothing in common. The human brain has done nothing that compares in complexity with this fusion of ideas involved in linking up the two forms of language. But the result of the fusion is that once it is achieved in our early years, we are for ever after unable to think clearly, independently and surely about any one aspect of the matter. We cannot think of sounds without thinking of letters; we believe letters have sounds. We think that the printed page is a picture of what we say, and that the mysterious thing called "spelling" is sacred. . . . The invention of printing broadcast the printed language and gave to print a degree of authority that it has never lost."

Stressing the latent kinesthetic effects even in silent reading Chaytor refers to the fact that "some doctors forbid patients with severe throat affections to read, because silent reading provokes motions of the vocal organs, though the reader may not be conscious of them." He also considers (p. 6) the interplay that is between the auditory and the visual in reading:

So also when we speak or write, ideas evoke acoustic combined with kinesthetic images, which are at once transformed into visual word images. The speaker or writer can now hardly conceive of language, except in printed or written form; the reflex actions by which the process of reading or writing is performed have become so 'instinctive' and are performed with such facile rapidity, that the change from the auditory to the visual is concealed from the reader or writer, and makes analysis of it a matter of great difficulty. It may be that acoustic and kinesthetic images are inseparable, and that 'image' as such is an abstraction made for purposes of analysis, but which is non-existent considered in itself and as pure. But whatever account the individual may render of his own mental processes, and most of us are far from competent in this respect, the fact remains that his idea of language is irrevocably modified by his experience of printed matter.

The alternating of modes or ratios between habitual patterns of sight and sound experience creates a large gap between the mental processes of the medieval and the modern reader. Chaytor writes (p. 10):

Nothing is more alien to medievalism than the modern reader, skimming the headlines of a newspaper and glancing down its columns to glean any point of interest, racing through the pages of some dissertation to discover whether it is worth his more careful consideration, and pausing to gather the argument of a page in a few swift glances. Nor is anything more alien to modernity than the capacious medieval memory which, untrammelled by the associations of print, could learn a strange language with ease and by the methods of a child, and could retain in memory and reproduce lengthy epic and elaborate lyric poems. Two points, therefore, must be emphasized at the outset. The medieval reader, with few exceptions, did not read as we do; he was in the stage of our muttering childhood learner; each word was for him a separate entity and at times a problem which he whispered to himself when he had found the solution; this fact is a matter of interest to those who edit the writings which he produced. Further, as readers were few and hearers numerous, literature in its early days was produced very largely for public recitation; hence, it was rhetorical rather than literary in character, and rules of rhetoric governed its composition.

As the present book was going to press, the observations of Dom Jean Leclercq concerning reading aloud in the patristic and medieval period came most opportunely to attention. His *The Love of Learning and the Desire for God* (pp. 18–19) puts this neglected matter in the central position in which it belongs:

If then it is necessary to know how to read, it is primarily in order to be able to participate in the *lectio divina*. What does this consist of? How is this reading done? To understand this, one must recall the meaning that the words *legere* and *meditari* have for St. Benedict, and which they are to keep throughout the whole of the Middle Ages; what they express will explain one of the characteristic features of monastic literature of the Middle Ages: the phenomenon of reminiscence, of which more must be said later. With regard to literature, a fundamental observation must be made here; in the Middle Ages, as in antiquity, they read usually, not as today, principally with the eyes, but with the lips, pronouncing what they saw, and with the ears, listening to the words pronounced, hearing what is called the "voices of the pages." It is a real acoustical reading; *legere* means at the same time *audire*; one understands only what one hears, as we still say: "entendre le latin," which means to "comprehend" it. No doubt, silent reading, or reading in a low voice, was not unknown; in that case it is designated by expressions like those of St. Benedict: *tacite legere* or *legere sibi*, and according to St. Augustine: *legere in silentio*, as opposed to the *clara lectio*. But most frequently, when *legere* and *lectio* are used without further explanation, they mean an activity which, like chant and writing, requires the participation of the whole body and the whole mind. Doctors of ancient times used to recommend reading to their patients as a physical exercise on an equal level with walking, running or ball-playing. The fact that the text which was being composed or copied was often written to dictation given aloud, either to oneself or to a secretary, satisfactorily explains the errors apparently due to hearing in medieval manuscripts: the use of the dictaphone today produces similar mistakes.

Further on (p. 90), Leclercq discusses the ways in which the inevitable action of reading aloud entered into the whole conception of meditation, prayer, study, and memory:

This results in more than a visual memory of the written words. What results is a muscular memory of the words pronounced and an aural memory of the words heard. The *meditatio* consists in applying oneself with attention to this exercise in total memorization; it is, therefore, inseparable from the *lectio*. It is what inscribes, so to speak, the sacred text in the body and in the soul.

This repeated mastication of the divine words is sometimes described by use of the theme of spiritual nutrition. In this case the vocabulary is borrowed from eating, from digestion, and from the particular form of digestion belonging to ruminants. For this reason, reading and meditation are sometimes described by the very expressive word *ruminatio*. For example, in praising a monk who prayed constantly Peter the Venerable cried: "Without resting, his mouth ruminated the sacred words." Of John of Gorze it was claimed that the murmur of his lips pronouncing the Psalms resembled the buzzing of a bee. To meditate is to attach oneself closely to the sentence being recited and weigh all its words in order to sound the depths of their full meaning. It means assimilating the content of a text by means of a kind of mastication which releases its full flavor. It means, as St. Augustine, St. Gregory, John of Fécamp and others say in an untranslatable expression, to taste it with the *palatum cordis* or in *ore cordis*. All this activity is, necessarily, a prayer; the *lectio divina* is a prayerful reading. Thus, the Cistercian, Arnoul of Bohériss, will give this advice:

> When he reads, let him seek for savor, not science. The Holy Scripture is the well of Jacob from which the waters are drawn which will be poured out later in prayer. Thus there will be no need to go to the oratory to begin to pray; but in reading itself, means will be found for prayer and contemplation.

Not only did this oral aspect of manuscript culture deeply affect the manner of composing and writing, but it meant that writing, reading, and oratory remained inseparable until well after printing.

The traditional lore of school children points to the gap between the scribal and typographic man.

✱ The difference between the man of print and the man of scribal culture is nearly as great as that between the non-literate and the literate. The components of Gutenberg technology were not new. But when brought together in the fifteenth century there was an acceleration of social and personal action tantamount to "take off" in the sense that W. W. Rostow develops this concept in *The Stages of Economic Growth* "that decisive interval in the history of a society when growth becomes its normal condition."

In his *Golden Bough* (vol. I, p. xii), James Frazer points to the similar acceleration introduced into the oral world by literacy and visuality:

"Compared with the evidence afforded by living tradition, the testimony of ancient books on the subject of early religion is worth very little. For literature accelerates the advance of thought at a rate which leaves the slow progress of opinion by word of mouth at an immeasurable distance behind. Two or three generations of literature may do more to change thought than two or three thousand years of traditional life. . . . and so it has come about that in Europe at the present day the superstitious beliefs and practices that have been handed down by word of mouth are generally of a far more archaic type than the religion depicted in the most ancient literature of the Aryan race . . ."

Just how this comes about is the theme of Iona and Peter Opie in their *Lore and Language of Schoolchildren* (pp. 1–2):

While a nursery rhyme passes from a mother or other adult to the small child on her knee, the school rhyme circulates simply from child to child, usually outside the home, and beyond the influence of the family circle. By its nature a nursery rhyme is a jingle preserved and propagated not by children but by adults, and in this sense it is an 'adult' rhyme. It is a rhyme which is adult approved. The schoolchild's verses are not intended for adult ears. In fact part of their fun is the thought, usually correct, that adults know nothing about them. Grown-ups have outgrown the schoolchild's lore. If made aware of it they tend to deride it; and they actively seek to suppress its livelier manifestations. Certainly they do nothing to encourage it. And the folklorist and anthropologist can, without travelling a mile from his door, examine a thriving unselfconscious culture (the word 'culture' is used here deliberately) which is as unnoticed by the sophisticated world, and quite as little affected by it, as is the culture of some dwindling aboriginal tribe living out its helpless existence in the hinterland of a native reserve. Perhaps, indeed, the subject is worthy of a more formidable study than is accorded it here. As Douglas Newton has pointed out: 'The word-wide fraternity of children is the greatest of savage tribes, and the only one which shows no sign of dying out.'

In communities widely separated in space and time there is a continuity and tenacity of tradition quite unknown to written forms.

No matter how uncouth schoolchildren may outwardly appear, they remain tradition's warmest friends. Like the savage, they are respecters, even venerators, of custom; and in their self-contained community their basic lore and language seems scarcely to alter from generation to generation. Boys continue to crack jokes that Swift collected from his friends in Queen Anne's time; they play tricks which lads used to play on each other in the heyday of Beau Brummel; they ask riddles which were posed when Henry VIII was a boy. Young girls continue to perform a magic feat (levitation) of which Pepys heard tell ('One of the strangest things I ever heard'): they hoard bus tickets and milk-bottle tops in distant memory of a love-lorn girl held to ransom by a tyrannical father; they learn to cure warts (and are successful in curing them) after the manner which Francis Bacon learnt when he was young. They call after the tearful the same jeer Charles Lamb recollected: they cry 'Halves!' for something found as Stuart children were accustomed to do; and they rebuke one of their number who seeks back a gift with a couplet used in Shakespeare's day. They attempt, too, to learn their fortune from snails, nuts, and apple-parings—divinations which the poet Gay described nearly two and a half centuries ago; they span wrists to know if someone loves them in the way that Southey used at school to tell if a boy was a bastard; and when they confide to each other that the Lord's Prayer said backwards will make Lucifer appear, they are perpetuating a story which was gossip in Elizabethan times.

The medieval monks' reading carrell was indeed a singing booth.

✻ Chaytor, in his *From Script to Print* (p. 19), was the first to tackle the problem of the medieval monk's carrell or reading-singing booth:

Why this attempt to secure privacy in establishments where the inmates as a rule spent most of their time among their fellows? For the same reason that the reading-room of the British Museum is not divided into sound-proof compartments. The habit of silent reading has made such an arrangement unnecessary; but fill the reading-room with medieval readers and the buzz of whispering and muttering would be intolerable.

These facts deserve greater attention from the editors of medieval texts. When the eye of a modern copyist leaves the manuscript before him in order to write, he carries in his mind a visual reminiscence of what he has seen. What the medieval scribe carried was an auditory memory, and probably in many cases, a memory of one word at a time.[22]

It is almost uncanny that the modern telephone booth should also reflect another aspect of the medieval book world, namely the chained work of reference. But in Russia, until recently quite oral, there are no phone books. You memorize your information—which is even more medieval than the chained book. But memorization presented little problem for the pre-print student, and much less for non-literate persons. Natives are often bewildered by their literate teachers and ask: "Why do you write things down? Can't you remember?"

Chaytor was the first to explain (p. 116) why print should impair our memories so notably, and why the manuscript should not:

Our memories have been impaired by print; we know that we need not 'burden our memories' with matter which we can find merely by taking a book from a shelf. When a large proportion of a population is illiterate and

[22]See also J. W. Clark, *The Care of Books*.

books are scarce, memories are often tenacious to a degree outside modern European experience. Indian students are able to learn a text-book by heart and to reproduce it word for word in an examination room; sacred texts are preserved intact by oral transmission alone. 'It is said that if all the written and printed copies of the Rigveda were lost, the text could be restored at once with complete accuracy.' This text is about as long as the *Iliad* and *Odyssey* combined. Russian and Jugoslav oral poetry is recited by ministrels who show great powers both of memory and improvisation.

But the more fundamental reason for imperfect recall is that with print there is more complete separation of the visual sense from the audile-tactile. This involves the modern reader in total translation of sight into sound as he *looks* at the page. Recall of material read by the eye then is confused by the effort to recall it both visually and auditorially. People with "good memories" are the ones with "photographic memories." That is, they do not translate back and forth from eye to ear and do not have things "on the tip of the tongue," which is our state when we do not know whether to see or hear a past experience.

Before turning to the oral and auditory world of the Middle Ages in its erudite and artistic aspects, there are two passages, one from the earliest and one from the latest phases of the medieval world that indicate the ordinary assumption that the act of reading was oral and even dramatic.

The first passage is from *The Rule of Saint Benedict*, chap. 48: "After the sixth hour, having left the table let them rest on their beds in perfect silence; or if anyone wishes to read by himself, let him read so as not to disturb the others."

The second passage is from a letter of St. Thomas More to Martin Dorp, reproving Dorp for his letters: "However I am certainly surprised if any person should take it into his head to be so flattering as to extol such matters even in your presence; and, as I began to say, I wish you could watch through a window and see the facial expression, the tone of voice, the emotion with which those matters are read."[23]

In the chantry schools grammar served, above all, to establish oral fidelity.

✻ Once it is understood that oral culture has many features of stability, quite non-existent in a visually organized world, it is quite easy to enter the

[23]E. F. Rogers, ed., *St. Thomas More: Selected Letters*, p. 13.

medieval situation. It is also easier to grasp some of the basic changes in twentieth century attitudes.

I turn briefly now to an unusual book by Istuan Hajnal[24] about the teaching of writing in medieval universities. I had opened this book in the expectation of finding, between the lines, as it were, evidence of the ancient and medieval practice of private reading aloud. I was not prepared to discover that "writing" to a medieval student was not only profoundly oral but inseparable from what is now called oratory and what was then called *pronuntiatio*, which was and remained the fifth major division of standard rhetorical study. Just why delivery or *pronuntiatio* was taken so seriously in the ancient and medieval worlds, gets new meaning from Hajnal's work: "The art of writing was held in great esteem because they saw in it the proof of a solid oral training."

The story of writing as oral training helps to explain the early age of entry to the medieval university. For the proper study of the development of writing we must consider that the students began their course at the university at the age of twelve or fourteen. "In the twelfth and thirteenth centuries, the necessity of knowing Latin grammar, as well as material obstacles like the rarity of parchment, could push back the age at which writing might acquire its definitive form."

We have to keep in mind that there was no organized system of education outside the universities. So that after the Renaissance "we find frequent allusions to the fact at Paris in the small classes of certain colleges, teaching commenced with the alphabet." We have, moreover, data on students in the college who were under ten years of age. But, certainly, for the medieval university we have to keep in mind that it "embraced all the levels of instruction from the most elementary to the most advanced." Specialism in our sense was unknown and all levels of instruction tended to be inclusive rather than exclusive. Certainly this inclusive character applies to the art of writing at this period; for writing implied all that to the ancient and medieval world was *grammatica* or *philologia*.

At the opening of the twelfth century, says Hajnal (p. 39), there had been "for some centuries an important system of teaching designed to train advanced students. This training included in addition to knowledge of the liturgy, practical skills associated with it. At the level of the choir or chantry school one learned to read Latin and thus grammar was necessary in order to recite and to copy properly the Latin texts. Grammar served above all to insure oral fidelity."

This stress on oral fidelity was to the medieval man the equivalent of our own visual idea of scholarship as involving exact quotation and proof-

---

[24]*L'Enseignement de l'écriture aux universités mediévales*, p. 74; translations by the present author.

reading. But the reason for this state of affairs Hajnal clears up in his section on "methods of teaching writing at the university."

By the middle of the thirteenth century the Faculty of Arts at Paris was at a crossroads as regards methods. Presumably, the growing volume of available books had made it possible for many teachers to forego the method of the *dictamen* or dictation, and to move at a fast pace. But the slow method of dictation was also still in vogue. According to Hajnal (pp. 64–5), "after careful consideration, [the Faculty] decided in favour of the first method; that the professor should speak fast enough to be understood, but too fast for the pen to follow him. . . . Students who in order to oppose this statute themselves, or by means of their servants and followers, should shout or whistle or stamp their feet would be excluded from the Faculty for one year."

The medieval student had to be paleographer, editor, and publisher of the authors he read.

✱ The clash was between the old form of dictation or the new form of dialogue and oral disputation. And it was this clash which enables us to learn about the details of medieval teaching procedure. On pages 65 and 66 of Hajnal's work we learn:

The mention that courses were conducted without dictation outside the Arts Faculty shows that the Arts Faculty had broken with the method in use in its courses till that time. And what is more striking the Faculty of Arts expected the opposition of the students . . . The students clung to dictation. For dictation up to that time served not only to slow down the lecture, it served not only to give students complementary texts, but it constituted the method of the principal courses: *modus legendi libros.* . . . Dictation was in use even in the lectures given by the candidates at their examinations when they had to offer evidence of reading the written texts.

Hajnal proceeds to another basic aspect:

There can be no doubt that one of the essential reasons for the custom of dictation finds its explanation in the fact that, before the era of printing, schools and scholars had no adequate supply of texts. A manuscript book cost much; the simplest way of getting them was for the teacher to dictate the texts to his pupils. It is possible that there were students who wrote by dictation texts for commercial ends. Yes, in a certain degree, dictation

95

would have been a commercial affair, both on the part of the student who wrote and sold the book and on the part of the teacher who by this means was assured of a large audience, and, by the same token, substantial revenue. The manual was necessary to the student, not only so far as it served for his university courses, but also because it would be useful in his future career. ... Moreover the university required that students present themselves at their courses furnished with books they had made, and if not that at least there be a book shared among every three students. ... Finally, in presenting himself for his candidature for a degree, the candidate was required to present the books which belonged to him. In the liberal careers, it was the corps of the profession in question that examined the candidates for a post in order to see in what measure they were furnished with books.[25]

The separation of words and music by the print technology was no more decisive than its separation of visual and oral reading. Moreover, until printing the reader or consumer was literally involved as producer. Hajnal describes (p. 68) how:

The method of 'la dictee' (*dictamen*, dictation) in medieval schools had beyond doubt the goal of producing a definitive written text, usable on the spot, suitable to be read by anybody, and being eligible for commercial sale should the occasion arise. The one dictating said the words not once or twice but several times. Indeed, even after the banning of dictation courses it was permitted that the teacher dictate certain theses to be retained. . .

Quite distinct from the precise and thorough mode of dictation in the Arts courses called *modus pronuntiantium*, there was: "a special form of dictation that followed the *modus pronuntiantium*; there was this other method of doing a course, speaking in a speedier fashion, a method destined for the use of the *reportateurs*, advanced students, who were able to teach the others on the basis of notes they had taken."

But the slow and precise mode of *dictamen* or dictation was not only aimed at the production of usable private editions, as it were:

... in taking the course in this manner, they took into account the skimpy preparation of the students. ... It is clear that the students followed these

[25]These considerations put Chaucer's clerk in an interesting light and offer some reason for preferring the reading "worthy" to "worldly" in the disputed text:

> A Clerk ther was of Oxenford also,
> That unto logyk hadde longe ygo.
> As leene was his hors as is a rake,
> And he nas nat right fat, I undertake,
> But looked holwe, and therto sobrely.
> Ful thredbare was his overeste courtepy;
> For he hadde geten hym yet no benefice,
> Ne was so worldly for to have office.
> For hym was levere have at his beddes heed
> Twenty bookes, clad in blak or reed,
> Of Aristotle and his philosophie,
> Than robes riche, or fithele, or gay sautrie.

courses not only to procure texts but also because they were obliged to learn the texts in the process of writing them correctly and legibly. . . .

The expression *modus pronuntiantium* was not used in the statutes simply to designate a course procedure of speaking aloud and duly articulating the words. It was a technical term. The teaching of *pronuntiatio* was one of the fundamental tasks of Latin *grammatica*; and the manuals of grammar devoted a good deal of detail to this question. It was an accepted and established method whose aim was to inculcate good pronunciation of spoken Latin, to teach the careful distinction of the letters, to separate and modulate words and phrases. Manuals of grammar took care to say clearly that all this training served the ends of teaching writing. At this time, good pronunciation was considered essential. It was indeed essential at that time and was the prerequisite for the teaching of writing. The act of writing silently without intervention of the reading the text aloud, was not yet possible at that period. The beginner did not yet see around him a world strewn with writings and printed texts. He needed clear and disciplined pronunciation of the text if he would learn to write without faults. (p. 69)

A fringe benefit of the need for reading and writing aloud is noted by Hajnal (pp. 75–6):

Writing in the mode of dictation did not constitute a copying exercise as simple as might at first appear. It is a curious fact but it is precisely owing to this system that studies had been able to revive and a new literature was born in the heart of these Faculties. For every professor strove to give to the matter taught a new form suited to its own assumptions and inherent conceptions; and mostly he dictated to his students the results of these personal insights. That is how the university movement, from its inception, appears to us now as really modern.

Aquinas explains why Socrates, Christ, and Pythagoras avoided the publication of their teachings.

✱ Hajnal then notes (p. 76) an aspect of personal book making that gives needed insight into a characteristic mode of manuscript culture. Not only did it foster minute textual attention, meditation in depth, and much memorization:

The old traditional manuals, mostly stemming from late antiquity, were always to hand for the professors, but they could see little point in recopying them ad infinitum. To learn and to teach every day, individual by individual,

97

adjusting the work to the preparation of each, they proceeded to condense and to simplify the matter taught in order to facilitate its study and to present it in a compact form.

Summing up, Hajnal says the teaching of writing

was a method of teaching that had multiple objectives: the scribal training, practice in composition, and at the same time the introduction of minds to awareness of new concepts and reasonings and their means of expression. It was a vital and steady movement, adding the pleasure of the practice and use of writing to the acquisition of the texts themselves. This was perhaps the original cause that university teaching in the Middle Ages was more and more characterized by the practice of writing. It is not strange that from the fourteenth century the practice of writing was considered as constituting the essence of university life at Paris.

It is in the light of Hajnal's presentation of medieval writing that we can make more sense of the view of Aquinas that Socrates and Christ, being teachers, did not connect their teachings to writing. It is in question 42 of the third part of the *Summa Theologica* (that is, textbook of theology) that Aquinas asks: "Utrum Christus debuerit doctrinam Suam Scripto tradere?" Aquinas rejects the idea of the learner as a page that is to be written on—a *tabula rasa*. He says:

I answer by saying that it is fitting that Christ did not commit his teaching to writing. First on account of his own dignity; for the more excellent the teacher, the more excellent his manner of teaching ought to be. And therefore it was fitting that Christ, as the most excellent of teachers, should adopt that manner of teaching whereby his doctrine would be imprinted on the hearts of his hearers. For which reason it is said in Matthew vii, 29, that 'he was teaching them as one having power'. For which reason even among the pagans Pythagoras and Socrates, who were most excellent teachers, did not want to write anything.

Had not medieval writing itself been so near to the oral mode of teaching the idea of the written form as merely a gimmick and not teaching, would not have been plausible.

With the splendid introduction that Hajnal provides for a unified approach to the teaching medieval writing as a branch of rhetoric, and as co-extensive with grammar and literary training, it is easy to tie the matter in for both earlier and later phases of studies. For example, in the *De oratore* (I, xvi) Cicero says that the poet is the rival and almost the equal of the orator. That poetry or *grammatica* is the handmaid of rhetoric is a commonplace in Quintilian, Augustine, and throughout the Middle Ages and the Renaissance.[26]

[26]See C. S. Baldwin, *Medieval Rhetoric and Poetic*, and D. L. Clark, *Rhetoric and Poetry in the Renaissance*. They find this Ciceronian fusion of poetic and rhetoric puzzling. But Milton accepted it. He takes the Ciceronian view in his tract *On Education*. After grammar, he says, just so much logic should be studied as is useful to "a

The Ciceronian concept of *doctus orator* and of eloquence as a kind of wisdom, as knowledge in action, became the basic charter of medieval education thanks to Augustine. But Augustine, an eminent professor of rhetoric, did not deliver this Ciceronian charter to the Middle Ages as a speech program for pulpit oratory. As Marrou states the matter in his great study,[27] "la culture chrétienne, augustinienne, emprunte moins à la technique du rheteur qu'à celle du grammairien." In a word, ancient *grammatica* and *philologia* were encyclopedic, linguistically oriented programs which Augustine took over for the Doctrina Christiana. It was not so much preaching as the understanding and expounding of the *sacra pagina* for which Augustine co-opted the world of *grammatica*. And just as Hajnal has shown how mere writing and the teaching of grammar could be completely one with the art of *pronuntiatio* or oratorical delivery,[28] so Marrou shows how it could happen that ancient *grammatica* became the basis for the study of the Bible in the Middle Ages. We shall see how in the sixteenth and seventeenth centuries the ancient and medieval techniques of exegesis flourished as never before. They became the basis for the Baconian scientific program and were thoroughly sidetracked by the new mathematics and the new techniques of quantification.

A brief look at the changes in the various methods of medieval exegesis will prepare the reader for some of the later effects of printing on the arts and sciences. Beryl Smalley's *Study of the Bible in the Middle Ages* is an admirable survey entirely suited to this purpose. For knowing the "take-off" or new dimensions for visual experience and organization which began shortly after printing, it is interesting to observe how much this visual stress was anticipated in a variety of areas quite unrelated to Gutenberg technology. The look we have just taken at the ways in which ancient *grammatica* persisted in oral relation to medieval writing and textual study, helps to show how little the manuscript culture was designed to intensify the visual faculty to the point of splitting it away from the other senses.

Smalley observes (p. xiv): "Teachers in the middle ages regarded the Bible as a school book par excellence. The little clerk learned his letters from the Psalter, and the Bible would be used in teaching him the liberal arts. Hence Bible study is linked with the history of institutions from the very beginning."

---

graceful and ornate rhetoric." To these "poetry would be made subsequent, or indeed rather precedent, as being less subtle and fine, but more simple, sensuous and passionate." These latter words of Milton have often been cited out of context and without any regard for the precise technical sense of Milton's language.

[27] H.-I. Marrou, *Saint Augustin et la fin de la culture antique*, p. 530, note.

[28] In the sixteenth century the Elizabethan actors were sometimes referred to as "the rhetoricians." This was natural in a time that studied *pronuntiatio* as much as the other four parts of rhetoric: *inventio, dispositio, elocutio*, and *memoria*. See B. L. Joseph's fine study, *Elizabethan Acting*, in which from the sixteenth century manuals of grammar and rhetoric he derives the numerous techniques of dramatic delivery and action with which every Elizabethan school child was acquainted.

The rise of the schoolmen or *moderni* in the twelfth century made a sharp break with the *ancients* of traditional Christian scholarship.

❋ We have seen how Marrou had shown that, thanks to Augustine, Bible study incorporated the ancient *egkuklios paideia* or encyclopedic program of *grammatica* and *rhetorica* as it reached definition at the hands of Cicero. Thus it was scriptural exegesis that ensured the continuity of classical humanism in the monastic schools from Augustine to Erasmus. But the rise of the universities in the twelfth century constituted a radical break with the classical tradition. The program of the new universities was much centred in *dialectica* or scholastic method which had had a heyday at Rome as we read in S. F. Bonner's *Roman Declamation* (p. 43):

> Under the Republic, oratory had been essential for success in public life, and the whole subject was alive and keenly debated; but under the principate it had lost much of its political value. It was not so much that the courts had lost a great deal of their power; there were still civil and criminal cases to attract the advocate. It was rather the lack of assured success in public life, which the good orator in Republican days could naturally expect. Under the principate, so much depended upon Imperial and Court patronage; and it became necessary to choose one's words rather too carefully when speaking in public for the practice to be a popular one. Writing under Tiberius (if not Caligula) the elder Seneca could look back upon the Augustan Age as a time when there was 'so much liberty of speech'; but even then that freedom which the author of the *Dialogues* and the philosopher in *Longinus* consider so essential for good oratory, was fast disappearing from Roman public life.
>
> And so oratory betook itself to the safer arena of the schools, where a man might air his Republicanism without fear of consequences, and where one might be recompensed for the loss of political prestige by the plaudits of one's fellow-citizens. The term *scholastica* came into vogue—a 'school-oration' as opposed to the genuine public speech, and the exponents of these display-speeches became known as 'schoolmen'—*scholastici*.

The break between political oratory and scholastic or academic disputation, then, took place long before the Middle Ages. Bonner refers to the *Controversiae* of the elder Seneca and notes (p. 2): "From this it appears that Seneca recognized three main stages of development: (i) the pre-

Ciceronian *thesis* (ii) the privately rehearsed declamations of Cicero and his contemporaries, known to them as *causae* (iii) the declamation proper, known as *controversia* and subsequently also as *scholastica*."

These scholastic exercises in ancient Rome depended on the *sic et non* examination of theses. And in his *Topics* (1, 9) Aristotle refers to such theses as an assertion or negation of some exceptional philosophical tenet, giving as examples "that everything is in a state of flux" or "that all existence is One."

Moreover, "thesis" meant that the topic might not only be paradoxical but that it would be considered in abstraction from particular circumstances and from "given person place or time." Bonner adds (p. 3):

It is in the *Rhetorica* of Cicero, the *Institutio Oratoria* of Quintilian, and the later Greek and Roman rhetoricians, that specific examples of subjects of *theses* are found. They represent the major problems of the world and its meaning, of human life and conduct, which the Greeks debated through the ages, from the cities of Asia Minor to the groves of the Academy, from the Garden and the Porch to the villas of Italy and the colonnades of Rome.

The reason for bringing up the character of scholastic form is that from the twelfth to the sixteenth centuries this kind of highly oral activity broke away from the *grammatica* that formed the base of monastic and later humanist procedures. For *grammatica* is concerned very much with particular historical circumstances and with given person, place and time. With the advent of the printed book *grammatica* surged back to a dominance it had enjoyed before scholasticism and the *moderni* and the new universities had swept it aside. Scholasticism in ancient Rome was also an oral affair, and Bonner points out Cicero's letter to Atticus in which Cicero mentions a list of theses which he himself declaimed in private:

They are almost exclusively concerned with the subject of tyrants and tyranny—'Should one work for the tyrant's downfall, even though it may jeopardise the State, or merely prevent his overthrower's elevation?' . . . 'Should one attempt to help one's country, when subject to a tyrant, by opportune speech rather than by force of arms?' There are eight such subjects, which Cicero says he declaimed in Greek and Latin, both for and against, in order to take his mind off his present troubles . . .[29]

[29]*Roman Declamation*, p. 10. Somewhere Cicero states "Philosophy shall be the declamation of my old age." At any rate, it was the declamation of the Middle Ages.

Scholasticism, like Senecanism, was directly related to the oral traditions of aphoristic learning.

✱ When it is understood how entirely oral these thesis defenses were, it is easier to see why the students of such arts would need to have memories furnished with a large repertory of aphorisms and *sententiae*. This is a factor in the prevalence of Senecan stylistic in later Roman times and for the long association of Senecan style with "scientific method" both in the middle ages and in the Renaissance. For Francis Bacon, as much as for Abelard, "writing in aphorisms" rather than in "methods" was the difference between keen analysis and mere public persuasion.

In *The Advancement of Learning*, which is itself shaped as a public oration, Bacon prefers, on intellectual grounds, the scholastic technique of aphorism to the Ciceronian method of explicit spelling out of information in the form of continuous prose:

> Another diversity of Method, whereof the consequence is great, is the delivery of knowledge in Aphorisms, or in Methods; wherein we may observe that it hath been too much taken into custom, out of a few axioms or observations upon any subject, to make a solemn and formal art, filling it with some discourses, and illustrating it with examples, and digesting it into a sensible Method.
>
> But the writing in aphorisms hath many excellent virtues, whereto the writing in Method doth not approach. For first, it trieth the writer, whether he be superficial or solid: for Aphorisms, except they should be rediculous, cannot be made but of the pith and heart of sciences; for discourse of illustration is cut off: recitals of examples are cut off; discourse of connection and order is cut off; descriptions of practice are cut off. So there remaineth nothing to fill the Aphorisms but some good quantity of observation: and therefore no man can suffice, nor in reason will attempt to write Aphorisms, but he that is sound and grounded. But in Methods,
>
> > Tantum series juncturaque pollet,
> > Tantum de medio sumptis accedit honoris;
>
> as a man shall make a great shew of an art, which, if it were disjointed, would come to little. Secondly, methods are more fit to win consent or belief, but less fit to point to action; for they carry a kind of demonstration in orb or circle, one part illuminating another, and therefore satisfy; but particulars, being dispersed, do best agree with dispersed directions. And lastly, Aphorisms, representing a knowledge broken, do invite men to inquire

farther; whereas Methods, carrying the show of a total, do secure men, as if they were at farthest. (p. 142)

We find it hard to grasp that the Senecan Francis Bacon was in many respects a schoolman. Later, it will appear that his own "method" in science was straight out of medieval *grammatica*.

Noting that the Roman scholastics or declaimers used sensational themes (such as the Senecan drama used in Roman and Renaissance times alike), Bonner adds (*Roman Declamation*, p. 65):

But apart from these characteristics their diction is much the same as that of contemporary writers, and is typical of the earliest 'Silver Latin'.

In composition, the chief faults are the excessive use of short and disjointed sentences, giving an abrupt effect to the style, the rarity of well-balanced periods, and the use by some declaimers of weak and ineffective rhythms. The style of these extracts is what the Greek critics would have called κατακεκομμένη or κεκερματισμένη as an antidote to periodic structure, this feature would have been most effective, but it is so frequently used that the mind wearies of the repeated pungency and point.

But the "disjointed sentences" and endless alliterations such as Augustine used for his popular "rhymed sermons" are the necessary norm of oral prose and poetry alike. (Witness the Elizabethan *Euphues*.) It is easy to gauge the degree of acceptance of print culture in any time or country by its effect in eliminating pun, point, alliteration, and aphorism from literature. Thus, the Latin countries even today retain maxims, *sententiae*, and aphorism at a respectable level. And the *symboliste* revival of oral culture not only began first in Latin countries but relied much on "disjointed sentences" and aphorism. Seneca and Quintilian, like Lorca and Picasso, were Spaniards for whom auditory modes were of great authority. Bonner (p. 71) is puzzled by the favourable light in which Quintilian sets the Euphuistic devices of Latin eloquence in spite of being "distinguished by his commonsense and liberal educational outlook."

Even this brief attention to Senecanism and scholasticism in ancient Rome will help to understand how oral tradition in Western literature is transmitted by the Senecan vogue, and was gradually obliterated by the printed page in the later eighteenth century. The paradox that Senecanism is both highbrow in medieval scholasticism and lowbrow in the Elizabethan popular drama will be found to be resolved by this oral factor. But for Montaigne, as for Burton, Bacon, and Browne, there was no enigma. Senecan antithesis and "amble" (as described in *Senecan Amble* by George Williamson) provided the authentic means of scientific observation and experience of mental process. When only the eye is engaged, the multi-levelled gestures and resonances of Senecan oral action are quite impertinent.

Only two more items in this part of our mosaic of *The Gutenberg Galaxy* are needed. One of them is timeless, and the other is right on the focal point of the sixteenth century metamorphosis *via* print. First, then, the matter of the proverb, the maxim, the aphorism, as an indispensable mode of oral society. Chapter 18 of J. Huizinga's *The Waning of the Middle Ages* is devoted to this theme of how in an oral society, ancient or modern,

... every event, every case, fictitious or historic, tends to crystallize, to become a parable, an example, a proof, in order to be applied as a standing instance of a general moral truth. In the same way every utterance becomes a dictum, a maxim, a text. For every question of conduct Scripture, legends, history, literature, furnish a crowd of examples or of types, together making up a sort of moral clan, to which the matter in question belongs. (p. 227)

Huizinga sees clearly that even written materials are strongly urged into the oral pattern of proverb and aphorism and exemplum or instance, by the oral form of discourse. That is why: "In the Middle Ages everyone liked to base a serious argument on a text, so as to give it a foundation." But the "text" was felt to be the immediate voice of an *auctor*, and was authoritative in an oral way. We shall see that with the advent of printing the feeling for authority is completely confused by the intermingling of the old oral and the new visual organization of knowledge.

The second point concerning the oral bias towards *Sentences* and aphorisms, as both compressed and authoritative, is that this preference is rapidly altered in the sixteenth century. Walter Ong has devoted a great deal of attention to this change as it appears in the work and vogue of Peter Ramus. Saving Father Ong's important work for attention a little later, it is only necessary to cite here his article on "Ramist Method and the Commercial Mind."[30] Ong stresses the change in human sensibility resulting from the rise of typography, showing "how the use of printing moved the word away from its original association with sound and treated it more as a 'thing' in space."

The implication of this visual approach for the oral aphorism, and for the compendia of sentences, adages, and maxims which had been the medieval staple of learning, was recession. As Ong puts it (p. 160), "... Ramus tends to regard the knowledge which he purveys in his arts as a commodity rather than as a wisdom." The printed book will naturally tend to become a work of reference rather than a speaking wisdom.

[30]In *Studies in the Renaissance*, vol. VIII, 1961, pp. 155–72.

Scribal culture and Gothic architecture were both concerned with light through, *not light* on.

✻ The scholastic deviation from the monastic literary humanism was soon to be confronted by the flood of ancient texts from the printing presses. Four centuries of dialectical intensity seemed to end there; but the spirit and achievement of scholastic science and abstraction was carried along, as men like Clagett have shown, into the full tide of modern science.

The scholastic discovery of visual means of graphing non-visual relationships of force and motion is quite at variance with the textual positivism of the humanist. Yet both humanist and the schoolman have been justly nominated for scientific honours. This natural confusion we shall see reaching explicit conflict in the mind of Francis Bacon. His own confusion will help to clarify many issues for us a little later on.

The exegesis of the Bible had its own conflicts of method, and as Smalley indicates in her *Study of the Bible in the Middle Ages* they concerned the letter and the spirit, the visual and the non-visual. She cites Origen:

I published three books (on Genesis) from the sayings of the Holy Fathers
concerning the letter and the spirit . . . For the Word came into the world
by Mary, clad in flesh; and seeing was not understanding; all saw the flesh;
knowledge of the divinity was given to a chosen few. . . . The letter appears
as the flesh; but the spiritual sense within is known as divinity. This is what
we find in studying Leviticus . . . Blessed are the eyes which see divine
spirit though the letters veil. (p. 1)

The theme of the letter and the spirit, a dichotomy deriving from writing, was frequently alluded to by Our Lord in his "It is written, but I say unto you." The prophets had usually been at war with the scribes in Israel. This theme enters into the very texture of medieval thought and sensibility, as in the technique of the "gloss" to release the light from within the text, the technique of the illumination as light *through* not *on*, and the very mode of Gothic architecture itself. As Otto von Simson states in *The Gothic Cathedral* (pp. 3–4):

In a Romanesque church, light is something distinct from and contrasting
with the heavy, somber, tactile substance of the walls. The Gothic wall seems
to be porous: light filters through it, permeating it, merging with it,
transfiguring it. . . . Light, which is ordinarily concealed by matter, appears
as the active principle; and matter is aesthetically real only insofar as it

105

partakes of, and is defined by, the luminous quality of light. . . . In this decisive aspect, then, the Gothic may be described as transparent, diaphanous architecture.

These effects of diaphanous stone are obtained by stained glass, but they are quite relevant to the medieval approach to the human senses and to the senses of scripture above all. It is interesting that Simson points out the tactile quality of stone. An oral manuscript culture had no fear of tactility, the very crux of the interplay of the senses. For it was in this interplay that all lattice or sense *ratio* was formed that let light through. The "literal" level which was thought to possess all the meanings was such an interplay. "We then discover that what we should now call exegesis, which is based on a study of the text and of biblical history, in its widest sense, belongs to the 'literal exposition.' "

In *The Study of the Bible in the Middle Ages,* Smalley cites from *Carolingian Art* by R. Hinks: "It is as though we were invited to focus our eyes not on the physical surface of the object, but on infinity as seen through the lattice . . . ; the object . . . exists—as it were—merely to define and detach a certain portion of infinite space, and make it manageable and apprehensible." Smalley then comments (p. 2): "This description of 'pierced technique' in early northern art is also an exact description of exegesis as understood by Claudius . . . We are invited to look not at the text but through it."

Probably any medieval person would be puzzled at our idea of looking through something. He would assume that the reality looked through at us, and that by contemplation we bathed in the divine light, rather than looked at it. The quite different sensuous assumptions of manuscript culture, ancient and medieval, from anything since Gutenberg, obtrude from the ancient doctrine of the senses and the *sensus communis.*[31] Erwin Panofsky in his study of *Gothic Architecture and Scholasticism* also stresses the medieval bias for light through and found it helpful to tackle the architectural problem *via* the schoolmen:

"Sacred doctrine," says Thomas Aquinas, "makes use of human reason, not to prove faith but to make clear (*manifestare*) whatever else is set forth in this doctrine." This means that human reason can never hope to furnish direct proof of such articles of faith . . . but that it can, and does, elucidate or clarify these articles . . .
   Manifestatio, then, elucidation or clarification, is what I would call the first controlling principle of Early and High Scholasticism . . . if faith had to be "manifested" through a system of thought complete and self-sufficient within its own limits yet setting itself apart from the realm of revelation, it became necessary to "manifest" the completeness, self-sufficiency, and

[31]Edmund Joseph Ryan gives a history of the idea of the *sensus communis* as it was understood in the Greek and Arab world, in his *Role of the Sensus Communis in the Psychology of St. Thomas Aquinas.* It is a doctrine that found a key place for tactility, and it pervades European thought as late as the work of Shakespeare.

limitedness of the system of thought. And this could be done only by a scheme of literary presentation that would elucidate the very processes of reasoning to the reader's imagination just as reasoning was supposed to elucidate the very nature of faith to his intellect. (pp. 29–31)

Panofsky then notes (p. 43) the "principle of transparency" in architecture: "It was, however, in architecture that the habit of clarification achieved its greatest triumphs. As High Scholasticism was governed by the principle of *manifestatio*, so was High Gothic architecture dominated—as already observed by Suger—by what may be called the "principle of transparency." Panofsky gives us (p. 38) the medieval sense doctrine as stated by Aquinas: "The senses delight in things duly proportioned *as in something akin to them; for, the sense, too, is a kind of reason as is every cognitive power*." Armed with this principle that there is a ratio or rationality in the senses themselves, Panofsky is able to move freely among the ratios that are between medieval scholasticism and medieval architecture. But this principle of ratio in the senses as light through Being is everywhere in study of the senses of scripture as well. But all of these matters became much confused by the growing demand for light *on*, rather than light *through*, as the later technology set the visual faculty in ever sharper separation from the other senses. The dilemma ahead is perfectly defined by Otto von Simson in *The Gothic Cathedral* (p. 3): "Not that Gothic interiors are particularly bright . . . in fact, the stained-glass windows were such inadequate sources of light that a subsequent and blinder age replaced many of them by grisaille or white windows that today convey a most misleading impression."

After Gutenberg the new visual intensity will require light *on* everything. And its idea of space and time will change to regard them as containers to be *filled* with objects or activities. But in a manuscript age when the visual stood in closer relation to the audile-tactile, space was not a visual container. There was scarcely any furniture in a medieval room, as Siegfried Giedion explains in *Mechanization Takes Command* (p. 301):

And yet there was a medieval comfort. But it must be sought in another dimension, for it cannot be measured on the material scale. The satisfaction and delight that were medieval comfort have their source in the configuration of space. Comfort is the atmosphere with which man surrounds himself and in which he lives. Like the medieval Kingdom of God, it is something that eludes the grasp of hands. Medieval comfort is the comfort of space.

A medieval room seems finished even when it contains no furniture. It is never bare. Whether a cathedral, refectory, or a burgher chamber, it lives in its proportions, its materials, its form. This sense for the dignity of space did not end with the Middle Ages. It lasted until nineteenth-century industrialism blurred the feelings. Yet no later age so emphatically renounced bodily comfort. The ascetic ways of monasticism invisibly shaped the period to its own image.

Medieval illumination, gloss, and sculpture alike were aspects of the art of memory, central to scribal culture.

✻ In this lengthy consideration of the oral aspects of manuscript culture, whether in the ancient or medieval phase, we gain this advantage: we shall not be inclined to look here for literary qualities that were the later product of print culture.

Moreover, we begin to know what to expect of print technology in the diminution of oral qualities. And today in the electronic age we can understand why there should be a great diminishing of the special qualities of print culture, and a revival of oral and auditory values in verbal organization. For verbal organization, whether on the page or in speech, can have a visual bias such as we associate with the clipped and rapid speech of highly literate people. Again, verbal organization, even on the written page can have an oral bias, as in the scholastic philosophy. The unconscious literary bias of Rashdall is quite involuntary when he says in *The University of Europe in the Middle Ages* (vol. II, p. 37): "The mysteries of logic were indeed intrinsically better calculated to fascinate the intellect of the half-civilized barbarian than the elegancies of classical poetry and oratory." But Rashdall is right in considering the oral man to be a barbarian. For technically the "civilized" man is, whether crude or stupid, a man of strong visual bias in his entire culture, a bias derived from only one source, the phonetic alphabet. It is the concern of this book to discover how far the visual bias of this phonetic culture was pushed, first by the manuscript, and then by typography, or "this mechanical kind of writing," as it was early called. Scholastic philosophy was deeply oral in its procedures and organization, but so, in different ways, was scriptural exegesis. And the centuries of study of the Bible in the Middle Ages that embraced both ancient *grammatica* (or literature) also prepared the materials indispensable to scholastic dialectic techniques. Both *grammatica* and *dialectica* or scholastic philosophy were extremely oral in their orientation compared to the new visual orientation fostered by print.

A favourite nineteenth century theme was that the medieval cathedrals were the "books of the people." Kurt Seligman's statement of this aspect of the cathedral (*The History of Magic*, pp. 415–16) serves to bring out their resemblance to the page of medieval scriptural commentary:

In this quality, the Tarot cards resemble the images of other arts: the paintings, sculpture, and stained glass windows of the cathedrals, which also clothed ideas in human form. Their world, however, is the one above, while the world of the Tarot is below. The trumps depict the relation of the powers and the virtues to man; the cathedrals on the other hand embody man's relation to the divine. But both images impress themselves upon the mind. They are mnemonic. They contain a wide complex of ideas that would fill volumes were they written down. They can be "read" by the illiterate and the literate alike, and they are destined for both. The Middle Ages were concerned with techniques that would enable man to remember and to compare many such areas of ideas. Under this impulse, Raymond Lully wrote his *Ars Memoria*, the Art of Memory. Similar preoccupations also resulted in the early block print, *Ars Memorandi*, printed about 1470. The author undertook the difficult task of making concrete the themes contained in the Four Gospels. For each Gospel, he created a few images, angels, bulls, lions, and eagles, emblems of the four Evangelists, upon which he imposed objects that were to suggest the stories treated in each chapter. Figure 231 shows the angel (Matthew), containing eight smaller emblems that were to recall Matthew's eight first chapters. In visualizing every figure of *Ars Memorandi* with all their emblems, one would remember the stories of the entire Gospel.

To us, such visual memory would seem prodigious, but it was surely not unusual in times when only a few could read and write, and when images played the role of writing.

Seligman has here grasped another essential feature of oral culture, the training of the memory. Just as *pronuntiatio*, the fifth division of classical rhetoric, was cultivated, as Hajnal has shown, for the art of writing and making books, so *memoria*, the fourth division of ancient oratory was a needful discipline in the manuscript age, and was served by the very arts of gloss and marginal illumination. Smalley, indeed, records (p. 53) that the marginal gloss, although of unknown origin, served among its users "as notes for the delivery of oral *lecturae*."

In an unpublished master's thesis[32] John H. Harrington observes that in the early Christian centuries "Both the book, and the written word were identified with the message they carried. They were considered as being magically potent instruments, especially against the devil and his snares." Harrington has many sections that bear on the oral character of "reading" and on the need for memorization as this from the rule of Pachomius: "And if he be unwilling to read, he is to be forced, so that there will never be one in a monastery who cannot read and memorize portions of Sacred Scripture." (p. 34) "Often while travelling two monks would read to one another, or recite from memory the Book of Scripture." (p. 48)

[32]"The Written Word as an Instrument and a Symbol in the First Six Centuries of the Christian Era," Columbia University, 1946, p. 2.

For the oral man the literal text contains all possible levels of meaning.

✳ It will be useful now to notice a few more points in Smalley's *Study of the Bible in the Middle Ages*, that indicate the steady development of new visual bias in later medieval study of the Bible.

There was the early scholastic drive to break away from literary contextual constraints: "Drogo, Lanfranc, and Berengar use dialectic in order to tunnel underneath their text; they attempt to reconstruct the logical process in the mind of their author. Dialectic could also be used for building up a new theological structure with the text as a base." (p. 72).

To get at this process, of disengagement from the literary context, had been one of the attractions of the great collection of sentences of Peter Lombard, of the *Sic et Non* of Abelard, and the concordances of Discordant Canons that were great literary labours of this time: "*Quaestiones* were not only excerpted from their original commentary and issued separately; they were also transferred to a different kind of work. . . . Hence we are faced with the difficult problem of distinguishing between exegesis and systematic doctrinal teaching." (p. 75)

The *Adagia* and *Similia* of Erasmus, excerpted from every sort of work, were later transferred into sermons, essays, plays, and sonnets in the sixteenth century. The real pressure towards visual schemes and organization came from the mounting volume of matters to be processed:

This one-sided development was quite natural. The innumerable problems arising from the reception of Aristotelian logic and the study of canon and civil law, the new possibilities of reasoning, the urgent need for speculation and discussion, all these produced an atmosphere of haste and excitement which was unfavourable to biblical scholarship. The masters of the cathedral schools had neither the time nor the training to specialize in a very technical branch of Bible study. This applied to the philosophers and humanists of Chartres as much as to the theologians of Paris and Laon. Even Bec, the last of the great monastic schools, had been no exception. Lanfranc was a theologian and logician; the genius of his pupil, St. Anselm of Canterbury, took another direction. His philosophical works eclipsed his biblical, which seem to have been lost. (p. 77)

And it was the same pressure of quantity that told, in the long run, in favour of typography. But the point where the visual and the oral approaches to scripture came into sharp medieval conflict was, as might have been predicted, axial or polar to the area where conflict occurred in the new visual culture of the Renaissance. Hugh of St. Victor conveys the matter clearly:

> The mystical sense is only gathered from what the letter says, in the first place. I wonder how people have the face to boast themselves teachers of allegory, when they do not know the primary meaning of the letter. "We read the Scriptures", they say, "but we don't read the letter. The letter does not interest us. We teach allegory." How do you read Scripture then, if you don't read the letter? Subtract the letter and what is left? "We *read* the letter" they say, "but not according to the letter. We read allegory, and we expound the letter not literally but allegorically . . . ; as *lion*, according to the historical sense means a beast, but allegorically it means Christ. Therefore the word *lion* means Christ." (p. 93)

To the oral man the literal is inclusive, contains all possible meanings and levels. So it was for Aquinas. But the visual man of the sixteenth century is impelled to separate level from level, and function from function, in a process of specialist exclusion. The auditory field is simultaneous, the visual mode is successive. Of course, the very notion of "levels of exegesis," whether literal, figurative, topological, or anagogic, is strongly visual, a clumsy sort of metaphor. Yet: "Living over a century before St. Thomas, Hugh seems to have grasped the Thomist principle that the clue to prophecy and metaphor is the writer's intention; the literal sense includes everything which the sacred writer meant to say. But he has occasional lapses from his own standard." (p. 101)

The Thomistic notion of the simultaneous interplay among the senses is as unvisualizable as analogical proportionality: "St. Thomas, perfecting the tentative efforts of his predecessors, has supplied a theory of the relations between the senses which lays the stress on the literal interpretation, now defined as the full meaning of the author." (p. 368)

The sheer increase in the quantity of information movement favoured the visual organization of knowledge and the rise of perspective even before typography.

✻ As the literal or "the letter" later became identified with light *on* rather than light *through* the text, there was also the equivalent stress on "point of view" or the *fixed* position of the reader: "from where I am sitting." Such a visual stress was quite impossible before print stepped up the visual intensity of the written page to the point of entire uniformity and repeatability. This uniformity and repeatability of typography, quite alien to manuscript culture, is the necessary preliminary to unified or pictorial space and "perspective." *Avant-garde* painters like Masaccio in Italy and the Van Eycks in the North began to experiment with pictorial or perspective space early in the fifteenth century. And in 1435, a mere decade before typography, the young Leone Battista Alberti wrote a treatise on painting and perspective which was to be the most influential of the age.

The other thing in Alberti's book that marked the coming of a new attitude far removed from that of the Greeks was his description of the earliest known geometrical scheme for depicting objects in a unified space, or in other words what we today call perspective. Just as it was a major event in the history of pictorial representation, so it was in the history of geometry, for in it was stated for the first time the now familiar process of central projection and section, the subsequent development of which has been the outstanding feature of modern synthetic geometry. It is an idea that was unknown to the Greeks, and it was discovered at a time so ignorant of geometry that Alberti thought it necesary to explain the words diameter and perpendicular.[33]

It is necessary for the understanding of the visual take-off that was to occur with Gutenberg technology, to know that such a take-off had not been possible in the manuscript ages, for such a culture retains the audile-tactile modes of human sensibility in a degree incompatible with abstract visuality or the translation of all the senses into the language of unified, continuous, pictorial space. That is why Ivins is entirely justified in maintaining in his *Art and Geometry* (p. 41):

Perspective is something quite different from foreshortening. Technically, it is the central projection of a three-dimensional space upon a plane. Untechnically, it is the way of making a picture on a flat surface in such a manner that the various objects represented in it appear to have the same sizes, shapes, and positions, *relatively to each other*, that the actual objects as located in actual space would have if seen by the beholder from a single determined point of view. I have discovered nothing to justify the belief that the Greeks had any idea, either in practice or theory, at any time, of the conception contained in the italicised words in the preceding sentence.

The study of the Bible in the Middle Ages achieved conflicting patterns of expression which the economic and social historian is also familiar with. The conflict was between those who said that the sacred text was a complex unified at the literal level, and those who felt that the levels of meaning should be taken one at a time in a specialist spirit. This conflict between an auditory and a visual bias seldom reached a high degree of intensity until after mechanical and typographical technology had conferred on the visual

[33]Ivins, *Art and Geometry*, p. 82.

great preponderance. Prior to this ascendancy, the relative equality among the senses of sight, sound, touch, and movement in interplay in manuscript culture, had fostered the preference for light *through*, whether in language, art or architecture. Panofsky's view in *Gothic Architecture and Scholasticism* (pp. 58–60) is:

A man imbued with the scholastic habit would look upon the mode of
architectural presentation just as he looked upon the mode of literary
presentation, from the point of view of *manifestatio*. He would have taken
it for granted that the primary purpose of the many elements that compose
a cathedral was to ensure stability, just as he took it for granted that the
primary purpose of the many elements that constitute a *Summa* was to ensure
validity.

But he would not have been satisfied had not the membrification of the
edifice permitted him to re-experience the very processes of cogitation. To
him, the panoply of shafts, ribs, buttresses, tracery, pinnacles, and crockets
was a self-analysis and self-explication of architecture much as the customary
apparatus of parts, distinctions, questions, and articles was, to him, a self-
analysis and self-explication of reason. Where the humanistic mind demanded
a maximum of "harmony" (impeccable diction in writing, impeccable
proportion, so sorely missed in Gothic structures by Vasari, in architecture),
the Scholastic mind demanded a maximum of explicitness. It accepted and
insisted upon a gratuitous clarification of function through form just as it
accepted and insisted upon a gratuitous clarification of thought through
language.

The student of medieval poetry could readily parallel these features. The *dolce stil nuovo* of Dante and others was achieved, as Dante explains, by looking within and following the very contours and process of passionate thought. It is in Canto XXIV of the *Purgatorio* that Dante says:

"Count of me but as one
Who am the scribe of love; that when he breathes,
Take up my pen, and, as he dictates, write."

To which his friend Forese replies:

"Brother!" said he, "the hindrance, which once held
The notary, with Guittone and myself,
Short of that new and sweeter style I hear,
Is now disclosed: I see how ye your plumes
Stretch, as the inditer guides them;"

Artistic and verbal fidelity to the very modes of experience is the secret of the sweet new style.

This concern to follow the very process of intellection rather than to arrive at a private point of view, is what lends the air of "universalism" to much scholastic meditation. The same concern with the inherent modalities of thought and being enable us to feel that "Dante is many men and suffers as many."[34]

Paolo Milano introducing Dante to an English public writes:

The main point about Dante is this: what he says is never more, is never less, than his initial and total response to the object before him. (Art for him is the form that truth takes on when it is fully perceived.) . . . Dante never indulges in fancy; he never adorns, or magnifies. As he thinks and sees (whether with his outer, or his inner eye), so he writes. . . . His sensory apprehension is so sure, and his intellectual grasp so direct that he never doubts that he is at the very centre of perception. This is probably the secret of Dante's celebrated conciseness.[35]

With Dante, as with Aquinas, the literal, the surface is a profound unity, and Milano adds (p. xxxvii):

We live in an age where the split between mind, matter and soul (to use Dante's terms) has become so complete that we feel it is about to be reversed. . . . A slow dissociation of these three qualities has been at work for centuries, and we are reduced to admire, as if in separate wings of a gallery, the flesh according to Matisse, the mind according to Picasso, and the heart according to Rouault.

A sculpturally contoured universalism of experience such as Dante's is quite incompatible with the unified pictorial space which houses the Gutenberg configuration ahead. For the modalities of mechanical writing and the technology of movable types were not kind to synesthesia or "the sculpture of rhyme."

The same clash between written and oral structures of knowledge occurs in medieval social life.

✱ In Henri Pirenne's *Economic and Social History of Medieval Europe* there are numerous structural parallels to the patterns of manuscript culture that have so far come to the attention here. The advantage in seeing the clash of forms before typography is that it enables us to see the turn to the struggle which was given by Gutenberg:

[34]Ezra Pound, *The Spirit of Romance*, p. 177.
[35]*The Portable Dante*, p. xxxiii.

It is quite plain, from such evidence as we possess, that from the end of the eighth century Western Europe had sunk back into a purely agricultural state. Land was the sole source of subsistence and the sole condition of wealth. All classes of the population, from the Emperor, who had no other revenues than those derived from his landed property, down to the humblest serf, lived directly or indirectly on the products of the soil, whether they raised them by their labour, or confined themselves to collecting and consuming them. Movable wealth no longer played any part in economic life. (p. 7)

Pirenne is explaining how the feudal estate structure that grew up after the Roman collapse was that of numerous "centres without margins." By contrast, the Roman pattern had been centralist-bureaucratic, with much interplay between centre and margins. The feudal estate fits the approach to scripture that found the total wealth of meaning in the literal text as inclusive. However, the new towns and burgesses begin to approach that phase of "one level at a time" and of specialist knowledge. In the same way, as Pirenne observes, there was no nationalism until the fifteenth century:

It was not until the fifteenth century that the first symptoms of protection began to reveal themselves. Before that, there is no evidence of the slightest desire to favour national trade by protecting it from foreign competition. In this respect, the internationalism which characterized medieval civilisation right into the thirteenth century was manifested with particular clarity in the conduct of the states. They made no attempt to control the movement of commerce and we should seek in vain for traces of an economic policy deserving of the name. (p.91)

Just why typography should have fostered nationalism will become plainer later on. But the role of literacy and papyrus in making possible the structures of early empires is the theme of Harold Innis in *Empire and Communications* (p. 7): "Media which emphasize time are those which are durable in character such as parchment, clay and stone. . . . Media which emphasize space are apt to be less durable and light in character such as papyrus and paper."

With the availability of quantities of manufactured paper, especially after the twelfth century, the growth of bureaucratic and centralist organization of distant areas got under way again. Pirenne writes (p. 211):

One of the most striking phenomena of the fourteenth and fifteenth centuries is the rapid growth of great commercial companies, each with its affiliations, correspondents and factors in different parts of the Continent. The example of the powerful Italian companies in the thirteenth century had now found followers north of the Alps. They had taught men the management of capital, bookkeeping and the various forms of credit, and though they continued to dominate the trade in money, they found themselves faced by a growing number of rivals in the trade in merchandise.

115

The peculiar character of medieval town life was its juxtaposition of two populations. There were the burgesses or guildsmen for whom the town mainly existed, and whose effort was to fix prices and standards for goods and conditions of citizenship:

> The period in which the craft gilds dominated or influenced the economic regime of the towns is also that in which urban protectionism reached its height. However divergent their professional interests might be, all industrial groups were united in their determination to enforce to the utmost the monopoly which each enjoyed and to crush all scope for individual initiative and all possibility of competition. Henceforth the consumer was completely sacrificed to the producer. The great aim of workers in export industries was to raise wages, that of those engaged in supplying the local market to raise, or at least to stabilise, prices. Their vision was bounded by the town walls, and all were convinced that their prosperity could be secured by the simple expedient of shutting out all competition from outside. Their particularism became more and more rabid; never has the conception that each profession is the exclusive possession of a privileged body been pressed to such extremes as it was in these medieval crafts. (pp. 206–7)

But side by side with these exclusive persons living the centre-without-margin life, was a growing population of second-class citizens who were engaged in international trade. They were the *avant-garde* of what later became the dominant middle class:

> But urban industry was not everywhere the same. In many towns, and precisely in those which were the most developed, there was, side by side with the craftsmen-*entrepreneurs* living by the local market, an entirely different group, which worked for export. Instead of producing only for the limited clientèle of the town and its environs, these were the purveyors of the wholesale merchants carrying on international commerce. From these merchants they received their raw material, for them they worked, and to them they delivered it in the form of a manufactured article. (p. 185)

Paradoxically, it will be these international deviationists from medieval town and guild life who form the nationalist core in the Renaissance. It is Chaucer's Host and Wyf of Bath, among others, who are the "outsiders" of their society. They belong to the international set, as it were, who will become the middle class in the Renaissance.

> The term *hôtes* (literally "guests"), which appears more and more frequently from the beginning of the twelfth century, is characteristic of the movement which was then going on in rural society. As the name indicates the *hôte* was a new-comer, a stranger. He was, in short, a kind of colonist, an immigrant in search of new lands to cultivate. These colonists were undoubtedly drawn either from the vagrant population, from which at the same period the first merchants and the artisans of the towns were being recruited, or from among the inhabitants of the great estates, whose serfdom they thus shook off. (p. 69)

The medieval world ended in a frenzy of applied knowledge–new medieval knowledge applied to the recreation of antiquity.

✽ The great study of *The Waning of the Middle Ages* by J. Huizinga is almost entirely concerned with the feudal nobility, whose tenure had been greatly modified by the medieval guildsmen, and was to be quite diminished by the middle class that later came with typography. In many ways, Huizinga is baffled by the medieval world as much as Heinrich Wolfflin was by medieval art. Both men hit upon the idea of applying to it the formulas of primitive and child art and living. And this approach works up to a point, since the tactile bounding lines of childhood visual life are not far from those of non-literate sensibility. Huizinga writes (p. 9):

To the world when it was half a thousand years younger, the outlines of all things seemed more clearly marked than to us. The contrast between suffering and joy, between adversity and happiness, appeared more striking. All experience had yet to the minds of men the directness and absoluteness of the pleasure and pain of child-life. Every event, every action, was still embodied in expressive, and solemn forms, which raised them to the dignity of a ritual. For it was not merely the great facts of birth, marriage and death which, by the sacredness of the sacrament, were raised to the rank of mysteries; incidents of less importance, like a journey, a task, a visit, were equally attended by a thousand formalities: benedictions, ceremonies, formulae.

Calamities and indigence were more afflicting than at present; it was more difficult to guard against them, and to find solace. Illness and health presented a more striking contrast; the cold and darkness of winter were more real evils. Honours and riches were relished with greater avidity and contrasted more vividly with surrounding misery. We, at the present day, can hardly understand the keenness with which a fur coat, a good fire on the hearth, a soft bed, a glass of wine, were formerly enjoyed.

Then, again, all things in life were of a proud or cruel publicity. Lepers sounded their rattles and went about in processions, beggars exhibited their deformity and their misery in churches. Every order and estate, every rank and profession, was distinguished by its costume. The great lords never moved about without a glorious display of arms and liveries, exciting fear and envy. Executions and other public acts of justice, hawking, marriages and funerals, were all announced by cries and processions, songs and music.

117

Associating the developments of five hundred years of Gutenberg technology with uniformity, quiet privacy, and individualism, Huizinga finds it easy to give us the pre-Gutenberg world in terms of diversity, passionate group life, and communal rituals. That is exactly what he does on page 40: "Here, then, we have attained a point of view from which we can consider the lay culture of the waning Middle Ages; aristocratic life decorated by ideal forms, gilded by chivalrous romanticism, a world disguised in the fantastic gear of the Round Table."

The magnificent Hollywood sets which Huizinga provides as an image of the medieval decline blend perfectly with the evocations of the ancient world done by the Medici craftsmen. What Huizinga may have chosen to disregard was the rise of middle-class wealth and skill and organization which made possible both the splendours of the Dukes of Burgundy and of the Medicis. He says of the great Dukes (p. 41):

The court was pre-eminently the field where this aestheticism flourished. Nowhere did it attain to greater development than at the court of the dukes of Burgundy, which was more pompous and better arranged than that of the kings of France. It is well known how much importance the dukes attached to the magnificence of their household. A splendid court could, better than anything else, convince rivals of the high rank the dukes claimed to occupy among the princes of Europe. "After the deeds and exploits of war, which are claims to glory," says Chastellain, "the household is the first thing that strikes the eye, and which it is, therefore, most necessary to conduct and arrange well." It was boasted that the Burgundian court was the richest and best regulated of all. Charles the Bold, especially, had the passion of magnificence.

It was the new middle-class wealth and skill that translated the chivalric dream into the visual panorama. Surely we have here an early phase of "know-how" and practical *applied* knowledge such as in centuries to come was to create complex markets, price-systems, and commercial empires unconceivable to oral and even to manuscript cultures.

The same urge to translate the tactile skills of the older crafts into the visual magnificence of the Renaissance rituals provided an esthetic medievalism in the North, and in Italy inspired the recreation of ancient art, letters and architecture. The same sensibility that led the Dukes of Burgundy and Berry to their *très riches heures* led the Italian merchant princes to restore ancient Rome. It was a kind of applied archeological knowledge in both cases. The same applied knowledge in the interests of new visual intensity and control inspired Gutenberg and led to two centuries of medievalism of a scope and degree unknown to the Middle Ages themselves. For until printing, very few books ancient or medieval were available at all. Those that existed were seen by few. The same situation obtained in painting until recent colour-engraving developed, as André Malraux has explained in his *Museum Without Walls*.

*Renaissance Italy became a kind of
Hollywood collection of sets of antiquity,
and the new visual antiquarianism of the
Renaissance provided an avenue to power
for men of any class.*

❉ Wyndham Lewis in *The Lion and the Fox* (p. 86) has given a fine
statement of the Italian antiquarianism:

The prince or commander of the army of a state had often started as a free
captain; and birth or training, in this age that has been called that of bastards
and adventurers, never mattered less. Muzio Sforza started life as a field
labourer: Niccolo Piccinini as a butcher: Carmagnola as a herdsman. We
can agree that it must have been "singular to see these men—generally of
low origin and devoid of culture—surrounded in their camps by ambassadors,
poets and learned men, who read to them Livy and Cicero, and original
verses, in which they were compared to Scipio and Hannibal, to Caesar and
Alexander." But they were all acting on a tiny scale the past that was
being unearthed, just as English statesmen were modelling themselves at the
time of England's great expansion on the statesmen of Roman antiquity.
With the more intelligent of them, like Cesare Borgia, this archaeological
and analogic habit of mind assumed the proportion of a mania. His "Aut
Caesar aut nihil" is the same type of literature as is concentrated in the small
maniacal figure of Julien Sorel, Stendhal's little domestic Napoleon. Borgia's
motto itself is reminiscent of the title of a book popular before the war in
Germany: *Wordly Power or Downfall.*

Lewis is right in pointing up the frequently shoddy and immature inspiration of much of this:

The Republican would call himself Brutus, the *littérateur* would be Cicero, and
so forth. They attempted to bring to life the heroes of antiquity, and recall
in their own lives the events recorded in the codices, and it was this immediate
application of everything to life in Italian Renaissance society (like the
substitution of a cinema for a history-book in a school) that made the Italian
influence so vivid in the rest of Europe. Renaissance Italy was very exactly
a kind of Los Angeles, where historical scenes were tried out, antique
buildings imitated and roughly run up, and dramatic crimes reconstructed.

How the association of learning and political crime came about is shown
by Villari as follows:

119

"Those were days in which every Italian seemed a born diplomatist: the merchant, the man of letters, the captain of adventures, knew how to address and discourse with kings and emperors, duly observing all conventional forms, . . . The dispatches of our ambassadors were among the chief historical and literary monuments of those times . . .

"It was then that adventurers, immovable by threats, prayers or pity, were sure to yield to the verses of a learned man. Lorenzo de' Medici went to Naples, and by force of argument persuaded Ferrante d'Aragona to put an end to the war and conclude an alliance with him. Alfonso the Magnanimous, a prisoner of Filippo Maria Visconti, and whom all believed dead, was instead honourably liberated because he had the skill to convince that gloomy and cruel tyrant that it would better serve his turn to have the Aragonese at Naples than the followers of Anjou. . . . In a revolution at Prato, got up by Bernardo Nardi, this leader . . . had already thrown the halter round the neck of the Florentine Podestà when the latter's fine reasoning persuaded him to spare his life . . ." (pp. 86–7)

Such was also the world which Huizinga portrays in *The Waning of the Middle Ages*. It was medievalism plus a visual slickness and pomp and opulence made possible by the new wealth and applied knowledge of the middle class. As we move into the Renaissance it is needful to understand that the new *age of applied knowledge* is an age of translation not only of languages but of centuries of accumulated audile-tactile experience into visual terms. Therefore what Huizinga and Villari stress as vivid and new in the applied historical antiquarianism will be found to prove equally characteristic in mathematics and science and economics.

Medieval idols of the king

✻ The mounting passion for visualizing knowledge and separating functions in the later Middle Ages is given extensive documentation in a major study by Ernst H. Kantorowicz. *The King's Two Bodies: A Study in Mediaeval Political Theology* illustrates in detail how medieval jurists were animated by the same passion that led later medieval scientists to separate kinematics and dynamics, as is described by A. C. Crombie in *Medieval and Early Modern Science*.

Late in his great study, Kantorowicz summarizes a good deal of his theme in a way that indicates how the legal fictions clustering about the separation of the King's two bodies led to such characteristic fantasies as the *danses macabres*. These, indeed, made up a kind of animated cartoon world which dominated even Shakespearean imagery, and continued to flourish in the eighteenth century, as Gray's *Elegy* testifies. It was the English in the fourteenth century who developed the effigy in funerary rites as a visible expression of the King's two bodies. Kantorowicz writes (pp. 420–1):

No matter how we may wish to explain the introduction of the effigy in 1327, with the funeral of Edward II there begins, to our knowledge, the custom of placing on top of the coffin the "roiall representation" or "personage", a figure or image *ad similitudinem regis*, which—made of wood or of leather padded with bombast and covered with plaster—was dressed in the coronation garments or, later on, in the parliamentary robe. The effigy displayed the insignia of sovereignty: on the head of the image (worked apparently since Henry VII after the death mask) there was the crown, while the artificial hands held orb and scepter. Wherever the circumstances were not to the contrary, the effigies were henceforth used at the burials of royalty: enclosed in the coffin of lead, which itself was encased in a casket of wood, there rested the corpse of the king, his mortal and normally visible—though now invisible—body natural; whereas his normally invisible body politic was on this occasion visibly displayed by the effigy in its pompous regalia: a *persona ficta*—the effigy—impersonating a *persona ficta*—the *Dignitas*.

The division between the ruler's private and his corporate Dignity, elaborated by Italian jurists for centuries, flourished in France, also. Kantorowicz quotes (p. 422) a French lawyer, Pierre Grégoire, in the later sixteenth century, writing (as if he were commenting of *King Lear*): "The Majesty of God appears in the Prince *externally*, for the utility of the subjects; but *internally* there remains what is human." And the great English jurist Coke observed that the mortal king was God-made, but the immortal King man-made.

Actually, the importance of the king's effigy in the funerary rites of the sixteenth century soon matched or even eclipsed that of the dead body itself. Noticeable as early as 1498, at the funeral of Charles VIII, and fully developed in 1547, at the rites held for Francis I, the display of the effigy was connected successively with the new political ideas of that age, indicating, for example, that the royal Dignity never died and that in the image of the dead king's jurisdiction continued until the day he was buried. Under the impact of those ideas—strengthened by influences deriving from the medieval *tableaux vivants*, the Italian *trionfi*, and the study as well as the application of classical texts—the ceremonial connected with the effigy began to be filled with new contents and to affect fundamentally the funerary mood itself: a new triumphal element came into the ceremony which was absent in earlier times. (p. 423)

Kantorowicz here and in many other passages helps us to understand how the analytic separation of functions was steadily intensified by visual manifestation. The long passage that follows (from pages 436 and 437 of *The King's Two Bodies*) will reinforce the Huizinga themes and further illuminate

Shakespeare's *King Lear*, which has a great relevance to the Gutenberg motifs of the Renaissance:

Our rapid digression on funerary ceremonial, effigies, and sepulchral monuments, though not directly related to the rites observed for English kings, has nevertheless yielded at least one new aspect of the problem of the "two Bodies"—the human background. Never perhaps, except in those "late Gothic" centuries, was the Western mind so keenly conscious of the discrepancy between the transience of the flesh and the immortal splendor of a Dignity which that flesh was supposed to represent. We understand how it could happen that the juristic distinctions, though developing quite independently and in a totally different thought compartment, eventually fell in with some very general sentiments, and that the jurists' imaginative fictions met with certain feelings which in the age of the *Danses macabres*, where all Dignities danced with Death, must have been peculiarly close to the surface. The jurists, as it were, discovered the immortality of the Dignity; but by this very discovery they made the ephemeral nature of the mortal incumbent all the more tangible. We should not forget that the uncanny juxtaposition of a decaying corpse and an immortal Dignity as displayed by the sepulchral monuments, or the sharp dichotomy of the lugubrious funeral train surrounding the corpse and the triumphant float of an effigy-dummy wrapped in regalia, was fostered, after all, in the same ground, came from the same world of thought and sentiment, evolved in the same intellectual climate, in which the juridical tenets concerning the "King's two Bodies" achieved their final formulation. In both instances, there was a body mortal, God-made and therefore "subject to all Infirmities that come by Nature or Accident," set against another body, man-made and therefore immortal, which is "utterly void of Infancy and old Age and other Defects and Imbecilities."

In short, one revelled in strong contrasts of fictitious immortality and man's genuine mortality, contrasts which the Renaissance, through its insatiable desire to immortalize the individual by any contrivable *tour de force*, not only failed to mitigate, but rather intensified: there was a reverse side to the proud reconquest of a terrestrial *aevum*. At the same time, however, immortality—the decisive mark of divinity, but vulgarized by the artifice of countless fictions—was about to lose its absolute, or even its imaginary, values: unless it manifested itself incessantly through new mortal incarnations, it practically ceased to be immortality. The King could not die, was not allowed to die, lest scores of fictions of immortality were to break down; and while kings died, they were granted the comfort of being told that at least "as King" they "never died." The jurists themselves, who had done so much to build up the myths of fictitious and immortal personalities, rationalized the weakness of their creatures, and while elaborating their surgical distinctions between the immortal Dignity and its mortal incumbent and talking about two different bodies, they had to admit that their personified immortal Dignity was unable to act, to work, to will, or to decide without the debility of mortal men who bore the Dignity and yet would return to dust.

Nevertheless, since life becomes transparent only against the background of death, and death against the background of life, the bone-rattling vitality of the late Middle Ages appears not devoid of some deeper wisdom. What one did was to build up a philosophy according to which a fictitious immortality became transparent through a real mortal man as its temporary incarnation, while mortal man became transparent through that new fictitious immortality which, being man-made as immortality always, was neither that of life eternal in another world nor that of the godhead, but that of a very terrestrial political institution.

The Roman jurists had also conceived an "objectivication" of the ruler's *persona publica,* and the Roman emperor is sometimes called "a corporation sole." But neither Greek nor Roman antecedents can explain the concept of the King's *two bodies.* It was the aggressive Pauline concept of the Church as *corpus Christi,* says Kantorowicz (pp. 505–6), that "eventually endowed the late antique "corporations" with a philosophico-theological impetus which apparently those bodies were lacking before Constantine the Great referred to the Church as a *corpus* and thereby introduced that philosophical and theological notion into the language of law."

As with any medieval development at all, the later phases show a preference for an increasingly visual stress. And so it is with the King's two bodies. In 1542 Henry VIII addressed his council: "We be informed by our judges that we at no time stand so highly in our estate royal as in the time of Parliament, wherein we as head and you as members are conjoined and knit together in one body politic."

The organological idea of mystical tribal unity was in itself only partly visual. Merely visual stress in the Renaissance "now served Henry VIII to incorporate the *Anglicana Ecclesia,* so to speak, the genuine *corpus mysticum* of his "empire, into the *corpus politicum* of England, of which he as king was the head." That is to say, Henry translated the non-visible into the visible exactly in keeping with the science of his age, which was giving visual form to non-visual forces. And the same transformation of the audible into the visual word was the prime effect of typography.

In a very interesting passage (vol. II, pp. 103–4) of his *Medieval and Early Modern Science,* A. C. Crombie argues that:

Many scholars now agree that 15th-century humanism, which arose in Italy and spread northwards, was an interruption in the development of science. The 'revival of letters' deflected interest from matter to literary style and, in turning back to classical antiquity, its devotees affected to ignore the scientific progress of the previous three centuries. The same absurd conceit that led the humanists to abuse and misrepresent their immediate predecessors for using Latin constructions unknown to Cicero and to put out the propaganda which, in varying degrees, has captivated historical opinion until quite recently, also allowed them to borrow from the scholastics

123

without acknowledgment. This habit affected almost all the great scientists of the 16th and 17th centuries, whether Catholic or Protestant, and it has required the labours of a Duhem or a Thorndike or a Maier to show that their statements on matters of history cannot be accepted at their face value.

Crombie grants that some of the older science became more accessible *via* printing; but does he not simply ignore the dynamic of later medieval science towards visual formulation? For, to translate force and energy into visual graphs and experiments was, as it continued to be until the discovery of electro-magnetic waves, the heart of modern science. Today, visualization is recessive and this makes us aware of its peculiar strategies during the Renaissance.

The invention of typography confirmed and extended the new visual stress of applied knowledge, providing the first uniformly repeatable commodity, the first assembly-line, and the first mass-production.

✱ The invention of typography, as such, is an example of the application of the knowledge of traditional crafts to a special visual problem. Abbott Payson Usher devotes the tenth chapter of his *History of Mechanical Inventions* to "The Invention of Printing," saying (p. 238) that more than any other single achievement, it "marks the line of division between medieval and modern technology . . . We see here the same transfer to the field of the imagination that is clearly evident in all the work of Leonardo da Vinci." From now on "imagination" will tend more and more to refer to the powers of visualization.

The mechanization of the scribal art was probably the first reduction of any handicraft to mechanical terms. That is, it was the first translation of movement into a series of static shots or frames. Typography bears much resemblance to cinema, just as the reading of print puts the reader in the role of the movie projector. The reader moves the series of imprinted letters before him at a speed consistent with apprehending the motions of the author's mind. The reader of print, that is, stands in an utterly different relation to the writer from the reader of manuscript. Print gradually made reading aloud pointless, and accelerated the act of reading till the reader could feel "in the hands of" his author. We shall see that just as print was the first mass-produced thing, so it was the first uniform and repeatable "commodity." The assembly line of movable types made possible a product that was uniform and as repeatable as a scientific experiment. Such a character does not belong to the manuscript. The Chinese in printing from blocks in the eighth century, had been mainly impressed by the repetitive character of print as "magical" and had used it as an alternative form to the prayer wheel.

William Ivins has made a more thorough analysis of the esthetic effects of prints and typography on our human habits of perception than anybody else. In *Prints and Visual Communication* (pp. 55–6) he writes:

Each written or printed word is a series of conventional instructions for the making in a specified linear order of muscular movements which when fully carried out result in a succession of sounds. These sounds, like the forms of the letters, are made according to arbitrary recipes or directions, which indicate by convention certain loosely defined classes of muscular movements but not any specifically specified ones. Thus any printed set of words can actually be pronounced in an infinitely large number of ways, of which, if we leave aside purely personal peculiarities, Cockney, Lower East Side, North Shore, and Georgia, may serve as typical specimens. The result is that each sound we hear when we listen to anyone speaking is merely a representative member of a large class of sounds which we have agreed to accept as symbolically identical in spite of the actual differences between them.

In this passage he not only notes the ingraining of lineal, sequential habits, but, even more important, points out the visual homogenizing of experience in print culture, and the relegation of auditory and other sensuous complexity to the background. The reduction of experience to a single sense, the visual, as a result of typography leads him to speculate that "the more closely we confine our data for reasoning about things to data that come to us through one and the same sense channel the more apt we are to be correct in our reasoning." (p. 54) However, this type of reduction or distortion of all experience to the scale of one sense only is in tendency the effect of typography on the arts and sciences as well as upon human sensibility. Thus the habit of a fixed position or "point of view" so natural to the reader of typography, gave popular extension to the *avant-garde* perspectivism of the fifteenth century:

Perspective rapidly became an essential part of the technique of making informative pictures, and before long was demanded of pictures that were not informative. Its introduction had much to do with that western European preoccupation with verisimilitude, which is probably the distinguishing mark of subsequent European picture making. The third of these events was Nicholas of Cusa's enunciation, in 1440, of the first thorough-going doctrines of the relativity of knowledge and of the continuity, through transitions and middle terms, between extremes. This was a fundamental challenge to definitions and ideas that had tangled thought since the time of the ancient Greeks.

These things, the exactly repeatable pictorial statement, a logical grammar for representation of space relationship in pictorial statements, and the concepts of relativity and continuity, were and still are superficially so unrelated that they are rarely thought of seriously in conjunction with one another. But, between them, they have revolutionized both the descriptive sciences and the mathematics on which the science of physics rests, and in addition they are essential to a great deal of modern technology. Their effects on art have been very marked. They were absolutely new things in the world. There was no precedent for them in classical practice or thought of any kind or variety. (pp. 23–4)

A *fixed point of view* becomes possible with print and ends the image as a plastic organism.

✳ Ivins is right in pointing to the interplay among many factors in this way. But the technology and social effects of typography incline us to abstain from noting interplay and, as it were, "formal" causality, both in our inner and external lives. Print exists by virtue of the static separation of functions and fosters a mentality that gradually resists any but a separative and compartmentalizing or specialist outlook. As Gyorgy Kepes explains in *The Language of Vision* (p. 200):

Literary imitation of nature tied to a fixed point of observation had killed the image as a plastic organism. . . . Non-representational art clarified the structural laws of the plastic image. It reestablished the image in its original role as a dynamic experience based upon the properties of the senses and their plastic organization. But it threw overboard the meaningful signs of the visual relationships.

That is, the explicit visual linking of components in a composition, verbal or non-verbal, began to fascinate and compel most minds in the later fifteenth century. Kepes specifies this explicit visual linking as "literary" and as the immediate occasion of the dissociation of the interplay of the various properties of all the senses. He adds (p. 200):

The image was 'purified'. But this purification overlooked the fact that the distortion and disintegration of the image as a plastic experience had not been due to represented meaningful signs as such but rather to the prevailing representation-concept which was static and limited, and consequently in contradiction to the dynamic plastic nature of the visual experience. The structure of meaning had been based upon the same conception which generated the fixed point of view of space representation, linear perspective and modelling by shading.

The involuntary and subliminal character of this private or "fixed point of view" depends on the isolation of the visual factor in experience.[36] It is upon this "fixed point of view" that the triumphs and destructions of the Gutenberg era will be made. Since there is widespread misunderstanding about the flat, two-dimensional, mosaic form in art and experience, the evidence which Kepes provides in *The Language of Vision* is very much needed. In fact, the two-dimensional is the opposite of inert, as Georg von Bekesy discovered in the study of hearing. For dynamic simultaneity is the effect of the two-dimensional, and inert homogeneity the effect of three-dimensionality. Kepes explains (p. 96):

Early medieval painters often repeated the main figure many times in the same picture. Their purpose was to represent all possible relationships that affected him, and they recognized this could be done only by a simultaneous description of various actions. This connectedness in meaning, rather than the mechanical logic of geometrical optics, is the essential task of representation.

There is then this great paradox of the Gutenberg era, that its seeming activism is cinematic in the strict movie sense. It is a consistent series of static shots or "fixed points of view" in homogeneous relationship. Homogenization of men and materials will become the great program of the Gutenberg era, the source of wealth and power unknown to any other time or technology.

---

[36]But the tendency for the visual to become "explicit" and to break off from the other senses has been noted even in the development of Gothic script. E. A. Lowe remarks: "The Gothic script is difficult to read . . . It is as if the written page was to be looked at and not read" (in "Handwriting" in G. C. Crump and E. F. Jacob, eds., *The Legacy of the Middle Ages*, p. 223).

How the *natural magic* of the *camera obscura* anticipated Hollywood in turning the spectacle of the external world into a consumer commodity or package.

✳ A quite celebrated novelty and pastime of the Renaissance relates directly to the increasing visual stress in experience, namely the delight which was taken in the use of the *camera obscura*. Erik Barnouw has an excellent brief account of this form of entertainment in his *Mass Communication* (pp. 13–14):

> In the days when Johann Gutenberg's Bible, printed from movable type, was stirring wonder in Germany, another innovation was gaining a foothold in Italy. It was a kind of game, having at first no apparent relationship to the dissemination of information or ideas.
>
> The device was described in Leonardo da Vinci's unpublished notes. If on a sunny day you sit in a darkened room with only a pinhole open on one side, you see on an opposite wall or other surface images of the outside world—a tree, a man, a passing carriage.
>
> The principle was described in detail in the book, *Natural Magic*, by Giovanni Battista della Porta, published in 1558. A few years later it became known that a lens, in place of the pinhole, would sharpen the image.
>
> A group of people in a darkened room, watching images on a wall— thrown by a beam of light cutting through the darkness—must have resembled a group watching home movies. There was one difference: the picture was upside down.
>
> Presently the lens was being put in one side of a box instead of in the wall of a room. Through mirrors the image could be thrown on a glass screen in the box, and seen right side up.
>
> The box, still thought of as a small room, was called a "dark room" or "*camera obscura*". This camera could be aimed at a landscape, street, garden party. A group of people looking in amazement at the moving images in the box may well have resembled a group watching television.
>
> Magicians began using the device for mystification and delight. It became a pastime among the well-to-do throughout Europe.
>
> By the 1600's, painters in many countries were using it to solve problems of perspective. Some artists found it easier to trace the two-dimensional image of the *camera obscura* than to work from three-dimensional reality.
>
> The next step was obvious. Could the image be preserved, saving the artist even more work? The idea seems to have been present for two centuries, awaiting the development of chemistry—and of demand.

St. Thomas More offers a plan for a bridge over the turbulent river of scholastic philosophy.

✻ As we stand on the frontiers between the manuscript and the typographical worlds, it is indispensable that a good deal of comparison and contrast of the traits of these two cultures be done here. Much insight into the Gutenberg era can be had from observation of the scribal era. A familiar passage from St. Thomas More's popular *Utopia* (pp. 39–40) will serve as a start:

'That is yt whyche I mente' (quod he), 'when I said phylosophye hadde no place amonge kinges.' 'In dede' (quode I) 'this schole philosophie hath not; whiche thinketh all thynges mete for euery place. But ther is an other philosophye more cyuyle, whyche knoweth as ye wolde saye her owne stage, and thereafter orderynge and behauynge herselfe in the playe that she hathe in hande, playethe her parte accordynglye wyth comlynes, vttcringc nothynge owte of dewe ordre and fassyon.

Writing in 1516, More is aware that the medieval scholastic dialogue, oral and conversational, is quite unsuited to the new problems of large centralist states. A new kind of processing of problems, one thing at a time, "nothing out of due order and fashion," must succeed to the older dialogue. For the scholastic method was a simultaneous mosaic, a dealing with many aspects and levels of meaning in crisp simultaneity. This method will no longer serve in the new lineal era. A recent book, *Ramus: Method and the Decay of Dialogue*, by Father Ong is entirely concerned with this previously obscure subject, which he illuminates brilliantly. His investigation of the transformation of later scholasticism into visual "method," will be a major aid in the next phase of the Gutenberg configuration of events. More in the second book of his *Utopia* (p. 82) also shows his entire awareness of the homogenizing process of the later scholasticism of his own day. He is happy to record that Utopians are old-fashioned: "But as they in all thynges be almost equall to our olde auncyente clerkes, so our new Logiciens in subtyll inventyons have farre passed and gone beyonde them. For they have not devised one of all those rules of restryctyons, and amplyfycatyons, and supposytyons, very wittelye invented in the small Logycalles, whyche heare oure chyldren in euerye place do learne."

Both *L'Apparition du livre* by Febvre and Martin, and Curt Buhler's *The Fifteenth Century Book* are extensive studies of the transition from scribal to typographical culture. Together with Ong's *Ramus*, it will be possible to

129

use these three great studies to give an entirely new understanding of the events that make up the Gutenberg galaxy. As might be expected, the printed book was a long time in being recognized as anything but a typescript, a more accessible and portable kind of manuscript. It is this kind of transitional awareness that in our own century is recorded in words and phrases such as "horseless carriage," "wireless," or "moving-pictures." "Telegraph" and "television" seem to have registered a more direct impact than mechanical forms such as typography and movies. Yet it would have been just as difficult to explain the Gutenberg innovation to a man in the sixteenth century as it is now to explain the utter diversity of TV and film images. Today we like to think that there is much in common between the mosaic image of television and the pictorial space of the photograph. In fact, they have nothing in common. Neither did the printed book and the manuscript. Yet both the producer and consumer of the printed page conceived of it as a direct continuation of the manuscript. In the same way the nineteenth century newspaper underwent complete revolution with the advent of the telegraph. The mechanical printed page was crossed with a new organic form that changed layout as it changed politics and society.

Today with the arrival of automation, the ultimate extension of the electro-magnetic form to the organization of production, we are trying to cope with such new organic production as if it were mechanical mass-production. In 1500 nobody knew how to market or distribute the mass-produced printed book. It was handled in the old manuscript channels. And the manuscript, like any other handicraft produce, was sold in the way in which we now handle "old masters." That is, the manuscript market was mainly a second-hand market.

Scribal culture could have neither authors nor publics such as were created by typography.

❋ Although we have seen with Hajnal a good deal about the scribal making of books, the assumptions and attitudes of authors about books and readers has not been looked at. Since it was precisely these assumptions that were to undergo very great changes, it is necessary to specify them, however succinctly. For this purpose the work of E. P. Goldschmidt, *Medieval Texts and Their First Appearance in Print*, is indispensable. His study of the habits and procedures of authorship under manuscript conditions leads him to conclude (p. 116):

What I have tried to demonstrate is that the Middle Ages for various reasons and from various causes did not possess the concept of 'authorship' in exactly the same significance as we have it now. Much of the prestige and glamour with which we moderns invest the term, and which makes us look upon an author who has succeeded in getting a book published as having progressed a stage nearer to becoming a great man, must be a recent accretion. The indifference of medieval scholars to the precise identity of the authors whose books they studied is undeniable. The writers themselves, on the other hand, did not always trouble to 'quote' what they took from other books or to indicate where they took it from; they were diffident about signing even what was clearly their own in an unambiguous and unmistakable manner.

The invention of printing did away with many of the technical causes of anonymity, while at the same time the movement of the Renaissance created new ideas of literary fame and intellectual property.

It is not entirely self-evident today that typography should have been the means and occasion of individualism and self-expression in society. That it should have been the means of fostering habits of private property, privacy, and many forms of "enclosure" is, perhaps, more evident. But most obvious is the fact of printed publication as the direct means of fame and perpetual memory. For, until the modern movie, there had been in the world no means of broadcasting a private image to equal the printed book. Manuscript culture did not foster any grand ideas in this department. Print did. Most of the Renaissance megalomania from Aretino to Tamburlaine is the immediate child of typography which provided the physical means of extending the dimensions of the private author in space and time. But to the student of manuscript culture, as Goldschmidt says (p. 88): "One thing is immediately obvious: before 1500 or thereabouts people did not attach the same importance to ascertaining the precise identity of the author of a book they were reading or quoting as we do now. We very rarely find them discussing such points."

Oddly enough, it is a consumer-oriented culture that is concerned about authors and labels of authenticity. Manuscript culture was producer-oriented, almost entirely a do-it-yourself culture, and naturally looked to the relevance and usability of items rather than their sources.

The practice of multiplying literary texts by typography has brought about such a profound change in our attitude towards the book and in our appraisal of different literary activities, that it requires some effort of historical imagination to realize vividly the very different conditions under which books were produced, acquired, disseminated, and procured in medieval times. I must ask you to be a little patient in following some of the reflections I am about to set down which may well appear to be obvious and self-evident. But it can hardly be denied that these material conditions are much too often lost sight of in discussing literary problems of the Middle Ages, and that our mental inertia tends to make us apply criteria of value and of conduct to the writers of medieval books which have originated in our minds under totally different modern conditions. (p. 89)

Not only was private authorship in the later print meanings unknown, but there was no reading public in our sense, either. This is a matter that has usually been confused with ideas about "the extent of literacy." But even if literacy were universal, under manuscript conditions an author would still have no public. An advanced scientist today has no public. He has a few friends and colleagues with whom he talks about his work. What we need to have in mind is that the manuscript book was slow to read and slow to move or be circulated. Goldschmidt asks (p. 90) us to

try to visualize a medieval author at work in his study. Having conceived the plan to compose a book, he would first of all proceed to collect material and to accumulate notes. He would search for books on kindred subjects, firstly in the library of his own monastery. If he found something he could use, he would write out relevant chapters or entire pieces on sheets of vellum, which he would keep in his cell to be made use of in due course. If in the course of his reading he came upon a mention of a book which was not available in his library, he would be anxious to find out where he could obtain sight of it, not an easy matter in those days. He would write to friends in other abbeys reputed to have big libraries to inquire whether they knew of a copy, and he would have to wait a long time for their replies. A large part of the extant correspondence of medieval scholars consists of such requests for search after the whereabouts of some book, requests for copies of books which are said to exist in the place of the addressee's residence, requests for the loan of books for copying purposes . . .

Authorship before print was in a large degree the building of a mosaic:

Nowadays, when an author dies, we can see clearly that his own printed works standing in his bookcases are those works which he regarded as completed and finished, and that they are in the form in which he wished to transmit them to posterity; his handwritten 'papers', lying in his drawers, would obviously be regarded differently; they were clearly not considered by him as ultimately finished and done with. But in the days before the invention of printing this distinction would not by any means be so apparent. Nor could it be determined so easily by others whether any particular piece written in the dead author's handwriting was of his own composition or a copy made by him of somebody else's work. Here we have an obvious source of a great deal of the anonymity and ambiguity of authorship of so many of our medieval texts. (p. 92)

Not only was the assembly of the parts of the book often a collective scribal affair, but librarians and users of books took a large hand in composition since small books which only took a few pages, could never be transmitted except in volumes of miscellaneous content. "These volumes comprising many pieces, which probably constituted the majority of the books in the library, were created as units not by the authors or even by the scribes but by the librarians or bookbinders (very often identical)." (p. 94)

Goldschmidt then points out (pp. 96–7) many other circumstances of pre-print book-making and -using that rendered authorship very secondary:

Whatever the method adopted, a volume containing twenty different pieces by ten different authors would necessarily have to be listed under one name, whatever the librarian might decide to do about the other nine names. And if the first tract in the volume was by St. Augustine, under St. Augustine it would go. If you wanted to see the volume you would have to ask for St. Augustine, even if it should be the fifth treatise in the volume you wanted to consult, which might be by Hugo de Sancto Caro. And if you asked a friend in another abbey to copy something for you which you had noted on a former visit you would have to write to him: 'Please copy the treatise on fols. 50 to 70 in your "Augustinus".' This would not necessarily imply that the writer was not aware that the author of this treatise was not Augustinus; whether he thought so or not, he would have to request this book 'ex Augustino'. In another library this same text, say the *De duodecim abusivis*, would be bound third in a volume beginning with something by St. Cyprian. There the same treatise would be 'ex Cypriano'. This is but one prolific source of 'authorship' attributions, which cause one and the same text to be referred to by a variety of names.

There is another circumstance, much too often forgotten, which greatly adds to the confusion. To the medieval scholar the question: Who wrote this book? would not necessarily or even primarily mean: Who composed this book? It might convey that the inquiry was for the identity of the scribe not of the author. And this would often be a much easier question to answer, for in any abbey the characteristic hand of a brother who wrote many fine books did remain traditionally familiar for generations.

The medieval book trade was a second-hand trade even as with the dealing today in old masters.

✱ Then, from the twelfth century onwards the rise of the universities brought masters and students into the field of book production in class time, and these books found their way back to the monastic libraries when students returned after completing their studies: "A number of these standard textbooks, of which approved exemplars were kept for copying by the stationarii of the universities, naturally found their way into print quite early, for many of them continued in undiminished request in the fifteenth century as before. These official university texts offer no problems of origin or nomenclature . . ." (p. 102) Goldschmidt then adds, "Soon after 1300 the expensive vellum could be dispensed with and the cheaper paper made the accumulation of many books a matter of industry rather than of wealth." Since, however, the student went to lectures pen in hand and "it was the lecturer's task to dictate the book he was expounding to his audience," there is a great body of these *reportata* which constitute a very complex problem for editors.[37]

Circumstances such as these described by Goldschmidt serve to illustrate the extent of the Gutenberg revolution which made possible uniform and repeatable texts:

It cannot be doubted that for many medieval writers the exact point at which they ceased to be 'scribes' and became 'authors' was not at all clear. What amount of 'comportation' of acquired information entitled a man to claim the standing of an 'author' of a new unit in the chain of transmitted knowledge? We are guilty of an anachronism if we imagine that the medieval student regarded the contents of the books he read as the expression of another man's personality and opinion. He looked upon them as part of that great and total body of knowledge, the *scientia de omni scibili*, which had once been the property of the ancient sages. Whatever he read in a venerable old book he would take to be not somebody's assertion but a small piece of knowledge acquired by someone long ago from someone else still more ancient. (p. 113)

Not only were users of manuscripts, writes Goldschmidt, mostly indifferent to the chronology of authorship and to the "identity and personality of the author of the book he was reading, or in the exact period at which this

[37]Under "textbook," the O.E.D. tells us that such arrangements continued into the eighteenth century.

particular piece of information was written down, equally little did he expect his future readers to be interested in himself." (p. 114) In the same way we do not concern ourselves with the authors of the multiplication table or with the personal lives of natural scientists. And so it was also when the student undertook to "imitate" the style of ancient writers.

Perhaps enough has been said about the nature of manuscript culture to illuminate the drastic changes in the relation of author to author and of author to reader in the Gutenberg years ahead. When the "higher critics" began to explain the nature of manuscript culture to the Bible-reading public in the later nineteenth century, it seemed to many educated people that the Bible was finished. But these people had lived mainly with the illusions of the Bible produced by print technology. The scriptures had had none of that uniform and homogeneous character during the centuries before Gutenberg. It was, above all, the concept of homogeneity, which typography fosters in every phase of human sensibility, that began to invade the arts, the sciences, industry, and politics from the sixteenth century forward.

But lest it be inferred that this effect of print culture is a "bad thing," let us consider rather that homogeneity is quite incompatible with electronic culture. We now live in the early part of an age for which the meaning of print culture is becoming as alien as the meaning of manuscript culture was to the eighteenth century. "We are the primitives of a new culture," said Boccioni the sculptor in 1911. Far from wishing to belittle the Gutenberg mechanical culture, it seems to me that we must now work very hard to retain its achieved values. For the electronic age, as de Chardin insisted, is not mechanical but organic, and has little sympathy with the values achieved through typography, "this mechanical way of writing" (*ars artificialiter scribendi*), as it was called at first.

Until more than two centuries after printing nobody discovered how to maintain a single tone or attitude throughout a prose composition.

✱ Once ensconced in the unified pictorial space of Gutenberg culture, many things which were in fact utter novelties began to be generalized as holding also for the pre-print author and reader. "Scholarship" consists very much in getting rid of such irrelevant assumptions. Thus the nineteenth-century editions of Shakespeare have become a sort of monument to irrelevant assumptions. Their editors had little idea that punctuation in 1623 and earlier was for the ear and not for the eye.

Until Addison, as we shall see, the author felt litle pressure to maintain a single attitude to his subject or a consistent tone to the reader. In short, prose remained oral rather than visual for centuries after printing. Instead of homogeneity there was heterogeneity of tone and attitude, so that the author felt able to shift these in mid-sentence at any time, just as in poetry.[38] It was disturbing to scholars to discover in recent years that Chaucer's personal pronoun or his "poetic self" as narrator was not a consistent *persona*. The "I" of medieval narrative did not provide a point of view so much as immediacy of effect. In the same way grammatical tenses and syntax were managed by medieval writers, not with an idea to sequence in time or in space, but to indicate importance of stress.[39]

E. T. Donaldson writing on "Chaucer the Pilgrim,"[40] says, regarding Chaucer the Pilgrim, Chaucer the Poet, and Chaucer the Man: "The fact that there are three separate entities does not naturally exclude the probability—or rather the certainty—that they bore a closer resemblance to one another, and that, indeed, they frequently got together in the same body. But that does not excuse us from keeping them distinct from one another, difficult as their close resemblance makes our task."

There simply was no available exemplar for author or man of letters in the first age of print, and Aretino, Erasmus, and More were, like Nashe, Shakespeare, and Swift later on, led to adopt in varying degrees the only available soothsayer mask, that of the medieval clown. Looking for the "point of view" of Erasmus or Machiavelli builds up a sense of their "inscrutability." Arnold's sonnet to Shakespeare is a useful point of reference for anybody who needs to observe the literary man baffled by the non-literary.

It was some time after printing began that authors or readers discovered "points of view." Earlier, it was shown how Milton was the first to introduce visual perspective into poetry, and his work had to wait till the eighteenth century for acceptance. For the world of visual perspective is one of unified and homogeneous space. Such a world is alien to the resonating diversity of spoken words. So language was the last art to accept the visual logic of Gutenberg technology, and the first to rebound in the electric age.

[38]See "Effects of Print on the Written Word in the Sixteenth Century," *Explorations in Communication*, pp. 125 ff.

[39]Helmut Hatzfeld in *Literature Through Art* illustrates the plastic and pictorial aspect of this question. Stephen Gilman's article on "Time in Spanish Poetry" (*Explorations*, no. 4, 1955, pp. 72–81) reveals "the hidden system or order" in the tenses of *Le Cid*.

[40]In R. J. Schoeck and Jerome Taylor, eds., *Chaucer Criticism*, p. 2. See also B. H. Bronson, "Chaucer and his Audience" in *Five Studies in Literature*.

Later medieval visual stress muddied liturgical piety as much as electronic-field pressure has clarified it today.

✱ One massive area to which scholars have turned recently is that of history of Christian liturgy. In an article on "Liturgy and Spiritual Personalism" in *Worship* (October, 1960, p. 494) Thomas Merton points out:

Liturgy is, in the original and classical sense of the word, a *political* activity. *Leitourgeia* was "a public work", a contribution made by a free citizen of the *polis*. As such, it was distinct from the economic activity or the private and more material concern of making a living and managing the productive enterprises of the "household" . . . Private life was properly the realm of those who were not fully "persons", like women, children and slaves, whose appearance in public was without significance because they had no ability to participate in the life of the city.

The Liturgical Piety of Louis Bouyer considers the later Middle Ages to have been quite decadent liturgically and to have already begun the translation of corporate prayer and worship into those visual terms that are so inseparable from Gutenberg technology. On page 16, we read:

Dom Herwegen's ideas on this point greatly shocked most of his early readers. But it must be admitted today that the whole tendency of contemporary research tends to bear out his conclusions, and to prove them even more convincingly than, perhaps, he himself would have expected. In the greatest scholarly work of our times on the history of the Roman Mass, Jungmann's *Missarum Sollemnia*, an overwhelming weight of evidence goes to show that the history of the Roman Mass during the Middle Ages is the history of how it came to be increasingly misunderstood by the clergy as well as by the Faithful, and of how it began to disintegrate through the fault of the medieval liturgists themselves. A prominent feature of that process as Father Jungmann's book shows, was the appearance, in the medieval *Expositiones Missae*, of those wrong conceptions we have already discussed: disproportionate emphasis on the Presence in the Holy Eucharist and a very sentimental notion of that Presence, which came to play so disastrous a part in the worship of the Romantic as well as the Baroque period.

With regard only to our new electronic technology, it might baffle many to explain why there should be such a profound liturgical revival in our time, unless they were aware of the essentially oral character of the electric "field." Today there is a "High Church" movement within Presbyterianism as well

137

as in many other sects. The merely individual and visual aspects of worship no longer satisfy. But here our concern is to understand how before typography there was already a powerful drive towards the visual organization of the non-visual. There grew up in the Catholic world a segmenting and also sentimental approach in which, writes Bouyer (p. 16), "it was taken for granted that the Mass was meant to reproduce the Passion by a kind of mimetic reproduction, each action of the mass representing some action of the Passion itself:—for example, the priest's moving from the Epistle side of the altar to the Gospel side being a representation of Jesus' journey from Pilate to Herod . . ."

It is plain that there was in liturgy precisely the same drive towards cinematic reconstruction by visual segmentation that we have seen in Huizinga's story of *The Waning of the Middle Ages* and in the Italian princes and their great Hollywood sets of antiquity. And segmentation equals sentimentality. The isolation of the sense of sight quickly led to the isolation of one emotion from another, which is sentimentality. "Sophistication" today is a negative version of sentimentality, in which conventionally appropriate feelings are simply anesthetized. But the due interplay of the emotions is not unrelated to synesthesia or interplay of the senses. So that Huizinga is quite justified in opening his story of the later Middle Ages as a period of emotional violence and decay, as well as a period of intense visual stress. Separation of the senses would be sensuality, as the separation of the emotions is sentimentality. Bouyer nowhere refers to the operation of typography in affecting Renaissance sensibility. But his entire book is a valid companion for the student of the Gutenberg revolution. He does note (p. 6) of this period that "it craved the super-human instead of the supernatural, as witness the paintings of Michaelangelo; and it took pleasure in the enormous rather than in the great, as witness the statues of St. John Lateran with their hysterical gesticulations, and the tomb of Alexander VII in St. Peter's."

Print as an immediate technological extension of the human person gave its first age an unprecedented access of power and vehemence. Visually, print is very much more "high definition" than manuscript. Print was, that is to say, a very "hot" medium coming into a world that for thousands of years had been served by the "cool" medium of script. Thus our own "roaring twenties" were the first to feel the hot movie medium and also the hot radio medium. It was the first great consumer age. So with print Europe experienced its first consumer phase, for not only is print a consumer medium and commodity, but it taught men how to organize all other activities on a systematic lineal basis. It showed men how to create markets and national armies. For the hot medium of print enabled men to *see* their vernaculars for the first time, and to visualize national unity and power in terms of the vernacular bounds: "We must be free or die who speak the tongue that Shakespeare spake." Inseparable from a nationalism of homogeneous English or French speakers was individualism. We shall discuss this later. But a visually homogeneous mass consists of individuals in a new subjective sense. Bouyer cites (p. 17) the medieval turn from objective to subjective piety: "This tendency goes along with a shift of emphasis from a union of the whole church with God to an emphasis on the union of the individual soul with Him."

A Catholic liturgist like Bouyer, quite unconcerned with segmental practices such as private interpretation of the Bible, sees, however, the same fragmenting tendency in "the insistence of priests on having each a separate celebration of his own, when it is not needed for the people," for this "tends only to obscure and break that unity of the Church which is not a detail of secondary importance in the Eucharist, but its own proper end." Once Catholic scholarship had transcended the idea of the Middle Ages as "the Christian era *par excellence*, and [the idea] that their civilization and culture provided the outstanding example of a Catholic ideal incarnated in earthly realities, it became easy to see that the medieval period in fact paved the way for the abandonment of the liturgy by Protestantism and its final disgrace and neglect in so much of post-Tridentine Catholicism." (p. 15)

Examining later, how medieval piety is a progressive alienation of the people from the liturgy, in the interest of grand visual effects, Bouyer (p. 249) feels great sympathy with the Protestant reformers who missed the real opportunity for inclusive reform in favour of exclusive segmentation:

This is true not only because the Reformers reacted against the extreme transformations of traditional piety which had been progressively achieved by these novelties, but also for the reason that had Protestantism been such a reaction through and through, in fact as well as in precept, it could have become a true reformation instead. But Protestantism is much more truly the product of medieval piety because it is the fruit of what lay in that piety in seed-form: a naturalistic outlook on religion, a systematic ignoring of the Mystery, a sentimental kind of religious "experience" in place of the sober mysticism, completely grounded on faith, of the great Christian tradition.

It is not the aim of this book to do more than to explain the configuration or galaxy of events and actions associated with Gutenberg technology. And rather than speak of "the rise of Protestantism" as a result of typography with its innovation of the visual text—the same for all—in place of the oral word, it is more helpful to note how the liturgy of the Catholic Church itself still carries deep marks of the effects of visual technology and the break-up of the unity of the senses. "The Elizabethan world picture" was to become much more visually hierarchical than anything medieval had ever been, if only because hierarchy came to be merely visual. Bouyer points (p. 155) to the inadequacy of visualizing "hierarchy": "The hierarchy is a hierarchy of ministries (services); according to Christ's word, he who is the high priest among his brethren should be the man who, like Christ himself, stands out more perfectly than anyone else, as the Lord's Servant." And

139

as the Catholic tendency in the past had been the splitting up of sacraments and the visualizing of functions, the present liturgical revival seeks an inclusive rather than an exclusive unity (p. 253):

This means that the first and fundamental condition for any liturgical revival which is truly a revival of piety must be a personal knowledge of the whole Bible and meditation on it, both to be achieved along the lines laid out for us by the liturgy; such a revival implies a full acceptance of the Bible as the Word of God, and as the framework and ever-living source of all authentic Christianity. The monks of the Middle Ages remained alive to the liturgy for so long a time only because, in spite of their own defects, they held so persistently to this biblical way of accepting Christianity, of meditating on its truths and of living in them.

Allusion to the changing patterns of liturgical worship in the twentieth century will recall to some readers the parallel changes in the world of management and of industrial organization. What occurs at the opening of *King Lear* in regard to the delegation of the king's authority and functions is now in a reverse phase in the electronic age. Dr. B. J. Muller-Thym, leading business analyst, states:[41]

The older, many-layered, highly functionalized organizations were characterized by the separation of thinking from doing; thinking was generally allocated to the top rather than the bottom of the pyramid and to "staff" as against "line" components. Whatever the wishes of the company about the decentralized exercises of authority, authority inexorably gravitated toward the top of the structure. There was created a numerous middle management class, spread over an indefinite number of supervisory layers whose actual roles, as many work studies showed, was predominantly the passing of information through the system.

In our electronic age the specialist and pyramidal forms of structure, which achieved vogue in the sixteenth century and later, are not any longer practical:

The first thing to be discovered was that pyramidal organizational structures, with many layers of supervision, and with functional division by specialty, simply did not work. The communication chain between top scientific or engineering leadership and work centers was too long for either the scientific or managerial message to be communicated. But in these research organizations where work actually got done, when one studied them he found that whatever the organization chart prescribed, groups of researchers with different competences as required by the problem in hand were working together, cutting across organizational lines; that they were establishing most of their own design criteria for the work as well as their intended patterns of

[41]In "New Directions for Organization Practice" in *Ten Years Progress in Management, 1950–1960*, pp. 48, 45.

association; that the patterns of their group association at work followed the organization of their competences as human knowledges.

The "simultaneous field" of electric information structures, today reconstitutes the conditions and need for dialogue and participation, rather than specialism and private initiative in all levels of social experience. Our present involvement in these new kinds of interdependence produces in many an involuntary alienation from our Renaissance heritage. But for the readers of this book it is hoped that we can deepen our understanding both of the typographic and the electronic revolutions.

The interface of the Renaissance was the meeting of medieval pluralism and modern homogeneity and mechanism—a formula for blitz and metamorphosis.

✱ An age in rapid transition is one which exists on the frontier between two cultures and between conflicting technologies. Every moment of its consciousness is an act of translation of each of these cultures into the other. Today we live on the frontier between five centuries of mechanism and the new electronics, between the homogeneous and the simultaneous. It is painful but fruitful. The sixteenth century Renaissance was an age on the frontier between two thousand years of alphabetic and manuscript culture, on the one hand, and the new mechanism of repeatability and quantification, on the other. It would have been strange, indeed, if the age had not approached the new in terms of what it had learned from the old. This matter is well understood by psychologists today as can be found in such a handbook as *The Psychology of Human Learning* by John A. McGeoch. He says (p. 394): "The influence of prior learning (retained until the present) upon the learning of, response to, new material has traditionally been called *transfer of learning.*" Mostly, transfer effect is quite subliminal. But overt or conscious transfer can occur. We have seen some of both kinds of transfer at the beginning of this book where the response of African natives to alphabet and film was discussed. Our own Western response to new media like film and radio and TV, has been overtly a book culture response to the "challenge." But the actual *transfer of learning* and change in mental process and attitude of mind that has occurred has been almost entirely subliminal. What we

141

acquire as a system of sensibility by our mother tongue will affect our ability in learning other languages, verbal or symbolic. That is perhaps why the highly literate Westerner steeped in the lineal and homogeneous modes of print culture has much trouble with the non-visual world of modern mathematics and physics. The "backward" or audile-tactile countries have a great advantage here.

Another basic advantage of cultural clash and transition is that people on the frontier between different modes of experience develop a great power of generalization. McGeoch says (p. 396): "Generalization, likewise, is a form of transfer, whether at the comparatively elementary level of conditioned responses . . . or at the complex level of abstract scientific generalization, where a single statement sums up a myriad of particulars."

We can generalize this statement at once by pointing out that the mature phase of print culture which proceeds by segmenting and homogenizing situations will not favour the interplay between fields and disciplines such as characterized the first age of print. When print was new it stood as a challenge to the old world of manuscript culture. When the manuscript had faded and print was supreme, there was no more interplay or dialogue but there were many "points of view." There is, however, one massive aspect of the "transfer of training" that occurred with the Gutenberg technology that is stressed throughout the work of Febvre and Martin (*L'Apparition du livre*). It is that during the first two centuries of print, until the end of the seventeenth century, the great body of printed matter was of medieval origin. The sixteenth and seventeenth centuries saw more of the Middle Ages than had ever been available to anybody in the Middle Ages. Then it had been scattered and inaccessible and slow to read. Now it became privately portable and quick to read. As today, the insatiable needs of TV have brought down upon us the backlog of the old movies, so the needs of the new presses could only be met by the old manuscripts. Moreover, the reading public was atuned to this earlier culture. Not only were there no modern writers at first, but they had no public ready to accept them so Febvre and Martin say (p. 420): "Thus print facilitated the work of scholars in some fields, but on the whole one can say that it contributed nothing to hasten the adoption of theories or new knowledge."[42]

This, of course, is to consider only the "content" of new theories, and to ignore the role of print in providing new models for such theories, and in processing new publics to accept them. Looked at merely from the "content" point of view the achievement of print is modest indeed: "Already in the fifteenth century fine editions of classical texts coming off the Italian presses, Venetian and Milanese in particular, . . . had begun to make better known such authors of antiquity as the Middle Ages had not forgotten . . ." (p. 400)

[42]My translation, as are the other quotations below from this work.

But the tiny public for these humanist offerings should not obscure the real work of the early age of print. Febvre and Martin (p. 383) see it thus:

To render the Bible directly accessible to a larger number of readers, not only in Latin but also in the vernacular, to furnish to students and teachers at the universities the major treatises in the traditional scholastic arsenal, to multiply above all the common books, breviaries, book of hours necessary for the practice of liturgical ceremonies and daily prayers, the writings of the mystical writers and books of popular piety, to render, above all, the reading of these works more easily accessible to a very large public, such was one of the principal tasks of print in its beginnings.

The largest public by far was for the medieval romances of chivalry, almanacs (shepherds' calendars) and, above all, illustrated books of hours. Of the penetrating force of printing in the shaping of market and capital organization, Febvre and Martin have much to say. For the moment, it is relevant to bring out here their stress on the early effort of the printers to attain "homogenéité de la page" in spite of poor equilibrium of types, and "in spite of defective fonts and in spite of precarious lineality." It is precisely these new effects which were still insecure that would strike the age as having the utmost charge of meaning and novelty of achievement. Homogeneity and lineality are the formulas for the new science and art of the Renaissance. For the infinitesimal calculus, as a means of quantifying forces and spaces, depends as much on the fiction of homogeneous particles as perspective depends upon the illusion of the third dimension on flat surfaces.

The student of the work of St. Thomas More knows how frequently More confronted the new passion for homogeneity in the sectaries of his day. We are here concerned not with theology but only the new psychic demand for homogeneity, no matter in what field. This is from "A letter of Sir Thomas More, Knight, impugning the erroneous writings of John Frith against the Blessed Sacrament of the Altar."[43]

If he sayd that the wordes of Chryste might beside the lyttarall sence bee vnderstanden in an allegorye, I would wel agre wyth him. For so may euery worde almost through the whole scripture, calling an allegory euerye sense, wherby the wordes be translated vnto some other spirituall vnderstanding, beside the true playne open sence that ye letter firste entended. But on the other side because yt in some wordes of scrypture is there none other thing entended but an allegorye, to goe therfore and in another place of scripture to take away wyth an allegory, the very true litterall sense as he doth here, thys is the faute that we fynde in hym. Whych if it may be suffered, must nedes make al ye scripture as touching anye poynte of oure fayth, of none effecte or force at all. I meruaile me therfore much that he is not aferde to affirme that these wordes of Christe, of his bodye and hys bloode, must

[43]More, *English Works*, 1557, p. 835.

143

needes be vnderstanden onely by way of a similitude or an allegory as yᵉ
wordes be of the vine and the dore.

Now this he woteth well, yᵗ thoughe some woordes spoken by the
mouthe of Christ written in scripture, be to be vnderstanden only by way
of a similitude or an allegory: it foloweth not therupō that of necessitye
euerye like woorde of Christ in other places was none other but an allegory.

More is saying that Frith understands the whole of Scripture to be continuous, uniform, and homogeneous space, exactly as in the new painting of
the time. The new homogeneity of the printed page seemed to inspire a
subliminal faith in the validity of the printed Bible as bypassing the traditional
oral authority of the Church, on one hand, and the need for rational critical
scholarship on the other. It was as if print, uniform and repeatable commodity
that it was, had the power of creating a new hypnotic superstition of the book
as independent of and uncontaminated by human agency. Nobody who had
read manuscripts could achieve this state of mind concerning the nature of
the written word. But the assumption of homogeneous repeatability derived
from the printed page, when extended to all the other concerns of life, led
gradually to all those forms of production and social organization from which
the Western world derives many satisfactions and nearly all of its characteristic traits.

---

*Peter Ramus and John Dewey were the
two educational surfers or wave-riders of
antithetic periods, the Gutenberg and
the Marconi or electronic.*

✳ In our time John Dewey worked to restore education to its primitive,
pre-print phase. He wanted to get the student out of the passive role of
consumer of uniformly packaged learning. In fact, Dewey in reacting against
passive print culture was surf-boarding along on the new electronic wave.
That wave has now rolled right over this age. In the sixteenth century the
great figure in educational reform was Peter Ramus (1515–1572), a Frenchman who rode the Gutenberg wave. Walter Ong has finally given us adequate
studies of Ramus, placing him in relation to the later scholasticism from
which he came and in relation to the new print-oriented classrooms for which
he devised his visual programs. The printed book was a new visual aid

available to all students and it rendered the older education obsolete. The book was literally a teaching machine where the manuscript was a crude teaching tool only.

Had any of our current testers of media and various educational aids been available to the harassed sixteenth century administrator they would have been asked to find out whether the new teaching machine, the printed book, could do the full educational job. Could a portable, private instrument like the new book take the place of the book one made by hand and memorized as one made it? Could a book which could be read quickly and even silently take the place of a book read slowly aloud? Could students trained by such printed books measure up to the skilled orators and disputants produced by manuscript means? Using the methods the testers now use for radio, film, and TV, our testers would have reported in due course: "Yes, strange and repugnant as it may sound to you, the new teaching machines enable students to learn as much as before. Moreover, they seem to have more confidence in the new method as giving them the means of acquiring many new kinds of knowledge."

The testers, that is to say, would have entirely missed the character of the new machine. They would have offered not one clue to its effects. There is no need to speculate about this situation. There is a recent work which attempts to assess these effects: *Television in the Lives of Our Children* by Wilbur Schramm, Jack Lyle, and Edwin B. Parker. When we see the reason for the total failure of this book to get in touch with its announced theme, we can understand why in the sixteenth century men had no clue to the nature and effects of the printed word. Schramm and his colleagues make no analysis of the TV image. They assume that apart from the "program" or "content" TV is a "neutral" medium like any other. To know otherwise, these men would have to have a thorough knowledge of the various art forms and scientific models of the past century. In the same way nobody could discover anything about the nature or effect of print without careful study of Renaissance painting and the new scientific models.

But there is one especially revealing assumption made by Schramm and his colleagues. It is one that they share with Don Quixote, and it is that print is the criterion of "reality." Schramm assumes (p. 106) that the non-print media are "fantasy"-oriented: "Looking at these children in another way, 75% of the highest socioeconomic group were high users of print. . . . whereas the lowest socioeconomic children were more likely to depend on television, and television alone."

Since print is of such importance as a parameter or frame of reference to people like Schramm in their scientific testing, we had best get on with finding out what it is and does. And that is where the work of Ramus can help us a lot. For just as Dewey, in a very confused way, was trying to explain the meaning of the electronic age to educators, Ramus had a new program for all phases of education in the sixteenth century. Father Ong at the end of a recent article on "Ramist Classroom Procedure and the Nature of Reality"[44] says that for Ramus and his followers, it is their version of the school curriculum which holds the world together. "Nothing is accessible for 'use' ... until it has first been put through the curriculum. The schoolroom is by implication the doorway to reality, and indeed the only doorway." Now that idea, new in the sixteenth century, is the one that Schramm has been saddled with, unconsciously, in the twentieth. Dewey, on the other hand, is the perfect foil to Ramus in his striving to dislodge the school from the fantastic Ramist idea of it as immediate adjunct to the press and as the supreme processer or hopper through which the young and all their experience must pass in order to be available for "use." Ramus was entirely right in his insistence on the supremacy of the new printed book in the classroom. For only there could the homogenizing effects of the new medium be given heavy stress in young lives. Students processed by print technology in this way would be able to translate every kind of problem and experience into the new visual kind of lineal order. For a nationalist society keen on exploiting its entire manpower for the common tasks of commerce and finance, of production and marketing, it needed very little vision to see that education of this kind should be compulsory. Without universal literacy it is hard, indeed, to tap the manpower pool. Napoleon had great trouble in getting peasants and semi-literates to march and drill, and took to tying their feet with 18-inch lengths of rope to give them the necessary sense of precision, uniformity and repeatability. But the fuller development of manpower resources by literacy in the nineteenth century had to wait for the intervening commercial and industrial applications of print technology, to all phases of learning, work, and entertainment.

Rabelais offers a vision of the future of print culture as a consumer's paradise of applied knowledge.

✱ Anybody who looks at the Gutenberg question at all, runs very soon into Gargantua's Letter to Pantagruel. Rabelais, long before Cervantes, produced an authentic myth or prefiguration of the whole complex of print technology. The Cadmus myth that the sowing of the dragon's teeth, or the letters of the

[44]*Studies in English Literature, 1500-1900*, vol. I, no. 1, winter, 1961, pp. 31–47.

alphabet, by King Cadmus, caused armed men to spring up is a concise and accurate oral myth. As befits the medium of print, Rabelais is a verbose mass-production entertainment. But his vision of giganticism and the consumer's paradises ahead was quite accurate. There are, indeed, four massive myths of the Gutenberg transformation of society. Besides *Gargantua*, they are *Don Quixote*, the *Dunciad*, and *Finnegans Wake*. Each of them deserves a separate volume in relation to the world of typography, but some attention will be given to each in the following pages.

If we first take a moment to glance at mechanization in its advanced stages it will be easier to see what Rabelais was excited about in its earlier phase. In his study of the democratization of the privileged consumer commodities, *Mechanization Takes Command*, Siegfried Giedion considers the meaning of the assembly-line in its explicit later phases (p. 457):

Eight years later, in 1865, Pullman's sleeping car, the *Pioneer*, began to democratize aristocratic luxury. Pullman possessed the same instinct as Henry Ford half a century later, for stirring the dormant fancies of the public until they grew into demands. Both careers centered round the same problem: How might the instruments of comfort, that in Europe were unquestionably reserved to the financially privileged class, become democratized?

Rabelais is concerned with the democratization of knowledge by the abundance of wines from the printing press. For the press is named from the technology it borrowed from the wine-press. Applied knowledge from the press led eventually to comfort as much as to learning.

If there is any doubt whether the Cadmus myth uses "dragon's teeth" as an allusion to the technology of the hieroglyph, there need be none at all about Rabelais's insistence on *pantagruelion* as the symbol and image of printing from movable types. For this is the name of the hemp plant from which rope was made. From the teasing and shredding and weaving of this plant there came the lineal cords and bonds of greatest social enterprises. And Rabelais had a vision of the entire "world in Pantagruel's mouth," which is quite literally the idea of the giganticism that issues from mere additive association of homogeneous parts. And again his vision was accurate as we in this century can easily testify by retrospect. It is in his letter to Pantagruel at Paris that Gargantua proclaims the praise of typography:

Now is it that the minds of men are qualified with all manner of discipline, and the old sciences revived, which for many ages were extinct: now it is, that the learned languages are to their Pristine purity restored, *viz.* Greek, (without which a man may be ashamed to account himself a scholar) Hebrew, Arabick, Chaldean and Latine. Printing likewise is now in use, so elegant, and so correct, that better cannot be imagined, although it was found out but in my time by divine inspiration, as by a diabolical suggestion on the other side was the invention of Ordnance. All the world is full of knowing men, of most learned Schoolmasters, and vast Libraries: and it appears to me as a truth, that neither in Plato's time nor Cicero's, nor Papinian's, there was ever such conveniency for studying, as we see at this day there is. . . . I see robbers, hangmen, free-booters, tapsters, ostlers, and such like, of the very rubbish of the people, more learned now, than the doctors and the preachers were in my time. . . . What shall I say? The very women and children have aspired to this praise and celestial Manna of good learning.[45]

Although the main work was done by Cromwell and Napoleon, "ordnance" (or cannon) and gunpowder had at least begun the levelling of castles, classes, and feudal distinctions. So print, says Rabelais, has begun the homogenizing of individuals and of talents. Later in the same century Francis Bacon was prophesying that his scientific method would level all talents and enable a child to make scientific discoveries of consequence. And Bacon's "method" we shall see was the extension of the idea of the new printed page to the whole encyclopedia of natural phenomena. That is, Bacon's method literally puts the whole of nature in Pantagruel's mouth.

Albert Guérard's comment on this aspect of Rabelais in *The Life and Death of an Ideal* (p. 39) is as follows:

This triumphant Pantagruelism inspires the chapters, full of quaint erudition, practical knowledge and poetic enthusiasm, which, at the end of the third book, he devotes to the praise of the blessed herb Pantagruelion. Literally, Pantagruelion is mere hemp; symbolically, it is human industry. Capping the wildest achievements of his own times with wilder boast and prophecy, Rabelais first shows man, by virtue of this Pantagruelion, exploring the remotest regions of his globe, "so that Taproban hath seen the heaths of Lapland, and both the Javas, the Riphaean Mountains." Men "scoured the Atlantic Ocean, passed the tropics, pushed through the torrid zone, measured all the Zodiac, sported under the equinoctial, having both poles level with their horizon." Then, "all marine and terrestrial gods were on a sudden all afraid." What is to prevent Pantagruel and his children from discovering some still more potent herb, by means of which they shall scale the very heavens? Who knows but they may "contrive a way to pierce into the high aerian clouds, and shut and open as they please the sluices from whence proceed the floodgates of the rain . . . then, prosecuting their ethereal voyage, they may step into the lightning workhouse and shop. . . where, seizing on the magazine of heaven, they may discharge a bouncing peal or two of thundering ordnance for joy of their arrival at these new supernal places. . . . And we the Gods shall then not be able to resist the impetuosity of their intrusion, . . . whatever regions, domiciles or mansions of the spangled firmament they shall have a mind to see, to stay in, or to travel through for their recreation."

[45]*The Works of Mr. Francis Rabelais*, translated by Sir Thomas Urquhart, p. 204.

The Rabelais vision of new means and patterns of human interdependence was a vista of power through applied knowledge. The price of conquering the new world of gigantic dimensions was simply to enter Pantagruel's mouth. Erich Auerbach devotes the eleventh chapter of *Mimesis: The Representation of Reality in Western Literature* to "The World in Pantagruel's Mouth." Auerbach notes (p. 269) some of the predecessors of Rabelais' fantasy in order to do justice to the originality of Rabelais who "maintains a constant interplay of different locales, different themes and different levels of style." Like Robert Burton's *Anatomy of Melancholy* later on, Rabelais follows the "principle of the promiscuous intermingling of the categories of event, experience, and knowledge, as well as of dimensions and styles."

Again, Rabelais is like a medieval glossator of the Roman law in supporting his absurd opinions with a welter of learning which manifests "rapid shifts between a multiplicity of viewpoints." That is to say, Rabelais is a scholastic in his mosaic procedures, consciously juxtaposing this ancient farrago with the new individual single-point-of-view technology of print. Like the poet John Skelton at the same time in England, of whom C. S. Lewis writes, "Skelton has ceased to be a man and become a mob,"[46] Rabelais is a collective rout of oral schoolmen and glossators suddenly debouched into a visual world newly set up on individualist and nationalist lines. It is just the incongruity of these two worlds as they mix and mingle in the very language of Rabelais that gives us a special feeling of his relevance for us, who also live ambivalently in divided and distinguished cultures. Two cultures or technologies can, like astronomical galaxies, pass through one another without collision; but not without change of configuration. In modern physics there is, similarly, the concept of "interface" or the meeting and metamorphosis of two structures. Such "interficiality" is the very key to the Renaissance as to our twentieth century.

The celebrated earthy tactility of Rabelais is a massive backwash of receding manuscript culture.

✳ A most significant feature of Rabelais as a man on the frontier between cultures, is the way in which the tactile sense in him gets such exaggeration as almost to become isolated. This extreme tactility in him advertises his

[46]*English Literature in the Sixteenth Century*, p. 140.

149

medievalism by consciously splattering it against tidy new visual wall of print culture. John Cowper Powys in his *Rabelais* puts it this way (p. 57):

One exceptional characteristic of Rabelais was his power, a power possessed also by Walt Whitman, of concentrating a tremendous magnetic energy upon the enjoyment—almost as if these inanimate elements were responsive to embraces and good to eat!—of the solid substances of wood and stone, making these things actually porous, you might say, to planetary desire. This characteristic was kept in humorous and very positive control; but that when so kept it is one of the chief characteristics of a born architect I used to be always finding out from my own brother, A. R. Powys, and his ways with wood and stone.

What Powys says here of tactility and affinity for wood and stone ties in with much said earlier about the audile-tactile features of scholasticism and Gothic architecture. It is in this tactile and audile, and ever so unliterary, mode that Rabelais gets his naughty, "earthy" effects. Like James Joyce, another modern master of medieval tactile mosaic, Rabelais expected the public to devote its life to study of his work. "I intend each and every reader to lay aside his business, to abandon his trade, to relinquish his profession, and to concentrate wholly upon my work." Joyce said the same thing, and like Rabelais, was free with the new medium in an especial way. For Joyce, throughout *Finnegans Wake*, television is "the Charge of the Light Brigade," and the whole world is comprised in a single book.

In addition Rabelais gives the reader a good tactile drubbing:

And therefore, to make an end of this Prologue, even as I give my selfe to an hundred Pannier-fulls of faire devils, body and soul, tripes and guts, in case that I lie so much as one single word in this History, after the like manner St. Anthonies fire burn you, Mahoom's disease whirle you, the squinance with a stitch in your side and the Wolfe in your stomack trusse you, the bloody Flux seize upon you, the curst sharp inflammations of wilde fire, as slender and thin as Cowes haire, strengthened with quick silver, enter into your Fundament, and like those of Sodom and Gomorrha, may you fall into sulphur, fire and bottomless pits in case you do not firmly beleeve all that I shall relate unto you in this present Chronicle.

Typography as the first mechanization of a handicraft is itself the perfect instance not of a new knowledge, but of applied knowledge.

✻ But the amazing splitting away of the tactile quality in language appears as an extreme development of this quality in Rabelais and some Elizabethans like Nashe. Then it divides steadily from language until Hopkins and the symbolists began to work at it in the nineteenth century. The point in all this will appear more plainly when we turn to the sixteenth century obsession with quantification. For number and measure are the mode of the tactile, and they are soon to be found departing from the visual humanist camp of letters. A great divorce between number, the language of science, and letters, the language of civilization, occurred in the later Renaissance. But the earlier phase of this divorce, as we shall see, was the Ramist method for "use" and applied knowledge by means of printed literature. For it cannot be sufficiently explained that the mechanization of the ancient handicraft of the scribe was itself "applied" knowledge. And the application consisted in the visual arresting and splitting up of the scribal action. That is why, once this solution to the problem of mechanization was worked out, it could be extended to the mechanizing of many other actions. Moreover, the mere accustomation to the repetitive, lineal patterns of the printed page strongly disposed people to transfer such approaches to all kinds of problems. Febvre and Martin say in *L'Apparition du livre* (p. 28), for example, that a great spur was applied to paper manufacture as early as the eleventh century by the discovery of a method which transformed "le movement circulaire en movement alternatif." The change was from mill to mallets, much like the shift from periodic Ciceronian prose to Senecan "cutted period" at the same time. A change from mill to mallets implies the breaking up of continuous into segmental operations, and the authors add: "This invention had been the origin of numerous industrial upsets." And print, which was to be the mother of all the *bouleversements* to come, was itself a veritable cluster or galaxy of previously achieved technologies. Usher's statement in his *History of Mechanical Inventions* (p. 239) is masterly:

> The entire achievement embodied in the printed book with illustrations presents a striking example of the multiplicity of individual acts of invention that are requisite to bring about a new result. In its entirety, this accomplish-

ment involves: the invention of paper and of inks made with an oil base; the development of engraving on wood and . . . of wood blocks; the development of the press and the special technique of press work involved in printing.

The history of paper is in some ways a separate subject, but it must be evident that the generalization of printing could not have proceeded significantly with any other basic medium. Parchment is difficult to handle, costly, and narrowly limited in supply. Books would have remained an article of luxury if parchment had been the only available medium of issue. Papyrus is hard, brittle, and unsuitable for printing. The introduction of linen-paper making into Europe from China was thus an important preliminary condition. The origin of this product in the Far East and the stages of its transfer overland to Europe are now fairly well ascertained, so that the chronology of the transfers is adequately established . . .

That printing from movable types was an event nearly related to the earlier technology of the phonetic alphabet is a fact that has been a main reason for studying all these centuries that preceded Gutenberg. Phonetic script was the indispensable prelude. Thus Chinese ideogrammic script proved a complete block against the development of print technology in their culture. Today when they are determined to alphabetize their writing they find that they must also break up their verbal structures polysyllabically before the phonetic alphabet will apply to them. Reflection on this situation will help us to understand why alphabetic writing at first, and print later, led to the analytic separation of interpersonal relations and inner and outer functions in the Western world. Thus everywhere in *Finnegans Wake* Joyce reiterates the theme of the effects of the alphabet on "abced-minded man," ever "whispering his ho (here keen again and begin again to make sound sense and sense sound kin again)" (p. 121) and urges all to "harmonize your abecedeed responses" (p. 140).

The new oil base for printing came "from the painters rather than the calligraphers," and "the smaller cloth and wine presses embodied most of the features required by the printing press. . . . the primary problems of innovation centered around the arts of engraving and casting . . ."[47] The goldsmiths and many others were needed to make up the family of inventions that add up to "printing." So complex is the story that a query has arisen: "What did Gutenberg invent?" Usher says (p. 247): "Unfortunately, no wholly decisive answer can be given, because we really have no competent contemporary evidence as to the details of the processes by which the various early books were produced." In the same way the Ford company has no record of the actual procedures followed in making its first cars.

The concern in the present book is to point out the contemporary response to this new technology, as in years to come historians will chart the effects of

[47]Usher, *History of Mechanical Inventions*, p. 240.

radio on the movie and of TV in disposing people towards the new kinds of space as, for example, of the small car. It seemed quite natural to Rabelais to hymn the printed book, product of the new wine press. The following passage from the disputed "fifth" book of the work would seem, in terms of my suggestion about the dominant continuing metaphor of the new printing press in the entire conception, to be integral to Rabelais.

> Bottle whose Mysterious Deep
> Does ten thousand secrets keep,
> With attentive ear I wait;
> Ease my Mind and speak my Fate,
> Soul of joy. Like Bacchus, we
> More than India gain by thee.
> Truths unborn thy juice reveals,
> Which Futurity conceals.
> Antidote to Frauds and Lies,
> Wine that mounts up to the skies,
> May thy Father Noah's Brood
> Like him drown, but in thy Flood.
> Speak, so may the Liquid Mine
> Of Rubies, or of Diamonds shine.

Every technology contrived and outered by man has the power to numb human awareness during the period of its first interiorization.

✱ That wisdom and knowledge should be distilled from the *press* seemed an obvious metaphor to anybody in the sixteenth century. Just how deeply the printed book was embedded in the preceding culture is made manifest by Curt Bühler in *The Fifteenth Century Book: the Scribes; the Printers; the Decorators*. Buhler tells of the "very considerable number of such manuscripts, copied from printed books" that have survived to our day; "Actually, of course, there is very little real difference between the fifteenth-century manuscripts and the incunabula—and the student of the earliest printing would be well advised if he viewed the new invention, as the first printers did, as simply another form of writing—in this case, "artificialiter scribere." (p. 16) The "horseless carriage" was for a time in the same ambiguous state as the printed book.

153

Buhler's data about the peaceful co-existence between scribe and printer will be new and welcome to many readers:

What, then, became of the book-scribes? What happened to the various categories of writers of literary works, who practiced their trade prior to 1450, once the printing press was established? The professionals previously employed by the large scriptoria seem to have done no more than to change their titles and thereupon became calligraphers; in any event, they went right on doing what had been their task for centuries. On the one hand, it should be remembered that calligraphers necessarily catered principally, if not exclusively, to the "de luxe-bespoke" trade. On the other, it was not apparent until the very late fifteenth century—or more fully, perhaps, in the sixteenth—that calligraphy had turned into an applied art or, at worst, a mere hobby. The scriptoria themselves seem to have been unable to compete with the printing firms and the publishing houses which subsequently came into being—although some managed to survive by becoming book-sellers. Their employees, however, enjoyed a variety of alternate choices, in that they could contrive to attach themselves to well-to-do patrons, to carry on a bespoke trade, or to become the itinerant scribes (mostly of Germanic or of Low Country origin) who wandered all over Europe in these years, even working in Italy. Some scribes joined forces with the enemy and became printers themselves—though some of those upon whom Fortune did not smile later forsook the press and returned to their former occupation. This is rather strong evidence for the belief that a scribe, in the closing years of the fifteenth century, could still make a living for himself with his pen. (pp. 26–7)

Usher has made it plain that the cluster of events and technologies that got together in the mind and age of Gutenberg is quite opaque. Nobody is today prepared to say even what it was that Gutenberg invented. In the laughing phrase of Joyce we must "sink deep or touch not the Cartesian spring." Only in our own time have people begun to analyse: "what is a business?" B. J. Muller-Thym answers that it is a machine for making wealth, successor to the family as the wealth-making unit of the pre-industrial ages. G. T. Guilbaud in asking the question *What is Cybernetics?* refers to the work of Jacques Lafitte, engineer and architect, saying (pp. 9–10) that whereas today nobody doubts "the importance of the study of machines for their own sake"

... twenty-five years ago, as Lafitte pointed out in his book, the science of machines did not exist. Elementary fragments of it could be found here and there among the works of engineers, in the writings of philosophers or sociologists, in novels or essays—but nothing systematic had so far taken shape.

'The *organised* constructions of man' ... these are our machines. From the primitive flint knife to the modern lathe, from the rude shanty to the perfected dwellings of the present day, from the simple abacus to the enormous calculating machine—what variety from which to extract common characteristics and attempt a useful classification! The notion of a machine is as hard to define as that of a living organism; a great engineer once spoke indeed of an 'artificial zoology'. But it is not definition or classification that is needed most urgently.

Here is how Lafitte put it: 'Because we are their makers, we have too often deluded ourselves into believing that we knew all there was to know about machines. Although the study and construction of machines of all sorts owes much to advances in mechanics, physics and chemistry, nevertheless mechanology—the science of machines as such, the science of the organized constructions of man—is not a branch of these sciences. Its place is elsewhere in the ranks of scientific disciplines.'

It will seem more and more strange to us why men have chosen to know so little about matters about which they have done so much. Alexander Pope may have noticed this matter ironically when he wrote:

> One science only will one genius fit
> So vast is art, so narrow human wit.

For he well knew that this was the formula for the Tower of Babel. At any rate, with the Gutenberg technology we move into the age of the take-off of the machine. The principle of segmentation of actions and functions and roles became systematically applicable wherever desired. Basically it is the principle of visual quantification discovered in the later Middle Ages, as Clagett explained. This principle of translating non-visual matters of motion and energy into visual terms is the very principle of "applied" knowledge in any time or place. The Gutenberg technology extended this principle to writing and language and the codification and transmission of every kind of learning.

With Gutenberg Europe enters the technological phase of progress, when change itself becomes the archetypal norm of social life.

✱ In an age which discovered this technique of translation as the means of *applied* knowledge, it is to be expected that it will be found everywhere as a consciously experienced novelty. Sir Philip Sidney, in his *Defence of Poetry*, felt he had hit upon a quite necessary principle. Whereas the philosopher

155

teaches and the historian gives examples of philosophical principle, only the poet applies the whole matter to the correction of the human will and the erection of the human spirit:

Now doth the peerless poet perform both: for whatsoever the philosopher saith should be done, he giveth a perfect picture of it in some one by whom he presupposeth it was done; so as he coupleth the general notion with the particular example. A perfect picture I say, for he yieldeth to the powers of the mind an image of that whereof the philosopher bestoweth but a wordish description: which doth neither strike, pierce, nor possess the sight of the soul so much as that other doth.[48]

A more unexpected translation into the new mode appears in a letter of Descartes prefacing his *Principles of Philosophy*: ". . . it may first of all be run through in its entirety like a novel, without forcing the attention unduly upon it. . . . It is only necessary to mark with a pen the places where difficulty is found, and continue to read without interruption to the end."

The instruction of Descartes to his readers is one of the more explicit recognitions of the change in language and thought resulting from print. Namely, that there is no more need, as there had been in oral philosophy, to probe and check each term. The context will now do. The situation is not unlike the meeting of two scholars today. When one asks, "How do you use the term 'tribal' in that connection?", the other can say, "Read my article on it in the current issue of . . ." Paradoxically, a close attention to precise nuance of word use is an oral and not a written trait. For large, general visual contexts always accompany the printed word. But if print discourages minute verbal play, it strongly works for uniformity of spelling and uniformity of meaning, since both of these are immediate practical concerns of the printer and his public.

In the same way, a written philosophy, and especially a printed one, will naturally make "certitude" the primary object of knowledge, just as the scholar in a print culture can have acceptance for his accuracy even though he have nothing to say. But the paradox of the passion for certitude in print culture is that it must proceed by the method of doubt. We shall find abundance of such paradoxes in the new technology that made each book reader the centre of the universe and also enabled Copernicus to toss man to the periphery of the heavens, dislodging him from the centre of the physical world.

Equally paradoxical is the power of print to install the reader in a subjective universe of limitless freedom and spontaneity:

My mind to me a Kingdom is;
Such perfect joy therein I find
That it excels all other bliss
Which God or Nature hath assigned.

[48]In W. J. Bates, ed., *Criticism: the Major Texts*, p. 89.

But by the same token print induces the reader to order his external life and actions with visual propriety and rigour, until the appearance of virtue and stability usurp all inner motive and

> Shades of the prison-house begin to close
> Upon the growing Boy.

The celebrated "To be or not to be" of Hamlet is the scholastic *sic et non* of Abelard translated into the new visual culture where it has a reverse significance. Under oral scholastic conditions the *sic et non* is a mode of experiencing the very sinuosities of the dialectical movements of the inquiring mind. It corresponds to the verbal sensing of the poetic process in Dante and the *dolce stil nuovo*. But in Montaigne and Descartes it is not the process but the product that is sought. And the method of arresting the mind by snapshot, which Montaigne calls *la peinture de la pensée*, is itself the method of doubt. Hamlet presents two pictures, two *views* of life. His soliloquy is an indispensable point of reorientation between the old oral and new visual cultures. He concludes with an explicit recognition of the contrast between the old and the new, putting "conscience" against "resolution":

> And thus the native hue of resolution
> Is sicklied o'er with the pale cast of thought,
> And enterprises of great pith and moment
> With this regard their currents turn awry
> And lose the name of action. (III, i)

This is the identical division we have already seen in Thomas More's contrast: "Your scholastic philosophy is not unpleasant among friends in familiar communication, but in the councils of Kings where great matters be debated and reasoned with great authority these things have no place."

Hamlet is repeating a commonplace conflict of his century, that between the old oral "field" approach to problems and the new visual approach of applied or "resolute" knowledge. And "resolution" is the cant or conventional term used by the Machiavellians. So the conflict is between "conscience" and "resolution," not in our sense at all, but between an over-all awareness and a merely private point of view. Thus, today the conflict goes the other way. The highly literate and individualist liberal mind is tormented by the pressure to become collectively oriented. The literate liberal is convinced that all real values are private, personal, individual. Such is the message of mere literacy. Yet the new electric technology pressures him towards the need for total human interdependence. Hamlet, on the other hand, saw the advantages of corporate responsibility and awareness ("conscience") with each man in a *role*, not at his private peephole or "point of view." Is it not obvious that there are always enough moral problems without also taking a moral stand on technological grounds?

Having asked myself this question some time ago, the following feature emerged: the printed word is an arrested moment of mental movement. To read print is to act both as movie projector and audience for a mental movie. The reader attains a strong feeling of participation in the total motions of a mind in the process of thinking. But is it not basically the printed word's 'still shot' that fosters a habit of mind which tackles all problems of movement and change in terms of the unmoved segment or section? Has not print inspired a hundred different mathematical and analytical procedures for explaining and controlling change in terms of the unchanging? Have we not tended to apply this very static feature to print itself and talked only of its quantitative effects? Do we not speak more of the power of print to increase knowledge and to extend literacy than the most obvious features of song, dance, painting, perception, poetry, architecture, and town planning?[49]

Print is the extreme phase of alphabet culture that detribalizes or decollectivizes man in the first instance. Print raises the visual features of alphabet to highest intensity of definition. Thus print carries the individuating power of the phonetic alphabet much further than manuscript culture could ever do. Print is the technology of individualism. If men decided to modify this visual technology by an electric technology, individualism will also be modified. To raise a moral complaint about this is like cussing a buzz-saw for lopping off fingers. "But," someone says, "we didn't know it would happen." Yet even witlessness is not a moral issue. It is a problem, but not a moral problem; and it would be nice to clear away some of the moral fogs that surround our technologies. It would be good for morality.

As for the technique of doubt in Montaigne and Descartes, it is inseparable, technologically, as we shall see from the criterion of repeatability in science. The print reader is subjected to a black and white flicker that is regular and even. Print presents arrested moments of mental posture. This alternating flicker is also the very mode of projection of subjective doubt and peripheral groping.

[49]H. M. McLuhan, "Printing and Social Change," *Printing Progress: A Mid-Century Report*, The International Association of Printing House Craftsmen, Inc., 1959.

Applied knowledge in the Renaissance had to take the form of translation of the auditory into visual terms, of the plastic into retinal form.

❋ The Renaissance discoveries of Father Ong, detailed in his *Ramus: Method, and the Decay of Dialogue* (from which we quote below) and numerous articles, are of direct relevance to the student of the effects of Gutenberg technology. Ong's investigation of the role of visualization in later medieval logic and philosophy is our direct concern here, for visualization and quantification are near twins. Earlier we have seen how, for the humanists, medieval glosses, illumination, and architectural modes had all served the art of memory. Also, the medieval dialecticians pursued their oral courses well into the sixteenth century:

The invention of printing invited large-scale manipulation of words in space and gave new urgency to the drive toward handling logic or dialectic quantitatively, a drive long manifest in the medieval arts scholostics. . . . The tendency for quantitative or quasi-quantitative manipulation of logic to dissipate itself in memory devices will be a noteworthy feature of Ramism. (p. xv)

The manuscript culture had not been able to duplicate visual knowledge on a mass scale and was less tempted to seek the means of reducing non-visual processes of mind to diagrams. Yet, even so, there is steady pressure in the later scholasticism to strip language to a kind of neuter mathematical counters. The "nominalists" were those who specialized in the logical treatises of Peter of Spain. The opening words of his *Summulae* have a ring, as Ong notes (p. 60), that would be familiar at any time from Cicero to Emerson: "Dialectic is the art of arts and the science of sciences, possessing the way to the principles of all curriculum subjects. For dialectic alone disputes with probability concerning the principles of all other arts, and thus dialectic must be the first science to be acquired." The humanists, especially after printing extended the boundaries of literature, complained bitterly that boys should have to comb through the divisions and distinctions of Peter of Spain.

The point of all this is that the drive to deal spatially and geometrically with words and logic, while useful as an art of memory, proved *cul de sac* in philosophy. It needed the mathematical symbolism we have devised today. But it did contribute directly to the spirit of quantification that expressed

itself in the mechanization of writing and what followed long before Gutenberg, "the advance in quantification which medieval logic exhibits is one of
the chief differences between it and the earlier Aristotelian logic." (p. 72)
And quantification means the translation of non-visual relations and realities
into visual terms, a procedure inherent in the phonetic alphabet, as was
shown earlier. But with Ramus in the sixteenth century it is not enough to
make trees and schemes of knowledge:

For at the heart of the Ramist enterprise is the drive to tie down words
themselves, rather than other representations, in simple geometrical patterns.
Words are believed to be recalcitrant insofar as they derive from a world of
sound, voices, cries; the Ramist ambition is to neutralize this connection by
processing what is of itself nonspatial in order to reduce it to space in the
starkest way possible. The spatial processing of sound by means of the
alphabet is not enough. Printed or written words themselves must be
deployed in spatial relationships, and the resulting schemata thought of
as a key to their meanings. (pp. 89–90)

Confronted with the numerous relationships between Ramus and "applied
knowledge," Father Ong has published an article, "Ramist Method and the
Commercial Mind,"[50] which makes an admirable approach to the obsession
with quantification in the Renaissance:

One of the persistent puzzles concerning Peter Ramus and his followers is
the extraordinary diffusion of their works during the sixteenth and seventeenth
centuries. The general pathway of this diffusion has been well known since
Waddington's Ramus in 1855. It proceeds chiefly through bourgeois
Protestant groups of merchants and artisans more or less tinged with
Calvinism. These groups are found not only in Ramus' native France, but
especially in Germany, Switzerland, the Low Countries, England, Scotland,
Scandinavia, and New England. Perry Miller's work, The New England
Mind: the Seventeenth Century, is the most detailed study of Ramism in any
such group. Such groups were moving into more openly influential positions
socially and were improving themselves intellectually, and Ramism appeals
to them as they move up. Ramus' works thus enjoyed particular favor not
in highly sophisticated intellectual circles but rather in elementary or
secondary schools or along the fringe where secondary schooling and
university education meet . . .

What is necessary to understand here is that the key to any kind of *applied*
knowledge is the translation of a complex of relations into explicit visual
terms. The alphabet itself as applied to the complex of the spoken word
translates speech into a visual code that can be uniformly spread and transported. Print had given an intensity to this latent process that was a virtual
educational and economic take-off. Ramus, with the whole scholastic drive

[50]*Studies in the Renaissance*, vol. VIII, 1961, pp. 155–72.

behind him was able to translate it into the visual "humanism of the new merchant classes." Such is the simplicity and crudity of the spatial models promoted by Ramus that no cultivated mind, and nobody sensitive to language, could be bothered with them. And yet it was this crudity that gave him his appeal to the self-educated and to the merchant classes. Just how large a section of the new reading public these were has been demonstrated in the great study of *Middle-Class Culture in Elizabethan England* by L. B. Wright.

Typography tended to alter language from a means of perception and exploration to a portable commodity.

✱ As for the mere stress on use and practicality, it is not only Ramus but the entire humanist corps that insists upon that. From the Sophists to Cicero training in language and oratory had been accepted as the road to power and top executive action. The Ciceronian program of encyclopedic knowledge in the arts and sciences came back with printing. The essentially dialogue character of scholasticism gave way to a more extensive program in languages and literature for the training of the Courtier and the Governor and the Prince. What we have come to consider as an impossibly genteel curriculum of authors, languages, and history was in the Renaissance held necessary for the statesman, on one hand, and the study of Scripture, on the other. Shakespeare presents (I, i) his Henry the Fifth as combining both:

> Hear him but reason in divinity,
> And, all-admiring, with an inward wish
> You would desire the King were made a prelate;
> Hear him debate of commonwealth affairs,
> You would say it hath been all in all his study;
> List his discourse of war, and you shall hear
> A fearful battle rend'red you in music;
> Turn him to any cause of policy,
> The Gordian knot of it he will unloose,
> Familiar as his garter: that, when he speaks,
> The air, a charter'd libertine, is still,
> And the mute wonder lurketh in men's ears,
> To steal his sweet and honey'd sentences;
> So that the art and practic part of life

161

Must be the mistress to this theoric;
Which is a wonder how his Grace should glean it,
Since his addiction was to courses vain,
His companies unletter'd, rude and shallow,
His hours fill'd up with riots, banquets, sports;
And never noted in him any study,
Any retirement, any sequestration
From open haunts and popularity.

But the practical qualities fostered by Ramism are more immediately related to numbers than to letters: "While Adam Smith attacked the system which emerged, he was aware of its advantages in defence. He saw it as part of the spread of the price system which had swept aside the feudal system, and led to the discovery of the New World . . ."[51] Innis is here writing on "The Penetrative Powers of the Price System," by which he means the power to translate one set of functions into a new mode and language. The feudal system was based on oral culture and self-contained system of centres-without-margins, as Pirenne showed us earlier. This structure was translated by visual, quantitative means into great centre-margin systems of a nationalist mercantile kind, a process greatly assisted by printing. It is interesting to see the way in which Adam Smith viewed this process of drastic translation carried out in the English Civil War. It was just about to take place in France:

A revolution of the greatest importance to public happiness was in this manner brought about by two different orders of people, who had not the least intention to serve the public. To gratify the most childish vanity was the sole motive of the great proprietors. The merchants and artificers, much less ridiculous, acted merely from a view to their own interest, and in pursuit of their own pedlar principles of turning a penny wherever a penny was to be got. Neither of them had either knowledge or foresight of that great revolution which the folly of the one, and the industry of the other, was gradually bringing about. It is thus that through the greater part of Europe the commerce and manufacture of cities, instead of being the effect, have been the cause and occasion of the improvement and cultivation of the country.[52]

The French Revolution, long prepared by the homogenizing print process, as de Tocqueville will show us, followed the pattern of Ramist reasonings which as Ong stresses "while seldom advertised as serving the purposes of debate, they frequently manifest an express concern for simplification":

Hooykaas makes less of Ramus' talk about 'induction' than of his enthusiasm for *usus*, that is, classroom practice or exercise, in establishing the relationship of Ramus' educational aims and procedures to bourgeois

[51]Harold Innis, *Essays in Canadian Economic History*, p. 253.
[52]Quoted in *ibid.*, p. 254.

culture. The break with older ways both among burghers generally and among Ramists in particular consisted more in an interest in pupil activity than in anything we should recognize today as experimentation or 'induction'. These points Hooykas makes are valid and follow recent lines of thinking in discerning a certain intellectual fertility in the meeting of the artisan and academic minds during the sixteenth and seventeenth centuries.[53]

Ong here points to a basic fact about print culture. Printed books, themselves the first uniform, repeatable, and mass-produced items in the world, provided endless paradigms of uniform commodity culture for sixteenth and succeeding centuries. Shakespeare makes frequent play with this fact as in *King John* (II, i):

> That smooth-faced gentleman, tickling Commodity,
> Commodity, the bias of the world—
> The world, who of itself is peised well,
> Made to run even upon even ground
> Till this advantage, this vile drawing bias,
> This sway of motion, this Commodity,
> Makes it take head from all indifferency,
> From all direction, purpose, course, intent—
> And this same bias, this Commodity,
> This bawd, this broker, this all-changing word,
> Clapp'd on the outward eye of fickle France,
> Hath drawn him from his own determin'd aid,
> From a resolved and honourable war,
> To a most base and vile-concluded peace.
> And why rail I on this Commodity?
> But for because he hath not woo'd me yet.
> Not that I have the power to clutch my hand
> When his fair angels would salute my palm;
> But for my hand, as unattempted yet,
> Like a poor beggar, raileth on the rich.
> Well, whiles I am a beggar, I will rail
> And say there is no sin but to be rich;
> And being rich, my virtue then shall be
> To say there is no vice but beggary.
> Since kings break faith upon commodity,
> Gain, be my lord, for I will worship thee!

[53]"Ramist Method and the Commercial Mind," p. 159.

163

Typography is not only a technology but is in itself a natural resource or staple, like cotton or timber or radio; and, like any staple, it shapes not only private sense ratios but also patterns of communal interdependence.

❋ Print, as it were, translated the dialogue of shared discourse into packaged information, a portable commodity. It put a spin or bias in language and human perception which Shakespeare studies here as "Commodity." How could it do otherwise? It created the price system. For until commodities are uniform and repeatable the price of an article is subject to haggle and adjustment. The uniformity and repeatability of the book not only created modern markets and the price system inseparable from literacy and industry. Lewis Mumford writes in *Sticks and Stones* (pp. 41–2):

> Victor Hugo said in Notre Dame that the printing-press destroyed architecture, which had hitherto been the stone record of mankind. The real misdemeanor of the printing-press, however, was not that it took literary values away from architecture, but that it caused architecture to derive its value from literature. With the Renaissance the great modern distinction between the literate and the illiterate extends even to building; the master mason who knew his stone and his workmen and his tools and the tradition of his art gave way to the architect who knew his Palladio and his Vignola and his Vitruvius. Architecture, instead of striving to leave the imprint of a happy spirit on the superficies of a building, became a mere matter of grammatical accuracy and pronunciation; and the seventeenth century architects who revolted from this regime and created the baroque were at home only in the pleasure gardens and theaters of princes . . .

In his youth a student of the Scottish biologist Patrick Geddes, Mumford has always given us a civilized example of how unnecessary and unrewarding are the ways of the specialist who sees nothing in relation to anything else: "It was by means of the book that the architecture of the eighteenth century from St. Petersburg to Philadelphia seemed cast by a single mind." (p. 43)

Print was in itself a commodity, a new natural resource which also showed us how to tap all other kinds of resources including ourselves. Media as staples or natural resources are the theme of the later work of Harold Innis. His early work concerns staples in the ordinary sense. In his maturity he hit on the discovery that technological media like writing, papyrus, radio, photoengraving, and such are themselves wealth.[54]

Without a technology tending to process experience homogeneously, a society cannot go far toward the control of natural forces nor even the organization of human effort. This was the ironic theme of *The Bridge Over the River Kwai*. The Japanese Buddhist Colonel has no technology to tackle the job. The English Colonel has it all diagrammed and segmented in no time. Of course, he has no proper end in view. His technology is his way of life. He lives by the book of the Geneva Convention. To an oral Frenchman all this is hilarious. English and American audiences found the picture profound, subtle, elusive.

In his *Two-Edged Sword*, John L. McKenzie shows (p. 13) how Biblical studies in the twentieth century have abandoned the concept of the lineal, homogeneous structure of Scriptural narration:

Modern control and use of natural forces was not known to the Hebrews, nor did the wildest fancy dream of anything like it. . . . The ancient Hebrews were prephilosophical; the most ordinary patterns of modern thought were unknown to them. Logic as a form of mental discipline they lacked. Their language is the speech of the simple man who sees motion and action rather than static reality, static reality as concrete rather than abstract.

In our legal world words are carefully reduced to homogeneous entities so that they can be applied. If allowed any grace or life such as is naturally theirs, they would not serve their practical, applied function.

I have shown that the theory I offer you is based on a natural virtue in words themselves. Let me state this theory of interpretation dogmatically before I turn the coin over to show that it conforms with the actual practices of draftsmanship.

Words in legal documents—I am not talking about anything else—are simply delegations to others of authority to apply them to particular things or occasions. The only meaning of the word meaning, as I am using it, is an application to the particular. And the more imprecise the words are, the greater is the delegation, simply because then they can be applied or not to more particulars. This is the only important feature of words in legal draftsmanship or interpretation.

They mean, therefore, not what their author intended them to mean, or even what meaning he intended, or expected, reasonably or not, others to give them. They mean, in the first instance, what the person to whom they are addressed makes them mean. Their meaning is whatever occasion or thing he may apply them to or what in some cases he may only propose to

[54]See H. M. McLuhan, "The Effects of the Improvements of Communication Media," *Journal of Economic History*, December, 1960, pp. 566–75.

apply them to. The meaning of words in legal documents is to be sought, not in their author or authors, the parties to a contract, the testator, or the legislature, but in the acts or the behavior with which the person addressed undertakes to match them. This is the beginning of their meaning.

In the second instance, but only secondarily, a legal document is also addressed to the courts. This is a further delegation, and a delegation of a different authority, to decide, not what the word means, but whether the immediate addressee had authority to make them mean what he did make them mean, or what he proposes to make them mean. In other words, the question before the court is not whether he gave the words the right meaning, but whether or not the words authorized the meaning he gave them.[55]

What Curtis so correctly discerns in the nature of applied terminology, equally concerns populations, civil and military. Unless processed in a uniform way, it would be quite impossible to have delegation of functions and duties, and thus there could be no centralized national groupings such as came into existence after printing. Without similar uniform processing by literacy, there could be no market or price system, a factor which constrains "backward" countries to be "communist," or tribal. There is no known means of having our price and distribution system without long and extensive experience of literacy. But we are swiftly becoming aware of these matters as we move into the electronic era. For telegraph, radio and TV do not tend towards the homogeneous in their effects of print culture and dispose us to easier awareness on non-print cultures.

The passion for exact measurement began to dominate the Renaissance.

✱ Just as Father Ong in his work on Ramus has provided the necessary insight into the strange similarities of form and motive between medieval logicians and Renaissance merchants, so John U. Nef has given us the connection between Renaissance science and commerce. His *Cultural Foundations of Industrial Civilization* is a study of quantification, especially as it intruded into the commercial world.

The spirit of rigorous separation and translation of functions by stress on visual quantity had beset the later scholastic centuries and contributed to the mechanization of the scribal craft, as we have seen. The pursuit of

[55]Charles P. Curtis, *It's Your Law*, pp. 65–6.

dichotomies and divisions carried over from scholasticism to mathematics and science, as Nef indicates (pp. 4–5):

The very separation of science from faith, from ethics and from art, which is so characteristic of our times, is at the roots of the industrialized world in which we live. In a letter destined for Fermat, which he sent to Father Mersenne in 1637, Descartes remarked that the great Toulouse mathematician seemed to suppose 'that in saying a thing is easy to believe, I meant only to say that it is probable. This is far from my position: I consider everything that is only probable as almost false. . . .' Such a position has led to the admission as true of only what is verifiable in tangible and increasingly in measurable terms, or in terms of mathematical demonstrations which start from propositions artificially divorced from the actual experience of living. Since it is impossible, as Pascal seems to have been the first to recognize, to offer the same kind of tangible proof and to get the same kind of assent in matters of faith, of morals and of beauty, the truths of religion, moral philosophy and art have come to be treated as subjects of private opinion rather than of public knowledge. Their contributions to the contemporary world are *indirect*, though not for that reason necessarily inferior to those of science.

Artificial separation of mental modes in the interests of homogeneity conveyed a sentiment of certitude to Descartes and his time. A century of more and more rapid movement of information by print had developed new sensibilities. In Nef's words (p. 8):

During the hundred years that followed Rabelais' death in 1553, there are many indications that exact time, exact quantities, exact distances were coming to have a greatly increased interest for men and women in connexion with private and public life. One of the most impressive examples of the new concern with precision was the action taken by the Church of Rome to provide a more exact calendar. Throughout the Middle Ages the ways in which the Christian peoples measured the passage of time were based on calculations made before the fall of the Roman Empire. The Julian calendar of A.D. 325 was still in use in the age of Rabelais.

The rise of statistics permitted the isolation of economics from the general social fabric of the sixteenth century:

The Europeans were striving after a higher degree of quantitative accuracy in many domains during the span of the eighty years or so that followed. Some of them attached a novel importance to the amassing of statistics, and notable of statistics concerning rates of increase, as guides to economic policy, at the very period when, with Bodin, Malynes, Laffemas, Montchretien and Mun, economics first emerged as a separate subject of human speculative inquiry, independent both of housekeeping, the concern of each of us in his daily active life, and of moral philosophy, the concern of us all for the guidance of our inner lives. (p. 10)

167

Already Europe was moving so far in the direction of visualized measurement and quantification of life that it "came to occupy for the first time a place apart from both the Near and Far East." In other words, under manuscript conditions Europe was not very sharply distinct from the East which was also a manuscript culture.

Let us turn a moment from Nef to Ong for confirmation of the new passion for quantity and measurement, we find that "the Ramist method appealed primarily to a desire for order, not to a desire for experimentation. . . . Ramus takes what might be called an itemizing approach to discourse."[56]

That the new commercial classes took to the itemizing approach can be documented from many quarters. Its novelty and oddity provided hilarity on the Elizabethan stage. Ben Jonson's Sir Politick Would-Be in *Volpone* is a would-be Machiavel, and Jonson naturally links the new statecraft with the new techniques of visual observation and organization of action:

> I do love
> To note and to observe: though I live out,
> Free from the active torrent, yet I'd mark
> The currents and the passages of things,
> For mine own private use; and know the ebbs
> And flows of state.

Sir Politick in Venice inquires of Peregrine:

> Why came you forth
> Empty of rules for travel?
> *Peregrine*: Faith, I had
> Some common ones from out of that vulgar grammar
> Which he that cried Italian to me, taught me. (II, i)

Later in Act IV, Sir Politick is doing some itemizing for Peregrine:

> *Sir P.* Nay, sir, conceive me. It will cost me in onions,
> some thirty livres—
> *Per.* Which is one pound sterling.
> *Sir P.* Beside my water-works: for this I do, sir
> First, I bring in your ship 'twixt two brick walls;
> But those the state shall venture: On the one
> I strain me a fair tarpauling, and in that
> I stick my onions, cut in halves: the other
> Is full of loop-holes, out at which I thrust
> The noses of my bellows; and those bellows
> I keep, with water-works, in perpetual motion,
> Which is the easiest matter of a hundred.
> Now, sir, your onion, which doth naturally
> Attract the infection, and your bellows blowing
> The air upon him, will show, instantly,

[56]Walter Ong, "Ramist Method and the Commercial Mind," p. 165.

By his changed colour, if there be contagion;
Or else remain as fair as at the first.
—Now it is known, 'tis nothing.
Per. You are right, sir.
Sir P. I would I had my note.
Per. 'Faith, so would I':
But you have done well for once, sir.
Sir P. Were I false,
Or would be made so, I could shew you reasons
How I could sell this state now to the Turk,
Spite of their gallies, or their—[*Examining his papers*]
Per. Pray you, sir Pol.
Sir P. I have them not about me.
Per. That I fear'd:
They are there, sir.
Sir P. No, this is my diary,
Wherein I note my actions of the day.
Per. Pray you, let's see, sir. What is here? *Notandum*, [Reads]
A rat had gnawn my spur-leathers; notwithstanding,
I put on new, and did go forth: but first
I threw three beans over the threshold. Item,
I went and bought two tooth-picks, whereof one
I burst immediately, in a discourse
With a Dutch merchant, 'bout ragion del stato.
From him I went and paid a moccinigo
For piecing my silk stockings; by the way
I cheapen'd sprats; and at St. Mark's I urined.
'Faith these are politic notes!
Sir P. Sir, I do slip
No action of my life, but thus I quote it.
Per. Believe me, it is wise!
Sir P. Nay, sir, read forth.

There can be, then, no mystery about why Sam Pepys kept just this kind of diary half a century later. It was a discipline of observation and precision for the would-be Machiavellian merchant. To the Elizabethan audience Iago's apologia in the first scene of Othello would have labelled him an obvious goon of the Politick Would-be stamp:

O, sir, content you.
I follow him to serve my turn upon him.
We cannot all be masters, nor all masters
Cannot be truly follow'd. You shall mark
Many a duteous and knee-crooking knave
That, doting on his own obsequious bondage,
Wears out his time, much like his master's ass,
For naught but provender; and when he's old, cashier'd.

169

Whip me such honest knaves! Others there are,
Who, trimm'd in forms and visages of duty,
Keep yet their hearts attending on themselves;
And, throwing but shows of service on their lords,
Do well thrive by them, and, when they have lin'd their coats,
Do themselves homage: these fellows have some soul;
And such a one do I profess myself. For, sir,
It is as sure as you are Roderigo,
Were I the Moor, I would not be Iago.
In following him, I follow but myself;
Heaven is my judge, not I for love and duty,
But seeming so, for my peculiar end;
For when my outward action doth demonstrate
The native act and figure of my heart
In compliment extern, 'tis not long after
But I will wear my heart upon my sleeve
For daws to peck at. I am not what I am.

The print-made split between head and heart is the trauma which affects Europe from Machiavelli till the present.

✱ What seemed fantastic in the early phases of print and the isolation of visuality, was that it appeared to create a comic hypocrisy or split between head and heart. It is interesting to see how the same split appeared to an Irishman and an Englishman just two hundred years later, at the end of the eighteenth century. Here is Edmund Burke, the sentimental Gael, commenting on the itemizing, calculating spirit in his *Reflections on the Revolution in France*:

It is now sixteen or seventeen years since I saw the queen of France, then the dauphiness, at Versailles; and surely never lighted on this orb, which she hardly seemed to touch, a more delightful vision. I saw her just above the horizon, decorating and cheering the elevated sphere she just began to move in,—glittering like the morning-star, full of life, and splendour, and joy. Oh! what a revolution! and what a heart must I have to contemplate, without emotion that elevation and that fall! Little did I dream when she added titles of veneration to those of enthusiastic, distant, respectful love, that she should ever be obliged to carry the sharp antidote against disgrace concealed in that bosom; little did I dream that I should have lived to see such disasters fallen upon her in a nation of gallant men, in a nation of men of honour, and of cavaliers. I thought ten thousand swords must have leaped from their scabbards to avenge even a look that threatened her with insult. But the age of chivalry is gone. That of sophisters, economists, and calculators, has succeeded; and the glory of Europe is extinguished for ever. Never, never more shall we behold that generous loyalty to rank and sex, that proud submission, that dignified obedience, that subordination of the heart, which kept alive, even in servitude itself, the spirit of an exalted freedom. The unbought grace of life, the cheap defence of nations, the nurse of manly sentiment and heroic enterprise, is gone! It is gone, that sensibility of principle, that charity of honour, which felt a stain like a wound, which inspired courage whilst it mitigated ferocity, which ennobled whatever it touched, and under which vice itself lost half its evil, by losing all its grossness.

And here is William Cobbett, the cool Saxon, in his *A Years' Residence in America* (1795) recording his amazement at the new kind of man made there by print culture:

356. There are very few really *ignorant* men in America of native growth. Every farmer is more or less of a *reader*. There is no *brogue*, no *provincial dialect*. No class like that which the French call *peasantry*, and which degrading appellation the miscreant spawn of the Funds have, of late years, applied to the whole mass of the most useful of the people in England, those who do the work and fight the battles. And, as to the men, who would naturally form *your* acquaintances, they, I know from experience, are as kind, frank, and sensible men as are, on the general run, to be found in England, even with the power of selection. They are all well-informed; modest without shyness; always free to communicate what they know, and never ashamed to acknowledge that they have yet to learn. You never hear them *boast* of their possessions, and you never hear them *complaining* of their wants. They have all been *readers* from their youth up; and there are few subjects upon which they cannot converse with you, whether of a political or scientific nature. At any rate, they always *hear* with patience. I do not know what I ever heard a native American interrupt another man while he was speaking. Their *sedateness* and *coolness*, the *deliberate* manner in which they say and do every thing, and the *slowness* and *reserve* with which they express their assent; these are very wrongly estimated, when they are taken for marks of a *want of feeling*. It must be a tale of woe indeed, that will bring a tear from an American's eye; but any trumped up story will send his hand to his pocket, as the ambassadors from the beggars of France, Italy and Germany can fully testify.
357. However, you will not, for a long while, know what to do for want of the *quick responses* of the English tongue, and the *decided* tone of the English expression. The *loud voice*: the *hard squeeze* by the hand; the *instant assent* or *dissent*: the *clamorous joy*: the *bitter wailing*: the *ardent friendship*: the *deadly enmity*: the *love that makes people kill themselves*:

the *hatred that makes them kill others*. All these belong to the characters of Englishmen, in whose minds and hearts every feeling exists in the *extreme*. To decide the question, which character is, upon the whole, *best*, the American or the English, we must appeal to some *third party* ...

That most Englishmen still retained the oral, passionate wholeness of character seemed as obvious to Cobbett as to Dickens. And Cobbett does not hesitate to observe that book culture had created the new man in America. The new man has literally taken to *heart* the message of print, and put on "the napless vesture of humility." He has stripped himself like Lear till he fulfils the ideal of Thomas Huxley, who wrote in 1868 in his essay on "A Liberal Education":

"That man, I think, has had a liberal education who has been so trained in
his youth that his body is the ready servant of his will, and does with ease
and pleasure all the work, that as a mechanism, it is capable of; whose
intellect is a clear, cold, logic engine, with all the parts of equal strength,
and in smooth working order; ready like a steam engine to be turned to any
kind of work. . . ."[57]

Close on the sentimental heels of this scientific vision came the figure of Sherlock Holmes of whom Doyle said in *A Scandal in Bohemia*:

He was, I take it, the most perfect reasoning and observing machine that
the world has seen; but, as a lover, he would have placed himself in a false
position. He never spoke of the softer passions save with a gibe and a
sneer. . . . Grit in a sensitive instrument, or a crack in one of his own
high-power lenses, would not be more disturbing than a strong emotion in a
nature such as his.[58]

It will become even plainer in the present volume why the Gutenberg drive to apply knowledge by translation and uniformity encounters such resistance in the matters of sex and race.

The process of "uniformatization" in its social and political bearings is explained by de Tocqueville very clearly in *L'Ancien Régime* (pp. 83–4, 103, 125):

I have already pointed out how almost throughout the whole kingdom
the special life of the different provinces had long since perished; that had
helped very much to make all Frenchmen very like each other. Despite the
diversities which still existed, the unity of the nation was already clear;
it is disclosed by the uniformity of the legislation. The farther down the
eighteenth century we come there is a corresponding increase in the number
of royal edicts, royal declarations, decrees of Council, which apply the same
rules in the same manner to all parts of the governed, who conceived the

[57]Printed in *Lay Sermons, Addresses and Reviews*, pp. 34–5. See also H. M. McLuhan, *The Mechanical Bride: Folklore of Industrial Man*, p. 108.
[58]See *The Mechanical Bride*, p. 107.

idea of a legislation quite general and quite uniform, the same everywhere, the same for all; this idea is revealed in all the successive projects of reform that appeared during the thirty years which preceded the outbreak of the Revolution. Two centuries before, the very material for such a conception would, so to speak, have been wanting.

Not only did the provinces resemble each other more and more, but in each province the men of different classes, at least all those who ranked above the common people, became more and more alike, despite the differences of rank.

Nothing shows this more clearly than the reading of the 'instructions' presented by the different orders in 1789. Those who drew them up differed profoundly in their interests, but in everything else they showed themselves alike.

What is still more strange is that all these men, who kept themselves so apart from each other, had become so much alike that it would have been impossible to distinguish them if their places had been changed. Nay more, if a man had been able to sound their innermost spirit, he would have discovered that these tiny barriers, which divided people so much alike, appeared to the men themselves as contrary alike to the public interest and to good sense and that in theory they already adored unity. Each of them stuck to his own particular condition simply because every one else was particularized by his condition but they were all ready to be confounded in one mass, provided that no one had any separate position nor rose superior to the common level.

Inseparable from the homogenizing of men and manners in the literacy process was the equally pervasive concern with consumer goods:

The men of the eighteenth century hardly knew that kind of passion for material comfort, which is, so to speak, the mother of servitude, an enervating but tenacious and unalterable passion, which readily mingles with and twines itself round many private virtues such as love of family, respectability of life, regard for religious beliefs, and even the assiduous if lukewarm practice of the established worship, which is partial to respectability but forbids heroism, which excels in making men steady but citizens mean-spirited. The men of the eighteenth century were both better and worse.

The French of that date loved joy and adored pleasure; they were perhaps more irregular in their habits and more unbridled in their passions and in their ideas than men of to-day; but they knew nothing of that judicious and well-regulated sensualism that *we* see around us. The upper classes were more concerned to adorn life than to make it comfortable, to make themselves illustrious rather than rich.

Even in the middle classes a man was not entirely devoted to the pursuit of comfort; the pursuit was often abandoned for the desire of higher and more refined pleasures; some other good rather than money was everywhere the objective. 'I know my countrymen,' wrote a contemporary, in a style fantastic but not wanting in pride, 'clever at melting and dissipating the

173

metals, but not ready to give them continuous worship; they will be quite
ready to return to their ancient idols—valor, glory, and, I make bold to say,
magnanimity.'

The Machiavellian mind and the merchant mind are at one in their simple faith in the power of segmental division to rule all—in the dichotomy of power and morals and of money and morals.

✳ As de Chardin explains in his *Phenomenon of Man*, new invention is
the interiorization in man of the structures of earlier technology; and therefore it stockpiles, as it were. What we are studying here is the interiorization
of print technology and its effect in shaping a new kind of man. De Chardin
speaks of our own day when there are so many new technologies to interior-
ize: "Firstly, the power of invention, so rapidly intensified at the present time
by the rationalised recoil of all the forces of research that it is already possible
to speak of a forward leap of evolution." (p. 305)

Applied knowledge has no mysteries then. It consists in segmentation of
any process or any situation or any human being. The Machiavellian power
technique is exactly the one ridiculed by Ben Jonson and Shakespeare in the
passages above. One observes a human being to see "what makes him tick."
That is, you reduce him to a machine. Then you isolate his ruling passion,
the fuel of the machine. Then you have him. Wyndham Lewis has given a
fine account of these Machiavellian techniques as they appear in Elizabethan
drama in *The Lion and the Fox*, from which we had seen earlier his description of the Hollywood aspect of Italian princely architecture.

It is not only people that are reduced to things by the segmental itemizing
methods of the new print culture. Father Ong points out in "Ramist Method
and the Commercial Mind" (p. 167):

> The mass-production methods utilized for bookmaking made it possible
> and indeed necessary to think of books less as representations of words
> serving for the communication of thought and more as things. Books came
> to be regarded more and more as products of crafts and as commodities to
> be merchandised. The word, living human speech, is here in a sense reified.
> Even before the advent of typography a marked reification of the word had

been begun by the medieval terminist logicians, and elsewhere I have
discussed in detail the psychological connections between terminist logic,
the topical logic which succeeded it in the humanist age, and the development
of attitudes toward communication favoring typography. The terminist
logic was indeed still represented at Paris in Ramus' youth or not long before
by persons such as Juan de Celaya, John Dullaert, and John Major, and
even later by Ramus' own defender Jean Quentin. But the terminist tradition
had favored the reification of the word for intellectual purposes. This
impulse to reification had come from the academy. When we view
typographical developments from the burghers' standpoint, we see another
type of drive to reification joining forces with the first. If the logicians
wanted to hypostatize expression so as to subject it to formal analysis, the
merchants were willing to hypostatize expression in order to sell it. . . .

It is not surprising that the Ramist visual methods of itemizing and
classifying should sound, as Ong says (p. 167–8) "highly reminiscent of
printing processes themselves, so that it enables one to impose organization
on a subject by imagining it as made up of parts fixed in space much in the
way in which words are locked into a printer's form."

This overwhelming example of print as visual, sequential, uniform, and
lineal was not lost on human sensibility in the sixteenth century. But before
turning to its more dramatic manifestations it is necessary to indicate, as
Ong has done, that the obsession with "method" in the Renaissance finds its
archetype in "the process of setting up type taken from a font. In each
instance, the composition of continuous discourse is a matter of building up
discourse by arranging preëxisting parts in a spatial pattern." (p. 168) And
it is obvious that Ramus exercised his extraordinary appeal by being close to
the new patterns of sensibility that people experienced in their contact with
typography. The new "typographic man" who shot into prominence with
printing will get full attention a little later on in connection with individualism
and nationalism. Here we are concerned to find out the ways in which print
structured ideas of *applied* knowledge by separation and division, moving
always towards sharper visualization. In Ong's words (p. 168): "This
increased sophistication in visual presentation is not restricted, of course, to
Ramist writings, but is part of the evolution of typography, showing clearly
how the use of printing moved the word away from its original association
with sound and treated it more and more as a 'thing' in space."

Ong makes the extremely important point (p. 169) that the Ramist
hostility to Aristotle was based on his incompatibility with print culture:

In manuscripts, diagrams are much more laborious productions than
straight text, for manuscript copying only with great difficulty controls the
position of material on the page. Typographical reproduction controls it
automatically and inevitably. . . . If Ramus did indeed defend his reputed
anti-Aristotelian thesis, *Quaecumque ab Aristotele dicta essent commentitia*

esse, . . . he quite evidently meant this to say not that Aristotle was untruthful (a common interpretation of the reported thesis) but rather that Aristotle's material was poorly organized, not properly controlled by 'method'.

In other words, it was unsuited for the Gutenberg era.

The accommodation of studies by Ramist diagrams and divisions was the first large move of learning in the direction of the merchant mind. So we shall leave Father Ong after quoting a last passage from page 170 which will help bring us back to Professor Nef:

> But there was another aspect of Ramist method which gave it appeal to the bourgeois groups among whom it was a favorite. It was very much like account keeping. The merchant not only deals in wares, but he has a way of keeping record of them which levels all sorts of items to the pages of an account book. Here the most diverse products are mingled on an equal footing—wool, wax, incense, coal, iron, and jewels—although they have nothing in common except commercial value. To handle a merchant's wares in terms of his account books, one need not trouble oneself with the nature of the wares. One has to know only the principles of accounting.

Dantzig explains why the language of number had to be increased to meet the needs created by the new technology of letters.

✱ The unremitting pressure on society to discover accurate means of quantification is in ratio to the individualist pressures in the society. Print intensified the tendency to individualism as all historians have testified. It also provided the means of quantification in its very technology. The monumental work of William I, Thomas and Florian Znaniecki, *The Polish Peasant in Europe and America*, is indispensable to any serious analyst of the effects of print culture on peasant culture. They write (vol. I, p. 182):

> But of course when once the egotistic attitude is introduced into economic relations, these relations have to be objectively regulated. And thus ultimately the principle of economic equivalence of services is introduced and becomes fundamental, while there still remains always some place beside it for the old valuation based upon the efficiency of the help and for the transitory valuation based upon the subjective sacrifice.

The exceeding usefulness of *The Polish Peasant* for understanding the Gutenberg galaxy is that it offers a mosaic study of events in our time that correspond to what happened in the first Gutenberg age. What happened to the Polish peasant confronted with print technology and industrial organization, has happened in lesser degree to the Russian and the Japanese, and is beginning to happen in China.

Before concluding Professor Nef's testimony on the development of quantification and applied knowledge in the first phase of Western industrialism, it will be well to notice the role of number and mathematics concurrent with the rise of movable types. Tobias Dantzig, in his *Number: The Language of Science*, has provided a cultural history of mathematics which led Einstein to declare: "This is beyond doubt the most interesting book on the evolution of mathematics that has ever fallen into my hands." The explanation of the rise of Euclidean sensibility from the phonetic alphabet was given in the early part of this book. Phonetic letters, the language and mythic form of Western culture, have the power of translating or reducing all of our senses into visual and "pictorial" or "enclosed" space.

More than anybody else, the mathematician is aware of the arbitrary and fictional character of this continuous, homogeneous visual space. Why? Because number, the language of science, is a fiction for retranslating the Euclidean space fiction back into auditory and tactile space.

The example Dantzig uses on page 139 concerns the measurement of the length of an arc:

Our notion of the length of an arc of a curve may serve as an illustration. The physical concept rests on that of a bent wire. We imagine that we have *straightened* the wire without *stretching* it; then the segment of the straight line will serve as the measure of the length of the arc. Now what do we mean by 'without stretching'? We mean without a change in length. But this term implies that we already know something about the length of the arc. Such a formulation is obviously a *petitio principii* and could not serve as a mathematical definition.

The alternative is to inscribe in the arc a sequence of rectilinear contours of an increasing number of sides. The sequence of these contours approaches a limit, and the length of the arc is defined as the limit of this sequence.

And what is true of the notion of length is true of areas, volumes, masses, movements, pressures, forces, stresses and strains, velocities, accelerations, etc., etc. All these notions were born in a 'linear', 'rational' world where nothing takes place but what is straight, flat, and uniform. Either, then, we must abandon these elementary rational notions—and this would mean a veritable revolution, so deeply are these concepts rooted in our minds; or we must adapt those rational notions to a world which is neither flat, nor straight, nor uniform.

Now Dantzig is quite wrong in supposing that Euclidean space, linear, flat, straight, uniform, is rooted in our minds at all. Such space is a product of literacy and is unknown to pre-literate or archaic man. We have seen earlier that Mircea Eliade has recently devoted a volume to this theme (*The Sacred and the Profane*), showing how the Western notions of space and time as continuous and homogeneous are quite absent from the lives of archaic man. They are equally absent from Chinese culture. Pre-literate man conceives always of uniquely structured spaces and times in the manner of mathematical physics.

The invaluable demonstration of Dantzig is that in order to protect our vested interest in Euclidean space (i.e., literacy) Western man devised the parallel but antithetic mode of number in order to cope with all of the non-Euclidean dimensions of daily experience. He continues (p. 140):

But how can the flat and the straight and the uniform be adapted to its very opposite, the skew and the curved and the non-uniform? Not by a finite number of steps, certainly! The miracle can be accomplished only by that miracle-maker the *infinite*. Having determined to cling to the elementary rational notions, we have no other alternative than to regard the 'curved' reality of our senses as the ultra-ultimate step in an infinite sequence of *flat* worlds which exist only in our imagination.

The miracle is that it works!

How the Greeks encountered the confusion of tongues when numbers invaded Euclidean space.

✱ Again let us ask why should the phonetic alphabet have created the fiction of flat, straight and uniform space? The phonetic alphabet, unlike the complex pictographics evolved by priestly groups of scribes for temple administration, was a streamlined code for commerce. It was easy for anybody to learn and to use and it was adaptable to any language whatever.

Number, that is to say, is itself an audile-tactile code which is meaningless without a highly developed phonetic-literate culture to complement it. Together, letters and number constitute a powerful systole-diastole engine for translating and retranslating the modes of human awareness in a system of "double translation" such as appealed deeply to the early humanists of the Renaissance. Yet today number is as obsolete as the phonetic alphabet as a means of endowing and applying experience and knowledge. We are now as post-number as we are post-literate in the electronic age. There is a mode of calculation that is pre-digital Dantzig points out (p. 14):

There exists among the most primitive tribes of Australia and Africa a system of numeration which has neither 5, 10, nor 20 for base. It is a *binary* system, i.e., of base two. These savages have not yet reached finger counting. They have independent numbers for one and two, and composite numbers up to six. Beyond six everything is denoted by "heap".

Dantzig indicates that even digital counting is a kind of abstraction or separation of the tactile from the other senses, whereas the yes-no which precedes it is a more "whole" response. Such, at any rate, are the new binary computers that dispense with number, and make possible the structuralist physics of Heisenberg. For the ancient world, numbers had not been just tactile for measurement as they became in the split visual world of the Renaissance. As de Chardin states it in his *Phenomenon of Man* (p. 50):

What ancient thought half perceived and imagined as a natural harmony of numbers, modern science has grasped and converted in the precision of formulae dependent on measurement. Indeed, we owe our knowledge of the macro-structure and micro-structure of the universe far more to increasingly accurate measurements than to direct observations. And, again, it is ever bolder measurements that have revealed to us the calculable conditions to which every transformation of matter is subject according to the force it calls into play.

Back in the visual space in abstraction from the other senses, the Renaissance and eighteenth-century world "seemed to rest, static and fragmentable on the three axes of its geometry. Now it is a casting from a single mould." It is not here a question of values but rather of the need to understand how the achievements of the Renaissance were associated with the separation of functions and senses. But the discovery of the visual techniques of separation and static arrest in a traditional milieu of audile-tactile culture was of immense fruitfulness. The same techniques used in a world that has been homogenized by these techniques may have much less advantage. De Chardin says (p. 221):

Our habit is to divide up our human world into compartments of different sorts of 'realities': natural and artificial, physical and moral, organic and juridical, for instance.
In a space-time, legitimately and perforce extended to include the movements of the mind within us, the frontiers between these pairs of opposites tend to vanish. Is there after all such a great difference from the point of view of the expansion of life between a vertebrate either spreading its limbs like a bat or equipping them with feathers, and an aviator soaring on wings with which he has had the ingenuity to provide himself?

It may not be necessary to enlarge here on the role of the infinitesimal calculus as an extension of print technology. More neutral than the alphabet, calculus permits the translation or reduction of any kind of space or motion or energy into a uniform repeatable formula. Dantzig explains in his *Number: The Language of Science* a great step in numeration and calculation taken by the Phoenicians under commercial pressure: "The ordinal numeration in which numbers are represented by the letters of an alphabet in their spoken succession." (p 24; see also p. 221.)

But using letters, Greek and Roman alike never got near a method suited to arithmetical operations: "This is why, from the beginning of history until the advent of our modern *positional* numeration, so little progress was made in the art of reckoning." (p. 25) That is, until number was given a visual, spatial character and abstracted from its audile-tactile matrix it could not be separated from the magical domain. "A man skilled in the art was regarded as endowed with almost supernatural powers. . . . even the enlightened Greeks never completely freed themselves from this mysticism of number and form." (pp. 25–6)

It is easy to see with Dantzig how the first crisis in mathematics arose with the Greek attempt to apply arithmetic to geometry, to translate one kind of space into another before printing had given the means of homogeneity: "This confusion of tongues persists to this day. Around infinity have grown up all the paradoxes of mathematics: from the arguments of Zeno to the antinomies of Kant and Cantor." (p. 65) It is difficult for us in the twentieth century to realize why our predecessors should have had such trouble in recognizing the various languages and assumptions of visual as opposed to audile-tactile spaces. It was precisely the habit of being with one kind of space that made all other spaces seem so opaque and intractable. From the eleventh to the fifteenth centuries the Abacists fought the Algorists. That is, the literate fought the numbers people. In some places the Arabic numerals were banned. In Italy some merchants of the thirteenth century used them as a secret code. Under manuscript culture the outward appearance of the numerals underwent many changes and, says Dantzig (p. 34): "In fact, the numerals did not assume a stable form until the introduction of printing. It can be added parenthetically that so great was the stabilizing influence of printing that the numerals of today have essentially the same appearance as those of the fifteenth century."

The great sixteenth century divorce between art and science came with accelerated calculators.

✳ Print assured the victory of numbers or visual position early in the sixteenth century. By the later sixteenth century the art of statistics was already growing. Dantzig writes (p. 16):

The late sixteenth century was the time when in Spain figures were printed giving the population of provinces and the population of towns. It was the time when the Italians also began to take a serious interest in population statistics—in the making of censuses. It was the period when in France a controversy was carried on between Bodin and a certain Monsieur de Malestroict concerning the relations of the quantity of money in circulation to the level of prices.

There was soon great concern with ways and means of speeding up arithmetical calculations:

It is hard for us to realize how laborious and slow were the means at the disposal of medieval Europeans for dealing with calculations 'which seem to us of the simplest character'. The introduction of Arabic numbers into Europe provided more easily manipulated counters than the Roman numbers, and the use of Arabic numbers seems to have spread rapidly towards the end of the sixteenth century, at least on the Continent. Between about 1590 and 1617 John Napier invented his curious 'bones' for calculating. He followed this invention with his more celebrated discovery of logarithms. This was widely adopted all over Europe almost at once, and in consequence arithmetical calculations were immensely accelerated. (p. 17)

There then occurred an event that dramatizes the separation of letters and numbers in a most striking way. In *Cultural Foundations of Industrial Civilization* (pp. 17–18), Nef cites the studies of Lucien Febvre concerning the sudden reversal in calculation, so that "the ancient habit of adding and subtracting from left to right, which still prevailed according to Lucien Lefebvre, until the end of the sixteenth century, began to be superseded by the much quicker way of making them from right to left." That is to say that the separation of letters and numbers which had taken so long to achieve was finally accomplished by dropping the reading habit of left to right in the use of numbers. Nef spends time (p. 19) trying to resolve the problem of integrating faith, art, and science. Religion and art are automatically excluded from a quantified, uniform, and homogenous system of thought:

181

"One of the major distinctions that has to be made between the work of the two periods relates to the place occupied by faith and art in scientific inquiry. It was hardly until the later period that they began to lose their importance as the basis for scientific reasoning."

Today when science also has turned from the segmental to the configurational, or structural mode of observation, it is hard to discover the grounds of difficulty and confusion that invested these matters from the sixteenth to the nineteenth centuries. It was notably Claude Bernard's approach to experimental medicine in the later nineteenth century that reconquered the heterogeneous dimensions of the *milieu intérieur* at exactly the same time that Rimbaud and Baudelaire shifted poetry to the *paysage intérieur*. But for three centuries before this the arts and sciences were engaged in the conquest of the *milieu extérieur* by means of new visual quantity and homogeneity derived especially from the printed word. And it was print that enabled letters and numbers to go their specialist and divergent ways to the confusion of arts and sciences ever since. But at the start, writes Professor Nef in his *Cultural Foundations of Industrial Civilization* (p. 21).

The novel desire, which was then arising, to see nature, including animal and human bodies, as they appear directly to man's senses, was of much help to science. The researches of a few great Renaissance artists, who were almost universal men in the range of their interests and artistic achievements, helped men to see bodies, plants and landscapes afresh in their material reality. But the ways in which the artist and the modern scientist employ sense impressions to create their independent worlds are fundamentally different, and the phenomenal development of science depended partly on a separation of science from art.

This is only to say that what began as a separation of the senses in science became the ground of all artistic opposition. The artist struggled to retain and to regain the integral, the interplay of sense in a world that was seeking madness by the simple road of isolation of the senses. As was indicated in the first pages of this book, the theme of *King Lear* is precisely what Nef is describing as the origins of modern science.

"Strike flat the thick rotundity of the world," cries Lear as a curse to snap "the most precious square of sense." And the striking flat, the isolation of the visual is the great achievement of Gutenberg and the Mercator projection. And Dantzig (p. 125) notes: "Thus the alleged properties of the straight line are of the geometer's own making. He deliberately disregards thickness and breadth, deliberately assumes that the thing common to two such lines, their point of intersection, is deprived of all dimension . . . but the assumptions themselves are arbitrary, a convenient fiction at best." It is easy for Dantzig to see how fictional classical geometry was. It got huge nourishment from printing after being engendered by the alphabet. And the non-Euclidean geometries familiar to our time also depend on electric technology for their nutriment and plausibility, and this is no more seen by mathematicians now than the relations to alphabet and print were seen by mathematicians in the past. It has been assumed till now that so long as everybody is hypnotized by the same isolated sense or spell, that the resulting homogeneity of mental states will suffice for human association. That print increasingly hypnotized the Western world is nowadays the theme of all historians of art and science alike, because we no longer live under the spell of the isolated visual sense. We have not yet begun to ask under what new spell we exist. In place of spell it may be more acceptable to say "assumptions" or "parameters" or "frame of reference." No matter what the metaphor, is it not absurd for men to live involuntarily altered in their inmost lives by some mere technological extension of our inner senses? The shift in our sense ratios brought about by exteriorizations of our senses is not a situation before which we need be helpless. Computers can now be programmed for every possible variety of sense ratio. We can then read off exactly what would be the resulting cultural assumptions in the arts and sciences, of such a new specific ratio as was produced by TV, for example.

Francis Bacon, PR voice for the moderni, had both his feet in the Middle Ages.

✱ Throughout *Finnegans Wake* Joyce specifies the Tower of Babel as the tower of Sleep, that is, the tower of the witless assumption, or what Bacon calls the reign of the Idols. The figure of Francis Bacon has always seemed full of contradictions. As the PR man for modern science, he has been found to have both feet firmly planted in the Middle Ages. His prodigious Renaissance reputation baffles those who can find nothing scientific in his method. Much more highbrow than the furious pedagogue Petrus Ramus, he yet shares with Ramus an extreme visual bias which links him with his relative Roger Bacon in the twelfth century and with Newton in the eighteenth. Everything said so far in this book applies as an introduction to Francis Bacon. And without the work of Ong, Dantzig, and Nef already introduced, it would not be easy to make sense of Bacon. Simply on his own terms, however, he does make sense. He hangs together once you grant his assumption that Nature is a Book whose pages have been smudged by the Fall of Man. But because he belongs to the history of modern science nobody has been disposed to grant him his medieval assumptions. Ong and

183

Nef and Dantzig will have helped to clear this point. The drive towards science was, from the ancient world to the time of Bacon, a drive to extricate the visual from the other senses. But this stress was inseparable from the cultivation of manuscript and print culture. Thus the medievalism of Bacon would not have been amiss in his time. As Febvre and Martin explain in *L'Apparition du livre*, the first two centuries of print culture were almost wholly medieval in *content*. More than ninety per cent of all books printed were of medieval origin. And Professor Nef insists in *Cultural Foundations of Modern Industrialism* (p. 33) that it was medieval universalism or faith in the adequacy of intellect to the understanding of all created beings that "gave men the courage to read anew the book of nature, which almost every European assumed had been made by God whom Christ revealed. . . . Leonardo da Vinci and Copernicus and Vesalius were reading that book anew, but they were not the discoverers of the vital new methods of reading it. They belong to what was in the main a transition period from the older science to the new sciences. Their methods of examining natural phenomena were derived mainly from the past."

Thus the grandeur of Aquinas is in his explanation of how the modalities of Being are proportional to the modalities of our intellection.

Observation and experiment were not new. What was new was insistence on tangible, repeatable, visible proof. Nef writes (p. 27) : "Such insistence on tangible proofs hardly goes back beyond the times of William Gilbert of Colchester, who was born in 1544. In his *De magnete*, published in 1600, Gilbert wrote that there was no description or explanation in the book that he had not verified several times 'with his own eyes'." But before printing had had a century and more to build up the assumptions of uniformity, continuity, and repeatability, such an impulse as Gilbert felt or such a proof as he offers would have attracted little interest. Bacon himself was aware of the discontinuity between his age and previous history as consisting in the rise of mechanism. He writes in *Novum Organum* (aphorism 129) :

It is well to observe the force and effect and consequences of discoveries. These are to be seen nowhere more conspicuously than in those three which were unknown to the ancients, and of which the origin, though recent, is obscure; namely, printing, gunpowder, and the magnet. For these three have changed the whole face and state of things throughout the world; the first in literature, the second in warfare, the third in navigation; whence have followed innumerable changes; insomuch that no empire, no sect, no star seems to have exerted greater power and influence in human affairs than these mechanical inventions.

"With Bacon we enter a new mental climate," writes Benjamin Farrington in *Francis Bacon: Philosopher of Industrial Science* (p. 141). "When we analyze it we find that it consists not so much in a scientific advance as in the well-founded confidence that the life of man can be transformed by science." Farrington is saying that had things turned out less well for man and science he would have had to regard Bacon's confidence as so much hot air and blather. A person with some acquaintance with Bacon's medieval roots can make a better case for his intellectual plausibility. The very phrase "experimental science" was invented and used in the thirteenth century by Roger Bacon of the same family as Francis. Roger makes the full distinction between deductive reasoning, insisting upon particularity of evidence in his discussion of the rainbow.[59]

Bacon was more impressed by the meaning of print as applied knowledge than anybody else except Rabelais. The entire Middle Ages had regarded Nature as a Book to be scanned for the *vestigia dei*. Bacon took the lesson of print to be that we could now literally get Nature out in a new and improved edition. An encyclopedia is envisaged. It is his complete acceptance of the idea of the Book of Nature that makes Bacon so very medieval and so very modern. But the gap is this. The medieval Book of Nature was for *contemplatio* like the Bible. The Renaissance Book of Nature was for *applicatio* and use like movable types. A closer look at Francis Bacon will resolve this problem and elucidate the transition from the medieval to the modern world.

Another view of the book as bridge between the medieval and the modern is given by Erasmus. His new Latin version of the New Testament in 1516 was entitled *Novum Organum* in 1620. Erasmus directed the new print technology to the traditional uses of *grammatica* and rhetoric and to tidying up the sacred page. Bacon used the new technology for an attempt to tidy up the text of Nature. In the different spirit of these works one can gauge the efficacy of print in preparing the mind for applied knowledge. But such change is not as rapid or as thorough as many suppose. Again and again Samuel Eliot Morison in his *Admiral of the Ocean Sea* is baffled by the inability of Columbus' sailors to fend for themselves in the circumstances of the New World: "Columbus embraced him, as well he might; for there was not a crust left to eat aboard the grounded caravels, and the Spaniards were starving. I cannot understand why they were unable to catch fish . . ." (p. 643) After all, the point of *Robinson Crusoe* is the very novelty of man as adaptable and resourceful, able to translate one kind of experience into new patterns. Defoe's work is the epic of applied knowledge. In the first age of print people had not yet acquired this ability.

[59]See Etienne Gilson, *La Philosophie au Moyen Age*, p. 481.

A strange wedding of the medieval Book of Nature and the new book from movable types was conducted by Francis Bacon.

✱ In order to clarify Bacon's strange ideas about science and the text of the Book of Nature a brief look at this idea in the Middle Ages is necessary.

Ernst Robert Curtius has taken up the subject of "The Book as Symbol" in chapter XVI of *European Literature and the Latin Middle Ages*. Greece and Rome had made little use of book symbol or metaphor, and it "was through Christianity that the book received its highest consecration. Christianity was a religion or the Holy Book. Christ is the only god whom antique art represents with a book-scroll. . . . The Old Testament itself contained a large stock of metaphors from the book." (p. 130) It is naturally with the coming of paper in the twelfth century and the ensuing increase of books that there is also an efflorescence of book metaphors. Curtius dips here and there among the poets and theologians and begins his section on the Book of Nature (pp. 319–20):

It is a favorite cliché of the popular view of history that the Renaissance shook off the dust of yellowed parchments and began instead to read in the book of nature or the world. But this metaphor itself derives from the Latin Middle Ages. We saw that Alan speaks of the "book of experience." . . . Omnis mundi creatura / Quasi liber et pictura / Nobis est et speculum. In later authors, especially the homilists, "scientia creaturarum" and "liber naturae" appear as synonyms. For the preacher the book of nature must figure with the Bible as a source of material.

However, it is in Dante himself, according to Curtius (p. 326), that "the entire book imagery of Middle Ages is brought together, intensified, broadened . . . from the first paragraph of the *Vita Nuova* to the last canto of the *Divina Commedia*. In fact, the very concept of *summa* inherent in all medieval organization of knowledge is the same as that of textbook: "Now to reading conceived as the form of reception and study, corresponds writing as the form of production and creation. The two concepts belong together. In the intellectual world of the Middle Ages they represent, as it were, the two halves of a sphere. The unity of this world was shattered by the invention of printing." (p. 328) And as the work of Hajnal showed earlier, the oral training involved in writing and reading constituted much more of a cultural unity for the book than Curtius suspects. Printing, Curtius sees, split apart the roles of producer and consumer. But it also created the means and the motive for *applied* knowledge. The means creates the want.

It was this homiletic use of the book of nature, the mirror of St. Paul in which we now see in *aenigmatate*, that enthroned Pliny as a resource of grammatical exegesis from St. Augustine forward. Summing up, Curtius finds (p. 321) "that the concept of the world or nature as a "book" originated in pulpit eloquence, was then adopted by medieval mystico-philosophical speculation, and finally passed into common usage."

Curtius then turns (p. 322) to Renaissance writers like Montaigne, Descartes, Thomas Browne, who took over the book metaphor, and Bacon: "The theological concept is preserved by Francis Bacon: "Num salvator noster inquit: Erratis nescientes Scripturas et potentiam Dei (Matt. 22, 29), ubi duos libros, ne inerrores, proponit nobis evolvendos. (*De Augmentis Scientiarum*, Bk. I.)" Since, however, our present goal is merely to relate Bacon's notion of science to the medieval tradition of the two Scriptures of Revelation and Nature, it is possible to limit discussion to *The Advancement of Learning* readily accessible in the Everyman edition. Here, too, Bacon makes use of the same text from Matthew (pp. 41–2):

... for as the Psalms and other Scriptures do often invite us to consider and magnify the great and wonderful works of God, so if we should rest only in the contemplation of the exterior of them, as they first offer themselves to our senses, we should do a like injury unto the Majesty of God, as if we should judge or construe of the store of some excellent jeweller, by that only which is set out toward the street in his shop. The other, because they minister a singular help and preservative against unbelief and error: for our Saviour saith, *You err, not knowing the Scriptures, nor the power of God*; laying before us two books or volumes to study, if we will be secured from error; first, the Scriptures, revealing the Will of God; and then the creatures expressing His Power; whereof the latter is a key unto the former: not only opening our understanding to conceive the true sense of the Scriptures, by the general notions of reason and rules of speech; but chiefly opening our belief, in drawing us into a due meditation of the omnipotency of God, which is chiefly signed and engraven upon His works. Thus much therefore for divine testimony and evidence concerning the true dignity and value of Learning.

The next passage gives Bacon's ever-recurrent theme that all of the arts are forms of applied knowledge for the sake of diminishing the effects of the Fall:

Concerning speech and words, the consideration of them hath produced the science of grammar: for man still striveth to reintegrate himself in those benedictions, from which by his fault he hath been deprived; and as he hath striven against the first general curse by the invention of all other arts, so hath he sought to come forth of the second general curse, which was the confusion of tongues, by the art of grammar; whereof the use in a mother tongue is small, in a foreign tongue more; but most in such foreign tongues as have ceased to be vulgar tongues, and are turned only to learned tongues. (p. 138)

It is the Fall of Man which engenders the arts of applied knowledge for the relief of man's fallen estate:

> So in the age before the flood, the holy records within those few memorials which are there entered and registered have vouchsafed to mention and honour the name of the inventors and authors of music and works in metal. In the age after the flood, the first great judgment of God upon the ambition of man was the confusion of tongues; whereby the open trade and intercourse of learning and knowledge was chiefly imbarred. (p. 38)

Bacon has the utmost regard for the kind of work done by unfallen man (p. 37):

> After the creation was finished, it is set down unto us that man was placed in the garden to work therein; which work, so appointed to him, could be no other than work of Contemplation; that is, when the end of work is but for exercise and experiment, not for necessity; for there being then no reluctation of the creature, nor sweat of the brow, man's employment must of consequence have been matter of delight in the experiment, and not matter of labour for the use. Again, the first acts which man performed in Paradise consisted of the two summary parts of knowledge; the view of creatures, and the imposition of names. As for the knowledge which induced the fall, it was, as was touched before, not the natural knowledge of creatures, but the moral knowledge of good and evil, but that they had other beginnings, which man aspired to know; to the end to make a total defection from God and to depend wholly upon himself.

Bacon's Adam is a medieval mystic and Milton's a trade union organizer.

✱ Before the Fall the purpose of work was just for experience or "experiment," "not for necessity," "nor matter of labour for the use." Strangely, although Bacon is quite explicit and repetitive in his derivation of the program of applied knowledge from the Scriptures, his commentators have avoided this issue. Bacon pushes Revelation into every part of his program stressing, not only the parallelism between the book of Nature and of Revelation, but also between the methods used in both.

Bacon's Adam would seem to correspond to Shakespeare's poet, using his unblemished intuition to pierce all mysteries and to name them like a nominalist magician:

> The poet's eye, in a fine frenzy rolling,
> Doth glance from heaven to earth, from earth to heaven;
> And as imagination bodies forth
> The forms of things unknown, the poet's pen
> Turns them to shapes, and gives to airy nothing
> A local habitation and a name.[60]

By comparison, Milton's unfallen Adam is a harassed agricultural labourer:

> Then commune how that day they best may ply
> Their growing work—for much their work outgrew
> The hands' dispatch of two gardening so wide:[61]

Milton must have some ironic intent.

Bacon's conception of applied knowledge concerns the means of restoring the text of the Book of Nature which has been defaced by the Fall, even as our faculties have been impaired. Just as Bacon strives to mend the text of Nature by his Histories, so he sought to repair our faculties by his *Essays or Counsels, Civil and Moral*, or public and private. The broken mirror or glass of our minds no longer lets "light through" but enchants us with broken lights, besetting us with Idols.

Just as Bacon draws on traditional inductive *grammatica* for his exegesis of the two books of Nature and Revelation, so he relies heavily on the Ciceronian conception of eloquence as applied knowledge, explicitly uniting Cicero and Solomon in this regard. In the *Novum Organum* (pp. 181–2) he writes:

> Neither needeth it at all to be doubted, that this knowledge should be so
> variable as it falleth not under precept; for it is much less infinite than
> science of government, which, we see, is laboured and in some part reduced.
> Of this wisdom, it seemeth some of the ancient Romans in the saddest and
> wisest times were professors; for Cicero reporteth that it was then in use for
> senators that had name and opinion for general wise men, as Coruncanius,
> Curius, Laelius, and many others, to walk at certain hours in the Place, and
> to give audience to those that would use their advice; and that the particular
> citizens would resort unto them, and consult with them of the marriage of
> a daughter, or of the employing of a son, or of a purchase or bargain, or of
> an accusation, and every other occasion incident to man's life. So as there is
> a wisdom of counsel and advice even in private causes, arising out of a
> universal insight into the affairs of the world; which is used indeed upon
> particular causes propounded, but is gathered by general observation of cases
> of like nature. For so we see in the book which Q. Cicero writeth to his
> brother, *De petitione consulatus*, (being the only book of business that I
> know written by the ancients,) although it concerned a particular action

[60]*Midsummer Night's Dream*, V, i.
[61]*Paradise Lost*, IX, 11. 201–3.

set on foot, yet the substance thereof consisteth of many wise and politic axioms, which contain not a temporary, but a perpetual direction in the case of popular elections. But chiefly we may see in those aphorisms which have place among divine writings, composed by Salomon the king, (of whom the Scriptures testify that his heart was as the sands of the sea, encompassing the world and all worldly matters, we see, I say, not a few profound and excellent cautions, precepts, positions, extending to much variety of occasions; whereupon we will stay awhile, offering to consideration some number of examples.

Bacon has much to say of Solomon as the forerunner of himself. In fact, he derives (pp. 39–40) his pedagogical theory of aphorism from Solomon:

So like wise in the person of Salomon the King, we see the gift or endowment of wisdom and learning, both in Salomon's petition and in God's assent thereunto, preferred before all other terrene and temporal felicity. By virtue of which grant or donative of God Salomon became enabled not only to write those excellent Parables or Aphorisms concerning divine and moral philosophy; but also to compile a Natural History of all verdure, from the cedar upon the mountain to the moss upon the wall (which is but a rudiment between putrefaction and a herb), and also of all things that breathe or move. Nay, the same Salomon the King, although he excelled in the glory of treasure and magnificent buildings, of shipping and navigation, of service and attendance, of fame and renown, and the like, yet he maketh no claim to any of those glories, but only to the glory of inquisition of truth; for so he saith expressly, *The glory of God is to conceal a thing, but the glory of the king is to find it out*; as if, according to the innocent play of children, the Divine Majesty took delight to hide His works, to the end to have them found out; and as if kings could not obtain a greater honour than to be God's playfellows in that game; considering the great commandment of wits and means, whereby nothing needeth to be hidden from them.

Bacon's allusion to scientific discovery as a children's game brings us close to another of his basic notions, that as man lost his Eden through pride he must regain it by humility:

So much concerning the several classes of Idols, and their equipage: all of which must be renounced and put away with a fixed and solemn determination, and the understanding thoroughly freed and cleansed; the entrance into the kingdom of man, founded on the sciences, being not much other than the entrance into the kingdom of heaven, where into none may enter except as a little child.[62]

Earlier in the *Essays* (pp. 289–90), Bacon insisted in the same way that "the course I propose for the discovery of sciences is such as leaves but little to the acuteness and strength of wits, but places all wits and understandings nearly on a level." Print had inspired Bacon not only with the idea of applied knowledge by means of the homogeneity of segmental pro-

[62]*Essays*, ed. R. F. Jones, p. 294.

cedure, but it gave him the assurance that men would be levelled in their capacities and performance as well. Some strange speculations have resulted from this doctrine, but few would care to dispute the power of print to level and to extend the learning process as much as cannon or ordnance did level castles and feudal privilege. Bacon, then, argues that the text of Nature can be restored by great encyclopedic fact-finding sweeps. Man's wits can be reconstructed so that they can once again mirror the perfected Book of Nature. His mind is now an enchanted glass, but the hex can be removed.

It is quite clear, then, that Bacon would have no respect for scholasticism any more than for the dialectics of Plato and Aristotle "because it is the duty of Art to perfect and exalt Nature; but they contrariwise have wronged, abused, and traduced Nature."[63]

How far did the mass-produced page of print become a substitute for auricular confession?

❋ Early in *The Advancement of Learning* (p. 23), Bacon has a compact history of Renaissance prose that illuminates the role of printing indirectly:

Martin Luther, conducted no doubt by a higher providence, but in discourse of reason finding what a providence he had undertaken against the bishop of Rome and the degenerate traditions of the church, and finding his own solitude, being no ways aided by the opinion of his own time, was enforced to awake all antiquity, and to call former times to his succours to make a party against the present time. So that the ancient authors, both in divinity and in humanity, which had long time slept in libraries, began generally to be read and revolved. Thus by consequence did draw on a necessity of a more exquisite travail in the languages original, wherein those authors did write, for the better understanding of those authors, and the better advantage of pressing and applying their words. And thereof grew again a delight in their manner of style and phrase, and an admiration of that kind of writing; which was much furthered and precipitated by the enmity and opposition that the propounders of those primitive but seeming new opinions had against the schoolmen; who were generally of the contrary part, and whose writings were altogether in a different style and form; taking liberty to coin and frame new terms of art to express their own sense, and to avoid circuit of speech, without regard to the pureness, pleasantness, and, as I may call it, lawfulness of the phrase or word.

[63]*Advancement of Learning*, p. 125.

Bacon says here that the entire humanist effort in languages and historical revival was incidental to religious differences. The printing presses made available authors of remote times. People began to imitate their styles. The schoolmen had such a technical terse way that they fell quite out of fashion, being utterly unable to develop any popularity with the new reading public. The growing public could only be won by flowery rhetoric and, Bacon goes on to say (p. 24):

for the winning and persuading of them, there grew of necessity in chief price and request eloquence and variety of discourse, as the fittest and forciblest access into the capacity of the vulgar sort: so that these four causes concurring, the admiration of ancient authors, the hate of the schoolmen, the exact study of languages, and the efficacy of preaching, did bring in an affectionate study of eloquence and copie of speech, which then began to flourish. This grew speedily to an excess; for men began to hunt more after words than matter; more after the choiceness of the phrase, and the round and clean composition of the sentence, and the sweet falling of the clauses, and the varying and illustration of their works with tropes and figures, than after the weight of matter, worth of subject, soundness of argument, life of invention or depth of judgment. Then grew the flowing and watery vein of Osorius the Portugal bishop, to be in price. Then did Sturmius spend such infinite and curious pains upon Cicero the Orator, and Hermogenes the Rhetorician, besides his own books of Periods and Imitation, and the like. Then did Car of Cambridge, and Ascham with their lectures and writings almost deify Cicero and Demosthenes, and allure all young men that were studious, unto that delicate and polished kind of learning. Then did Erasmus take occasion to make the scoffing Echo: *decem annos consumpsi in legendo Cicerone*; and the Echo answered in Greek, $\theta \nu \epsilon$ *Asine*. Then grew the learning of the schoolmen to be utterly despised as barbarous. In sum, the whole inclination and bent of those times was rather towards copie than weight.

There in a page or so Bacon renders a detailed image of the literary struggles and fashions of his day. Like his idea of scientific methods, his idea of the literary scene is rooted in religion. His outline of a history of English prose has yet to be examined seriously by literary historians. When, for example, Bacon says: "Then grew the learning of the Schoolmen to be utterly despised as barbarous" he does not say that he himself despises it. He has no respect for the ornate and affected eloquence that was currently trumped up.

After this outline of some of the features of applied knowledge in Bacon's medievalism, it is time to consider some of the applications of print technology to individual and national life. And here it is necessary to consider writers and the vernaculars as shaped by the new extension of the visual image by means of the press.

Some writers have recently suggested that we can almost regard the whole of creative writing since the Renaissance as an externalization of the medieval confessional. In his *Anatomy of Criticism* (p. 307) Northrop Frye points to the strong autobiographic strain in prose fiction, "following St. Augustine who appears to have invented it, and Rousseau who established a modern type of it. The earlier tradition gave *Religio Medici, Grace Abounding,* and Newman's *Apologia* to English literature, besides the related but subtly different type of confession favored by the mystics."

In particular the sonnet as a new form of public confessional fostered by print, is worth study as it relates to new verse forms. Wordsworth's familiar sonnet on the sonnet strikes some main notes of *The Gutenberg Galaxy*:

> Scorn not the Sonnet; Critic, you have frowned,
> Mindless of its just honours; with this key
> Shakespeare unlocked his heart; the melody
> Of this small lute gave ease to Petrarch's wound;
> A thousand times this pipe did Tasso sound;
> With it Camöens soothed an exile's grief;
> The Sonnet glittered a gay myrtle leaf
> Amid the cypress with which Dante crowned
> His visionary brow: a glow-worm lamp,
> It cheered mild Spenser, called from Faery-land
> To struggle through dark ways; and, when a damp
> Fell round the path of Milton, in his hand
> The Thing became a trumpet; whence he blew
> Soul-animating strains—alas, too few!

Many a trumpet solo was delivered by the press medium which would else never have been composed. The mere existence of the press created the need and possibility of new expression at the same time:

> Loving in truth, and fain in verse my love to show,
>   That she, dear she, might take some pleasure of my pain,—
>   Pleasure might cause her read, reading might make her know,
>   Knowledge might pity win, and pity grace obtain,—
> I sought fit words to paint the blackest face of woe;
>   Studying inventions fine, her wits to entertain,
>   Oft turning others' leaves to see if thence would flow
>   Some fresh and fruitful showers upon my sunburn'd brain.
> But words came halting forth, wanting Invention's stay;
>   Invention, Nature's child, fled step-dame Study's blows,
>   And others' feet still seem'd but strangers in my way.
> Thus, great with child to speak, and helpless in my throes,
>   Biting my truant pen, beating myself for spite;
>   "Fool," said my Muse to me, "look in thy heart, and write."[64]

[64]Sir Philip Sidney, *Astrophel and Stella.*

Aretino, like Rabelais and Cervantes, proclaimed the meaning of Typography as Gargantuan, Fantastic, Supra-human.

✱ The outering or uttering of mind under manuscript conditions, was, as we have seen, very restricted. The poet or author was far from being able to use the vernacular as a public address system. With print the discovery of the vernacular as a PA system was immediate. The figure of Pietro Aretino (1492–1556) will serve to illuminate this sudden development. He also illustrates the sudden reversal of the private self-accusation, of the confessional, into public denunciation of others. Aretino was known in his time as "the scourge of Princes":

> He was monster, it is true: to deny that is to belittle him; but above all he was a man of his day, perhaps the most free and complete expression of the age in which he lived—the sixteenth century. That, and his enormous ability, together with the fact that he founded the modern press and used the hitherto unsuspected weapon of publicity with an incomparable appreciation of its power, are his chief claims upon our notice.[65]

Born two years after Rabelais, he was, like Rabelais, just in time to seize the new instrument of the press. He became a one-man newspaper, a single-handed Northcliffe.

> He is, in a sense, in his "yellow" proclivities, the forerunner of Mr. Hearst, Lord Northcliffe and others, while he is also the father of the awful tribe of modern press agents, who, when they wish to put on airs, become "publicists". It is his boast that throughout the world, "Fame is sold by me." He had to have publicity; it was his living; and he certainly knew how to set about to get it. . . . Here, then, we have a man who may be called, in point of chronology, the first literary realist, the first journalist, the first publicist, the first art critic.[66]

Like his exact contemporary Rabelais, Aretino sensed the gigantism that is latent in the uniformity and repeatability of the printed word. Aretino, from lowly origins and without education, used the press as it has been used ever since. Putnam writes (p. 37):

> If Aretino, at this time, was probably the most powerful man in Italy, perhaps in the world, the reason is to be found in the new force which he

[65]Edward Hutton, *Pietro Aretino, The Scourge of Princes*, p. xl.

[66]*The Works of Aretino*, translated into English from the original Italian, with a critical and biographical essay, by Samuel Putnam, p. 13.

had discovered, that force which we today would call "the power of the press". Aretino himself regarded it as the power of his pen. He himself did not realize the right Promethean fire with which he was playing. All he knew was that he had a tremendous instrument in his hands, and he employed it quite as unscrupulously as it, consistently, has been employed since his time. He was capable—see his *Letters*—of being quite as hypocritical as the press of today.

Putnam goes on (p. 41) to mention that Aretino was "perhaps the greatest blackmailer in all history, the first truly modern exponent of the 'poison pen.' " That is to say, Aretino really regarded the printing press as a public confessional with himself as Father Confessor, pen or microphone in hand. Hutton cites Aretino on page xiv of his study: "Let others worry themselves about style and so cease to be themselves. Without a master, without a model, without a guide, without artifice I go to work and earn my living, my well-being and my fame. What do I need more? With a goose-quill and a few sheets of paper I mock myself of the universe."

We shall return to his "without a model, without a guide," for it was literally true. The press was an instrument without precedent. It had no writers and no reading public of its own, and had for a long time to make do with the kind of writer and public created by manuscript conditions. As Febvre and Martin explain in *L'Apparition du livre*, the press had to rely on medieval manuscripts almost entirely for the first two centuries. As for the role of author, it did not exist, so the writer tried on various masks of preacher and clown for the first two centuries, discovering the role of "man of letters" only in the eighteenth century:

> *Jaques*. . . . I must have liberty
> Withal, as large a charter as the wind,
> To blow on whom I please; for so fools have.
> And they that are most galled with my folly,
> They most must laugh. And why, sir, must they so?
> The why is plain as way to parish church:
> He that a fool doth very wisely hit
> Doth very foolishly, although he smart,
> Not to seem senseless of the bob. If not,
> The wise man's folly is anatomiz'd
> Even by the squand'ring glances of the fool.
> Invest me in my motley. Give me leave
> To speak my mind, and I will through and through
> Cleanse the foul body of th' infected world,
> If they will patiently receive my medicine.[67]

Though engaged in this cathartic enterprise, Shakespeare felt the absence of role bitterly. In his Sonnet cx, we read:

[67]*As You Like It*, II, vii.

> Alas, 'tis true I have gone here and there
> And made myself a motley to the view,
> Gor'd mine own thoughts, sold cheap what is most dear, . . .

He was little attracted into the print mode and made no effort to publish, since the circulation of his work in print form would have conferred no dignity on him. It was quite otherwise for the writer in divinity. When Ben Jonson published his plays as the *Works* of Ben Jonson in 1616, there was much derisive comment.

It is interesting that Shakespeare should comment on the confessional aspect of authorship, "sold cheap what is most dear," for whether as actor or playwright his going "here and there" would have seemed the same to him. And it is this confessional pouring forth of private news and views that seemed to Aretino and his contemporaries to warrant the association of the press with pornography and filth. This is the view that dominates Pope's *Dunciad* in the early eighteenth century. But for Aretino the switching of private confession into public accusation was a perfectly natural response to the print technology.

Indeed, remarks Raimondi, Aretino "is a prostitute". He has the prostitute's instinct of social rebellion. "He throws mud not merely in the face of his contemporaries, but of a whole past. It would seem that he lifts up the world and places it against the light of the sun. . . . All is obscene and libidinous, everything is for sale, everything is false, nothing is sacred. He himself makes merchandise of sacred things to gain money and writes romantic lives of the saints. And then? Like Nanna, like Pippa, he finds it convenient to stand above men and hold them with the reins of their own vices. . . . The discipline which Nanna gives to Pippa is the dicipline which guided the life of Aretino."[68]

Marlowe anticipated Whitman's barbaric yawp by setting up a national PA system of blank verse–a rising iambic system of sound to suit the new success story.

✱ It is necessary to keep in mind that print created gigantism not only for the author and for the vernaculars, but for markets. And the sudden expansion of enlarged markets and commerce under the inspiration of this first

[68]Aretino, *Dialogues*, p. 59.

form of mass-production, seemed to be a visible extension of all the latent venalities of mankind. This then is not the least of the effects of playing up the visual component in human experience. The technique of translation that is *applied* knowledge is impartially advanced to include the hidden crimes and motives of mankind in a new form of self-expression. Because print is visually a greatly intensified form of the written word, it is insatiable for intense or sensational materials to broadcast. This fact is no more basic for the understanding of current newspapers than for an appreciation of what was happening to language and expression in the sixteenth century:

> It is because Aretino is a man of genius, and because he sums up and expresses that disastrous age of anarchy, its complete moral disorder and collapse, its delight in insulting and disregarding the past, its repudiation of every ancient authority and tradition, that he is worth studying. And if we add to this that he contrived a weapon for his own ends which has in our own day come to be more powerful than any established government or elected parliament or hereditary monarchy—publicity, the Press—there is more than sufficient excuse for this book.[69]

Print as a public address system that gave huge power of amplification to the individual voice, soon made itself a new form of expression, namely the Elizabethan popular drama. The opening lines of the very popular *Tamburlaine the Great* by Christopher Marlowe provides all our new themes:

> From jigging veins of rhyming mother-wits,
> And such conceits as clownage keeps in pay,
> We'll lead you to the stately tent of war,
> Where you shall hear the Scythian Tamburlaine
> Threatening the world with high astounding terms,
>
> . . . .
>
> View but his picture in this tragic glass.
> And then applaud his fortunes as you please.

The first speaker, Mycetas, follows this with equally indicative words:

> Brother Cosroe, I find myself aggriev'd;
> Yet insufficient to express the same,
> For it requires a great and thundering speech:

What is especially significant is the discovery of blank verse as a broadcasting megaphone and the consciousness that jigging rhymes cannot provide the sweep and volume of public utterance that is resonating in the new age. Blank verse to the Elizabethan was as exciting a novelty as the "close up" in a Griffith's movie, and the two are much alike in the intensity of amplification and exaggeration of feeling. Even Whitman, impelled by the new visual intensities of the newspaper of his time, did not devise a louder vehicle for

[69]*Pietro Aretino*, p. xiv.

197

his barbaric yawp than blank verse. Nobody has been willing to offer a theory of the origin of English blank verse. It has no antecedents or exemplars except, perhaps, in the long melodic line of medieval music. I do not think Kenneth Sisam's idea of Old English meter has any bearing on blank verse. He writes in *Fourteenth Century Verse and Prose* (p. xiii): "Old English had a single metre—the long alliterative line without rime. It was best suited to narrative; it was unmusical in the sense that it could not be sung; it had marked proclivities toward rant and noise."

But the paradox is that the blank verse, being one of the first kinds of "spoken," as opposed to sung, poetry is very much faster than song, or perhaps even than speech itself. It is very safe, however, to commence with the consideration that blank verse, unlike rhymed poetry, answered the new need of the vernacular to have recognition and implementation as a public address system. Aretino had been the first to seize the vernacular as the mass medium which print had made it. His biographers note his extraordinary resemblance to the most vulgar press lords and emperors of our own century. Reviewing a biography *Citizen Hearst* by W. A. Swanberg, the *New York Times* headlined the review (September 10, 1961): "The Man Who Made Headlines Scream."

Blank verse was a means to make English roar and resonate in a way suited to the new extension and consolidation of the vernacular by typography. In our own century as the vernacular has met the non-verbal competition of photo, film, and television, a reverse effect has occurred. It was strikingly noted by Simone de Beauvoir in *The Mandarins*: "What a derisory triumph, to be a great writer of Guatemala or Hunduras! Yesterday he had thought himself the inhabitant of a privileged part of the world, from which every sound reverberated through the entire globe; but now he knew that his words died at his feet."

What an extraordinary insight this passage affords into the Gutenberg era and into blank verse! It is not strange that literary research has failed to reveal the origins of blank verse. Equally fruitless would be the seeking the origins of the long lines of the Roman road in engineering antecedents. The Roman road was a by-product of papyrus and fast-moving couriers. Cesare Folingo has the necessary approach to this kind of problem when writing on "Vernacular Literature" in *The Legacy of the Middle Ages* (p. 182): "Rome had produced no popular epics. . . . These undaunted builders were wont to construct their epics in stone; miles and miles of paved roads . . . must have possessed an almost emotional appeal such as the long sequences of single rhymed lines may have had for the French."

Print, in turning the vernaculars into mass media, or closed systems, created the uniform, centralizing forces of modern nationalism.

✱ The French, more than any other modern nation, have felt the unifying force of their vernacular as a national experience. It is fitting that they should be the first to record the break-up of this typographically created unity under the impact of non-verbal media. In the electronic age Simone de Beauvoir and Jean-Paul Sartre declaim in tragic mode in *What is Literature?* the dilemma of "For whom does one write?"

An editorial comment on Simone de Beauvoir in *Encounter* (August, 1955) helps very much to relate the new clamorous voices of the Gutenberg era with the phenomenon of nationalism. The editor is considering the nature of fame and enduring reputation:

... and to obtain this it is almost necessary, in our age, to be a member of
a national community that has, along with whatever moral and aesthetic
excellences, the quite vulgar quality of being in some degree powerful—
of being regarded attentively by the world and, most important, listened to.
The existence of such a community seems to be a precondition for the
emergence of a national literature sufficiently large in extent and weighty in
substance to fix the world's eye and give shape to the world's imagination; ...
it was the writers themselves who helped call into being this thing called
"national literature". At first, their activity had a pleasing artlessness about
it, ... Later under the spell of the Romantic movement, moribund languages
were revived, new national epics were composed for nations that as yet
barely existed, while literature enthusiastically ascribed to the idea of
national existence the most supernatural virtues. ...

Closely interrelated, then, by the operation and effects of typography are the outering or uttering of private inner experience and the massing of collective national awareness, as the vernacular is rendered visible, central, and unified by the new technology.

It is quite consistent that Chaucer, as much as Dryden, should have preferred the couplet as an intimate mode of conversation among friends. In this way the Chaucerian couplet would have struck St. Thomas More as quite close in character to the scholastic dialogue, much as the couplet of Pope and Dryden preserved the character of the Senecan amble. The important text of

199

More cited earlier makes the proper distinction between rhyme and blank verse when he contrasts scholastic philosophy as "not unpleasant among friends in familiar communication," and the new modes of discourse for the "councils of Kings, where great matters be debated and reasoned with great authority." More is talking of the centralist and nationalistic political organizatons which were new in his day. For these new forms of gigantism the blank verse of Marlowe was the objective correlative:

> Cheridamas: Tamburlaine!
> A Scythian shepherd so embellished
> With nature's pride and richest furniture!
> His looks do menace heaven and dare the gods;
> His fiery eyes are fix'd upon the earth,
> As if he now devis'd some stratagem,
> Or meant to pierce Avernus' darksome vaults
> To pull the triple-headed dog from hell.[70]

The divorce of poetry and music was first reflected by the printed page.

✱ Commenting on the melodic line of the Troubadours in *Music and Society* (p. 29) Wilfred Mellers provides a counter-point from which to observe the precipitate forward drive of Marlowe:

The immense length and arching plasticity of line in all these musics is evidence of the advantages, counterbalancing the obvious limitations, of music conceived in terms of a single line; if one sacrifices the possibilities of harmony and sonorous contrast, one gains the possibility of creating melody free of the inhibitions of mensuration. There is no limit to the subtleties of phrase, intonation and nuance one may use, except the limits implicit in the creation of a coherent linear organization.

Song is the slowing down of speech in order to savour nuance. Blank verse originated in an age that first split words and music asunder and which moved towards the specialist autonomy of musical instruments. According to Mellers, the role of polyphony was to break up the ancient monodic line. And polyphony was to have effects in music comparable to movable types and mechanical writing in language and literature. For especially after the printing of music quantification and measurement became necessary as a means of keeping the singers of various parts together. But medieval poly-

[70]*Tamburlaine the Great*, I, ii.

phony only had these separate parts and quantities in latency. Mellers writes (p. 31):

It seems possible that polyphony was in the first place a largely unconscious result of certain accidents that may occur in unison monophonic singing; it is certainly not surprising that during the later Middle Ages polyphony should be so deeply rooted in what are essentially monophonic attitudes that people of the modern world find it, at first at least, curiously difficult of approach. We know more or less what we expect from music conceived in "parts", and the mediaeval composer does not gratify our expectations. But before we dismiss him as 'primitive' or 'tentative' we ought to be sure that we understand what he thought he was trying to do. He was not really trying to break with the implications of the monophonic music on which he had been nurtured and which, as we have seen, symbolized the philosophy inherent in his world; he was perhaps trying to extend that music's resources, and in so doing he quite unwittingly introduced conceptions which were to produce a profound technical revolution.

Bruce Pattison's excellent study of *Music and Poetry of the English Renaissance* stresses that "song-form was virtually the only form up to the seventeenth century" (p. 83). But song-form having been for centuries inseparable from narrative and lineal development of themes, it penetrated and shaped literary practice as well. What we might call the story or "narrative line" today is not much more discernible in Nashe than in the Old Testament. Rather such a "line" is embedded in multitudinous effects of language. This quality of simultaneous interplay or tactile sensuousness is prominent in medieval music. As Pattison puts it (p. 82), "In a sense medieval music is often instrumental in conception, although it is not certain what part instruments took in its performance. Attention was largely concentrated on the sensuous effect of combining different voices rather than on the sentiments of the text or indeed on emotional expression at all."

The oral polyphony of the prose of Nashe offends against lineal and literary decorum.

✱ This sensuous relish for the complex interplay of qualities persists in the sixteenth century even in language intended for the printed page. And James Sutherland in *On English Prose* (p. 49) mistakes this polyphony in Nashe for a failure to be a sensible man of letters: "The trouble with Nashe is partly that he is a good deal less interested in making things easy for the reader than in enjoying his own superiority over him; or, if that seems too harsh a judgment, in exploiting the linguistic resources of the language for his own amusement." Read aloud by a trained rhetorician from the new grammar schools, the passage which Sutherland quotes (pp. 49–50) takes on the brash variety of a Louis Armstrong trumpet solo:

Hero hoped, and therefore she dreamed (as all hope is but a dream); her hope was where her heart was, and her heart winding and turning with the wind, that might wind her heart of gold to her, or else turn him from her. Hope and fear both combatted in her, and both these are wakeful, which made her at break of day (what an old crone is the day, that is so long a breaking) to unloop her luket or casement, to look whence the blasts came, or what gait or pace the sea kept; when forthwith her eyes bred her eye-sore, the first white whereon their transpiercing arrows struck being the breathless corps of Leander: with the sudden contemplation of this piteous spectacle of her love, sodden to haddock's meat, her sorrow could not choose but be indefinite, if her delight in him were but indifferent; and there is no woman but delights in sorrow, or she would not use it so lightly for everything.

Down she ran in her loose night-gown, and her hair about her ears (even as Semiramis ran out with her lie-pot in her hand, and her black dangling tresses about her shoulders with her ivory comb ensnarled in them, when she heard that Babylon was taken) and thought to have kissed his dead corpse alive again, but as on his blue jellied sturgeon lips she was about to clap one of those warm plaisters, boistrous woolpacks of ridged tides came rolling in, and raught him from her (with a mind belike to carry him back to Abydos). At that she became a frantic Bacchanal outright, and made no more bones but sprang after him, and so resigned up her priesthood, and left work for Musaeus and Kit Marlowe.

Just how much the circumstances affected not only the structure of music but of language and music, appears in John Hollander's discussion of the Elizabethan theatres (*The Untuning of the Sky*, p. 147) with their elaborate use of music in signalling functions and the necessity of incorporating all music except these signals into the plot of the play itself. "The small coterie theaters of the city . . . followed the masque . . ."

The printing press was at first mistaken for an engine of immortality by everybody except Shakespeare.

❋ The physical factors as restructuring the modes and areas of expression have so far occupied us only with regard to the sudden emergence of individual voices and the seizing of the vernacular as a unified and ready-made public address system. Simultaneously there occurred the realization that the printed word in the vernacular could confer an artificial eternity of fame. In a delightful essay on Cardano (1501–1576) in *Abinger Harvest* (p. 190) E. M. Forster points out that: "The printing press, then only a century old, had been mistaken for an engine of immortality, and men hastened to commit to it deeds and passions for the benefit of future ages." And Forster (p. 193) quotes Cardano:

It has been my peculiar fortune to live in the century which discovered the whole world—America, Brazil, Patagonia, Peru, Quito, Florida, New France, New Spain, countries to the North and East and South. And what is more marvellous than the human thunderbolt, which in its power far exceeds the heavenly? Nor will I be silent about thee, magnificent Magnet, who dost guide us through vast oceans, and night and storms, into countries we have never known. Then there is our printing press, conceived by man's genius, fashioned by his hands, yet a miracle equal to the divine.

About the same time Pierre Boaistuau wrote in his *Theatrum Mundi*:[71]

I can find nothing that may be equall or compare to the wonderfull invention, utility and dignitie of printing, the which surmounteth all that the antiquitie may conceive or imagine of excellencie, knowing that it conserveth and keepeth all the conceptions of our soules, it is the treasure that doth immortalize the monument of our spirits, and eternizeth world without end and also bringeth to light the fruits of our labours. And although somewhat may be added to all other acts and humane inventions, yet this alone has entred with such good hap and perfection in this world, that ther cannot be added nor diminished any thing that doth not render it defectious and deformed: these effects are so mervailous, and executed with such celerity and diligence, that one man alone in one day will print more letters, than the promptest scribe or scrivener may write with pen in the space of one whole year.

Self-expression is yet unknown as a concept; but "bringeth to light the fruits of our labours" is an excellent indication of the matrix from which the concept will be extracted much later. "Doth immortalize the monument of our spirits" renders perfectly the sixteenth-century idea of an immortality won through toil and mechanical repetition of that toil. In our own century the idea of such immortality has taken on a wry quality that is caught by Joyce in *Ulysses* (p. 41):

"When one reads these strange pages of one long gone, one feels that one is at one with one who once ...
    The grainy sand had gone from under his feet. His boots trod again a damp crackling mast, razorshells, squeaking pebbles, that on the unnumbered

[71]Translated by John Alday, 1581; STC 3170, R_{iii} to R_{iv}.

pebbles beats, wood sieved by the shipworm, lost Armada. Unwholesome sandflats waited to suck his treading soles, breathing upward sewage breath. He coasted them, walking warily. A porter bottle stood up, stogged to its waist, in the cakey sand dough. A sentinel: isle of dreadful thirst.

From meditation on books and libraries, that is, Stephen Dedalus turns to the message in the bottle, reaching it through a riot of audile-tactile-olfactory experience carefully counterpointed with the subjective vistas of authors, libraries, and literary immortality.

The theme of eternizing by means of the printed word had great plausibility in the early period of typography when so many forgotten and unknown writers of the past ages were being brought into a new and far more intense life, by typography, than they had ever known in their actual scribal existences. Shakespeare's inscribed sonnets in 1609 were "To the onlie begetter . . . all happinesses and that eternitie promised by our ever-living Poet, wisheth the well-wishing adventurer in setting forth."

The ever-living poet lives ever in print, that is, and promises that eternity of the printed word (ever so much more assured than the manuscript eternity of a message in a bottle) to "the onlie begetter." It is only proper that the identity of the begetter should be as mysterious as the poetic process by which the sonnets were created. Since, however, eternity is now assured for the begetter as he sets forth on a new life of printed poetic existence, the poet wishes him well, even as he is wishing himself well, in his printed voyage through eternity. And so follows the setting forth of (and in) the text of the sonnets, just ten years after the Elizabethan sonnet vogue had passed.

More double talk was seldom put in thirty-odd words than in these words of dedication. Similar irony occurs in a preface to Shakespeare's *Troilus and Cressida*, which appeared in front of the quarto text of 1609, the same year as the sonnets. It does not concern us here whether Shakespeare wrote this preface. It is too witty for Dekker, too restrained for Nashe. It is much on our theme of print as an engine of immortality:

A never writer, to an ever reader, Newes. Eternall reader, you have heere a new play, never estal'd with the Stage, never clapper-clawd with the palmes of the vulgar, and yet passing full of the palme comicall; for it is a birth of your braine, that never under-tooke anything commicall, vainlly: And were but the vaine names of commedies changde for the titles of Commodities, or of Playes for Pleas; you should see all those grand censors, that now stile them such vanities, flock to them for the maine grace of their gravities: especially this authors Commedies, that are so fram'd to the life, that they serve for the most common Commentaries, of all the actions of our lives, shewing such a dexteritie, and power of witte, that the most displeased with Playes, are pleasd with his Commedies. And all such dull and heavy-witted worldings, as were never capable of the witte of a Commedie, comming by report of them to his representations have found that witte there, that they never found in them-selves, and have parted better wittied then they came: feeling an edge of witte set upon them, more then ever they dreamd they had braine to grinde it on. So much and such savored salt of witte is in his Commedies, that they may seeme (for their height of pleasure) to be borne in that sea that brought forth Venus. Amongst all there is none more witty then this: And had I time I would comment upon it, though I know it needs not, (for so much as will make you thinke your testerne well bestowed) but for so much worth, as even poore I know to be stuft in it. It deserves such a labour, as well as the best Commedy in Terrence or Plautus. And believe this, that when hee is gone, and his Commedies out of sale, you will scramble for them, and set up a new English Inquisition. Take this for a warning, and at the perrill of your pleasures losse, and Judgements, refuse not, nor like this the lesse, for not being sullied, with the smoaky breath of the multitude; but thanke fortune for the scape it hath made amongst you. Since by the grand possessors wills I beleeve you should have prayd for them rather than beene prayd. And so I leave all such to bee prayd for (for the states of their wits healths) that will not praise it. Vale.

This piece of prose requires the same kind of agility of attention as *Troilus and Cressida* itself. It opens like James Joyce in the role of "Mr. Germ's Choice" saying "My consumers are they not my producers?" The play's never having been "clapper-clawd with the palmes of the vulgar" may indicate an Inns of Court performance. But the preface in its entirety is as much an analysis of communication theory as the play itself. At the hub of the play (III, iii) the theme of the preface is stated at much greater length, beginning:

> A strange fellow here
> Writes me, that man—how dearly ever parted,
> How much in having, or without or in—
> Cannot make boast to have that which he hath,
> Nor feels not what he owes, but by reflection;

The preface uses this idea that the producer is only his consumer to mock both readers and writers of the new age in a dazzling sequence of negative involutions. The author is as little impressed by the ultimate value of print as the Shakespeare who could not be bothered to print his plays.

There is no need to do more than mention many of the most popular of Shakespeare's sonnets as bodying forth the accepted ideas of his age on the subject of eternity *via* the printed vernacular word, as in sonnet LV, which opens:

> Not marble nor the gilded monuments
> Of princes shall outlive this pow'rful rhyme;

And because it has lived these centuries we suppose that the authors had no doubts either. But the learned of the age, whatever their attitude to print, had doubts concerning the staying powers of the vernaculars. And some of their doubts appear in Spenser's sonnet (*Amoretti*, LXXV):

> One day I wrote her name upon the strand,
>   But came the waves and washed it away:
>   Agayne I wrote it with a second hand,
>   But came the tyde and made my paynes his prey.
> Vayne man, sayd she, that doest in vaine assay
>   A mortall thing so to immortalize: . . .

"We must remember," writes J. W. Lever in *The Elizabethan Love Sonnet* (p. 57) "to what extent life itself is patterned on literary modes: how men in one age tend to conduct their amours in all earnestness, like the heroes of Stendhal; in another in all flippancy, like the heroes of Noël Coward." But whereas the Elizabethan was, like the Chaucerian "I," able to shift into a variety of public and private roles, so he was able to play with language on various levels. The old oral bond with its flexibility of pitch held between reader and writer. Lever in explaining the nineteenth-century failure to grasp Sidney's procedure comments (p. 57) "It was the atrophy of positive convention during the nineteenth century, and the consequent splitting of the individual into a public and a private self, that explains why so much personal verse of the Victorians evokes a sense of embarrassment."

S. L. Bethell's *Shakespeare and the Popular Dramatic Tradition* takes up this theme thoroughly, showing how the break-up of the older bonds between author and public led nineteenth-century critics "to treat Shakespeare as Ibsen is more appropriately treated: they fastened upon his characters as if they were historical personages, examining their psychology. . . . There was no atempt to consider the historical anomaly by which a naturalistic drama could so quickly have arisen out of a conventional tradition." (pp. 13–14) In the same way Hollywood could rise quickly because it built on the nineteenth century novel.

The portability of the book, like that of the easel-painting, added much to the new cult of individualism.

✱ Very arbitrarily we shall move on to a physical aspect of the printed book that contributed a great deal to individualism. I mean its portability. As easel painting deinstitutionalized pictures, so printing broke library monopoly. Moses Hadas mentions in *Ancilla to Classical Reading* (p. 7) that: "Papyrus made into rolls continued to be the regular material for books until the introduction, mainly by Christians for the convenience of having the Gospels in a single volume, of the codex form and hence of vellum which is more suitable to that form." He adds:

the codex, which is in effect the modern book, consisting of leaves arranged in quires, is obviously more compact than a roll. . . . could be reduced to the convenient size of a pocket edition, and that advantage is usually taken to explain the general adoption of the codex form by Christians in the fourth century . . . but through the third century the great majority of pagan remains are in rolls, while the great majority of Christian works are in codex form. The usual size of the codex was about 10 by 7 inches.

As Febvre and Martin report in *L'Apparition du livre* (p. 126), pocket-size books of devotion and books of hours were perhaps the most numerous among all the books printed in the first century and more of typography: "Moreover, thanks to printing and the multiplication of texts, the book ceased to seem a precious object to be consulted in a library: there was more and more need to be able to carry it about readily in order to refer to it or to read it anywhere at any time."

This very natural inclination towards accessibility and portability went hand in hand with greatly increased reading speeds which were possible with uniform and repeatable type, but not at all with manuscript. The same drive towards accessibility and portability created ever larger publics and markets which were indispensable to the whole Gutenberg undertaking. Febvre and Martin make clear (p. 162) that: "From the first, printing emerged as an industry regulated by the same laws as any other, and the book as a product concocted by men who had their living to make—even when, as with the Aldus family or the Eastiennes, they were at the same time humanists and scholars."

These authors, then, proceed to go into the question of the considerable capital needed for printing and publishing, the very high incidence of commercial failure, and the drive for sales and markets. Even to the sixteenth century eye there was a notable trend of book selection and circulation that boded "l'apparition d'une civilisation de masse et de standardisation." A new kind of consumer world was organized gradually. Out of the entire production of books till 1500, amounting to fifteen to twenty million copies of 30,000 to 35,000 separate publications, by far the greatest proportion, seventy-seven per cent, are in Latin. But just as the printed book had routed the manuscript between 1500 and 1510, so the vernacular was soon to supersede Latin. For it was inevitable that a larger market existed for the printed book within the bounds of a national speech than the international, clerical élite of Latin readers could ever muster. Book production was a heavy capital venture and needed the utmost markets to survive. Febvre and Martin write (p. 479): "Thus the sixteenth century, era of the renewal of ancient culture, was the time when Latin began to lose ground. From 1530 centainly this trend is clear. The reading public . . . becomes therefore more and more a lay public—often of women and the middle class among whom many were not familiar with Latin."

The problem of "what the public wants" is central to printing from the first. But just as book format long retained the characteristics of manuscript appearance, so bookselling long depended on the medieval fair as an outlet. "The trade in books throughout the Middle Ages, it need scarcely be stressed, was largely a second-hand business; only with the invention of printing did a new-book market become a commonplace."[72] The meaning of the medieval book trade as a second-hand operation can only be grasped in our time through the parallel that the market in great paintings is largely a second-hand market. For, in general, paintings and antiques are in the category of the manuscript book before printing. For the printed book retaining a manuscript format, this was necessary if only for sales, since readers were trained and disposed to the manuscript mode. Buhler has fascinating details (p. 16) about the early habit of sending printed books to the scribe to be copied, so that the student of the earliest printing would be well advised if he viewed the new invention, as the first printers did, as simply another form of writing.

The uniformity and repeatability of print created the political arithmetic of the seventeenth century and the hedonistic calculus of the eighteenth.

✻ Nevertheless, there was an inherent principle of uniformity in print just as there was the tendency for a manuscript book to become "a leisurely accumulation of heterogeneous texts." The principle of uniformity and repeatability was to find ever fuller expression as print raised visual quantification to eminence. By the seventeenth century we find ourselves in a world that speaks of "political arithmetic," which carries the separation of functions a step past Machiavelli. If Machiavelli could argue in the early sixteenth

[72]Buhler, *The Fifteenth Century Book*, p. 33.

century that "there is one rule for business and another for private life,"[73] he was really recording the effect and meaning of the printed word in separating writer and reader, producer and consumer, ruler and ruled, into sharply defined categories. Before printing these operations were much interfused in the same way as the scribe as producer was involved in reading, and the student was involved in the making of the books he studied.

It cannot be easily grasped, else it had been explained long ago, that the mechanical principle of visual uniformity and repeatability which is inherent in the press steadily extended itself to include many kinds of organization. Malynes wrote in his *Lex Mercatoria* (1622): "We see how one thing driveth or enforceth another, like as in a clock where there are many wheels, the first wheel being stirred driveth the next and that the third and so forth, till the last that moveth the instrument that striketh the clock; or like as in a press going in a strait, where the foremost is driven by him that is next to him, and the next by him that followeth him."[74]

More than two hundred years before Thomas Huxley's idea of the educated mind as a "clear cold logic engine with all its parts of equal strength" we encounter the principle of movable types and replaceable parts extended to social organization. But let us note that it is a meaningless principle where the uniform processing of minds by the habit of reading the printed word has not occurred. In a word, individualism, whether in the passive atomistic sence of drilled uniformed soldiery or in the active aggressive sense of private initiative and self-expression, alike assumes a prior technology of homogeneous citizens. This scabrous paradox has haunted literate men in every age. In the later nineteenth century it expressed itself in the emancipation of women which was accomplished by assigning men and women to the same jobs. It was thereby hoped they would be free. But this mechanical operation of the human spirit was also felt and furiously resisted in the first age of print. "One might almost say," writes Leo Lowenthal in *Literature and the Image of Man* (p. 41), "that the prevailing philosophy of human nature since the Renaissance has been based on the conception of each individual as a "deviant case whose existence consists very largely in his efforts to assert his personality against the restrictive and levelling claims of society."

Before considering the evidence from the world of Cervantes offered by Lowenthal, here are two peripheral items that also bear on these issues. Writing of Oxford University in the sixteenth century, C. E. Mallet opens his second volume of his *History of the University of Oxford*:

> The year 1485 marks an epoch in history at Oxford as elsewhere. Under the Tudors the mediaeval university passed imperceptibly away. The old customs lost to some extent their meaning. The old views of education

[73]R. H. Tawney, *Religion and the Rise of Capitalism*, p. 156.
[74]Quoted in *ibid.*, p. 151.

altered. The old lawless democratic spirit yielded unwillingly to discipline. The Renaissance set up new ideals of learning. The Reformation brought new energies to theological debate. The old Halls were fast disappearing. The Colleges, some of which had begun life as struggling little communities of theologians or Arts-students, grew into larger and wealthier societies, with a fuller share in the government of the place. Undergraduate Commoners, as we know them, came more definitely into view. Several Colleges had from the beginning elected undergraduates as Fellows, and in some cases young students had been admitted on a special footing. Merton had its *parvuli*. Queen's had its Poor Boys. Magdalen had some very young Demies. Poor Colleges had eked out their revenues by admitting boarders. Waynflete had sanctioned a system of Gentlemen Commoners, which Wykehan had been unwilling to permit. But it was not till the sixteenth century, when the Colleges became recognized centres of teaching, when the lectures in Schools Street were going out of fashion, when the training of priests was gradually ceasing to be the chief aim of Oxford education, and when, after the perils of the Reformation, the expansion of Oxford on new lines began, that the great class of undergraduate Commoners, with no direct share in College endowments, arose to take the College courts and gardens for their own.

The "old lawless democratic spirit" has reference to the decentralist, oral organization of society that preceded print and nationalism. Centralism of the newly released national energies required greatly increased interdependence. Here the printed text books made themselves felt very soon. And just as papyrus made the Roman road, print made for the speed and visual precision felt in the new monarchies of the Renaissance. It is fascinating to move ahead a century and to Cambridge to observe the strong centralist action of the printed book. Christopher Wordsworth tells the story of the strange reversals and interplay of the written and the oral modes in his *Scholae academicae: Some Account of the Studies at the English Universities in the Eighteenth Century* (p. 16):

Before entering upon the details of the university exercises and examinations, we ought to try to divest ourselves of a modern opinion, that study exists for examinations rather than examinations for study. Indeed, to apply the measure of their prevalence and efficiency to the education of past generations, would be to commit an anachronism.

We might look in vain for any public examination to justify the learning and research which in the seventeenth century made English students famous:—whose efforts were fostered, rather by the encouragement of tutors and friends, than by the disputations in the schools. Examinations in our modern acceptation there were none. As books became cheaper, the quicker and the more diligent students discovered that they could acquire knowledge for themselves where previous generations had been dependent on the oral teaching. Then arose the necessity of examination, and as this has come to be more scientifically conducted, and its results to be more public, and at last in a sense marketable, there has been a fresh demand for oral instruction.

Wordsworth is describing the rise of centralist examining which arose from access to decentralized learning. For it was easy under print conditions for a student to read in areas unvisited by his examiners. But the principle that the portable, uniform book creates the centralized uniform exam (in place of the older oral test) is one that applies at all levels. The printed word, we shall see, has quite strange organizational effects on the vernacular. And the eighteenth century business man whose political arithmetic was based on visual quantity, or the eighteenth century business man whose speculations were built on the mechanism of "the hedonistic calculus," alike relate to the uniform repeatability of print technology. Yet the calculating business man who used this principle at every turn, in production and distribution, fought its logic of centralism with anarchic bitterness. So Lowenthal observes in *Literature and the Image of Man* (pp. 41–2):

Very quickly after the downfall of feudalism, the literary artist developed a liking for figures who look at society not from the viewpoint of a participant but from the vantage point of an outsider. The further these figures are removed from the affairs of society, the greater is likely to be their social failure (which is almost, but not quite, a tautology); they are also more prone, as a result, to display unspoiled, uninhibited, and highly individual characteristics. The conditions—whatever they may be—that remove them from the affairs of society are viewed as the conditions that bring them closer to their inner natures. The more primitive and "natural" the setting into which they are cast, the better are they able to develop and maintain their humaneness.

Cervantes presents an array of such marginal figures and situations. There are, first, the mad people—Don Quixote and the Man of Glass—who though still operating in the social world are in continuous conflict with it by word and deed. Then in *Rinconete and Cortadillo*, we meet petty crooks and beggars who live parasitically off the social world. One step farther from the center we find the gypsies presented in *The Little Gypsy* (*La Gitana*); they are completely outside the main stream of affairs. Finally, we have the situation wherein Don Quixote, the marginal Knight, speaks to the simple goatherds about the Golden Age in which the unity of man and nature reaches its fulfillment.

To this catalog of marginal types and situations, we add the figure of woman, who almost throughout the entire course of modern literature from Cervantes to Ibsen has been treated as an individual closer to her own nature and truth than are men, since man is indissolubly bound up with the competitive processes of work, in contrast to the enforced removal of woman from professional activities. Not accidentally does Cervantes use Dulcinea as a symbol of human creativity.

211

The typographic logic created the outsider, the alienated man, as the type of integral, that is, intuitive and irrational, man.

✱ If Lowenthal is right, we have spent much energy and fury in recent centuries in destroying oral culture by print technology so that the uniformly processed individuals of commercial society can return to oral marginal spots as tourists and consumers, whether geographical or artistic. The eighteenth century began to spend its time at the Metropolitan Opera as it were. Having refined and homogenized and visualised itself to the point of self-alienation, it hied off to the Hebrides, the Indies, the Americas, the transcendental imagination, and especially to childhood, in search of natural man. D. H. Lawrence and others repeated this Odyssey in our day with much acclaim. It is a performance of automatic kind. Art tends to become a mere compensation for a top-sided life.

Lowenthal gives an excellent account of the new alienated man who refused to join the consumer rush and remained on the old feudal and oral margins of society. To the new crowd of visually and consumer-oriented society these marginal figures have great appeal.

"The figure of woman" joins this picturesque group of outsiders. Her haptic bias, her intuition, her wholeness entitle her to marginal status as a Romantic figure. Byron understood that men must be homogenized, splintered, specialists. But not women:

> Man's love is of man's life a thing apart,
> 'Tis woman's whole existence.

"Woman," wrote Meredith in 1859, "is the last thing to be civilized by man." By 1929 she had been homogenized by means of the movies and photo advertizing. Mere print had not been intense enough to reduce her to uniformity and repeatability and specialism.

What a fate, to be integral and whole in a fragmented and visual flat-land! But the homogenization of women was finally effected in the twentieth century after the perfection of photo-engraving permitted them to pursue the same courses of visual uniformity and repeatability that print had brought to men. I have devoted an entire volume, *The Mechanical Bride*, to this theme.

Pictorial advertisements and movies finally did for women what print technology had done for men centuries before. When raising these themes, one is beset by queries of the "Was it a good thing?" variety. Such questions seem to mean: "How should we *feel* about these matters?" They never suggest that anything could be done about them. Surely, understanding the formal dynamic or configuration of such events is the prime concern. That is really doing something. Control and action in terms of values must follow understanding. Value judgments have long been allowed to create a moral fog around technological change such as renders understanding impossible.

But how were people prevented during these centuries from understanding what they were doing to themselves by means of visual quantification and fragmentation? Boasts on all hands of the segmental analysis of every function and operation of person and society, and wild laments that this splintering is also affecting the inner life! The split man enters the scene as Mr. Entirely Normal. He is still here in that capacity, though increasingly in a panic about electric media, as he might well be. For the marginal man is a centre-without-a-margin, an integral independent type. That is, he is feudal, "aristocratic," and oral. The new urban or bourgeois man is centre-margin oriented. That is, he is visual, concerned about appearances and conformity or respectability. As he becomes individual or uniform, he becomes homogeneous. He belongs. And he creates and craves large centralist groupings, starting with nationalism.

Cervantes confronted typographic man in the figure of Don Quixote.

✳ There is no need to go into Cervantes' novel in detail, since it is well known. But Cervantes, in his life and in his work, presents the case of the feudal man confronted with a newly visually quantified and homogeneous world. In Lowenthal's *Literature and the Image of Man* (p. 21) we read how

Fundamentally the themes of his novel are those of an old way of life being replaced by a new order. Cervantes stresses the resulting conflicts in two ways: through the struggles of the Knight, and through the contrast between him and Sancho Panza. Don Quixote lives in a phantasy world of the vanishing feudal hierarchy; the people with whom he deals, however, are merchants, minor functionaries in the government, unimportant intellectuals —in short, they are, like Sancho, people who want to get ahead in the world and, therefore, direct their energies to the things which will bring them profit.

213

In choosing the great folios of medieval romances as his *reality*, Cervantes establishes an ambivalence of the utmost use. For print was the *new* reality and it was print that made the old reality of the Middle Ages popularly available for the first time. Thus, in our day, movie and TV have given a dimension and reality to the American frontier in all our lives, such as it had for very few people in historical fact. Next to the Books of Hours, medieval romances were by far the biggest item on the market. And whereas the Books of Hours were preferred in pocket editions, the romances came in folio.[75]

Lowenthal (p. 22) makes some further observations about Don Quixote that are especially relevant here for the understanding of print culture:

One might say that Don Quixote is the first figure in Renaissance literature who seeks by action to bring the world into harmony with his own plans and ideals. Cervantes' irony lies in the fact that while overtly his hero battles against the new (the early manifestations of middle-class life) in the name of the old (the feudal system), actually he attempts to sanction a new principle. This principle consists, basically, in the autonomy of individual thinking and feeling. The dynamics of society have come to demand a continuous and active transformation of reality; the world must be perpetually constructed anew. Don Quixote recreates his world even though he does so in a phantastic and solipsistic fashion. The honor for which he enters the lists is the product of his thinking, not of socially established and accepted values. He defends those whom he considers worthy of his protection and assails those he believes to be wicked. In this sense he is a rationalist as well as an idealist.

Enough has been said earlier apropos of the drive towards applied knowledge inherent in print technology to give additional significance to Lowenthal's words. This is the situation which David Riesman highlights in *The Lonely Crowd* as the pattern of "inner direction." Inner direction towards remote goals is inseparable from print culture and the perspective and vanishing point organization of space that are part of it. The fact that no such organization of space or culture is compatible with electronic simultaneity is what has involved Western man in new anxiety for a century. In addition to the solipsism and solitude and uniformity of print culture, there is now the immediate electric pressure for its dissolution.

In a study of *The Vanishing Adolescent* (p. 25) Edgar Z. Friedenberg casts the adolescent in the role of Don Quixote:

The process of becoming an American, as it goes on in high school, tends to be a process of renunciation of differences. This conflicts directly, of course, with the adolescent need for self-definition; but the conflict is so masked in institutionalized gaiety that the adolescent himself usually does not become aware of it. He must still deal with the alienation it engenders.

[75]See *L'Apparition du livre*, pp. 127, 429.

He may do this by marginal differentiation, like Riesman's glad-handing boy with the special greeting style. He may do it by erupting into bouts of occasionally violent silliness, which does not make him seem queer to other people because it is unconsciously recognized as a form of self-abnegation rather than self-assertion, and is not, therefore, threatening. He may, if he has sufficient ego-strength, become the adolescent equivalent of a genuine revolutionary—rather than a rebel—that is, he may actually succeed in rejecting the folkways of the school without identifying with them and becoming guilty and raucous; . . .

The school system, custodian of print culture, has no place for the rugged individual. It is, indeed, the homogenizing hopper into which we toss our integral tots for processing. Some of the most memorable poems of our language concern Wordsworth's Lucy, on the one hand, and Yeats *Among School-children*, on the other. Both of these are much concerned with the poignant conflict between the order of enclosed and uniform systems and the spontaneity of the world of spirit. The inherent conflict that Friedenberg defines so well is at the centre of print technology itself, which isolates the individual yet also creates massive groupings by means of vernacular nationalism. Friedenberg is speaking of a situation inherent in movable types from the first when he says (p. 54):

We conceive our country as having achieved a position of leadership and dominance by carefully subordinating personal and ethnic disparity to the interests of teamwork in a colossal technical and administrative enterprise. For us, a personal conformity is a moral mandate. When we insist on taking a personal stand and bucking the system, we feel not only anxious but guilty as well.

Donne's mention of his "hydroptic immoderate thirst for humane learning and languages" beset countless men in the sixteenth century. There was a furious consumer urge in that first age of mass production such as struck the United States in the 1920's with the movies and radio. The same consumer urge is only now reaching Europe and England after the Second World War. It is a phenomenon that goes with high-intensity visual stress and organization of experience.

Typographic man can express but is helpless to read the configurations of print technology.

✱ The subject of nationalism and print has been held back until now lest it usurp the entire book. It will be the easier to handle the complex of issues now that we have encountered similar groupings of issues in quite different areas of experience. The present volume to this point might be regarded as a gloss on a single text of Harold Innis: "The effect of the discovery of printing was evident in the savage religious wars of the sixteenth and seventeenth centuries. Application of power to communication industries hastened the consolidation of vernaculars, the rise of nationalism, revolution, and new outbreaks of savagery in the twentieth century."[76]

Innis in his later work tackled configurations rather than sequences of events in their interplay. In his earlier work, like *The Fur Trade in Canada*, he had been a conventional arranger of evidence in perspective packages of inert, static components. As he began to understand the structuring powers of media to impose their assumptions subliminally, he strove to record the interaction of media and cultures: "Improvements in communication, like the Irish bull of the bridge which separated the two countries, make for increased difficulties of understanding. The cable compelled contraction of language and facilitated a rapid widening between the English and American languages. In the vast realm of fiction in the Anglo-Saxon world, the influence of the newspaper . . . the cinema and the radio has been evident in the best seller and the creation of special classes of readers with little prospect of communication between them."[77] Innis is here speaking with ease of the interplay among literary and non-literary forms exactly as in the earlier quotation he was speaking of the interplay between the mechanization of the vernaculars and the rise of military, nationalist states.

There is nothing wilful or arbitrary about the Innis mode of expression. Were it to be translated into perspective prose, it would not only require huge space, but the insight into the modes of interplay among forms of organization would also be lost. Innis sacrificed point of view and prestige to his sense of the urgent need for insight. A point of view can be a dangerous luxury when substituted for insight and understanding. As Innis got more insights he abandoned any mere point of view in his presentation of knowl-

[76] *The Bias of Communication*, p. 29.
[77] *Ibid.*, p. 28.

edge. When he interrelates the development of the steam press with "the consolidation of the vernaculars" and the rise of nationalism and revolution he is not reporting anybody's point of view, least of all his own. He is setting up a mosaic configuration or galaxy for insight. It was a prime effect of print in altering human sense ratios, that it substituted static point of view for insight into causal dynamics. We shall consider this further on. But Innis makes no effort to "spell out" the interrelations between the components in his galaxy. He offers no consumer packages in his later work, but only do-it-yourself kits, like a symbolist poet or an abstract painter. *Literature and the Press* by Louis Dudek provides a straight-away perspective picture of the rise of the steam press, but the effects on language, on war, and on the emergence of new literary forms are not mentioned since they would require a non-literary or mythic form in order to be explained at all.

James Joyce devised an entirely new form of expression in *Finnegans Wake* in order to capture the complex interplay of factors in the very configuration that we are considering here. In the following passage "fowl" includes *La Patrie*, the Great Mother, and "foule" or mob created by the homogenizing powers of print. When, therefore, it is mentioned that "man will become dirigible," the way in which this happens is simply an inflation by accretion of homogeneous units.

Lead, kindly fowl! They always did: ask the ages. What bird has done yesterday man may do next year, be it fly, be it moult, be it hatch, be it agreement in the nest. For her socioscientific sense is sound as a bell, sir, her volucrine automutativeness right on normalcy: she knows, she just feels she was kind of born to lay and love eggs (trust her to propagate the species and hoosh her fluffballs safe through din and danger!); lastly but mostly, in her genesic field it is all game and no gammon, she is ladylike in everything she does and plays the gentleman's part every time. Let us auspice it! Yes, before all this has time to end the golden age must return with its vengeance. Man will become dirigible, Ague will be rejuvenated, woman with her ridiculous white burden will reach by one step sublime incubation, the manewanting human lioness with her dishorned discipular manram will lie down together publicly flank upon fleece. No, assuredly, they are not justified, those gloompourers who grouse that letters have never been quite their old selves again since that weird weekday in bleak Janiveer (yet how palmy date in a waste's oasis!) when to the shock of both, Biddy Doran looked ad literature. (p. 112)

It may well be that print and nationalism are axiological or co-ordinate, simply because by print a people *sees* itself for the first time. The vernacular in appearing in high visual definition affords a glimpse of social unity co-extensive with vernacular boundaries. And more people have experienced this visual unity of their native tongues *via* the newspaper than through the book. Carlton Hayes is most helpful in his *Historical Evolution of Modern Nationalism* (p. 293):

Nor is it at all certain that the "masses" in any country have been directly responsible for the rise of modern nationalism. The movement appears to have gotten under way first among the "intellectual" classes and to have received decisive impetus from the support of the middle classes. In England, where physical environment and political and religious circumstances were peculiarly favorable, a strong national consciousness developed considerable before the eighteenth century, and it may be that English nationalism did spring more or less spontaneously out of mass feeling and sentiment. Even here, the matter is debatable, though it is not within the scope of the present work to indicate the pros and cons in any detail.

Outside of England, however, there can be little question that in the first half of the eighteenth century the masses of Europe, as well as of Asia and America, whilst possessing some consciousness of nationality, thought of themselves chiefly as belonging to a province or town or an empire, rather than to a national state, and made no serious or effective protest against being transferred from one political domain to another, and that their later thought and action as nationalities were taught them by the intellectual and middle classes of their respective countries.

The historians, although aware that nationalism originated in the sixteenth century, have yet no explanation of this passion that preceded theory.

✱ It is important nowadays to understand why there cannot be nationalism where there has not first been an experience of a vernacular in printed form. Hayes here indicates that in non-literate areas, ferment and social action of a tribal kind is not to be confused with nationalism. Hayes had no clue about the rise of visual quantification in the later Middle Ages, nor of the visual effects of print on individualism and nationalism in the sixteenth century. He was keenly aware (p. 4) that there was no nationalism in the modern sense before the sixteenth century when the modern state system of Europe emerged:

The states which composed this new system were very different from the "nations" of primitive tribesmen. They were much larger and much looser. They were more in the nature of agglomerations of peoples with diverse languages and dialects and with divergent traditions and institutions. In most of them a particular people, a particular nationality, constituted the core and furnished the governing class and the official language, and in all of them minority as well as majority nationalities usually evinced a high degree of loyalty to a common monarch or "sovereign". They were referred to, in contradistinction to the older comprehensive Empire, as "nations" or "national states", and popular loyalty to their sovereigns has sometimes been described as "nationalism". But it must rigidly be borne in mind that they were not "nations" in the primitive tribal sense and that their "nationalism" had other foundation than that of present-day nationalism. The European "nations" of the sixteenth century were more akin to small empires than to large tribes.

Hayes is mystified by the peculiar character of modern internationalism which began with the primitivistic obsession of the eighteenth century: "Modern nationalism signifies a more or less purposeful effort to revive primitive tribalism on an enlarged and more artificial scale." (p. 12) But since the telegraph and radio, the globe has contracted, spatially, into a single large village. Tribalism is our only resource since the electro-magnetic discovery.

Alexis de Tocqueville in his *L'Ancien Régime* (p. 156) shows himself much more aware than Hayes of the causes and effects of nationalism. Not only had accustomation to print tended to create a uniform type of citizen but the political education of France was carried on by men of letters:

The writers furnished not merely their ideas to the people who made it, but also their temperament and disposition. As a result of their long education, in the absence of any other instructors, coupled with their profound ignorance of practice, all Frenchmen from reading their books finally contracted the instincts, the turn of mind, the tastes and even the eccentricities natural to those who write. To such an extent was this the case that, when finally they had to act, they transported into politics all the habits of literature.

A study of the history of our Revolution shows that it was conducted precisely in the same spirit, that has caused so many abstract books to be written on government—the same attraction for general theories, complete systems of legislation, and exact symmetry in the laws; the same contempt for existing facts; the same confidence in theory, the same taste for the original, the ingenious and the novel in institutions; the same desire to rebuild at once the entire constitution according to the rules of logic and a single plan, in the place of trying to amend it in its parts.

The mysterious "logic" mania of the French is easily recognizable as the visual component in isolation from other factors. Similarly, visual quantification as a collective mania yields the French Revolutionary military mania. Here the uniform and the homogeneous are *most* visibly at one. The modern soldier is especially the instance of the movable type, the replaceable part, the classic Gutenberg phenomenon. De Tocqueville has much to say of this in his *European Revolution* (pp. 140–1):

What the republican partisans took for love of the Republic was chiefly a love of the Revolution. In fact, the army was the only class in France in which every member, without exception, had gained by the Revolution and had a personal interest in supporting it. To it every officer owed his rank, and every soldier his chance of becoming an officer. The army was, in truth, the standing Revolution in arms. If it still fiercely exclaimed: "Long live the Republic!" this was really a challenge to the old regime, whose friends cried: "Long live the King!" Deep down the army cared nothing for civic liberties. Hatred of foreigners and a love of his native land are generally the only elements of the soldier's patriotism even in free nations; still more must this have been the case at that time in France. The army, like almost every other army in the world, could make nothing of the slow and complicated gyrations of a representative government; it detested and despised the Assembly, because it understood only powers that were strong and simple; all it wanted was national independence and victories.

Nationalism insists on equal rights among individuals and among nations alike.

✱ If rigorous centralism is a main feature of literacy and print, no less so is the eager assertion of individual rights. De Tocqueville notes in *The European Revolution* (p. 103): "In 1788 and 1789 all the pamphlets published even those by the future revolutionaries themselves, are opposed to centralization and in favor of local rule." He adds a little later (pp. 112–13) a note that indicates that, like Harold Innis, he had the habit not of presenting a picture of events but of meditating on their inner causes: "What is so extraordinary in the French Revolution is not so much the procedures it employed as the ideas it conceived. The new and astonishing thing is that so many nations should arrive at a stage where such procedures could be so efficiently employed and such ideas so easily accepted."

At this point it would be a joy to have a de Tocqueville to take over the writing of *The Gutenberg Galaxy*, for his mode of thought is the one that is here followed so far as possible. He defines his method perfectly when speaking of the old regime (p. 136): "I myself have tried to judge it not from my own ideas but from the feelings which it inspired in those who endured and then destroyed it."

Nationalism depends upon or derives from the "fixed point of view" that arrives with print, perspective, and visual quantification. But a fixed point of view can be collective or individual or both, thus causing great diversity of clash and outlook. Hayes writes in his *Historical Evolution of Modern*

Nationalism (p. 135): "By 1815 liberal nationalism was a fairly definite intellectual movement throughout western and central Europe. . . . It was surely not aristocratic, and, though paying lip-service to democracy, it tended to be middle-class." It is his next sentences that indicate the "fixed point of view" for the state, on one hand, and the individual, on the other: "It stressed the absolute sovereignty of the national state, but sought to limit the implications of this principle by stressing individual liberties—political, economic, and religious—within each national state."

The inevitable condition of fixed viewpoints arising from the visual stress in nationalism also led, writes Hayes (p. 178), to the principle that: "Because the national state does not belong to the citizens of any particular generation, it must not be revolutionized." This principle is made especially manifest in the written-visual fixity of the American Constitution, whereas pre-print and pre-industrial forms of political order have no such pattern.

Early in his book (pp. 10–11), Hayes points to the excitement about the discovery of the "equal" principle as it applied both to groups and individuals: equal rights of individuals to determine the state and government to which they would belong, equal rights of individual nations to self-determination.

In practice, therefore, nationalism does not develop its full potential of uniform lateral extension until after the application of print technology to the methods of work and production. Hayes can see the logic of this, but is puzzled to see how nationalism ever could have started in agrarian societies. He is entirely without perception of the role of print technology in disposing men to the uniform, repeatable patterns of association:

The putting forth of nationalist doctrines was one of the mental exercises of the eighteenth century. Primarily it was the work of intellectuals and an expression of current intellectual interests and tendencies. But what has chiefly enabled nationalist doctrines, once put forth, to take hold of the masses of mankind since then, has been a marvellous improvement in the mechanical arts, an improvement which is nowadays termed the Industrial Revolution—the invention of labor-saving machinery, the perfecting of the steam-engine and other motive devices, the extensive use of coal and iron, the mass production of commodities, and the speeding up of transportation and communication. This Industrial Revolution began in a large way in England about a hundred and forty years ago—about the time of the Jacobin Revolution in France—and its intensification in England and its extension throughout the world have paralleled the rise and spread of popular devotion to doctrines of nationalism. The doctrines themselves were originally crystallized in an agricultural society, before the advent of the new industrial machinery, but their acceptance has accompanied, and their complete triumph has followed, the introduction of the new machinery and the transition from an agricultural to an industrial society. It seems to have been a perfectly natural development. (pp. 232–3)

221

Since industrialism even the arts, philosophy, and religion have been patterned by nationalism. Hayes writes (p. 289):

> For a century and a half major improvements in technology, in the industrial arts, and in material comfort, as well as most developments in the realms of intellect and aesthetics, have been yoked to the service of nationalism. The Industrial Revolution, despite its cosmopolitan potentialities, has been largely nationalized in actual fact. Modern scholarship, despite its scientific claims and its ubiquitous nature, has been preponderantly enlisted in support of nationalism. Philosophies which in origin were not expressly nationalist and were sometimes definitely intended to be anti-nationalist, philosophies such as Christianity, Liberalism, Marxism, and the systems of Hegel, Comte, and Nietzche, have been copiously drawn upon and frequently distorted for nationalist purposes. The plastic arts, music, and belles-lettres, despite their universal appeal, have become increasingly the product or the pride of national patriots. So much is nationalism a commonplace in the modes of thought and action of the civilized populations of the contemporary world that most men take nationalism for granted. Without serious reflection they imagine it to be the most natural thing in the universe and assume that it must always have existed.

What has given such a vogue to nationalism in recent times? That is the first major question to be raised concerning this most vital phenomenon.

The citizen armies of Cromwell and Napoleon were the ideal manifestations of the new technology.

✷ As an historian Hayes knows well (p. 290) that there is a mystery about nationalism. It never existed before the Renaissance, and it was never originated as an idea: "But the philosophers of nationalism did not make its vogue. The vogue was there when they appeared on the scene. They merely expressed and gave some emphasis and guidance to it. For the historian they are extremely useful in that they afford him vivid illustrations of current tendencies in nationalist thought." He ridicules the idea that "the masses of mankind are instinctively nationalist," or that nationalism is natural at all: "During much the longest periods of recorded history the groups to which individuals have been predominantly loyal have been tribes, clans, cities, provinces, manors, guilds, or polyglot empires. Yet it is nationalism, far more than any other expression of human gregariousness, which has come to the fore in modern times." (p. 292)

The answer to Hayes' problem is in the efficacy of the printed word in first visualizing the vernacular and then creating that homogeneous mode of association which permits modern industry, markets, and the visual enjoyment of national status. He writes (p. 61):

> The "nation in arms" was one Jacobin concept of great significance for nationalist propaganda. The "nation in public schools" was another. Previous to the French Revolution, it had long and generally been held that children belonged to their parents and that it was for parents to determine what schooling, if any, their children should have.

Liberty, equality and fraternity found their most natural, if least imaginative, expression in the uniformity of the revolutionary citizen armies. They were not only exact repetitions of the printed page, but of the assembly line. The English were much ahead of Europe in nationalism as in industrialism, and in typographical organization of the army. Cromwell's Ironsides were in action a hundred and fifty years before the Jacobin armies.

> England preceded all countries on the Continent in the development of an acute popular consciousness of common nationality. Long before the French Revolution at a time when Frenchmen had thought of themselves primarily as Burgundians or Gascons or Provencals, Englishmen had been Englishmen and had rallied with real national patriotism to the secularizations of Henry VIII and the exploits of Elizabeth. There had been a nationalist spirit in the political philosophy of Milton and Locke hardly paralleled by their contemporaries on the Continent, and Bolingbroke, the Englishman, was a pioneer in the expounding of a formal doctrine of nationalism. It was natural, therefore, that any Englishman who would enter the lists against Jacobinism should be arrayed in trappings of nationalism.

So writes Hayes on page 86 of *Historical Evolution of Modern Nationalism*. Similar testimony of English precedence in national unity comes from a sixteenth century Venetian ambassador:

> In 1557 the Venetian ambassador Giovanni Micheli wrote to his government: 'In so far as religion [in England] is concerned, the example and authority of the sovereign are all-important. The English esteem and practise their religion only in so far as thereby they fulfil their duty as subjects towards their ruler; they live as he lives, believe what he believes: in one word, do everything he commands . . . they would accept Mohammedanism or Judaism if the king believed in it, and it was the king's will that they should believe in it.' To a foreign observer the religious behaviour of the English at that time looked most peculiar. Religious uniformity remained the rule, as on the Continent, but religion changed with each sovereign. After having been schismatic under Henry VIII, and Protestant under Edward VI, England became again, and without any serious upheaval, Roman Catholic under Mary Tudor.[78]

[78]Joseph Leclerc, *Toleration and the Reformation*, vol. II, p. 349.

Merely nationalist excitement about the English vernacular was embedded in religious controversy in the sixteenth and seventeenth centuries. Religion and politics had become so interfused as to be indistinguishable. The Puritan James Hunt wrote in 1642:

> For henceforth no man shall need the Universities,
> For to learn the wisedom of the wise;
> For there are very few mysteries in the Gospel
> that be so strong
> But they may be unfolded by the plaine
> true English tongue.[79]

At the present time the concern among Catholic liturgists about the question of the mass in English, is utterly confused by the new media such as movie, radio, and TV. For the social role and function of a vernacular are constantly being shifted by the means of interrelating it to private life. Thus the question of the mass in English today is as confused as the role of English in religion and politics in the sixteenth century. Nobody will question that it was the medium of print that then gave the vernaculars new functions, and utterly changed the uses and relevance of Latin. By the eighteenth century, on the other hand, the relations between language, religion, and politics had clarified. Language had become religion, in France at least.

If the original Jacobins were sluggish in translating all their theories of education into action, they were prompt to recognize the significance of language as the basis of nationality and to try to compel all inhabitants of France to use the French language. They contended that successful rule by "the people" and united action by the nation were dependent, not only on a certain uniformity of habits and customs, but even more on an identity of ideas and ideals which could be effected by speeches, the printing press, and other instruments of education, provided that these employed one and the same language. Confronted with the historic fact that France was not a linguistic unit—that, in addition to widely variant dialects in different parts of the country, "foreign" languages were spoken in the west by Bretons, in the south by Provencals, Basques, and Corsicans, in the north by Flemings, and in the northeast by Alsatian Germans—they resolved to stamp out the dialects and the foreign languages and to force every French citizen to know and employ the French language.[80]

Hayes in this passage makes it quite clear that the passion behind the vernacular drive was homogenization, a matter which the Anglo-Saxon world has always understood is much better managed by price rivalry and consumer goods. In a word, the English world understands that print means applied knowledge, while the Latin world has always held print at bay,

[79]Cited by Jones in *The Triumph of the English Language*, p. 321.
[80]Hayes, *Historical Evolution of Modern Nationalism*, pp. 63–4.

preferring to use it to enhance the drama of oral disputation or military virtuosity. Nowhere can this deep rejection of the print message be better seen than in *The Structure of Spanish History* by Americo Castro.

The Spaniards had been immunized against typography by their age-old quarrel with the Moors.

✱ As the Jacobeans got the military message of print as lineal levelling aggression, the English were applying print to production and markets. So while the English were extending print to prices, shop-keeping and do-it-yourself hand books of every kind, the Spaniards had abstracted from print the message of gigantism and supra-human effort. The Spaniard bypassed or ignored the entire aspect of print as applied, as levelling, homogenizing. There is no intent or wish to set up any other standards. Castro writes (p. 620):

They rebel against standards as such. There is a kind of personal separatism.
... If I had to locate, as it were, that which is most characteristic of Hispanic life, I would put it between the acceptance of inertia and the willful outburst through which the person reveals what there is—be it something insignificant or something of value—in the depths of his soul, as if he were his own theatre. Visible examples of this enormous contrast are the peasant and the conquistador—insensibility to the political and social situations and the insurrections and convulsions of the blind mass of the people, destroying everything; apathy toward the transformation of natural resources into wealth and the use of public wealth as if it were private; archaic and static ways of living and the hasty adoption of modern devices produced outside of Spain. The electric light, the typewriter, and the fountain-pen were popularized in Spain more quickly than in France. On the plane of the highest human values we find a manifestation of this sharp contrast in the poetic inwardness of Saint John of the Cross or of the quietist Miguel de Molinos, and the series of daring assaults to be found in Quevedo and Góngora, or in Goya's artistic transformation of the outer world.

The Spaniards are not in the least averse to the acceptance and import of things and ideas from outside: "In 1480 Ferdinand and Isabella authorized the free importation of foreign books." Later they were subjected to censorship, and Spain began to attenuate its lines of communication with the rest of the world. Castro explains (p. 664) how:

The Spaniards have expanded and contracted the objective zone of their life in a dramatic rhythm: they are not inclined to industrial activity, nor will they agree to live without industry. At certain moments the outward sallies, the efforts to break out of themselves, ... give rise to problems that have no "normal" mode of solution.

Perhaps the most spectacular effect of print in the Renaissance was the militant campaign of counter-Reformation mounted by Spaniards like St. Ignatius Loyola. His religious order, the first since printing began, embodied much visual stress in religious exercises, intense literary training, and military homogeneity of organization. Writing his *Apologie of Two English Seminaries* in 1581, Cardinal Allen explains the new militancy of missionary zeal among Catholics: "Books opened the way." The book as a militant missionary affair did appeal to the Spaniard who yet rejected commerce and industry. The Spaniard, according to Castro (p. 624), has always manifested hostility towards the written word:

The Spaniard wants a system of justice based on value judgements, not on firm and rationally deduced principles. It is not accident that casuistry was fostered by the Spanish Jesuits, nor that the Frenchman Pascal should find this casuistry perversely immoral. It is written laws that the Spaniard fears and despises: "I find twenty chapters against you and only one that is with you," says a lawyer to the unfortunate litigant in the *Rimado de palacio* by Pero López de Ayala ...

It is one of Castro's principal themes that the structure of Spanish history is axiologically inclined between the literate West and the oral Moorish East. "Even Cervantes expresses more than once a longing for Moorish justice, in spite of his long captivity in Algiers." And it was the Moorish strain which immunized the Spaniards against the visual quantifications of literacy. Study of the Spanish case offers especially significant light on the diverse effects of literacy as print technology encounters unique cultures. The Spanish preference for living at the passionate centre may have an analogue in Russia where, unlike Japan, the effects of print technology have not extended to the discovery of consumer goods. And the oral Russian attitude to technology has a passionate character that may inure them, too, against the uses of literacy.

Castro has a fine essay on "Incarnation in Don Quixote" in *Cervantes across the Centuries* (pp. 136–78) in which he observes that: "The preoccupation with noting the effects of reading upon the vital processes of readers is characteristically Spanish." Not only is this very fact the principal theme of Don Quixote:

The effect of books (religious or profane) upon the life of the reader is an ever-present theme in the letters of the 16th century. The youth of Ignatius of Loyola was spent very much in tune with the novels of chivalry, which "he was very curious and fond of reading. But chance placed in his hands a life of Christ and a *Flos Sanctorum*. Not only did he begin to find enjoyment, but his heart also began to change, and he was filled with the desire to imitate and put into action what he read. While still undecided between earthly and heavenly values, he sheltered within him both the person that he had been and the one that that great incited man aspired to be: "Then there followed a sovereign light and wisdom, that Our Lord *infused* into his mind." (p. 163)

By way of explanation of this peculiar Spanish consciousness of literary effects, Castro considers (p. 161) that: "To feel books as a living, animate, communicable and inciting reality is a human phenomenon belonging to Oriental tradition . . ." And it may be this oriental sensitivity to *form*, progressively numbed in the world of the alphabet, that accounts for the unique Spanish outlook on print: ". . . but the peculiarity of sixteenth-century Spain was the attention accorded to the vital effect of the printed word upon its readers; the communicative power of the word was stressed above even errors and literary defects of the books themselves." (p. 164)

The Spanish concern, then, was with the very medium of print as effecting a new ratio of the senses, a new mode of consciousness. As Casalduero puts it in *Cervantes across the Centuries* (p. 63): "Knight and Squire are neither opposites nor complements to one another. They are of the same nature with a difference in proportion. The comic spirit arises from the juxtaposition of these diverse proportions which are translated plastically." With regard to the peculiar Spanish stress on the medium of the printed word, Stephen Gilman in a chapter on "The Apocryphal 'Quixote' " in the same book notes (p. 248) that authorship in Spain was secondary: "The reader is more important than the writer." But this is a long way from the idea of "what the public wants," for it is the notion of the medium of the language itself as a public trust rather than of the reader as private consumer. R. F. Jones encountered this attitude in the early sixteenth century in England:

The refinement and adornment of the mother tongue were themselves considered the goal of literature. In other words, literature was considered instrumental to language, not language to literature. Writers are more frequently praised for what they have done for the medium of their expression than for the intrinsic value of their compositions. . . .[81]

---

[81] *The Triumph of the English Language*, p. 183.

Print had the effect of purifying Latin out of existence.

✱ Many great scholars have toiled at the study of the printed English vernacular. So rich is the field that any kind of approach is arbitrarily selective. Writing on "Tyndale and the English Language," G. D. Bone brings out: "Tyndale's task was to make real the common life of the gospels. He was to rediscover the parables. . . . Before they possessed the Bible in their own language few people considered that a story in some way acquired more weight if it were actually a reflection of common life."[82]

Implied here is the suggestion that the language of everyday life when *seen* evokes the need for a literature of everyday life. Print applied to vernaculars transformed them into mass media, which was not too strange since typography was the first form of mass production. But print applied to Latin was a disaster: "The efforts of the great Italian humanists, from Petrarch in his *Africa* to Cardinal Bembo, had the unexpected effect of purifying Latin out of active existence."[83]

C. S. Lewis in *English Literature in the Sixteenth Century* (p. 21) writes:

It is largely to the humanists that we owe the curious conception of the 'classical' period in a language, the correct or normative period before which all was immature or archaic and after which all was decadent. Thus Scaliger tells us that Latin was 'rude' in Plautus, 'ripe' from Terence to Virgil, decadent in Martial and Juvenal, senile in Ausonius (*Poetices* viii). Vives says much the same (*De tradendis disciplinis* iv). Vida, more wildly, makes all Greek poetry after Homer a decline (*Poeticorum* I, 139). When once this superstition was established it led naturally to the belief that good writing in the fifteenth or sixteenth century meant writing which aped as closely as possible that of the chosen period in the past. All real development of Latin to meet the changing needs of new talent and new subject-matter was thus precluded; with one blow of 'his Mace petrific' the classical spirit ended the history of the Latin tongue. This was not what the humanists had intended.

Febvre and Martin point also (in *L'Apparation du livre*, p. 479) to the role of the revival of ancient Roman script. "Even more, the return to the antique letters contributed to make of Latin a dead language." This is a basic point. The very letters which we associate with print itself were not medieval but Roman and were used by the humanists as part of their

[82]S. L. Greenslade, *The Work of William Tyndale*, with an essay . . . by G. D. Bone, p. 51.
[83]Guérard, *Life and Death of an Ideal*, p. 44.

archeological effort. But the high visual quality of Roman script, so congenial to the printing press, was the main factor in ending the reign of Latin, even more than the revival of ancient styles by means of the printed word.

Print permitted the direct visual confrontation of the ancient styles in all their fixity. The humanists were shocked to discover how far they were in their oral Latin modes from all classical precedent. They decided at once to teach Latin by the printed page rather than by discourse, as a means of stopping the further spread of their own barbarous medieval Latin speech and idiom. Lewis concludes (p. 21): "They succeeded in killing the medieval Latin: but not in keeping alive the schoolroom severities of their restored Augustanism."

Typography extended its character to the regulation and fixation of languages.

✱ Later (pp. 83–4), Lewis contrasts the Renaissance schoolroom "classicality" with the oral and auditory freedom and variety of the medieval Latinity of Gavin Douglas, Bishop of Dunkeld. Douglas shocks us by being closer to Virgil than we. Once a man's eyes have been opened to this, he will find instances everywhere. *Rosea cervice refulsit*: "her nek schane like unto the rois in May." Do you prefer Dryden's "She turned and made appear her neck refulgent"? But *refulsit* cannot possibly have had for a Roman ear the "classical" quality which "refulgent" has for an English. It must have felt much more like "schane."

What we feel as "classical" in the Augustans and the eighteenth century, that is to say, has to do with the large stratum of Latin neologism which was imported into English by the translators of the first age of print. R. F. Jones in his *The Triumph of the English Language* devotes much space to this basic matter of the vernacular and neologism. He also discusses at length two questions directly related to the printed form of any language at all, namely the drive for fixity of spelling and grammar.

Febvre and Martin devote a chapter of their *L'Apparition du livre* to "Printing and Languages," pointing to "the essential role of print in the formation and fixation of languages. Until the beginning of the sixteenth century," the forms of written discourse, Latin or vernacular, "had continued to evolve after the pattern of the spoken language." (p. 477) Manuscript culture had no power to fix language or to transform a vernacular into a mass medium of national unification. Medievalists point to the im-

229

possibility of a Latin dictionary for the Middle Ages, simply because a medieval author felt free to define his terms progressively by the changing contexts of his thought. The idea of a word having a definite meaning fixed by some lexicon simply could not have occurred to him. In the same way, before writing, words do not have any external "sign," reference or significance. The word "oak" is oak, says the non-literate man; how else could it evoke the idea of oak? But print had just as far-reaching results in every aspect of language as writing had earlier. Whereas medieval vernaculars changed very much even from the twelfth to the fifteenth centuries, "from the beginning of the sixteenth century these matters were no longer thus. By the seventeenth century vernaculars everywhere begin to appear crystalized."

Febvre and Martin then point to the efforts made in medieval chancelleries to standard verbal practices, and to the new centralism of Renaissance monarchies to fix languages. The new monarch would gladly have passed Acts of Uniformity, in the spirit of the printing press to extend not only to religion and thought but to spelling and grammar. Today in the electronic age of simultaneity all these policies have had to be reversed, beginning with the new drive for decentralism and pluralism in big business itself. That is why it is so easy now to understand the dynamic logic of printing as a centralizing and homogenizing force. For all the effects of print technology now stand in stark opposition to the electronic technology. In the sixteenth century the whole of ancient and medieval culture stood in equally conflicting relation to the new print technology. In Germany, more pluralistic and tribally diverse than the rest of Europe, "the unifying services of printing in the formation of a literary language" were strikingly effective. And, write Febvre and Martin (p. 483):

Luther made a language which in all domains approaches modern German. The enormous diffusion of his works, their literary quality, the quasi-sacred character which belonged in the eyes of the faithful to the text of the Bible and of the New Testament as established by him, all this soon made his language a model. Accessible immediately to all readers . . . the term employed by Luther finally conquered, and numerous words used only in medieval German were finally adopted universally. And his vocabulary imposed itself in so imperious a fashion that most printers did not dare to diverge from it in the least.

Before looking at the English evidence for the same concern with regularity and uniformity among printers and print uses alike, it is well to remind ourselves of the rise of structural linguistics in our day. Structuralism in art and criticism stemmed, like non-Euclidean geometrics, from Russia. Structuralism as a term does not much convey its idea of inclusive synesthesia, an interplay of many levels and facets in a two-dimensional mosaic. But it is a mode of awareness in art language and literature which the West took great pains to eliminate by means of Gutenberg technology. It has returned in our time, for good or ill, as this opening paragraph of a recent book[84] indicates:

Language gives evidence of its reality through three categories of human experience. The first may be considered as the meaning of words; the second, as those meanings enshrined in grammatical forms; and the third and, in the view of this author, the most significant, as those meanings which lie beyond grammatical forms, those meanings mysteriously and miraculously revealed to man. It is with the last category that this chapter will endeavor to deal, for its thesis is that thought itself must be accompanied by a critical understanding of the relation of linguistic expression to the deepest and most persistent intuitions of man. An effort will further be made to show that language becomes imperfect and inadequate when it depends exclusively upon mere words and forms and when there is an uncritical trust in the adequacy of these words and forms as constituting the ultimate content and extent of language. For man is that being on earth who does not have language. Man *is* language.

Print altered not only the spelling and grammar but the accentuation and inflection of languages, and made bad grammar possible.

✱ In our time it is extremely evident that man is language, though he now recognizes many non-verbal languages as well as the language of forms. And this structuralist approach to experience engenders the awareness that "unconsciousness in relation to the one who knows is nonexistence."[85] That is to say, that in so far as print structured language and experience and motivation in new ways not recognized in conscious ways, life was impoverished by mesmerism. Earlier in this volume, Shakespeare was shown as providing his contemporaries with a working model of print technology in action. For the separation of functions by mechanical inertia is the foundation of movable types and applied knowledge in all domains. It is a technique of reduction to a single level of problems, talents, and solutions alike. Thus Dr. Johnson "was scandalized by the untimeliness of many of Shakespeare's puns. For

[84]R. N. Anshen, *Language: An Enquiry into its Meaning and Function*, Science of Culture series, vol. VIII, p. 3.
[85]*Ibid.*, p. 9. See also Edward T. Hall, *The Silent Language*.

a character to quibble in the teeth of death, as many do in the plays, was contrary to 'reason, propriety and truth'."[86]

Not only did simultaneity of meanings have to go with the change from oral to visual culture, but pronunciation and pitch were flattened out so far as possible. Robert Hillyer writes in his *In Pursuit of Poetry* (p. 45):

For the most part, we Americans do not avail ourselves of changing pitch. Unconsciously we avoid it as an affectation and lose half the effectiveness of our native tongue in one long monotone of drone, drawl, or growl. The effect is flat and blurred, especially since we run our syllables and words together, like a piece of prose without any punctuation. We ought to let every syllable come out round and full like a golden bubble! But we don't. The result is hard on poetry. The American voice is, in general, far richer than the English. Leaving out Cockney—and that super-Cockney, the "Oxford accent"—we mistakenly accord superiority to the English *voice*, whereas actually it is the flexible *pitch* that makes the Englishman's talk so much more articulate than ours. Pitch is to our language as gesticulation is to the French, its expressiveness, its emphasis, and its point. The Elizabethans doubtless spoke the language up and down through its whole gamut, and echoes of that eloquence linger in the talk of Irishmen today. *Without sliding pitch the reading of verse cannot be effective.*

Americans have pursued the merely visual implications of print more whole-heartedly than anybody else, for reasons that will shortly appear. Gror Danielsson provides a wealth of specialist material to back up Hillyer in his *Studies on Accentuation of Polysyllabic Latin, Greek, and Romance Loan-words in English.*

It has already been shown in relation to art and science and scriptural exegesis how the Middle Ages had tended steadily towards visual stress. It is now time to mention the gradual shift in medieval language, preparatory to the leap towards visual fixity represented by print.

In general, then, in respect to the expression of the subject and object relations, the development in English has been away from inflectional devices which made it grammatically possible for subjects and objects to stand in *any* position among the words of a sentence, to the use of grammatically functioning fixed word order patterns which made the position before the verb "subject" territory and the position after the verb, "object" territory.[87]

Inflexion is natural to the oral or auditory culture, for it is a mode of simultaneity. Phonetic alphabetic culture strongly tends to reduce inflexion in favour of visual positional grammar. Edward P. Morris has a lucid statement of this principle in *On Principles and Methods in Latin Syntax* where the visual stress appears as

[86]M. M. Mahood, *Shakespeare's Wordplay*, p. 33.
[87]Charles Carpenter Fries, *American English Grammar*, p. 255.

movement toward the expression of relation by single words. . . .

The general movement by which single words have in part taken the place of inflection is the most sweeping and radical change in the history of the Indo-European languages. It is at once the indication and the result of a clearer feeling of concept-relation. *Inflection in the main rather suggests than expresses relations*; it is certainly not correct to say that in every case the expression of relation by a single word, e.g., a preposition, is clearer than the suggestion of the same relation by a case form, but it is correct to say that the relation can become associated with a single word only when it is felt with a considerable degree of clearness. The relation between concepts must itself become a concept. To this extent *the movement toward the expression of relation by single words is a movement toward precision.* . . . The adverb-preposition is the expression in more distinct form of some element of meaning which was latent in the case-form. It serves therefore as a definition of the meaning of the case-form. (pp. 102–4)

The levelling of inflexion and of wordplay became part of the program of applied knowledge in the seventeenth century.

✻ If there had never been a seventeenth century it could have been predicted that the continuing print-inspired movement towards visual word order meant elimination of the principle of verbal decorum, the ending of wordplay, and the insistence on homogeneity of utterance. Long before Bishop Sprat had worked out this implication of print for the Royal Society, Robert Cawdrey states it plainly. In 1604 he argues that wit (which implied erudition at that time) consisted not in strange words but

in wholsom matter and apt declaring on a man's mind. . . . we must of necessitie banish all affected Rhetorique and use altogether one manner of language. Those therefore that will avoyde this follie, and acquaint themselves with the plainest and best kind of speech, must seek from time to time for such words as are commonlie received, and such as properly may expresse in plaine manner, the whole conceit of their mind.[88]

That we must "use altogether one manner of language" is a perfectly natural deduction from visual experience of the printed vernacular. And as Bacon showed, the reduction of talents and experience to a single level is the very crux of *applied* knowledge. But it is quite destructive of "the criterion

[88]Quoted in Jones, *The Triumph of the English Language*, p. 202.

233

of decorum," as Rosamund Tuve designates, in *Elizabethan and Metaphysical Imagery*, the principle that had informed the language arts continuously from the Greeks to the Renaissance.

Levels of style like levels of exegesis were part of an entire cultural complex, and exercised the thoughts of the Fathers with regard to the style of the Bible a great deal. John Donne is merely rehearsing a patristic commonplace when he writes: "The Holy Ghost in penning Scriptures delights himself not only with a propriety, but with a delicacy, and harmony, and melody of language; with height of Metaphors and other figures, which may work great impressions on the Readers, and not with barbarous or triviall, or market or homely language . . .[89]

Ignorance of the continuous operation of the principle of decorum in styles misled people like R. W. Chambers into notions of plain simple styles as growing out of some happy new principle of literary practice. Thus Bede, who wrote in all styles, is congratulated in the *Cambridge History of English Literature* because in his *Ecclesiastical History*: "It seems to be one great service he rendered to English writers that he gave currency to direct and simple style."

R. W. Chambers confused the later nineteenth century cult of oral, colloquial simplicity with the sixteenth century practice of the low style in devotional treatises and sermons. Thomas More uses the high style in *Richard III*, and middle style for his satire the *Utopia*, and low style for his devotional work. Part of Donne's sophistication in decorum is a daring use of imagery from humble crafts in order to pose the paradoxes of the Divine humility of the Incarnation. The purpose here, however, is merely to indicate the range and depth of the tradition of decorum in the use of language for varied themes. For with print it had to be sheered off so that men could "use altogether one manner of language." The need to homogenize every kind of situation, in order to get the whole culture in rapport with the potential of the print technology, is an easily recognizable and understandable attitude. Bishop Sprat in his *History of the Royal Society* (1667) is prepared to dispense, not only with decorum and levels of style, but with poetry itself. Myths and fables were the fanciful rhetoric of the childhood of the race:

the first masters of knowledge among them were as well Poets, as Philosophers;
for Orpheus, Linus, Musaeus and Homer, first softened men's natural
rudeness, and by the charms of their Numbers, allur'd them to be instructed
by the severer doctrines of Solon, Thales and Pythagoras. This was a course
that was useful at first, when men were to be delightfully deceiv'd to their
own good. But perhaps it left some ill influence, on the whole Philosophy
of their Successors; and gave the Grecians occasion ever after of exercising

---

[89]Quoted in W. F. Mitchell, *English Pulpit Oratory from Andrews to Tillotson*, p. 189.

their wit, and their imagination, about the works of Nature, more than was consistent with a sincere Inquiry into them.[90]

By a kind of metamorphosis it follows from Sprat's position (which tries to follow Bacon) that the modern scientist or philosopher is the true poet. And in order to purge the dross of the past from the present, Sprat sees the Royal Society as having "endeavour'd to separate the knowledge of Nature from the colours of Rhetorick, the devices of Fancy, or the delightful deceit of Fables."

The procedure of separation and segmentation as the very technique of *applied* knowledge comes out clearly wherever a job of reducing antiquity arises. The members of the Royal Society being privy to this technique, repudiate "this vicious abundance of Phrase, this trick of Metaphors, this volubility of Tongue, which makes so great a noise in the world."

They have therefore been most rigorous in putting into execution, the only Remedy that can be found for this extravagance: and that has been, a constant Resolution, to reject all the amplifications, digressions, and swellings of style: *to return back to the primitive purity, and shortness,* when men deliver'd so many things, almost in an equal number of words. *They have exacted from all their members, a close, naked, natural way of speaking; positive expressions, clear senses; a native easiness; bringing all things as near the Mathematical plainness, as they can: and preferring the language of Artizans, Countrymen, and Merchants, before that, of Wits, or Scholars.*[91]

Print created national uniformity and government centralism, but also individualism and opposition to government as such.

✱ At this point of reduction of all language to one mode, we are not really disengaged from the original meaning of print in transforming the vernaculars into mass media of nationalist significance. It will repay us to dip more than a century behind Sprat in order to follow the contours of the original manifestation of print as a means of uniformity.

[90]Cited in Basil Willey, *The Seventeenth Century Background*, p. 207.
[91]*Ibid.*, p. 212.

Karl Deutsch writes in his *Nationalism and Social Communication* (pp. 78–9):

a nationality is a people pressing to acquire a measure of effective control over the behavior of its members. . . . nationalities turn into nations when they acquire power to back up their aspirations. Finally, if their nationalistic members are successful, and a new or old state organization is put into their service, then at last the nation has become sovereign, and a *nation-state* has come into being.

Carleton Hayes has made it plain that there was no nationalism before the Renaissance, and we have now seen enough of the character of print technology to know why this should be so. For if print made the vernaculars into mass media, they also constituted a means of central government control of society beyond anything that even the Romans had known with papyrus and alphabet and paved roads. But the very nature of print creates two conflicting interests as between producers and consumers, and between rulers and ruled. For print as a form of centrally organized mass-production ensures that the problem of "freedom" will henceforth be paramount in all social and political discussion. In Library Week, March 17, 1950, the *Minneapolis Morning Tribune*, in an editorial entitled "The Right to Read," quoted a joint statement by Herbert Hoover and Harry Truman: "We Americans know that if freedom means anything, it means the right to think. And the right to think means the right to read—anything, written anywhere, by any man, at any time." This is an impressive statement of consumer doctrine based on the homogeneity of print. If print is uniform, it should create uniform rights for writer and reader, publisher and consumer. The American colonies were first settled by people who had long had experience of the exactly opposite idea of the meaning of print. The producer-oriented or ruler-oriented version of the message of Gutenberg is simply that it is the ruler's right to impose uniform patterns of behaviour on society. The police state precedes the consumer society. It is interesting, therefore, to read an American account of *Freedom of the Press in England, 1476–1776: The Rise and Decline of Government Controls*, by F. S. Siebert, for it provides a fine view of the relative advantages in producer-imposed *versus* consumer-created uniformity. It is the perpetual and ironic alternation of these two positions that gives to Alexis de Tocqueville's *Democracy in America* its rich fascination. The same contrast between the interests of centralized government and those of settlers is the theme of *The Fur Trade in Canada* by Harold Innis. For, writes Innis (p. 388), it was the interest of the centre to organize the margins for the production of staples, not of consumer goods:

Large scale production of raw materials was encouraged by improvement of technique of production, of marketing, and of transport as well as by improvement in the manufacture of the finished product. As a consequence, energy in the colony was drawn into the production of the staple commodity both directly and indirectly. Population was involved directly in the production of the staple and indirectly in the production of facilities promoting production. Agriculture, industry, transportation, trade, finance, and governmental activities tend to become subordinate to the production of the staple for a more highly specialized manufacturing community. These general tendencies may be strengthened by governmental policy as in the mercantile system but the importance of these policies varies in particular industries. Canada remained British in spite of free trade and chiefly because she continued as an exporter of staples to a progressively industrialized mother country.

The War of Independence of 1776, Innis explains, was the clash between centre and margin, which is identical with the conflict between conformity and non-conformity, politics and literature, in the sixteenth century. And just as "a colony engaged in the fur trade was not in a position to develop industries to compete with manufactures of the mother country," so the margins also developed a merely consumer attitude to literature and the arts, such as has lingered until this century.

The non-conformists inclined to the reader or consumer side, interpreting the meaning of print to be private and individual. The conformists inclined to the author-publisher, ruler of the new force. It may or may not be significant that most of English literature since printing has been created by this ruler-oriented minority.

Says Siebert (p. 25): "The Tudor policy of strict control over the press in the interest of the safety of the state was maintained throughout the sixteenth century." It was inevitable that with printing the sixteenth century should also witness "a large increase in the powers—executive, legislative, and judicial—of the Council (or Privy Council) at the expense of both Parliament and the older courts, but to the distinct advantage of the crown." But as the book market enlarged and the habit of much reading spread widely toward the end of the century, the consumer revolt against central controls got ever stronger. L. B. Wright's splendid account of *Middle-Class Culture in Elizabethan England* provides an image of the complex uses of print to foster many varieties of self-education and self-help. It becomes obvious how the first age of readers was not merely seeking diversion but instruction in methods of applied knowledge.

The reader of Wright's work will easily appreciate how the centralist structure of Elizabeth was being undermined from within by a new variety of rugged individualists:

Isolated groups had already begun to challenge the system of government controls, the printers for economic reasons, the Puritans for religious reasons, and at least one member of Parliament for political reasons. Printers like Wolfe chafed under the rules of the Stationers Company. They rebelled against the printing privileges and the patents of monopoly. The religious nonconformists, denied the privilege of appealing to public opinion, darted about inserting wedges with which they eventually wrecked the entire structure.[92]

It would need a book in itself to explain how the Enclosure movement was related to the centralism of the print process. But no further example of the power of print to enhance central power need be sought beyond the Act of Uniformity of Elizabeth in 1559. The bill was opposed in the Lower House of Convocation on the ground that no government could possess "authority to treat of or to define whatever concerns the faith, the sacraments and ecclesiastical discipline . . ." But liturgy and church observance were an easy mark for print, depending as they long had on book form. As from June 24, 1559, the Prayer Book of 1552 was to be "in full force and effect," all ministers being thenceforth "bounden to say and use the Matins, Evensong, celebration of the Lord's Supper and administration of each of the sacraments, and all their common and open prayer" as these are in the book "and none other or other wise."

In 1562 the Book of Homilies was issued for universal public reading from every pulpit. Their content is not our concern, but rather their being uniformly imposed on the entire public. By making the vernacular a mass medium, print created a new instrument of political centralism previously unavailable. And at the same time, as personal and political conformity became matters of sharp formulation, scholars and teachers began a concerted drive for correct spelling and grammar.

Nobody ever made a grammatical error in a non-literate society.

✱ The intensity of the ferment concerning orthography is only a useful index to the novelty of print and its effects of central conformity. Charles Carpenter Fries, in his *American English Grammar*, studies the question of the clash between written and oral discourse: "Only the sixty-six most common strong verbs have resisted the pull of the regular pattern. . . . As a matter of fact, during the sixteenth and seventeenth centuries there was a strong tendency to eliminate the distinction of form between the past tense and the past participle in all of these verbs . . ." (p. 61)

[92]Siebert, *Freedom of the Press in England, 1476–1776*, p. 103.

Print had a levelling function on all verbal and social forms, it had been said over and over again. And where print has left some inflections unchanged, as in "who-whom," there yawns the great booby-trap of "correct grammar"—that is to say, the abyss between visual and oral modes. The status of these issues in the electronic age is sufficiently indicated in a *Time* report[93] from the British House of Lords:

In debating the merits of a bill concerning the rights and liabilities of
hotel proprietors, Britain's House of Lords found itself up against a
momentous question: should an *a* or an *an* precede *hotel*?
In favor of *an* was Lord Faringdon, who begged "your Lordships
to join me in making a demonstration in favor of elegance." Lord Conesford
agreed, pointed out that *h* words that are not accented on the first syllable
demand *an*. "I believe," said he, "that every one of your Lordships would
say 'a Harrow boy,' but would also speak of 'an Harrovian.' " But what,
asked Lord Rea, would Lord Conesford do with one-syllable words? "In the
case of an inn sign of a public house, would he look at it as 'A Horse and a
Hound' or 'An Orse and an Ound'?" Lord Merthyr fell back on no less an
authority than Fowler to prove that *an hotel* would be hopelessly old-
fashioned—but to no avail. When the debate was over, the *ans* won out.
Said *a*-man Lord Merthyr of *an*-man Lord Faringdon, an Etonian like
himself: "It is rather sad to think that the noble Lord and I should have been
educated in the same place, and at the same time, and that 40 years later
we should come here to differ upon this question."

It is presumably impossible to make a grammatical error in a non-literate society, for nobody ever heard one. The difference between oral and visual order sets up the confusions of the ungrammatical. In the same way the passion for spelling reform in the sixteenth century arose from the new effort to adjust sight and sound. Sir Thomas Smith had argued that "a letter had an inherent nature which made it appropriate to one sound only." This is the one-thing-at-a-time of the natural victim of print. And there were many who extended this logic to the meanings of words as well. But many rugged characters like Richard Mulcaster rallied against this visual logic, just as Dr. Johnson was to rally against the visual logic of the doctrine of the dramatic unities.

[93]July 2, 1956, p. 46.

The reduction of the tactile qualities of life and language constitute the refinement sought in the Renaissance and repudiated now in the electronic age.

✱ A major theme of the passionate vernacular nationalists brings us to the effect of print in swiftly depriving language of many of its tactile qualities. Until the nineteenth century there was a common boast of "refinement" of the English tongue that had occurred since the sixteenth century. In the sixteenth century there was still plenty of brogue and dialect to confer tactility and resonance. Even by 1577 Holinshed could feel happy about the gradual refinement between the language of the Saxons and the relative perfection of his own time. The old Saxon English was

and hard and rough kinde of speach, god wotte, when our nation was
brought first into acquaintance withall, but now chaunged with vs into a farre
more fine and easie kind of vtterunce, and so polished and helped with
new and milder wordes that it is to be adouched howe there is no one
speache vnder the sonne spoken in our time, that hath or can haue more
varietie of words, copie of phrases, or figures or floures of eloquence, than
hath our English tongue.[94]

The reduction of tactile quality in life and language is ever the mark of refinement. And it was not till the pre-Raphaelites and Hopkins that a deliberate campaign for Saxon tactile values in language was to begin in English. Yet tactility is the mode of interplay and of being rather than of separation and of lineal sequence. A brief look at the effects of print in reshaping our ideas of space and of time will bridge across into the next centuries after printing. For it is quite impossible to continue to advance on all fronts in the present book.

[94]Quoted in Jones, *The Triumph of the English Language*, p. 189.

The new time sense of typographic man is cinematic and sequential and pictorial.

✱ With the stepping up of the isolated intensity and quantity by print the individual is ushered into a world of movement and isolation. In every aspect of experience and affairs the stress is on separation of functions, analysis of components, and isolation of the moment. For with the isolation of the visual, the feeling of interplay and of *light through* the mesh of being yields, and "Human thought no longer feels itself a part of things." What Shakespeare refers to in *Lear* as the "precious square of sense" probably has reference to the traditional "square of opposition" in logic and to that four-part analogy of proportionality which is the interplay of sense and reason. But with the isolation of the visual by this new intensity, Reason is also

. . . isolated from exterior time, [and] it feels also equally detached from the time of its mental life. The modifications which happen to affect it by turns can, indeed, in succeeding each other, give it the idea of an interior duration. But this duration, consisting in modes which replace one another, is by no means the duration of the thinking being; it is solely the duration of the successive ensemble of man's thoughts. Separated from the duration of things, and even from that of the modes of its existence, the human consciousness finds itself reduced to existence without duration. It is always of the present moment.[95]

This is Macbeth's world of "Tomorrow and tomorrow and tomorrow." This, says Poulet, is the experience of modern man, and Montaigne, in his *Essays,* was the first to depict it. He set out to snapshot his own mind in the act of reading and reflection by way of *la peinture de la pensée.* In this respect Montaigne more than anybody else, perhaps, carried out the lesson of print as by a kind of applied knowledge. He bred up a great race of self-portrayers by means of the mental snapshot, of the sequence of the arrested and isolated moments of experience which anticipate the cinema: "At first, on this island of the moment which isolates him but which he fills with his presence, man still keeps something of the joy he experienced in the Renaissance when he felt that he existed in all the reaches of space and duration. He is now given no more than a moment at a time, but each moment can be one of illumination and fullness. . . ."[96]

Inseparably, however, from visual awareness and order, is the sense of discontinuity and a feeling of self-alienation: "Every hour we are swept away

[95]Poulet, *Studies in Human Time,* p. 13.
[96]*Ibid.,* p. 15.

241

from ourselves," says Boileau, and a hectic urgency invades the time sense: "Aware that the instant in which he thinks and wishes is slipping from under him, man hurls himself into a new instant, an instant of a new thought and a new wish: 'But man without rest in his mad course / Flutters incessantly from thought to thought.'"[97]

From the isolated present moment, Poulet writes (p. 19), "God the creator and preserver is absent. The principal actor is no longer on the scene. For the supereminent role of the first cause we find substituted the play of second causes. In place of God there are feelings, sensations, and whatever causes sensations." Well, what causes sensations such as the above is unmistakably print technology with its power like Lear's "darker purpose" to divide the little kingdom of man into a batch of jarring atoms, and uniformly homo-genized components. Existence becomes, then, not *being* but only "flux, shadow, and perpetual variation"; "I do not depict being," says Montaigne; "I depict passage." Nothing could be more cinematic than that. Renouncing the depiction of what is favour of an illusion achieved by a sequence of static "shots"—this is *typography in extenso*. Let us recall *King Lear* as a live model of the stripping of human institutions, and consciousness itself, by the progressive isolation of the senses. Parallel to this psychological experiment in our time is the deprivation of sense under controlled condi-tions. But to anybody first undergoing the print experience there was an extreme specialism of sense, not felt again, perhaps, until the movies and then, shortly afterwards, radio. The Baroque painters did exactly as did Montaigne in shifting attention to the peripheries of vision. Poulet is quite right in saying (p. 43), therefore:

> But to renounce the depiction of being for the depiction of passage is not only an enterprise of unprecedented denudation; it is a task of extreme difficulty. To depict passage is not simply to seize oneself in an object which fades away and by its own blurring lets the self appear more distinctly; it is not to paint a portrait of oneself which would be all the more faithful by the disappearance of all the traces of occasions which had led its creation. It is to seize the self at the instant when the occasions remove from it its old form and impose upon it a new one.

It may be a mistake for Poulet or anybody else to see in this new strategy of Montaigne some extraordinarily profound discovery of enterprise. But just as the infinitesimal calculus was devised to translate non-visual experience into homogeneous visual terms, so Montaigne's seizing the imperceptible instant or facet, as "diversely and imperceptibly our soul darts out her passions," is entering "the home of what Leibnitz was later to call the infinitely small entities. . . . It is a wager to attempt to 'choose and lay hold of so many nimble little motions'. . . . Thus the self is dissolved not only from

[97]*Ibid.*, p. 16.

instant to instant but even in the middle of the instant-passage, in a prismatic play like that of a spray of water."[98]

What is being presented here is identical with the methods of precise, visual quantification described by John U. Nef earlier. As Nef showed, these minute statistical methods were the means of applied or translated knowledge. Montaigne had all the experiences and techniques of the impressionist film of our own time. And both modes of awareness are direct extrapolations of typography when applied to the spoken word. In the midst of impressionism symbolism strove to recover the unified field of being once more. It is easy today in an electronic milieu to understand the novelty of segmental impressionist devices as they emerged from the sixteenth until the end of the nineteenth century. They are inseparable from the Gutenberg galaxy of events.

And so with Descartes, for whom science is the anticipation of causes with effects: "Foundation of an admirable science which his mind conceives as an ensemble of 'Concatenated' things: world of the *catena*, of pure determinism. Spontaneity, liberty, piety have no part in it."[99] Having reduced knowledge to a merely visual mode of sequence, "nothing can assure us of one instant's being continued in another; nothing can guarantee to us that a bridge will be built between this instant and the following instant. . . . This is the strongest anxiety of all; the 'terror,' as Descartes calls it; the terror of *failure in time* against which there is no recourse except by a veritable leap to God."[100] Poulet later (p. 357) describes this "leap":

In this manner the idea of God reappears to Descartes. Long neglected by the primary consciousness absorbed in the *"science admirable,"* it reappears in this spontaneous act of the secondary consciousness given to him by his dream. From this moment, so to speak, a change of atmosphere will occur in those dreamlike regions which seem to lead to some inevitable reality of despair. But in order for Descartes to arrive finally at the true "shelter" and to find the genuine "remedy," he must endure other trials. The spontaneous act by which he turns toward God does not possess at this moment the necessary efficacy: it is not *pure* spontaneity; it is not addressed directly to a God of the present, but to a God of the past . . .

[98]*Ibid.*, p. 45.
[99]*Ibid.*, p. 54.
[100]*Ibid.*, p. 58.

The denuding of conscious life and its reduction to a single level created the new world of the unconscious in the seventeenth century. The stage has been cleared of the archetypes or postures of individual mind, and is ready for the archetypes of the collective unconscious.

✳ It is thus that the seventeenth century, having emerged into a merely visual science in its conscious life, is reduced to recourse to the world of dreams. The mechanical spirit of movable types in precise lines, thus, could not have been given a more faithful reflection than by Descartes. We have earlier cited his new consumer idea of philosophy, exhorting his reader to go through his work "in its entirety like a novel without forcing the attention unduly upon it or stopping at difficulties." The notion of moving steadily along on single planes of narrative awareness is totally alien to the nature of language and of consciousness. But it is highly consistent with the nature of the printed word. Going closely with this lineal denudation of language is the associated impression of mechanical repetition and recurrence which came to weigh ever more heavily on the Renaissance mind:

> Like as the waves make towards the pebbled shore,
> So do our minutes hasten to their end;
> Each changing place with that which goes before,
> In sequent toil all forwards do contend.[101]

But it had first a comic aspect which not only Shakespeare but Sidney exploited in his *Astrophel and Stella*:

> You that do dictionary's method bring
> Into your rimes, running in rattling rows;

But the examples of the new power of visual lineality are innumerable, one of the most curious being the King James (1611) version of the Lord's Prayer in which "debt" becomes "trespass." The reduction of the multi-

[101]Shakespeare, Sonnet LX.

levelled idea of "debt" and duty is thus confined to the written legal meaning, and the idea of "stepping out of line" is substituted for a complex of theological and moral implication.

Paradoxically, then, the first age of print introduced the first age of the unconscious. Since print allowed only a narrow segment of sense to dominate the other senses, the refugees had to discover another home for themselves. We have seen how aware of this meaning of the effects of print were the Spaniards. *Don Quixote* is as much as *Lear* a demonstration of the dichotomies of mind and heart and sense instituted by the printed book. More practical nations preferred to *live out* these consequences rather than to meditate upon them in live art models.

Lancelot Law Whyte in his *The Unconscious before Freud* gives some idea of the rise of the "discovery" of the unconscious as a result of the restriction of conscious life within the extreme limits of print technology. "Sink deep or touch not the Cartesian spring" is the relevant jest of Joyce in *Finnegans Wake* (p. 301). But for centuries to come the West chose to be motivated by this simple mechanism and to live as in a dream from which artists strove to awaken us. Whyte says (pp. 59–60):

There have probably been individuals in every culture who knew that the factors of which we are not directly aware influence thought and behavior. As I have suggested, this recognition must have been widespread, for example in China where a more balanced and unified view of mind than that of Cartesian Europe was prevalent in some periods.

So far as the present book is concerned, it is not helpful to talk about the unconscious as the domain of the unknown, or as an area more profound than ordinary consciousness. Even a restricted consciousness is far more interesting than the unconscious profound. The concern here is to demonstrate how by stressing the visual sense component in the sense ratio, we have ourselves created that huge area of bathos and dulness which Pope celebrated in *The Dunciad* and Swift in *The Tale of a Tub*. The unconscious is a direct creation of print technology, the ever-mounting slag-heap of rejected awareness.

No thinker ever imagined that "body" and "mind"—insofar as the terms are valid—are without apparent interactions. We must leave it to the Cartesian scholars, as Descartes did, to explain what it meant to postulate, as one of the first products of clear thinking, two independent realms which are none the less so intimately interdependent. The lesson is that the more brilliant the light cast on two neighboring realms, the more profound the obscurity into which their interactions are thrown.[102]

[102]Whyte, *The Unconscious before Freud*, p. 60.

245

Philosophy was as naive as science in its unconscious acceptance of the assumptions or dynamic of typography.

✳ The massive and abounding presence of printed matter and its derivatives in new space and time organization gave prestige and authority to the absurdities here cited by Whyte. Thus, for example, today children in schools, when invited to consider the moronic quality of media offerings, are shocked. They entertain an unspoken assumption that whatever the adult world takes the time and trouble to perform is valid. They assume that grown-ups *en masse* would never be engaged in a depraved activity. It is only after teaching the languages of the media, from script to print and from print to TV, that this obvious fact is borne in on the mind. A Descartes is validated by his milieu, and by people engaged in living the mechanism he talks. Today in the new electronic milieu Descartes gets short shrift and people now give to the unconscious the same fragmentary attention and acceptance that they had previously given to the bright segmental moments of Cartesian awareness. Is it not possible to emancipate ourselves from the subliminal operation of our own technologies? Is not the essence of education civil defence against media fall-out? Since the effort has never been made in any culture the answer may seem to lie in doubt. There may be some hitherto unsuspected and wise motive for mental sleep and self-hypnosis in man which the confrontation of the effects of media technology would reveal. However this may be, it is plain that the pseudo-dichotomies and visual quantities imposed on our psychology by print began in the seventeenth century to assume the character of consumer packages or "systems" of philosophy. They are of the kind that can be described and presented in a few minutes, but, thanks to the mesmerism of print, were to occupy the attention of generations. Philosophies from Descartes onward are diverse in the way in which a steam engine differs from a gas or diesel engine. And Bergson, who tried to end it all, is as mechanical as his enemy Descartes, although he preferred a kind of cosmic fuel for his system. Once grant the stripping and segmenting process for language and experience such as Shakespeare indicates in *Lear*, and there is no possible stay. The roller-coaster is off over the Cartesian, Lockeian, Kantian course with all the built-in panic and *Angst* that could be asked for. Whyte sums it up (pp. 60–1):

During the late seventeenth century three main attitudes dominated European philosophical thought, corresponding to three interpretations of the nature of existence. Materialism treated physical bodies and their motions as the primary reality; idealism took it to be spirit or mind; while Cartesian dualism postulated two independent realms: the mental *res cogitans* and the material *res extensa*. For the first two schools there was no difficulty in recognizing unconscious mentality though under other names. To the materialists all mentality was physiological, and the existence of unconscious physiological processes, similar to and influencing thought, was an immediate consequence of the fact that our direct awareness of the processes in our bodies is restricted. And to the idealists all natural processes were the expression of a universal mind or world spirit of which the human individual has no direct knowledge, though it shares, in some degree, the characteristics of human mentality. Thus for the idealists also there was no problem; the unconscious mind of the individual was not in any way surprising; it was merely a part of the universal mind to which the individual awareness enjoyed no direct access. But to the third, Cartesian, school the admission of the existence of unconscious mental processes presented an acute philosophical challenge, for it demanded the discarding of the original conception of the dualism, as one of two independent realms, matter in motion and mind necessarily aware. For those who were loyal to Descartes, all that was not conscious in man was material and physiological, and therefore not mental.

The last sentence will suggest to some that the present book is material and physiological rather than mental in its assumptions. That is not the case, nor is it the theme. The point is, rather, how do we become aware of the effects of alphabet or print or telegraph in shaping our behaviour? For it is absurd and ignoble to be shaped by such means. Knowledge does not extend but restrict the areas of determinism. And the influence of un-examined assumptions derived from technology leads quite unnecessarily to maximal determinism in human life. Emancipation from that trap is the goal of all education. But the unconscious is no escape-hatch from a world of denuded categories any more than Leibnitzian or any other monism is a resolution of Cartesian dualism. There is still the full ratio or interplay of all the senses in concert, which permits light *through*. That concert comes to an end with the stepping up of *one* sense by technology, and by the insistence of light *on*. The nightmare of light *on* is the world of Pascal: "Reason acts slowly and with so many views upon so many principles which always must be present, that at any time it may fall asleep or get lost, for want of having all its principles present."[103]

---

[103]Poulet, *Studies in Human Time*, p. 78.

Heidegger surf-boards along on the electronic wave as triumphantly as Descartes rode the mechanical wave.

✱ This kind of ballet of mind choreographed by Gutenberg by means of the isolated visual sense, is about as philosophical as Kant's assumption of Euclidean space as *a priori*. But the alphabet and kindred gimmicks have long served man as a subliminal source of philosophical and religious assumptions. Certainly Martin Heidegger would seem to be on better ground in using the totality of language itself as philosophical datum. For there, at least in non-literate periods, will be the ratio among *all* the senses. But this is not to recommend non-literacy, any more than the uses made of print are a judgment against literacy. In fact, Heidegger seems to be quite unaware of the role of electronic technology in promoting his own non-literate bias in language and philosophy. An enthusiasm for Heidegger's excellent linguistics could easily stem from naive immersion in the metaphysical organicism of our electronic milieu. If the mechanism of Descartes looks paltry today, it may be for the same subliminal reasons that it looked resplendent in its own time. In that sense all fashions betoken somnambulism of some kind, and are one means of critical orientation to the psychic effects of technology. Perhaps this is the way to help those who want to say: "But is there nothing good about print?" The theme of this book is not that there is anything good or bad about print but that unconsciousness of the effect of *any* force is a disaster, especially a force that we have made ourselves. And it is quite easy to test the universal effects of print on Western thought after the sixteenth century, simply by examining the most extraordinary developments in any art or science whatever. Fragmented and homogeneous lineality, which appears as discovery in the sixteenth and seventeenth centuries, will become the popular novelty or utilitarian fashion of the eighteenth and nineteenth centuries. That is, mechanism persists as "novelty" into the electronic age that began with men like Faraday. Some may feel that life is too valuable and delightful a thing to be spent in such arbitrary and involuntary automatism.

Pascal uses the Montaigne kodak trick of snapshotting moments in order to get into a misery of dilemmas: "When we love ardently, it is always a novelty to see the person beloved." But this spontaneity is the product of simultaneity and instantaneous profusion. And the mind must take the elements one by one. Here then is the gratuitous and subliminal component of typography in Pascal. All experience is segmental and must be processed sequentially. Therefore, rich experience eludes the wretched mesh or sieve of our attention. "One does not show his greatness by being at one extreme, but in touching both extremes at once, and in filling in all the intermediate space."[104] Of course, by setting up this little Gutenberg rack to anguish his spirit, Pascal insured himself public notice and acceptance: "Those great efforts of the mind, which the soul occasionally reaches, are such as it cannot sustain. It reaches them only by a bound, not as on a throne, continuously, but for an instant only."[105]

Pascal indicates that the old kind of consciousness was kingly, continuous, "as on a throne." The old king had a role, not a job. He was an inclusive centre-without-a-margin. The new consciousness like the new prince is a harassed executive, exercising a job, applying knowledge to problems, and having only momentary contacts with his marginal subjects, who are all ambitious rival segments anyway.

Says Poulet in what must be an irony (p. 85): "For an instant! Shattering return to the misery of the human condition and to the tragedy of the experience of time: in the very instant man catches his prey, experience dupes him, and he knows he is duped. His prey is a shadow. In the instant he catches the instant, and the instant passes, for it is instant."

One gets the uneasy feeling that these philosophers have undertaken expressly to dramatize the mechanism of Gutenberg in our sensibilities, acting it out like all the King's horses and all the King's men, around old Humpty Dumpty. How can one discover the principle of human identity amidst lineal sequences of moments? The self is obliged, such is the discontinuity of these typographic moments, "each time to forget itself in order to re-invent itself, to reinvent itself in order to regain interest in itself, in short to effect a mocking simulacrum of continued creation, thanks to which it believes it will escape the authentication of its nothingness, and out of its nothingness refashion a reality."[106]

Yet homogeneous repetition à la Gutenberg still leaves something to be desired in the way of a self. How is one to reason with the person who feeds himself into a buzz-saw because the teeth are invisible? Such was the fate of the unified "self" in the age of print segmentation. But it is hard to believe in the reality of anybody who in any age could take seriously the Gutenberg assumptions when applied to the ordering of life.

James Joyce certainly thought he had found in Vico a philosopher who had some better cultural awareness than those moved by the "Cartesian spring." And Vico, like Heidegger, is a philologist among philosophers. His

[104]*Ibid.*, p. 80.
[105]*Ibid.*, p. 85.
[106]*Ibid.*, p. 87.

249

time theory of "*ricorsi*" has been interpreted by lineal minds to imply "recurrence." A recent study of him brushes this notion aside.[107]

Vico conceives the time-structure of history as "not linear, but contrapuntal. It must be traced along a number of lines of development . . ." For Vico all history is contemporary or simultaneous, a fact given, Joyce would add, by virtue of language itself, the simultaneous storehouse of all experience. And in Vico, the concept of recurrence cannot "be admitted at the level of the course of the nations through time": "The establishment of providence establishes universal history, the total presence of the human spirit to itself in idea. In this principle, the supreme 'ricorso' is achieved by the human spirit in idea, and it possesses itself, past, present, and future, in an act which is wholly consonant with its own historicity."[108]

Typography cracked the voices of silence.

✻ From the plastic and audile-tactile world of southern Italy came an answer to the lineal anguish of the segmenters of the Gutenberg milieu. So thought Michelet and Joyce.

Let us briefly return to the space question as affected by Gutenberg. Everybody is familiar with the phrase, "the voices of silence." It is the traditional word for sculpture. And if an entire year of any college program were spent in understanding that phrase, the world might soon have an adequate supply of competent minds. As the Gutenberg typography filled the world the human voice closed down. People began to read silently and passively as consumers. Architecture and sculpture dried up too. In literature only people from backward oral areas had any resonance to inject into the language— the Yeats, the Synges, the Joyces, Faulkners, and Dylan Thomases. These themes are linked in the following paragraph by le Corbusier, which makes plain why stone and water are inseparable:

Around the building, inside the building, there are definite places, mathematical points, which integrate the whole and establish platforms from which the sound of speech would reverberate in all parts. These are the predestined sites for sculpture. And that sculpture would be neither a metope, a tympanum, nor a porch. It would be much more subtle and precise. The site would be a place which would be like the focus of a parabola or an ellipse, like the precise point of intersection of the different planes which compose the architecture. From there the word, the voice

[107]A. Robert Caponigri, *Time and Idea: The Theory of History in Giambattista Vico.*
[108]*Ibid.*, p. 142.

would issue. Such places would be focal points for sculpture, as they are focal points for acoustics. Take up your stand here, sculptor, if your voice is worth hearing.[109]

It is merely trite to mention that man became the centre *via* Gutenberg only to be demoted at once by Copernicus to the status of a marginal speck. Dangling for centuries at the end of a chain of being, man's lineality was interrupted by Darwin whose lineality highlighted a missing segment in the sequence. Anyhow, Darwin broke up anthropocentric consciousness just as Copernicus had done for space. Yet till Freud, man somehow clung to some scrap of intuition of consciousness as tinged by spontaneity. But Freud ended that by his image of mind as ripple on the ocean of unconsciousness. Unless the West had long been processed by print these metaphors would have carried no interest whatever. Let us turn to a book by a mathematician, Sir Edmund Whittaker, which explains how some of this came to be. A passage of Kant's from the *Critique of Practical Reason* (p. 14) will usher us into this territory: "Since mathematics irrefutably proves the infinite divisibility of space which empiricism cannot allow, there is an obvious contradiction between the highest possible demonstrable evidence and the alleged inferences from empirical principles. . . . One might ask like Cheseldren's blind man, 'Which deceives me, sight or touch?' Empiricism is based on touch, but rationalism on a necessity which can be seen." Not only did Kant not know that number is audile-tactile and infinitely repeatable, but that the visual, in abstraction from the audile-tactile, sets up a world of antinomies and dichotomies of insoluble but irrelevant kind.

Sir Edmund Whittaker, in his *Space and Spirit* (p. 121), explains in terms of the recent mathematics and physics, the end of the Renaissance idea of continuous, uniform space that came in with the notion of visual quantification:

At this point we escape from the order of the Newtonian cosmos. . . . In the argument as usually presented the language used is appropriate to the case when each effect has only one cause, and each cause has only one effect, so that all chains of causation are simple linear sequences. If we now take into account the fact that an effect may be produced by the joint action of several distinct causes, and also that a cause may give rise to more than one effect, the chains of causation may be branched, and also may have junctions with one another; but since the rule still holds, that the cause always precedes the effect in time, it is evident that the proof is not essentially affected. Moreover, the argument does not require that all chains of causation, when traced backward, should terminate on the *same* ultimate point: in other words, it does not lead necessarily to the conclusion that the universe acquired its entire stock-in-trade in a single consignment at the Creation, and that it

[109]Carola Giedion-Welcker, *Contemporary Sculpture*, p. 205.

251

has received nothing since. Thus it does not warrant the view, so common among the deistic Newtonians of the eighteenth century, that the system of the world is absolutely closed and has developed according to purely mechanical laws, so that all the events of history must have been implicit in its specification at the primeval instant. On the contrary, the recent trend of physical thought (as will be evident from what has been said about the principle of causality) is in favor of the view that in the physical domain, there is a continual succession of intrusions or new creations. The universe is very far from being a mere mathematical consequence of the disposition of the particles at the Creation, and is a much more interesting and eventful place than any determinist imagines.

That passage explains the title and procedure of the present book, but is in no way necessary to the configurations with which we are dealing. Proneness to look for mono-linear causation may explain why print culture has long been blind to most other kinds of causation. And it has been the consensus of modern science and philosophy that we have now shifted from "cause" to "configuration" in all fields of study and analysis. This is why for a physicist like Whittaker, it seems as unfortunate for St. Anselm in the early Middle Ages to have tried to establish the existence of God by pure reason as for Newton to have taken the opposite tack (pp. 126–7): "Newton, though profoundly interested in theology, seems to have held that the physicist can give his undivided attention to investigating the laws which will enable him to predict phenomena, and can leave the deeper problems entirely out of account: he can make it his purpose to describe rather than to explain."

This was the Cartesian technique of separation that ensured that all the neglected aspects of experience would be rolled back into the unconscious. This strategy, which grew from lineal specialism and separation of functions, created the world of dulness, bathos, and mock-profundity that Swift and Pope and Sterne made fun of. Newton was quite eligible as hero for *The Dunciad* and certainly got a place in *Gulliver's Travels*.

We have seen how the alphabet involved the Greeks in a fictional "Euclidean Space."The effect of the phonetic alphabet in translating the audile-tactile world into a visual world, was both in physics and in literature to create the fallacy of "content." Whittaker writes thus (p. 79): "Aristotle regarded the *place* of a body as being defined by the inner surface of a body containing it: bodies which are not contained in other bodies are not in any place, and therefore the first or outermost heaven is not in any place: space and time do not exist beyond it. He concluded that the total extent of the universe is finite."

The Gutenberg galaxy was theoretically dissolved in 1905 with the discovery of curved space, but in practice it had been invaded by the telegraph two generations before that.

✽ Whittaker notes (p. 98) that the space of Newton and Gassendi was "so far as geometry was concerned, the space of Euclid: "it was infinite, homogeneous, and completely featureless, one point being just like another . . ." Much earlier our concern had been to explain why this fiction of homogeneity and uniform continuity had derived from phonetic writing, especially in print form. Whittaker says that from a physics point of view the Newtonian space was "mere emptiness into which things could be put." But even for Newton, the gravitational field seemed incompatible with this neutral space. "As a matter of fact, the successors of Newton felt this difficulty; and, having started with a space that was in itself simply nonentity having no property except a capacity for being occupied, they proceeded to fill it several times over with ethers designed to provide electric, magnetic, and gravitational forces, and to account for the propagation of light." (pp. 98–9)

Perhaps no more striking evidence of the merely visual and uniform character of the space was given than in the famous phrase of Pascal: "Le silence éternel des espaces infinis m'effraie." Some meditation on why silent space should be so terrifying yields much insight into the cultural revolution going on in human sensibilities by the visual stress of the printed book.

But the absurdity of speaking of space as a neutral container will never trouble a culture which has separated its visual awareness from the other senses. Yet, says Whittaker (p. 100) "in Einstein's conception, space is no longer the stage on which the drama of physics is performed: it is itself one of the performers; for gravitation, which is a physical property, is entirely controlled by curvature, which is a geometrical property of space."

With this recognition of curved space in 1905 the Gutenberg galaxy was officially dissolved. With the end of lineal specialisms and fixed points of view, compartmentalized knowledge became as unacceptable as it had always been irrelevant. But the effect of such a segregated way of thinking has been to make science a departmental affair, having no influence on eye and thought except indirectly through its applications. In recent years this isolationist attitude has weakened. And it has been the effort of this book to explain how the illusion of segregation of knowledge had become possible by the isolation of the visual sense by means of alphabet and typography. Perhaps it cannot be said too often. This illusion may have been a good or a bad thing. But there can only be disaster arising from unawareness of the causalities and effects inherent in our own technologies.

In the later seventeenth century there is a considerable amount of alarm and revulsion expressed concerning the growing quantity of printed books. The first hopes for a great reform of human manners by means of the book had met disappointment, and in 1680 Leibnitz was writing:

I fear we shall remain for a long time in our present confusion and indigence through our own fault. I even fear that after uselessly exhausting curiosity without obtaining from our investigations any considerable gain for our happiness, people may be disgusted with the sciences, and that a fatal despair may cause them to fall back into barbarism. To which result that horrible mass of books which keeps on growing might contribute very much. For in the end the disorder will become nearly insurmountable; the indefinite multitude of authors will shortly expose them all to the danger of general oblivion; the hope of glory animating many people at work in studies will suddenly cease; it will be perhaps as disgraceful to be an author as it was formerly honorable. At best, one may amuse himself with little books of the hour which will run their course in a few years and will serve to divert a reader from boredom for a few moments, but which will have been written without any design to promote our knowledge or to deserve the appreciation of posterity. I shall be told that since so many people write it is impossible for all their works to be preserved. I admit that, and I do not entirely disapprove those little books in fashion which are like the flowers of a springtime or like the fruits of an autumn, scarcely surviving a year. If they are well made, they have the effect of a useful conversation, not simply pleasing and keeping the idle out of mischief but helping to shape the mind and language. Often their aim is to induce something good in men of our time, which is also the end I seek by publishing this little work . . . [110]

Leibnitz here envisages the book as the natural successor, as well as executioner, of scholastic philosophy, which might yet return. The book as a spur to fame and as the engine of immortality now seems to him in the utmost danger from "the indefinite multitude of authors." For the general run of books he sees the function of serving as a furtherer of conversation "keeping the idle out of mischief" and "helping to shape the mind and language." It is clear that the book was yet far from having become the main mode of politics and society. It was still a surface fact which had only begun to obscure the traditional lineaments of Western society. With regard to the

[110]*Selections*, ed., Philip P. Wiener, pp. 29–30.

continuing threat of scholastic renewal there is the ever-present literary or visual complaint about oral scholasticism that it is words, words, words. Leibnitz, writing on the "Art of Discovery," says:

> Among the Scholastics there was a certain Jean Suisset called the Calculator, whose works I have not yet been able to find and I have seen only those of a few disciples of his. This Suisset began to use Mathematics in scholastic arguments, but few people imitated him because they would have to give up the method of disputation for that of book-keeping and reasoning, and a stroke of the pen would have spared much clamor.[111]

Pope's *Dunciad* indicts the printed book as the agent of a primitivistic and Romantic revival. Sheer visual quantity evokes the magical resonance of the tribal horde. The box office looms as a return to the echo chamber of bardic incantation.

✽ In 1683–84 there appeared in London by Joseph Moxon, *Mechanick Exercises on the Whole Art of Printing*. The editors point out (p. vii) that "it put in writing a knowledge that was wholly traditional", and that Moxon's book "was by forty years the earliest manual of printing in any languge." Like Gibbon in his retrospect of Rome, Moxon seems to have been animated by a sense of print as having reached a terminus. A similar sentiment inspires *The Tale of a Tub* and *The Battle of the Books* by Dean Swift. But it is to *The Dunciad* that we must turn for the epic of the printed word and its benefits to mankind. For here is the explicit study of plunging of the human mind into the sludge of an unconscious engendered by the book. It has been obscured to posterity, in keeping with the prophecy at the end of Book IV, just why literature should be charged with stupefying mankind, and mesmerically ushering the polite world back into primitivism, the Africa within, and above all, the unconscious. The simple key to this operation is that which we have had in hand throughout this book—the increasing separation of the visual faculty from the interplay with the other senses leads to the re-

[111]*Ibid.*, p. 52.

255

jection from consciousness of most of our experience, and the consequent hypertrophy of the unconscious. This ever-enlarging domain Pope calls the world "of Chaos and old Night." It is the tribal, non-literate world celebrated by Mircea Eliade in *The Sacred and the Profane*.

Martinus Scriblerus in his notes to *The Dunciad* reflects on how much more difficult it is to write an epic about the numerous scribblers and industrious hacks of the press than about a Charlemagne, a Brute, or a Godfrey. He then mentions the need for a satirist "to dissuade the dull and punish the wicked," and looks at the general situation that has brought on the crisis:

We shall next declare the occasion and the cause which moved our Poet
to this particular work. He lived in those days when (after providence had
permitted the Invention of Printing as a scourge for the Sins of the learned)
Paper also became so cheap, and printers so numerous, that a deluge of
authors cover'd the land: Whereby not only the peace of the honest
unwriting subject was daily molested, but unmerciful demands were made
of his applause, yea of his money, by such as would neither earn the one, or
deserve the other; At the same time, the Liberty of the Press was so unlimited,
that it grew dangerous to refuse them either: For they would forthwith
publish slanders unpunish'd, the authors being anonymous; nay the immediate
publishers thereof lay sculking under the wings of an Act of Parliament,
assuredly intended for better purposes.[112]

Next he turns (p. 50) from the general economic causes to the private moral motivation of authors inspired by "Dulness and Poverty; the one born with them, the other contracted by neglect of their proper talents . . ." In a word, the attack is on applied knowledge as it manifests itself in "Industry" and "Plodding." For authors inspired by self-opinion and the craving for self-expression are driven into "setting up this sad and sorry merchandise."

By means of the agglomerate action of many such victims of applied knowledge—that is, self-opinionated authors endowed with Industry and Plodding—there is now the restoration of the reign of Chaos and old Night and the removal of the imperial seat of Dulness their daughter from the City to the Polite world." As the book market expands, the division between intellect and commerce ends. The book trade takes over the functions of wit and spirit and government.

That is the meaning of the opening lines of the first editions of the poem:

> Books and the man I sing, the first who brings
> The Smithfield Muses to the ears of Kings.

It seemed quite unnatural to the "polite world" of the time that decision-making and kingly rule should be accessible to popular authors. We no longer consider it odd or revolting to be ruled by people for whom the book of the month might appear quite respectable fare. Smithfield, where Bar-

112*The Dunciad* (B), ed., James Sutherland, p. 49.

tholomew Fair was kept, was still a place for book-peddling. But in later editions Pope changed the opening:

> The mighty Mother, and her Son, who brings
> The Smithfield Muses to the ear of Kings.

He has encountered the public, the collective unconscious, and dubbed it "the mighty Mother," in accordance with the occultism of his time. It is Joyce's "Lead kindly Fowl" (foule, owl, crowd), which we have seen earlier.

As the book market enlarged and the gathering and reporting of news improved, the nature of authorship and public underwent the great changes that we accept as normal today. The book had retained from manuscript times some of its private and conversational character, as Leibnitz indicated in his evaluation. But the book was beginning to be merged in the newspaper as the work of Addison and Steele reminds us. Improved printing technology carried this process all the way by the end of the eighteenth century and the arrival of the steam press.

Yet Dudek in *Literature and the Press* (p. 46) considers that even after steampower had been applied to printing:

English newspapers in the first quarter of the century, however, were by no means designed to appeal to the whole population. By modern standards they would be considered too dull to interest more than a small minority of serious readers. . . . Early nineteenth century newspapers were run largely for the genteel. Their style was stiff and formal, ranging betwen Addisonian gracefulness and Johnsonian elevation. The contents consisted of small advertisements, of local affairs and national politics, especially of commercial news and long transcriptions of parliamentary reports. . . . the best current literature was noticed in the newspapers. . . . 'In those days', Charles Lamb recalled, 'every morning paper, as an essential retainer to its establishment, kept an author, who was bound to furnish daily a quantum of witty paragraphs. . . .' And since the divorce between the language of journalism (journalese) and the literary use of language had not yet been brought about, we find in the eighteenth and early nineteenth century that some of the principal men of letters contributed to the newspapers or made a living by writing.

But Pope peopled his *Dunciad* with these very figures, for his perceptions and criticisms were not personal or based on a private point of view. Rather he was concerned with a total change. It is significant that this change is not specified until the fourth book of *The Dunciad*, which came out in 1742. It is after introducing the famous classics master, Dr. Busby of Westminster school, that we hear the ancient and especially Ciceronian theme concerning the excellence of man (IV, ll. 147–50):

> The pale Boy-Senator yet tingling stands,
> And holds his breeches close with both his hands.

257

Then thus. 'Since Man from beast by Words is known,
Words are Man's province, Words we teach alone.'

Earlier we had noted the meaning of this theme for Cicero who regarded eloquence as an inclusive wisdom harmonizing our faculties, unifying all knowledge. Pope is here quite explicit in citing the destruction of this unity as deriving from word specialism and denudation. The theme of the denudation of consciousness we have followed continuously throughout the Renaissance. It is also the theme of Pope's *Dunciad*. The Boy-Senator continues:

> When Reason doubtful, like the Samian letter,
> Points him two ways, the narrower is the better.
> Plac'd at the door of Learning, youth to guide,
> We never suffer it to stand too wide.
> To ask, to guess, to know, as they commence,
> As Fancy opens the quick springs of Sense,
> We ply the Memory, we load the brain,
> Bind rebel Wit, and double chain on chain,
> Confine the thought, to exercise the breath;
> And keep them in the pale of Words till death.
> Whate'er the talents, or howe'er design'd,
> We hang one jingling padlock on the mind:
> A Poet the first day, he dips his quill;
> And what the last? a very Poet still.
> Pity! the charm works only in our wall,
> Lost, lost too soon in yonder House or Hall.

Pope has not received his due as a serious analyst of the intellectual *malaise* of Europe. He continues Shakespeare's argument in *Lear* and Donne's in the *Anatomy of the World*:

> 'Tis all in pieces, all coherence gone,
> All just supply and all relation.

It is the division of sense and the separation of words from their functions that Pope decries exactly as does Shakespeare in *King Lear*. Art and science had been separated as visual quantification and homogenization penetrated to every domain and the mechanization of language and literature proceeded:

> Beneath her foot-stool *Science* groans in Chains,
> And Wit dreads Exile, Penalties and Pains.
> There foam'd rebellious *Logic* gagg'd and bound,
> There, strip fair *Rhet'ric* languish'd on the ground;[113]

---

[113]*Ibid.*, IV, ll. 21–4.

The new collective unconscious Pope saw as the accumulating backwash of private self-expression.

✱ Pope had a very simple scheme for his first three books. Book I deals with authors, their egotism and desire for self-expression and eternal fame. Book II turns to the book sellers who provide the conduits to swell the tides of public confession. Book III concerns the collective unconscious, the growing backwash from the tidal wave of self-expression. It is Pope's simple theme that the fogs of Dulness and new tribalism are fed by the printing press. Wit, the quick interplay among our senses and faculties, is thus steadily anesthetized by the encroaching unconscious. Anybody who tried to get Pope's meaning by considering the content of the writers he presents would miss the needed clues. Pope is offering a formal causality, not an efficient causality, as an explanation of the metamorphosis from within. The entire matter is thus to be found in a single couplet (I, ll. 89–90):

> Now night descending, the proud scene was o'er,
> But liv'd, in Settle's numbers, one day more.

Print, with its uniformity, repeatability, and limitless extent, does give reincarnate life and fame to anything at all. The kind of limp life so conferred by dull heads upon dull themes formalistically penetrates all existence. Since readers are as vain as authors, they crave to view their own conglomerate visage and, therefore, demand the dullest wits to exert themselves in ever greater degree as the collective audience increases. The "human interest" newspaper is the ultimate mode of this collective dynamic:

> Now May'rs and Shrieves all hush'd and satiate lay,
> Yet eat, in dreams, the custard of the day;
> While pensive Poets painful vigils keep,
> Sleepless themselves to give their readers sleep.[114]

Of course, Pope does not mean that the readers will be bored by the products of sleepless poets or news writers. Quite the contrary. They will be thrilled, as by seeing their own image in the press. The readers' sleep is of the spirit. In their wits they are not pained but impaired.

Pope is telling the English world what Cervantes had told the Spanish world and Rabelais the French world concerning print. It is a delirium. It

---

[114]*Ibid.*, IV, ll. 91–4.

259

is a transforming and metamorphosing drug that has the power of imposing its assumptions upon every level of consciousness. But for us in the 1960's, print has much of the quaint receding character of the movie and the railway train. In recognizing its hidden powers at this late date we can learn to stress the positive virtues of print but we can gain insight into the much more potent and recent forms of radio and television also.

In his analysis of books, authors, and markets, Pope, like Harold Innis in *The Bias of Communication*, assumes that the entire operation of print in our lives is not only unconscious but that for this very reason it immeasurably enlarges the domain of the unconscious. Pope placed an owl at the beginning of *The Dunciad*, and Innis entitled the opening chapter of *The Bias of Communication*, "Minerva's Owl": "Minerva's Owl begins its flight only in the gathering dusk . . ."

Aubrey Williams has a fine treatment[115] of the second *Dunciad* of 1729 in which he quotes Pope's own words to Swift:

The Dunciad is going to be printed in all pomp. . . . It will be attended with
Proeme, Prolegomena, Testimonia Scriptorum, Index Authorum, and
Notes *Variorum*. As to the latter, I desire you to read over the text, and make
a few in any way you like best, whether dry raillery, upon the style and way
of commenting of trivial critics; or humorous, upon the authors in the poem;
or historical, of persons, places, times; or explanatory; or collecting the
parallel passages of the ancients.

Instead, that is, of a mere individual book attack on Dulness, Pope has provided a collective newspaper format and much "human interest" for the poem. He can thus render the plodding industry of Baconian applied knowledge and group toil with a dramatic quality that renders, yet irradiates, the very Dulness he decries. Williams points out (p. 60) that the reason why "the new material attached to the poem has never been adequately defined is due, I think, to the assumptions most critics and editors have made: that the notes are to be taken at the level of history, and that their main purpose is to continue the personal satire in a prose commentary."

[115]*Pope's Dunciad*, p. 60.

The last book of *The Dunciad* proclaims the metamorphic power of mechanically applied knowledge as a stupendous parody of the Eucharist.

✱ The entire fourth book of *The Dunciad* has to do with the theme of *The Gutenberg Galaxy*, the translation or reduction of diverse modes into a single mode of homogenized things. Right off, (ll. 44–5) this theme is rendered in terms of the new Italian opera.

> When lo' a Harlot form soft sliding by,
> With mincing step, small voice, and languid eye;

In the new chromatics, Pope finds (ll. 57–60) the all-reducing and homogenizing power that the book exercises on the human spirit:

> One Trill shall harmonize joy, grief, and rage,
> Wake the dull Church, and lull the ranting Stage;
> To the same notes thy sons shall hum, or snore,
> And all thy yawning daughters cry, *encore.*

Reduction and metamorphosis by homogenization and fragmentation are the persistent themes of the fourth book (ll. 453–6):

> O! would the Sons of Men once think their Eyes
> And Reason giv'n them but to study *Flies!*
> See Nature in some partial narrow shape,
> And let the Author of the Whole escape:

But these were the means by which, as Yeats tells us:

> Locke sank into a swoon;
> The Garden died;
> God took the spinning jenny
> Out of his side.

The popular mesmerism achieved by uniformity and repeatability, taught men the miracles of the division of labour and the creation of world markets. It is these miracles that Pope anticipates in *The Dunciad*, for their transforming power had long affected the mind. The mind now afflicted with the desire and power to climb by sheer sequential additive toil:

> Why all your Toils? Your Sons have learn'd to sing.
> How quick Ambition hastes to ridicule!
> The Sire is made a Peer, the Son a Fool.

Then follows a decisive passage of explicit comment (ll. 549–57) on the Gutenberg miracles of applied knowledge and human transformation:

> On some, a Priest succinct in amice white
> Attends; all flesh is nothing in his sight!
> Beeves, at his touch, at once to jelly turn,
> And the huge Boar is shrunk into an Urn:
> The board with specious miracles he loads,
> Turns Hares to Larks, and Pigeons into Toads.
> Another (for in all what one can shine?)
> Explains the *Seve* and *Verdeur* of the Vine.
> What cannot copious Sacrifice attone?

Pope deliberately makes the miracles of applied knowledge a parody of the Eucharist. It is the same transforming and reducing power of applied knowledge which has confounded and confused all the arts and sciences, for, says Pope, the new *translatio studii* or transmission of studies and disciplines by the printed book has not been so much a transmission as a complete transformation of the disciplines and of the human mind as well. Studies have been translated exactly as was Bottom the Weaver.

How closely Pope's progress of Dulness over the earth conforms to the concept of *translatio studii* can be seen easily if lines 65–112 of Dunciad III are compared to this statement of the historic theme by an English humanist of the fourteenth century, Richard de Bury: 'Admirable Minerva seems to bend her course to all the nations of the earth, and reacheth from end to end mightily, that she may reveal herself to all mankind. We see that she has already visited the Indians, the Babylonians, the Egyptians and Greeks, the Arabs and the Romans. Now she has passed by Paris, and now has happily come to Britain, the most noble of islands, nay, rather a microcosm in itself, that she may show herself a debtor both to the Greeks and to the Barbarians.'[116]

And Pope in making Dulness the goddess of the unconscious is contrasting her with Minerva, goddess of alert intellect and wit. It is not Minerva but her obverse complement, the owl, that the printed book has conferred on Western man. "However ill-fitting their heroic garb," Williams remarks (p. 59), "one at last finds the dunces invested with uncivilizing powers of epic proportions."

Supported by the Gutenberg technology, the power of the dunces to shape and befog the human intellect is unlimited. Pope's efforts to clarify this basic point have been in vain. His intense concern with the *pattern* of action in his armed horde of nobodies has been mistaken for personal spite. Pope was entirely concerned with the *formalistic pattern* and penetrative and con-

[116]*Ibid.*, p. 47.

figuring power of the new technology. His readers have been befogged by "content" obsession and the practical benefits of applied knowledge. He says in a note to Book III, 1. 337:

Do not gentle reader, rest too secure in thy contempt of the Instruments for such a revolution in learning, or despise such weak agents as have been described in our poem, but remember what the *Dutch* stories somewhere relate, that a great part of their Provinces was once overflow'd, by a small opening made in one of their dykes by a single *Water-Rat*.

But the new mechanical instrument and its mesmerized and homogenized servants, the dunces, are irresistible:

> In vain, in vain,—The all-composing Hour
> Resistless falls: The Muse obeys the Pow'r.
> She comes! she comes! the sable Throne behold
> Of *Night* Primaeval, and of *Chaos* old!
> Before her, *Fancy's* gilded clouds decay,
> And all its varying Rain-bows die away.
> *Wit* shoots in vain its momentary fires,
> The meteor drops, and in a flash expires.
> As one by one, at dread Medea's strain,
> The sick'ning stars fade off th'ethereal plain;
> As Argus' eyes by Hermes' wand opprest,
> Clos'd one by one to everlasting rest;
> Thus at her felt approach, and secret might,
> *Art* after *Art* goes out, and all is Night.
> See skulking *Truth* to her old Cavern fled,
> While the Great Mother bids Britannia sleep,
> And pours her Spirit o'er the Land and Deep.
> She comes! she comes! The Gloom rolls on,
> Mountains of Casuistry heap'd o'er her head!
> *Philosophy*, that lean'd on Heav'n before,
> Shrinks to her second cause, and is no more.
> *Physic* of *Metaphysic* begs defence,
> And *Metaphysic* calls for aid on *Sense*!
> See *Mystery* to *Mathematics* fly!
> In vain! they gaze, turn giddy, rave, and die.
> *Religion* blushing veils her sacred fires,
> And unawares *Morality* expires.
> Nor *public* Flame, nor *private*, dares to shine;
> Nor *human* Spark is left, nor Glimpse *divine*!
> Lo! thy dread Empire, CHAOS! is restor'd;
> Light dies before thy uncreating word:
> Thy hand, great Anarch! lets the curtain fall;
> And Universal Darkness buries All.[117]

This is the Night from which Joyce invites the Finnegans to wake.

[117]*Dunciad* (B), IV, 11. 627–56.

THE GALAXY RECONFIGURED
or the Plight of Mass Man in an Individualist Society

✳ The present volume has employed a mosaic pattern of perception and observation up till now. William Blake can provide the explanation and justification of this procedure. *Jerusalem*, like so much of his other poetry, is concerned with the changing patterns of human perception. Book II, chapter 34, of the poem contains the pervasive theme:

> If Perceptive organs vary, Objects of Perception
> seem to vary:
> If the Perceptive Organs close, their Objects seem to
> close also.

Determined as he was to explain the causes and effects of psychic change, both personal and social, he arrived long ago at the theme of *The Gutenberg Galaxy*:

> The Seven Nations fled before him: they became what
> they beheld.

Blake makes quite explicit that when sense ratios change, men change. Sense ratios change when any one sense or bodily or mental function is externalized in technological form:

> The Spectre is the Reasoning Power in Man, & when separated
> From Imagination and closing itself as in steel in a Ratio
> Of the Things of Memory, It thence frames Laws & Moralities
> To destroy Imagination, the Divine Body, by Martyrdoms & Wars.[1]

Imagination is that ratio among the perceptions and faculties which exists when they are not embedded or outered in material technologies. When so outered, each sense and faculty becomes a closed system. Prior to such outering there is entire interplay among experiences. This interplay or synesthesia is a kind of tactility such as Blake sought in the bounding line of sculptural form and in engraving.

When the perverse ingenuity of man has outered some part of his being in material technology, his entire sense ratio is altered. He is then compelled to behold this fragment of himself "closing itself as in steel." In beholding

---

[1]*Jerusalem*, III, 74.

265

this new thing, man is compelled to become it. Such was the origin of lineal, fragmented analysis with its remorseless power of homogenization:

The Reasoning Spectre
Stands between the Vegetative Man & his Immortal Imagination.[2]

Blake's diagnosis of the problem of his age was, like Pope's in *The Dunciad*, a direct confrontation of the forces shaping human perception. That he sought mythical form by which to render his vision was both necessary and ineffectual. For myth is the mode of simultaneous awareness of a complex group of causes and effects. In an age of fragmented, lineal awareness, such as produced and was in turn greatly exaggerated by Gutenberg technology, mythological vision remains quite opaque. The Romantic poets fell far short of Blake's mythical or simultaneous vision. They were faithful to Newton's single vision and perfected the picturesque outer landscape as a means of isolating single states of the inner life.[3]

It is instructive for the history of human sensibility to note how the popular vogue of the Gothic romance in Blake's time later unfolded into a serious esthetic with Ruskin and the French symbolists. This Gothic taste, trite and ridiculous as it first appeared to serious people, was yet a confirmation of Blake's diagnosis of the defects and needs of his age. It was itself a pre-Raphael or pre-Gutenberg quest for a unified mode of perception. In *Modern Painters* (vol. III, p. 91) Ruskin states the matter in a way which entirely dissociates Gothic medievalism from any historical concern about the Middle Ages. He states the matter in a way that won him the serious interest of Rimbaud and Proust:

A fine grotesque is the expression, in a moment, by a series of symbols thrown together in bold and fearless connection, of truths which it would have taken a long time to express in any verbal way, and of which the connection is left for the beholder to work out for himself; the gaps, left or overleaped by the haste of the imagination, forming the grotesque character.

For Ruskin, Gothic appeared as an indispensable means of breaking open the closed system of perception that Blake spent his life describing and fighting. Ruskin proceeds (p. 96) to explain Gothic grotesque as the best way of ending the regime of Renaissance perspective and single vision or realism:

It is with a view (not the least important among many others bearing upon art) to the reopening of this great field of human intelligence, long entirely closed, that I am striving to introduce Gothic architecture into daily domestic use; and to revive the art of illumination, properly so called; not

[2]*Ibid.*, II, 36.
[3]This Newtonian theme is developed by myself apropos "Tennyson and Picturesque Poetry" in John Killham, ed., *Critical Essays on the Poetry of Tennyson*, pp. 67–85.

the art of miniature-painting in books, or on vellum, which has ridiculously been confused with it; but of making *writing*, simple writing, beautiful to the eye, by investing it with the great chord of perfect colour, blue, purple, scarlet, white, and gold, and in that chord of colour, permitting the continual play of the fancy of the writer in every species of grotesque imagination, carefully excluding shadow; the distinctive difference between illumination and painting proper, being, that illumination admits *no* shadows, but only gradations of pure colour.

The student of Rimbaud will find that it was while reading this part of Ruskin that Rimbaud found his title for *Illuminations*. The technique of vision in the *Illuminations* or "painted slides," (as Rimbaud called them, in English, on his title page) is exactly as Ruskin delineates the grotesque. But even Joyce's *Ulysses* finds anticipatory designation in the same context:

Hence it is an infinite good to mankind when there is full acceptance of the grotesque, slightly sketched or expressed; and, if field for such expression be frankly granted, an enormous mass of intellectual power is turned to everlasting use, which, in this present century of ours, evaporates in street gibing or vain revelling; all the good wit and satire expiring in daily talk, (like foam on wine,) which in the thirteenth and fourteenth centuries had a permitted and useful expression in the arts of sculpture and illumination, like foam fixed into chalcedony.[4]

Joyce, that is to say, also accepted the grotesque as a mode of broken or syncopated manipulation to permit *inclusive* or simultaneous perception of a total and diversified field. Such, indeed, is symbolism by definition— a collocation, a *parataxis* of components representing insight by carefully established ratios, but without a point of view or lineal connection or sequential order.

Nothing, therefore, could be more remote from Joyce's ratios than the aim of pictorial realism. Indeed, he uses such realism and such Gutenberg technology as part of his symbolism. For example, in the seventh or Aeolus episode of *Ulysses* the technology of the newspaper is made the occasion for introducing all of the nine hundred and more rhetorical figures specified by Quintilian in his *Institutes of Oratory*. The figures of classical rhetoric are archetypes or postures of individual minds. Joyce by means of the modern press translates them into archetypes or postures of collective consciousness. He breaks open the closed system of classical rhetoric at the same time that he cuts into the closed system of newspaper somnambulism. Symbolism is a kind of witty jazz, a consummation of Ruskin's aspirations for the grotesque that would have shocked him a good deal. But it proved to be the only way out of "single vision and Newton's sleep."

Blake had the insights but not the technical resources for rendering his vision. Paradoxically, it was not through the book but through the develop-

[4]John Ruskin, *Modern Painters*, vol. III, p. 96.

ment of the mass press, especially the telegraph press, that poets found the artistic keys to the world of simultaneity, or of modern myth. It was in the format of the daily press that Rimbaud and Mallarmé discovered the means of rendering the interplay of all the functions of what Coleridge called the "esemplastic" imagination.[5] For the popular press offers no single vision, no point of view, but a mosaic of the postures of the collective conciousness, as Mallarmé proclaimed. Yet these modes of collective or tribal consciousness proliferating in the telegraphic (simultaneous) press, remain uncongenial and opaque to the bookmen locked in "single vision and Newton's sleep."

The principal ideas of the eighteenth century were so crude as to seem risible to the wits of the time. The great chain of Being was in its way as comical as the chains which Rousseau proclaimed in his *Social Contract*. Equally inadequate as an idea of order was the merely visual notion of goodness as a *plenum*: "The best of all possible worlds" was merely a quantitative idea of a bag crammed to the utmost with goodies—an idea which lurked still in the nursery world of R. L. Stevenson. ("The world is so full of a number of things.") But in J. S. Mill's *Liberty* the quantitative idea of truth as an ideal container packed with every possible opinion and point of view created mental anguish. For the suppression of any possible aspect of truth, any valid angle, might weaken the whole structure. In fact, the stress on the abstract visual evoked as standards of truth the mere matching of object with object. So unconscious were people of this matching theory as being dominant, that when a Pope or a Blake pointed out that truth is a ratio between the mind and things, a ratio made by the shaping imagination, there was nobody to note or comprehend. Mechanical matching, not imaginative making, will rule in the arts and sciences, in politics and education, until our own time.

Earlier, in presenting Pope's prophetic vision of the return of tribal or collective consciousness, the relation to Joyce's *Finnegans Wake* had been indicated. Joyce had devised for Western man individual pass-keys to the collective consciousness, as he declared on the last page of the *Wake*. He knew that he had solved the dilemma of Western individual man faced with the collective or tribal consequences of first his Gutenberg, and next his Marconi, technologies. Pope had seen the tribal consciousness latent in the new mass culture of the book-trade. Language and the arts would cease to be prime agents of critical perception and become mere packaging devices for releasing a spate of verbal commodities. Blake and the Romantics and the Victorians alike became obsessed with the actualization of Pope's vision in the new organization of an industrial economy embedded in a self-regulating system of land, labour, and capital. The Newtonian laws of mechanics, latent

[5]See H. M. McLuhan, "Joyce, Mallarmé and the Press," *Sewanee Review*, winter, 1954, pp. 38–55.

in Gutenberg typography, were translated by Adam Smith to govern the laws of production and consumption. In accordance with Pope's prediction of automatic trance or "robo-centrism," Smith declared that the mechanical laws of the economy applied equally to the things of the mind: "In opulent and commercial societies to think or to reason comes to be, like every other employment, a particular business, which is carried on by a very few people, who furnish the public with all the thought and reason possessed by the vast multitudes that labour."[6]

Adam Smith is always faithful to the fixed visual point of view and its consequent separation of faculties and functions. But in this passage Smith does seem to sense that the new role of the intellectual is to tap the collective consciousness of "the vast multitudes that labour." That is to say, the intellectual is no longer to direct individual perception and judgment but to explore and to communicate the massive unconsciousness of collective man. The intellectual is newly cast in the role of a primitive seer, *vates*, or hero incongruously peddling his discoveries in a commercial market. If Adam Smith was reluctant to push his view to this point of the transcendental imagination, Blake and the Romantics felt no qualms but turned literature over to the transcendental arm. Henceforth, literature will be at war with itself and with the social mechanics of conscious goals and motivations. For the matter of literary vision will be collective and mythic, while the forms of literary expression and communication will be individualist, segmental, and mechanical. The vision will be tribal and collective, the expression private and marketable. This dilemma continues to the present to rend the individual Western consciousness. Western man knows that his values and modalities are the product of literacy. Yet the very means of extending those values, technologically, seem to deny and reverse them. Whereas Pope fully faced up to this dilemma in *The Dunciad*, Blake and the Romantics tended to devote themselves to one side of it, the mythic and collective. J. S. Mill, Matthew Arnold, and a great many others devoted themselves to the other side of the dilemma, the problem of individual culture and liberty in an age of mass-culture. But neither side has its meaning alone, nor can the causes of the dilemma be found anywhere but in the total galaxy of events that constitute literacy and Gutenberg technology. Our liberation from the dilemma may, as Joyce felt, come from the new electric technology, with its profound organic character. For the electric puts the mythic or collective dimension of human experience fully into the conscious wake-a-day world. Such is the meaning of the title *Finnegans Wake*. While the old Finn cycles had been tribally entranced in the collective night of the unconscious, the new Finn cycle of totally interdependent man must be lived in the daylight of consciousness.

[6]Cited by Raymond Williams, *Culture and Society, 1780–1850*, p. 38.

269

At this point, *The Great Transformation* by Karl Polanyi, on "the political and economic origins of our time," assumes complete relevance in the mosaic of *The Gutenberg Galaxy*. Polanyi is concerned with the stages by which the Newtonian mechanics invaded and transformed society in the eighteenth and nineteenth centuries, only to encounter a reverse dynamic from within. His analysis of how prior to the eighteenth century "the economic system was absorbed in the social system" is exactly parallel to the situation of literature and the arts up till that time. This was true till the time of Dryden, Pope, and Swift, who lived to detect the great transformation. Polanyi enables us (p. 68) to face the familiar Gutenberg principle of practical advance and utility by separation of forms and functions:

As a rule, the economic system was absorbed in the social system, and whatever principle of behavior predominated in the economy, the presence of the market pattern was found to be compatible with it. The principle of barter or exchange, which underlies this pattern, revealed no tendency to expand at the expense of the rest. Where markets were most highly developed, as under the mercantile system, they throve under the control of a centralized administration which fostered autarchy both in the households of the peasantry and in respect to national life. Regulation and markets, in effect, grew up together. The self-regulating market was unknown; indeed the emergence of the idea of self-regulation was a complete reversal of the trend of development.

The principle of self-regulation repeating by reverberation from the New-tonian sphere swiftly entered all the social spheres. It is the principle that Pope mocked in "whatever is is right" and that Swift ridiculed in "the mechanickal operation of the Spirit." It derives from a merely vision image of an uninterrupted chain of Being or a visual *plenum* of the good as "the best of all possible worlds." Granted the merely visual assumptions of lineal continuity or of sequential dependence, the principle of non-interference in the natural order becomes the paradoxical conclusion of applied knowledge.

Through the sixteenth and seventeenth centuries the transformation of mechanization of crafts by the application of visual *method* had proceeded slowly. But it was a procedure of maximal interference with existing non-visual modes. By the eighteenth century the process of applied knowledge had reached such a momentum that it became accepted as a natural process which must not be impeded save at the peril of greater evil: "all partial evil universal good." Polanyi notes (p. 69) this automation of consciousness as follows:

A further group of assumptions follows in respect to the state and its policy. Nothing must be allowed to inhibit the formation of markets, nor must incomes be permitted to be formed otherwise than through sales. Neither must there be any interference with the adjustment of prices to changed market conditions—whether the prices are those of goods, labor, land, or money. Hence there must not only be markets for all elements of industry, but no measure of policy must be countenanced that would influence the action of these markets. Neither price, nor supply, nor demand must be fixed or regulated; only such policies and measures are in order which help to ensure the self-regulation of the market by creating conditions which make the market the only organizing power in the economic sphere.

The assumptions latent in typographic segmentation, and in applied knowledge by the method of fragmenting of crafts and the specializing of social tasks, these assumptions were the more acceptable in the degree that typography enlarged its markets. The same assumptions presided over the formation of Newtonian space and time and mechanics. So literature, industry, and economics were easily accommodated within the Newtonian sphere. Those who questioned these assumptions were simply denying the facts of science. Now that Newton is no longer synonymous with science, we can meditate on the dilemmas of the self-regulating economy and the hedonistic calculus with light hearts and clear heads. But eighteenth century man was locked into a closed visual system that had enveloped him he knew not how. So he proceeded, robo-centred, to carry out the behests of the new vision.

However, in 1709 Bishop Berkeley had published *A New Theory of Vision*, which revealed the lop-sided assumptions of Newtonian optics. Blake, at least, had understood the Berkeleyan critique and had restored tactility to its prime role as agent of unified perception. Today artists and scientists alike concur in praising Berkeley. But his wisdom was lost on his age that was wrapped in "single vision and Newton's sleep." The hypnotized patient carried out the behests of the abstract visual control. Polanyi observes (p. 71):

A self-regulating market demands nothing less than the institutional separation of society into an economic and political sphere. Such a dichotomy is, in effect, merely the restatement, from the point of view of society as a whole, of the existence of a self-regulating market. It might be argued that the separateness of the two spheres obtains in every type of society at all times. Such an inference, however, would be based on a fallacy. True, no society can exist without a system of some kind which ensures order in the production and distribution of goods. But that does not imply the existence of separate economic institutions; normally, the economic order is merely a function of the social, in which it is contained. Neither under tribal, nor feudal, nor mercantile conditions was there, as we have shown, a separate economic system in society. Nineteenth century society, in which economic activity was isolated and imputed to a distinctive economic motive, was, indeed, a singular departure.

Such an institutional pattern could not function unless society was somehow subordinated to its requirements. A market economy can exist only in a market society. We reached this conclusion on general grounds in our analysis of the market pattern. We can now specify the reasons for

271

this assertion. A market economy must comprise all elements of industry, including labor, land, and money. (In a market economy the last also is an essential element of industrial life and its inclusion in the market mechanism has, as we will see, far-reaching institutional consequences.) But labor and land are no other than the human beings themselves of which every society consists and the natural surroundings in which it exists. To include them in the market mechanism means to subordinate the substance of society itself to the laws of the market.

A market economy "can exist only in a market society." But to exist, a market society requires centuries of transformation by Gutenberg technology; hence, the absurdity in the present time of trying to institute market economies in countries like Russia or Hungary, where feudal conditions obtained until the twentieth century. It is possible to set up modern production in such areas, but to create a market economy that can handle what comes off the assembly lines presupposes a long period of psychic transformation, which is to say, a period of altering perception and sense ratios.

When a society is enclosed within a particular fixed sense ratio, it is quite unable to envisage another state of affairs. Thus, the advent of nationalism was quite unforeseen in the Renaissance, although its causes arrived earlier. The Industrial Revolution was well on the way in 1795, yet, as Polanyi points out (p. 89):

... the generation of Speenhamland was unconscious of what was on its way. On the eve of the greatest industrial revolution in history, no signs and portents were forthcoming. Capitalism arrived unannounced. No one had forecast the development of a machine industry; it came as a complete surprise. For some time England had been actually expecting a permanent recession of foreign trade when the dam burst, and the old world was swept away in one indomitable surge towards a planetary economy.

That every generation poised on the edge of massive change should later seem oblivious of the issues and the imminent event would seem to be natural enough. But it is necessary to understand the power and thrust of technologies to isolate the senses and thus to hypnotize society. The formula for hypnosis is "one sense at a time." And new technology possesses the power to hypnotize because it isolates the senses. Then, as Blake's formula has it: "They became what they beheld." Every new technology thus diminishes sense interplay and consciousness, precisely in the new area of novelty where a kind of identification of viewer and object occurs. This somnambulist conforming of beholder to the new form or structure renders those most deeply immersed in a revolution the least aware of its dynamic. What Polanyi observes about the insentience of those involved in the expediting of the new machine industry is typical of all the local and contemporary attitudes to revolution. It is felt, at those times, that the future will be a larger or greatly improved version of the *immediate past*. Just before revolutions the image of the immediate past is stark and firm, perhaps because it is the only area of sense interplay free from obsessional identification with new technological form.

No more extreme instance of this delusion could be mentioned than our present image of TV as a current variation on the mechanical, movie pattern of processing experience by repetition. A few decades hence it will be easy to describe the revolution in human perception and motivation that resulted from beholding the new mosaic mesh of the TV image. Today it is futile to discuss it at all.

Looking back to the revolution in literary forms in the later eighteenth century, Raymond Williams writes in *Culture and Society, 1780–1850* (p. 42) that "changes in convention only occur when there are radical changes in the general structure of feeling." Again, "while in one sense the market was specializing the artist, artists themselves were seeking to generalize their skills into the common property of imaginative truth." (p. 43) This can be seen in the Romantics who, discovering their inability to talk to conscious men, began by myth and symbol to address the unconscious levels of dream life. The imaginative reunion with tribal man was scarcely a voluntary strategy of culture.

One of the most radical of new literary conventions of the market society of the eighteenth century was the novel. It had been preceded by the discovery of "equitone prose." Addison and Steele, as much as anybody else, had devised this novelty of maintaining a single consistent tone to the reader. It was the auditory equivalent of the mechanically fixed view in vision. Mysteriously, it is this break-through into equitone prose which suddenly enabled the mere author to become a "man of letters." He could abandon his patron and approach the large homogenized public of a market society in a consistent and complacent role. So that with both sight and sound given homogeneous treatment, the writer was able to approach the mass public. What he had to offer the public was equally a homogenized body of common experience such as the movie finally took over from the novel. Dr. Johnson devoted his *Rambler no. 4* (March 31, 1750) to this theme:

> The works of fiction, with which the present generation seems more particularly delighted, are such as exhibit life in its true state, diversified only by accidents that daily happen in the world, and influenced by passions and qualities which are really to be found in conversing with mankind.

Johnson shrewdly notes the consequences of this new form of social realism, indicating its basic deviation from the forms of book learning:

> The task of our present writers is very different; it requires, together with that learning which is to be gained from books, that experience which can never be attained by solitary diligence, but must arise from general converse and accurate observation of the living world. Their performances have, as Horace expresses it, *plus oneris quantum veniae minus*, little indulgence,

and therefore more difficulty. They are engaged in portraits of which every one knows the original, and can detect any deviation from exactness of resemblance. Other writings are safe, except from the malice of learning, but these are in danger from every common reader; as the slipper ill executed was censured by a shoemaker who happened to stop in his way at the Venus of Apelles.

Johnson continues in this vein, pointing out further rivalries between the new novel and the older modes of book learning:

In the romances formerly written, every transaction and sentiment was so remote from all that passes among men, that the reader was in very little danger of making any applications to himself; the virtues and crimes were equally beyond his sphere of activity; and he amused himself with heroes and with traitors, deliverers and persecutors, as with beings of another species, whose actions were regulated upon motives of their own, and who had neither faults nor excellencies in common with himself.

But when an adventurer is levelled with the rest of the world, and acts in such scenes of the universal drama, as may be the lot of any other man; young spectators fix their eyes upon him with closer attention, and hope, by observing his behaviour and success, to regulate their own practices, when they shall be engaged in the like part.

For this reason these familiar histories may perhaps be made of greater use than the solemnities of professed morality, and convey the knowledge of vice and virtue with more efficacy than axioms and definitions.

Quite parallel with this extension of the book page into the form of a talking picture of ordinary life, was what Leo Lowenthal mentions in *Popular Culture and Society* (p. 75) as "the crucial shift from Patron to Public," citing the testimony of Oliver Goldsmith's 1759 *Enquiry into the Present State of Polite Learning in Europe*:

At present the few poets of England no longer depend on the Great for subsistence, they have now no other patrons but the public, and *the public, collectively considered, is a good and generous master.* . . . A writer of real merit now may easily be rich if his heart be set only on fortune: and for those who have no merit, it is but fit that such should remain in merited obscurity.

Leo Lowenthal's new study of popular literary culture is not only concerned with the eighteenth century and after, but studies the dilemmas of diversion *v.* salvation through art from Montaigne and Pascal to modern magazine iconology. In pointing out how Goldsmith made a great change in criticism by shifting attention to the *experience* of the reader, Lowenthal has broken rich new ground (pp. 107–8):

But perhaps the most far-reaching change which took place in the concept of the critic was that a two-way function was premised for him. Not only was he to reveal the beauties of literary works to the general public by means of which, in Goldsmith's terms, "even the philosopher may acquire popular applause"; he must also interpret the public back to the writer. In brief, the critic not only "teaches the vulgar on what part of a character to lay the emphasis of praise," he must also show "the scholar where to point his application so as to deserve it." Goldsmith believed that the absence of such critical mediators explained why wealth rather than true literary fame was the goal of so many writers. The result, he feared, might be that nothing would be remembered of the literary works of his time.

We have observed that Goldsmith, in his endeavor to come to grips with the dilemma of the writer, represented a variety of sometimes conflicting views. We have seen, however, that it was likely to be Goldsmith in his optimistic rather than in his pessimistic vein who set the tone for what was to come. So, too, his view of the "ideal" critic, of his function as one of mediation between the audience and the writer, was to prevail. Critics, writers, and philosophers—Johnson, Burke, Hume, Reynolds, Kames, and the Whartons—all adopted Goldsmith's premise as they began to analyze the experience of the reader.

As the market society defined itself, literature moved into the role of consumer commodity. The public became patron. Art reversed its role from guide for perception into convenient amenity or package. But the producer or artist was compelled, as never before, to study the effect of his art. This in turn revealed to human attention new dimensions of the function of art. As manipulators of the mass market tyrannized over the artist, the artist in isolation achieved new clairvoyance concerning the crucial role of design and of art as a means to human order and fulfilment. Art has become as total in its mandate for human order as the mass markets that created the plateau from which all can now share the awareness of new scope and potential for everyday beauty and order in all aspects of life at once. Retrospectively, it may well prove necessary to concede to the period of mass marketing the creation of the means of a world order in beauty as much as in commodities.

It is quite easy to establish the fact that the same means that served to create the world of consumer abundance by mass production served also to put the highest levels of artistic production on a more assured and consciously controlled basis. And, as usual, when some previously opaque area becomes translucent, it is because we have moved into another phase from which we can contemplate the contours of the preceding situation with ease and clarity. It is this fact that makes it feasible to write *The Gutenberg Galaxy* at all. As we experience the new electronic and organic age with ever stronger indications of its main outlines, the preceding mechanical age becomes quite intelligible. Now that the assembly line recedes before the new patterns of information, synchronized by electric tape, the miracles of mass-production assume entire intelligibility. But the novelties of automation, creating workless and propertyless communities, envelop us in new uncertainties.

275

A most luminous passage of A. N. Whitehead's classic *Science and the Modern World* (p. 141) is one that was discussed previously in another connection.

The greatest invention of the nineteenth century was the invention of the method of invention. A new method entered into life. In order to understand our epoch, we can neglect all the details of change, such as railways, telegraphs, radios, spinning machines, synthetic dyes. We must concentrate on the method in itself; that is the real novelty, which has broken up the foundations of the old civilisation. The prophecy of Francis Bacon has now been fulfilled; and man, who at times dreamt of himself as a little lower than the angels, has submitted to become the servant and the minister of nature. It still remains to be seen whether the same actor can play both parts.

Whitehead is right in insisting that "we must concentrate on the method itself." It was the Gutenberg method of homogeneous segmentation, for which centuries of phonetic literacy had prepared the psychological ground, that evoked the traits of the modern world. The numerous galaxy of events and products of that method of mechanization of handicrafts, are merely incidental to the method itself. It is the method of the fixed or specialist point of view that insists on repetition as the criterion of truth and practicality. Today our science and method strive not towards a point of view but to discover how not to have a point of view, the method not of closure and perspective but of the open "field" and the suspended judgment. Such is now the only viable method under electric conditions of simultaneous information movement and total human interdependence.

Whitehead does not elaborate on the great nineteenth century discovery of the method of invention. But it is, quite simply, the technique of beginning at the end of any operation whatever, and of working backwards from that point to the beginning. It is the method inherent in the Gutenberg technique of homogeneous segmentation, but not until the nineteenth century was the method extended from production to consumption. Planned production means that the total process must be worked out in exact stages, backwards, like a detective story. In the first great age of mass production of commodities, and of literature as a commodity for the market, it became necessary to study the consumer's experience. In a word it became necessary to examine the *effect* of art and literature before producing anything at all. This is the *literal* entrance to the world of myth.

It was Edgar Allan Poe who first worked out the rationale of this ultimate awareness of the poetic process and who saw that instead of directing the work to the reader, it was necessary to incorporate the reader in the work. Such was his plan in "the philosophy of composition." And Baudelaire and Valéry, at least, recognized in Poe a man of the Leonardo da Vinci stature. Poe saw plainly that the anticipation of effect was the only way to achieve organic control for the creative process. T. S. Eliot, like Baudelaire and

Valéry, gives his entire sanction to Poe's discovery. In a celebrated passage of his essay on *Hamlet*,[7] he writes:

> The only way of expressing emotion in the form of art is by finding an 'objective correlative'; in other words, a set of objects, a situation, a chain of events which shall be the formula of that *particular* emotion; such that when the external facts, which must terminate in sensory experience, are given, the emotion is immediately evoked. If you examine any of Shakespeare's more successful tragedies, you will find this exact equivalence; you will find that the state of mind of Lady Macbeth walking in her sleep has been communicated to you by a skilful accumulation of imagined sensory impressions; the words of Macbeth on hearing of his wife's death strike us as if, given the sequence of events, these words were automatically released by the last event in the series.

Poe set this method to work in many of his poems and stories. But it is most obvious in his invention of the detective story in which Dupin, his sleuth, is an artist-esthete who solves crimes by a method of artistic perception. Not only is the detective story the great popular instance of working backwards from effect to cause, it is also the form in which the reader is deeply involved as co-author. Such is also the case in symbolist poetry whose completion of effect from moment to moment requires the reader to participate in the poetic process itself.

It is a characteristic chiasmus that waits upon the utmost development of any process that the last phase shall show characteristics opposite to the early phases. A typical example of massive psychic chiasmus or reversal occurred when Western man fought the harder for individuality as he surrendered the idea of unique personal existence. The nineteenth century artists made a mass-surrender of that unique selfhood, that had been taken for granted in the eighteenth century, as the new mass pressures made the burdens of selfhood too heavy. Just as Mill fought for individuality even though he had given up the self, the poets and artists moved towards the idea of impersonal process in art production in proportion as they berated the new masses for impersonal process in the consumption of art products. A similar and related reversal or chiasmus occurred when the consumer of popular art was invited by new art forms to become participant in the art process itself.

This was the moment of transcendence of the Gutenberg technology. The centuries-old separation of senses and functions ended in a quite unexpected unity.

The reversal by which the presence of the new markets and the new masses encouraged the artist to surrender the unique self might have seemed a final consummation for art and technology alike. It was a surrender made

7In *Selected Essays*, p. 145.

277

almost inevitable when the symbolists began to work backwards from effect to cause in the shaping of the art product. Yet it was just at this extreme moment that a new reversal occurred. The art process had no sooner approached the rigorous, impersonal rationale of the industrial process, in the period from Poe to Valéry, than the assembly line of symbolist art was transformed into the new "stream of consciousness" mode of presentation. And the stream of consciousness is an open "field" perception that reverses all aspects of the nineteenth century discovery of the assembly-line or of the "technique of invention." As G. H. Bantock writes of it:

in a world of increasing socialization, standardization, and uniformity, the aim was to stress uniqueness, the purely personal in experience; in one of 'mechanical' rationality, to assert other modes through which human beings can express themselves, to see life as a series of emotional intensities involving a logic different from that of the rational world and capturable only in dissociated images or stream of consciousness musings.[8]

Thus the technique of the suspended judgment, the great discovery of the twentieth century in art and physics alike, is a recoil and transformation of the impersonal assembly-line of nineteenth century art and science. And to speak of the stream of consciousness as unlike the rational world is merely to insist upon visual sequence as the rational norm, handing art over to the unconscious quite gratuitously. For what is meant by the irrational and the non-logical in much modern discussion is merely the rediscovery of the ordinary transactions between the self and the world, or between subject and object. Such transactions had seemed to end with the effects of phonetic literacy in the Greek world. Literacy had made of the enlightened individual a closed system, and set up a gap between appearance and reality which ended with such discoveries as the stream of consciousness.

As Joyce expressed it in the *Wake*, "My consumers are they not my producers?" Consistently, the twentieth century has worked to free itself from the conditions of passivity, which is to say, from the Gutenberg heritage itself. And this dramatic struggle of unlike modes of human insight and outlook has resulted in the greatest of all human ages, whether in the arts or in the sciences. We are living in a period richer and more terrible than the "Shakespearean Moment" so well described by Patrick Cruttwell in his book of the same title. But it has been the business of *The Gutenberg Galaxy* to examine only the mechanical technology emergent from our alphabet and the printing press. What will be the new configurations of mechanisms and of literacy as these older forms of perception and judgment are interpenetrated by the new electric age? The new electric galaxy of events has already moved deeply into the Gutenberg galaxy. Even without collision, such co-

[8]"The Social and Intellectual Background" in *The Modern Age* (The Pelican Guide to English Literature), p. 47.

existence of technologies and awareness brings trauma and tension to every living person. Our most ordinary and conventional attitudes seem suddenly twisted into gargoyles and grotesques. Familiar institutions and associations seem at times menacing and malignant. These multiple transformations, which are the normal consequence of introducing new media into any society whatever, need special study and will be the subject of another volume on *Understanding Media* in the world of our time.

Bibliographic Index

ANSHEN, R. N., *Language: An Inquiry into its Meaning and Function*, Science of Culture
Series, vol. III (New York: Harper, 1957). page 231

AQUINAS, THOMAS, *Summa Theologica*, part III (Taurini, Italy: Marietti, 1932).
23, 98, 106

ARETINO, PIETRO, *Dialogues, including The Courtesan*, trans. Samuel Putnam (New
York: Covici-Friede, 1933). 194–6

———— *The Works of Aretino*, trans. Samuel Putnam (New York: Covici-Friede,
1933). 194–6

ATHERTON, JAMES S., *Books at the Wake* (London: Faber, 1959). 74–5

AUERBACH, ERICH, *Mimesis: The Representation of Reality in Western Literature*,
trans. Willard R. Trask (Princeton: Princeton University Press, 1953). 57

BACON, FRANCIS, *The Advancement of Learning*, Everyman 719 (New York: Dutton,
n.d. [original date, 1605]). 102, 187, 190–2

———— *Essays or Counsels, Civil and Moral*, ed. R. F. Jones (New York: Odyssey
Press, 1939). 189, 190, 233

BALDWIN, C. S., *Medieval Rhetoric and Poetic* (New York: Columbia University Press,
1928). 98

BANTOCK, G. H., "The Social and Intellectual Background," in Boris Ford, ed.,
The Modern Age, Pelican Guide to English Literature (London: Penguin Books,
1961). 278

BARNOUW, ERIK, *Mass Communication* (New York: Rinehart, 1956). 128

BARZUN, JACQUES, *The House of Intellect* (New York: Harper, 1959). 32

BÉKÉSY, GEORG VON, *Experiments in Hearing*, ed. and trans. E. G. Wever (New York:
McGraw-Hill, 1960). 41–2, 53, 63, 127

———— "Similarities Between Hearing and Skin Sensation," *Psychological Review*,
vol. 66, no. 1, Jan., 1959.

BERKELEY, BISHOP, *A New Theory of Vision* (1709), Everyman 483 (New York:
Dutton, n.d.). 17, 53, 271

BERNARD, CLAUDE, *The Study of Experimental Medicine* (New York: Dover
Publications, 1957). 3, 4

BETHELL, S. L., *Shakespeare and the Popular Dramatic Tradition* (London: Staples
Press, 1944). 206

Blake, The Poetry and Prose of William, ed. Geoffrey Keynes (London: Nonsuch
Press, 1932). 265–6

BOAISTUAU, PIERRE, *Theatrum Mundi*, trans. John Alday, 1581 (STC 3170). 203

BONNER, S. F., *Roman Declamation* (Liverpool: Liverpool University Press,
1949). 100–1

BOUYER, LOUIS, *Liturgical Piety* (Notre Dame, Ind.: University of Notre Dame,
1955). 137–40

BRETT, G. S., *Psychology Ancient and Modern* (London: Longmans, 1928). 74

BROGLIE, LOUIS DE, *The Revolution in Physics* (New York: Noonday Press, 1953). 5, 6

BRONSON, B. H., "Chaucer and His Audience," in *Five Studies in Literature*
(Berkeley, Calif.: University of California Press, 1940). 136

BUHLER, CURT, *The Fifteenth Century Book* (Philadelphia: University of
Pennsylvania Press, 1960). 129, 153–4, 208

BURKE, EDMUND, *Reflections on the Revolution in France* (1790), Everyman 460
    (New York: Dutton). 170–1
BUSHNELL, GEORGE HERBERT, *From Papyrus to Print* (London: Grafton, 1947). 62

CAPONIGRI, A. ROBERT, *Time and Idea: The Theory of History in Giambattista Vico*
    (London: Routledge and Kegan Paul, 1953). 250
CAROTHERS, J. C., "Culture, Psychiatry and the Written Word," in *Psychiatry*, Nov.,
    1959. 18–20, 22, 26–8, 32–4
CARPENTER, E. S., *Eskimo* (identical with *Explorations*, no. 9; Toronto: University
    of Toronto Press, 1960). 66–7
CARPENTER, E. S., and H. M. MCLUHAN, "Acoustic Space," in *idem*, eds., *Explorations in*
    Communication (Boston: Beacon Press, 1960). 19, 136
CARTER, T. F., *The Invention of Printing in China and its Spread Westward* (1931),
    2nd rev. ed., ed. L. C. Goodrich (New York: Ronald, 1955). 40
CASSIRER, ERNST, *Language and Myth*, trans. S. K. Langer (New York: Harper,
    1946). 25, 26
CASTRO, AMERICO, "Incarnation in Don Quixote," in Angel Flores and M. I. Bernadete,
    eds., *Cervantes Across the Centuries* (New York: Dryden Press, 1947). 225–7
—————— *The Structure of Spanish History* (Princeton: Princeton University Press,
    1954). 225–6
CHARDIN, PIERRE TEILHARD DE, *Phenomenon of Man*, trans. Bernard Wall (New York:
    Harper, 1959). 46, 174, 179
CHAUCER, GEOFFREY, *Canterbury Tales*, ed. F. N. Robinson, Student's Cambridge ed.
    (Cambridge, Mass.: Riverside Press, 1933). 96
CHAYTOR, H. J., *From Script to Print* (Cambridge: Heffer and Sons, 1945). 86–9, 92–3
CICERO, *De oratore*, Loeb Library no. 348–9 (Cambridge, Mass.: Harvard
    University Press, n.d.). 24, 98, 101
CLAGETT, MARSHALL, *The Science of Mechanics in the Middle Ages* (Madison, Wisc.:
    University of Wisconsin Press, 1959). 80–1
CLARK, D. L., *Rhetoric and Poetry in the Renaissance* (New York: Columbia
    University Press, 1922). 98
CLARK, J. W., *The Care of Books* (Cambridge: Cambridge University Press, 1909). 92
COBBETT, WILLIAM, *A Year's Residence in America*, 1795 (London: Chapman and
    Dodd, 1922). 171–2
CROMBIE, A. C., *Medieval and Early Modern Science* (New York: Doubleday Anchor
    books, 1959). 120, 123, 124
CRUMP, G. C., and E. F. JACOB, eds., *The Legacy of the Middle Ages* (Oxford: Oxford
    University Press, 1918). 127
CRUTTWELL, PATRICK, *The Shakespearean Moment* (New York: Columbia
    University Press, 1955; New York: Random House, 1960, Modern Library
    paperback). 1, 278
CURTIS, CHARLES P., *It's Your Law* (Cambridge, Mass.: Harvard University
    Press, 1954). 165–6
CURTIUS, ERNST ROBERT, *European Literature and the Latin Middle Ages*, trans.
    W. R. Trask (London: Routledge and Kegan Paul, 1953). 186–7

DANIELSSON, BROR, *Studies on Accentuation of Polysyllabic Latin, Greek, and Romance*
    Loan-Words in English (Stockholm: Almquist and Wiksell, 1948). 232
DANTZIG, TOBIAS, *Number: The Language of Science*, 4th ed. (New York:
    Doubleday, 1954, Anchor book). 81, 177–81
DESCARTES, RENE, *Principles of Philosophy*, trans. Holdvane and Rose (Cambridge:
    Cambridge University Press, 1931; New York: Dover Books, 1955). 243

DEUTSCH, KARL, *Nationalism and Social Communication* (New York: Wiley, 1953). 236

DIRINGER, DAVID, *The Alphabet* (New York: Philosophic Library, 1948). 47–50

DODDS, E. R., *The Greeks and the Irrational* (Berkeley: University of California Press, 1951; Boston: Beacon Press paperback, 1957). 51–2

DUDEK, LOUIS, *Literature and the Press* (Toronto: Ryerson Press, 1960). 217, 257

EINSTEIN, ALBERT, *Short History of Music* (New York: Vintage Books, 1954). 61

ELIADE, MIRCEA, *The Sacred and the Profane: The Nature of Religion*, trans. W. R. Trask (New York: Harcourt Brace, 1959). 51, 68–71, 256

ELIOT, T. S., *Selected Essays* (London: Faber and Faber, 1932). 276–7

FARRINGTON, BENJAMIN, *Francis Bacon, Philosopher of Industrial Science* (London: Lawrence and Wishart, 1951). 184–5

FEBVRE, LUCIEN, and MARTIN, HENRI-JEAN, *L'Apparition du livre* (Paris: Editions Albin Michel, 1950). 129, 142–3, 207–8, 214, 228–30

FISHER, H. A. L., *A History of Europe* (London: Edward Arnold, 1936). 26

FLORES, ANGEL, and M. I. BERNADETE, eds., *Cervantes Across the Centuries* (New York: Dryden Press, 1947). 225–7

FORD, BORIS, ed., *The Modern Age*, The Pelican Guide to English Literature (London: Penguin Books, 1961). 278

FORSTER, E. M., *Abinger Harvest* (New York: Harcourt Brace, 1936; New York: Meridian Books, 1955). 203

FRAZER, SIR JAMES, *The Golden Bough*, 3rd ed. (London: Macmillan, 1951). 90–1

FRIEDENBERG, EDGAR Z., *The Vanishing Adolescent* (Boston: Beacon Press, 1959). 214–15

FRIES, CHARLES CARPENTER, *American English Grammar* (New York: Appleton, 1940). 232, 238

FRYE, NORTHROP, *Anatomy of Criticism* (Princeton: Princeton University Press, 1957). 193

GIEDION, SIEGFRIED, *Mechanization Takes Command* (New York: Oxford University Press, 1948). 44, 147

———— *The Beginnings of Art* (in progress; quoted in *Explorations in Communication*). 65–6

GIEDION-WELCKER, CAROLA, *Contemporary Sculpture*, 3rd rev. ed. (New York: Wittenborn, 1960). 251

GILMAN, STEPHEN, "The Apocryphal Quixote," in Angel Flores and M. I. Bernadete, eds., *Cervantes Across the Centuries* (New York: Dryden Press, 1947). 227

GILSON, ETIENNE, *La Philosophie au Moyen Age* (Paris: Payot, 1947). 185

———— *Painting and Reality* (New York: Pantheon Books, Bollingen Series, xxxv. 4, 1957). 51

GOLDSCHMIDT, E. P., *Medieval Texts and Their First Appearance in Print* (Oxford: Oxford University Press, 1943). 130–5

GOLDSMITH, OLIVER, *Enquiry into the Present State of Polite Learning in Europe*, cited by Leo Lowenthal in *Popular Culture and Society*. 274

GOMBRICH, E. H., *Art and Illusion* (New York: Pantheon Books, Bollinger Series xxxc. 5, 1960). 16, 51, 52–3, 81–2

GREENSLADE, S. L., *The Work of William Tyndale* (London and Glasgow: Blackie and Son, 1938). 228

GRONINGEN, BERNARD VAN, *In the Grip of the Past* (Leiden: E. J. Brill, 1953). 56–8

GUÉRARD, ALBERT, *The Life and Death of an Ideal: France in the Classical Age*
    (New York: Scribner, 1928). 148, 228
GUILBAUD, G. T., *What is Cybernetics?* trans. Valerie Mackay (New York:
    Grove Press, Evergreen ed., 1960). 154–5

HADAS, MOSES, *Ancilla to Classical Learning* (New York: Columbia University Press,
    1954). 62, 85–6, 207
HAJNAL, ISTVAN, *L'Enseignement de l'écriture aux universités médiévales*, 2nd. ed.
    (Budapest: Academia Scientiarum Hungarica Budapestini, 1959). 94–9, 109
HALL, EDWARD T., *The Silent Language* (New York: Doubleday, 1959). 4, 231
HARRINGTON, JOHN H., "The Written Word as an Instrument and a Symbol of the
    Christian Era," Master's thesis (New York: Columbia University, 1946). 109
HATZFELD, HELMUT, *Literature through Art* (Oxford: Oxford University Press,
    1952). 136
HAYES, CARLETON, *Historical Evolution of Modern Nationalism* (New York:
    Smith Publishing Co., 1931). 217–24
HEISENBERG, WERNER, *The Physicist's Conception of Nature* (London: Hutchinson,
    1958). 29
HILDEBRAND, ADOLF VON, *The Problem of Form in the Figurative Arts*, trans.
    Max Meyer and R. M. Ogden (New York: G. E. Stechert, 1907, reprinted
    1945). 41
HILLYER, ROBERT, *In Pursuit of Poetry* (New York: McGraw-Hill, 1960). 232
HOLLANDER, JOHN, *The Untuning of the Sky* (Princeton: Princeton University Press,
    1961). 60, 202
HOPKINS, GERARD MANLEY, *A Gerard Manley Hopkins Reader*, ed. John Pick
    (New York and London: Oxford University Press, 1953). 83
HUIZINGA, J., *The Waning of the Middle Ages* (New York: Doubleday, 1954;
    Anchor book). 117–18, 120, 138
HUTTON, EDWARD, *Pietro Aretino, The Scourge of Princes* (London: Constable,
    1922). 194, 197
HUXLEY, T. H., *Lay Sermons, Addresses and Reviews* (New York: Appleton,
    1871). 172

INKELES, ALEXANDER, *Public Opinion in Russia* (Cambridge, Mass.: Harvard
    University Press, 1950). 21
INNIS, HAROLD, *Empire and Communications* (Oxford: University of Oxford Press,
    1950). 25, 50, 115
    ——— *Essays in Canadian Economic History* (Toronto: University of Toronto
    Press, 1956). 162
    ——— *The Bias of Communication* (Toronto: University of Toronto Press,
    1951). 25, 61, 216–17, 260
    ——— *The Fur Trade in Canada* (New Haven: Yale University Press, 1930). 216,
    236
IVINS, WILLIAM, JR., *Art and Geometry: A Study in Space Intuitions* (Cambridge,
    Mass.: Harvard University Press, 1946). 39, 40, 54, 81, 112
    ——— *Prints and Visual Communication* (London: Routledge and Kegan Paul,
    1953). 71–3, 77–9, 125–6

JAMES, A. LLOYD, *Our Spoken Language* (London: Nelson, 1938). 87
JOHNSON, SAMUEL, *Rambler* no. 4 (March 31, 1750). 273–4
JONES, R. F., *The Triumph of the English Language* (Stanford, Calif.: Stanford
    University Press, 1953). 224, 227, 229, 240

JONSON, BEN, *Volpone.* 168–9
JOSEPH, B. L., *Elizabethan Acting* (Oxford: Oxford University Press, 1951). 99
JOYCE, JAMES, *Finnegans Wake* (London: Faber and Faber, 1939).
74–5, 83, 150, 183, 217, 245, 263, 268, 278
———— *Ulysses* (New York Modern Library, 1934; New York: Random House,
1961 [new ed.]). 74, 203, 267

KANT, EMMANUEL, *Critique of Practical Reason*, 1788, Library of Liberal Arts ed. 251
KANTOROWICZ, ERNST H., *The King's Two Bodies: A Study in Medieval Political
Theology* (Princeton: Princeton University Press, 1957). 120–3
KENYON, FREDERICK, C., *Books and Readers in Ancient Greece and Rome* (Oxford:
Clarendon Press, 1937). 82, 84–5
KEPES, GYORGY, *The Language of Vision* (Chicago: Paul Theobald, 1939). 126–7
KILLHAM, JOHN, ed., *Critical Essays on Poetry of Tennyson* (London: Routledge
and Kegan Paul, 1960). 266

LATOURETTE, KENNETH SCOTT, *The Chinese, Their History and Culture* (New
York: Macmillan, 1934). 34–5
LECLERC, JOSEPH, *Toleration and the Reformation*, trans. T. L. Westow (New
York: Association Press; London: Longmans, 1960). 223
LECLERCQ, DOM JEAN, *The Love for Learning and the Desire for God*, trans.
Catherine Misrahi (New York: Fordham University Press, 1961). 89–90
Leibnitz, Selections from, ed. Philip P. Wiener (New York: Scribners, 1951). 254–5
LEVER, J. W., *The Elizabethan Sonnet* (London: Methuen, 1956). 206
LEWIS, C. S., *English Literature in the Sixteenth Century* (Oxford: Oxford
University Press, 1954). 149, 228–9
LEWIS, D. B. WYNDHAM, *Doctor Rabelais* (New York: Sheed and Ward,
1957). 147–8, 153
LEWIS, PERCIVAL WYNDHAM, *The Lion and the Fox* (London: Grant Richards,
1927). 119
———— *Time and Western Man* (London: Chatto and Windus, 1927). 63
LORD, ALBERT B., *The Singer of Tales* (Cambridge, Mass.: Harvard University
Press, 1960). 1
LOWE, E. A., "Handwriting," in *The Legacy of the Middle Ages*, ed. G. C. Crump
and E. F. Jacob (Oxford: Oxford University Press, 1928). 127
LOWENTHAL, LEO, *Literature and the Image of Man* (Boston: Beacon Press,
1957). 209, 211, 213–14
———— *Popular Culture and Society* (Englewood Cliffs, New York:
Prentice-Hall, 1961). 274
LUKASIEWICZ, JAN, *Aristotle's Syllogistic* (Oxford: Oxford University Press,
1951). 59

MAHOOD, M. M., *Shakespeare's Wordplay* (London: Methuen, 1957). 231–2
MALLET, C. E., *A History of the University of Oxford* (London: Methuen, 1924). 209
MALRAUX, ANDRÉ, *Psychologie de l'art*, vol. I, *Le Musée imaginaire* (Geneva:
Albert Skira Editeur, 1947). 118
MARLOWE, CHRISTOPHER, *Tamburlaine the Great.* 197, 200
MARROU, H. I., *Saint Augustin et la fin de la culture antique* (Paris: de Coddard,
1938). 99–100
MCGEOCH, JOHN A., *The Psychology of Human Learning* (New York: Longmans,
1942). 141

MCKENZIE, JOHN L., *Two-Edged Sword* (Milwaukee: Bruce Publishing Co., 1956). 165

MCLUHAN, HERBERT MARSHALL, ed. with E. S. Carpenter, *Explorations in Communication* (Boston: Beacon Press, 1960). 19, 136

———— "Inside the Five Sense Sensorium," in *Canadian Architect*, vol. 6, no. 6, June, 1961. 39

———— "Joyce, Mallarmé and the Press," in *Sewanee Review*, Winter, 1954. 268

———— "Myth and Mass Media," in Henry A. Murray, ed., *Myth and Mythmaking* (New York: George Braziller, 1960).

———— "Printing and Social Change," in *Printing Progress: A Mid-Century Report* (Cincinnati: The International Association of Printing House Craftsmen, Inc., 1959). 158

———— "Tennyson and Picturesque Poetry," in John Killham, ed., *Critical Essays of the Poetry of Tennyson* (London: Routledge and Kegan Paul, 1960). 266

———— "The Effects of the Improvement of Communication Media," in *Journal of Economic History*, Dec., 1960. 165

———— "The Effect of the Printed Book on Language in the Sixteenth Century," in *Explorations in Communications*. 84

———— *The Mechanical Bride: Folklore of Industrial Man* (New York: Vanguard Press, 1951). 172, 212

MELLERS, WILFRED, *Music and Society* (London: Denis Dobson, 1946). 200–1

MERTON, THOMAS, "Liturgy and Spiritual Personalism," in *Worship* magazine, Oct., 1960. 137

MILANO, PAOLO, ed., *The Portable Dante*, trans. Laurence Binyon and D. G. Rossetti (New York: Viking Press, 1955). 113–14

MILL, JOHN STUART, *On Liberty*, ed. Alburey Castell (New York: Appleton-Century-Crofts, 1947). 268

MITCHELL, W. F., *English Pulpit Oratory from Andrewes to Tillotson* (London: Macmillan, 1932). 234

MONTAGU, ASHLEY, *Man: His First Million Years* (Cleveland and New York: World Publishing Co., 1957). 76–7

MORE, THOMAS, *Utopia* (Oxford: Clarendon Press, 1904). 129

More, St. Thomas: Selected Letters (1557), ed. E. F. Rogers (New Haven: Yale University Press, 1961). 93, 143–4

MORISON, SAMUEL ELIOT, *Admiral of the Ocean Sea* (New York: Little Brown, 1942). 185

MORRIS, EDWARD P., *On Principles and Methods in Latin Syntax* (New York: Scribners, 1902). 232

MOXON, JOSEPH, *Mechanick Exercises on the Whole Art of Printing* (1683–84), ed. Herbert Davis and Harry Carter (London: Oxford University Press, 1958). 255

MULLER-THYM, B. J., "New Directions for Organization Practice," in *Ten Years Progress in Management, 1950–1960* (New York: American Society of Mechanical Engineers, 1961). 140–1

MUMFORD, LEWIS, *Sticks and Stones* (New York: Norton, 1934; 2nd rev. ed., New York: Dover Publications, 1955). 164

NEF, JOHN U., *Cultural Foundations of Industrial Civilization* (Cambridge: Cambridge University Press, 1958). 167, 181–2, 184

ONG, WALTER, "Ramist Classroom Procedure and the Nature of Reality," in *Studies in English Literature, 1500–1900*, vol. I, no. 1, Winter, 1961. 146

———— *Ramus: Method and the Decay of Dialogue* (Cambridge, Mass.: Harvard University Press, 1958).   129, 159–60

———— "Ramist Method and the Commercial Mind," in *Studies in the Renaissance*, vol. VIII, 1961.   104, 160, 162–3, 168, 174–6

OPIE, IONA and PETER, *Lore and Language of Schoolchildren* (Oxford: Oxford University Press, 1959).   91–2

PANOFSKY, ERWIN, *Gothic Architecture and Scholasticism*, 2nd ed. (New York: Meridian Books, 1957).   106–7, 113

PATTISON, BRUCE, *Music and Poetry of the English Renaissance* (London: Methuen, 1948).   201

PIRENNE, HENRI, *Economic and Social History of Medieval Europe* (New York: Harcourt Brace, 1937; Harvest book 14).   114–16

PLATO, *Dialogues*, trans. B. Jowett (New York: 1895).   25, 27

POLANYI, KARL, *The Great Transformation* (New York: Farrar Strauss, 1944; Boston: Beacon Press paperback, 1957).   270–2

———— Conrad M. Arenberg, and Harry W. Pearson, eds., *Trade and Market in Early Empires* (Glencoe, Ill.: The Free Press, 1957).   2

POPE, ALEXANDER, *The Dunciad*, ed. by James Sutherland, 2nd ed. (London: Methuen, 1953).   155, 255–63, 268–9

POPPER, KARL R., *The Open Society and Its Enemies* (Princeton: Princeton University Press, 1950).   7–9

POULET, GEORGES, *Studies in Human Time*, trans. E. Coleman (Baltimore: Johns Hopkins Press, 1956; New York: Harper Torch Books, 1959).   14–15, 241–3, 247, 249

POUND, EZRA, *The Spirit of Romance* (Norfolk, Conn.: New Directions Press, 1929).   114

POWYS, JOHN COWPER, *Rabelais* (New York: Philosophic Library, 1951).   150

Rabelais, The Works of Mr. Francis, trans. Sir Thomas Urquhart (New York: Harcourt, 1931).   147–8, 153

RASHDALL, HASTINGS, *The University of Europe in the Middle Ages*, 2nd ed. (Oxford: Oxford University Press, 1936).   108

RIESMAN, DAVID J., with REUEL DENNY and NATHAN GLAZER, *The Lonely Crowd* (New Haven: Yale University Press, 1950).   28–9, 214

ROSTOW, W. W., *The Stages of Economic Growth* (Cambridge: Cambridge University Press, 1960).   90

RUSKIN, JOHN, *Modern Painters*, Everyman ed. (New York: Dutton, n.d.).   266–7

RUSSELL, BERTRAND, *ABC of Relativity* (1st ed., 1925), rev. ed. (London: Allen and Unwin, 1958; New York: Mentor paperback, 1959).   41

———— *History of Western Philosophy* (London: Allen and Unwin, 1946).   22

RYAN, EDMUND JOSEPH, *Role of the Sensus Communis in the Psychology of St. Thomas Aquinas* (Cartagena, Ohio: Messenger Press, 1951).   106

RYLE, GILBERT, *The Concept of the Mind* (London: Hutchinson, 1949).   72–3

SAINT BENEDICT, "De opera manum cotidiana" in *The Rule of Saint Benedict*, ed. and trans. by Abbot Justin McCann (London: Burns Oates, 1951).   93

SARTRE, JEAN-PAUL, *What is Literature?* trans. Bernard Frechtman (New York: Philosophic Library, 1949).   199

SCHOECK, R. J., and JEROME TAYLOR, eds., *Chaucer Criticism* (Notre Dame, Ind.: Notre Dame University Press, 1960).   136

287

SCHRAMM, WILBUR, with JACK LYLE and EDWIN B. PARKER, *Television in the Lives of Our Children* (Stanford, Calif.: University of California Press, 1961).   145
SELIGMAN, KURT, *The History of Magic* (New York: Pantheon Books, 1948).   108
SELTMAN, CHARLES THEODORE, *Approach to Greek Art* (New York: E. P. Dutton, 1960).   61–4
Shakespeare, The Complete Works of, ed. G. L. Kittredge (Boston, New York, Chicago: Ginn and Co., 1936).   11–15, 161–3, 169–70, 188–9, 244
SHAKESPEARE, WILLIAM, *Troilus and Cressida*, First Quarto Collotype Facsimile, Shakespeare Association (Sidgwick and Jackson, 1952).   204–5
SIEBERT, F. S., *Freedom of the Press in England 1476–1776: The Rise and Decline of Government Controls* (Urbana, Ill.: University of Illinois Press, 1952).   236–8
SIMSON, OTTO VON, *The Gothic Cathedral* (London: Routledge and Kegan Paul, 1956).   105, 107
SISAM, KENNETH, *Fourteenth Century Verse and Prose* (Oxford: Oxford University Press, 1931).   198
SMALLEY, BERYL, *Study of the Bible in the Middle Ages* (Oxford: Oxford University Press, 1952).   99, 105–6, 110–11
SPENGLER, OSWALD, *The Decline of the West* (London: Allen and Unwin, 1918).   54–5
SUTHERLAND, JAMES, *On English Prose* (Toronto: University of Toronto Press, 1957).   201–2

TAWNEY, R. H., *Religion and the Rise of Capitalism*. Holland Memorial Lectures, 1922 (New York: Pelican books,1947).   209
THOMAS, WILLIAM I., and FLORIAN ZNANIECKI, *The Polish Peasant in Europe and America* (first published Boston: R. G. Badger, 1918–20; New York: Knopf, 1927).   176–7
TOCQUEVILLE, ALEXIS DE, *Democracy in America*, trans. Phillips Bradley (New York: Knopf paperback, 1944).   236
TUVE, ROSAMUND, *Elizabethan and Metaphysical Imagery* (Chicago: University of Chicago Press, 1947).   234

USHER, ABBOTT PAYSON, *History of Mechanical Inventions* (Boston: Beacon Press paperback, 1959).   6, 124, 152

WHITE, JOHN, *The Birth and Rebirth of Pictorial Space* (London: Faber and Faber, 1957).   55
WHITE, LESLIE A., *The Science of Culture* (New York: Grove Press, n.d.).   5
WHITE, LYNN, "Technology and Invention in the Middle Ages," in *Speculum*, vol. XV, April, 1940.   79
WHITEHEAD, A. N., *Science and the Modern World* (New York: Macmillan, 1926).   45, 276
WHITTAKER, SIR EDMUND, *Space and Spirit* (Hinsdale, Ill.: Henry Regnery, 1948).   57, 251–3
WHYTE, LANCELOT LAW, *The Unconscious Before Freud* (New York: Basic Books, 1960).   245–7
WILLEY, BASIL, *The Seventeenth Century Background* (London: Chatto and Windus, 1934).   234–5
WILLIAMS, AUBREY, *Pope's Dunciad* (Baton Rouge, La.: Louisiana State University Press, 1955).   260, 262
WILLIAMS, RAYMOND, *Culture and Society 1780–1950* (New York: Columbia University Press, 1958; Anchor books, 1959).   269, 273
WILLIAMSON, GEORGE, *Senecan Amble* (London: Faber and Faber, 1951).   103

WOLFFLIN, HEINRICH, *Principles of Art History* (New York: Dover Publications, 1915).   41, 81

WILSON, JOHN, "Film Literacy in Africa," in *Canadian Communications*, vol. I, no. 4, Summer, 1961.   38

WORDSWORTH, CHRISTOPHER, *Scholae Academicae: Some Account of the Studies at the English Universities in the Eighteenth Century* (Cambridge: Cambridge University Press, 1910).   211

WRIGHT, L. B., *Middle-Class Culture in Elizabethan England* (Chapel Hill, N.C.: University of North Carolina Press, 1935).   161

YOUNG, J. Z., *Doubt and Certainty in Science* (Oxford: Oxford University Press, 1961).   4

Index of Chapter Glosses

76 Until now a culture has been a mechanical fate for societies, the automatic interiorization of their own technologies.

77 The techniques of uniformity and repeatability were introduced by the Romans and the Middle Ages.

80 The word "modern" was a term of reproach used by the patristic humanists against the medieval schoolmen who developed the new logic and physics.

82 In antiquity and the Middle Ages reading was necessarily reading aloud.

84 Manuscript culture is conversational if only because the writer and his audience are physically related by the form of *publication as performance*.

86 The manuscript shaped medieval literary conventions at all levels.

90 The traditional lore of school children points to the gap between the scribal and typographic man.

92 The medieval monks' reading carrell was indeed a singing booth.

93 In the chantry schools grammar served, above all, to establish oral fidelity.

95 The medieval student had to be paleographer, editor, and publisher of the authors he read.

97 Aquinas explains why Socrates, Christ, and Pythagoras avoided the publication of their teachings.

100 The rise of the schoolmen or *moderni* in the twelfth century made a sharp break with the "ancients" of traditional Christian scholarship.

102 Scholasticism, like Senecanism, was directly related to the oral traditions of aphoristic learning.

105 Scribal culture and Gothic architecture were both concerned with light *through*, not light *on*.

108 Medieval illumination, gloss, and sculpture alike were aspects of the art of memory, central to scribal culture.

110 For the oral man the literal text contains all possible levels of meaning.

111 The sheer increase in the quantity of information movement favoured the visual organization of knowledge and the rise of perspective even before typography.

114 The same clash between written and oral structures of knowledge occurs in medieval social life.

117 The medieval world ended in a frenzy of applied knowledge—new medieval knowledge applied to the recreation of antiquity.

119 Renaissance Italy became a kind of Hollywood collection of *sets* of antiquity, and the new visual antiquarianism of the Renaissance provided an avenue to power for men of any class.

120 Medieval idols of the king

124 The invention of typography confirmed and extended the new visual stress of applied knowledge, providing the first uniformly repeatable "commodity," the first assembly-line, and the first mass-production.

126 A fixed point of view becomes possible with print and ends the image as a plastic organism.

128 How the "natural magic" of the *camera obscura* anticipated Hollywood in turning the spectacle of the external world into a consumer commodity or package.

129 St. Thomas More offers a plan for a bridge over the turbulent river of scholastic philosophy.

130 Scribal culture could have neither authors nor publics such as were created by typography.

134 The medieval book trade was a second-hand trade even as with the dealing today in "old masters."

135 Until more than two centuries after printing nobody discovered how to maintain

a single tone or attitude throughout a prose composition.

137 Later medieval visual stress muddied liturgical piety as much as electronic-field pressure has clarified it today.

141 The "interface" of the Renaissance was the meeting of medieval pluralism and modern homogeneity and mechanism—a formula for blitz and metamorphosis.

144 Peter Ramus and John Dewey were the two educational "surfers" or wave-riders of antithetic periods, the Gutenberg and the Marconi or electronic.

146 Rabelais offers a vision of the future of print culture as a consumer's paradise of applied knowledge.

149 The celebrated earthy tactility of Rabelais is a massive backwash of receding manuscript culture.

151 Typography as the first mechanization of a handicraft is itself the perfect instance not of a new knowledge, but of applied knowledge.

153 Every technology contrived and "outered" by man has the power to numb human awareness during the period of its first interiorization.

155 With Gutenberg Europe enters the technological phase of progress, when change itself becomes the archetypal norm of social life.

159 Applied knowledge in the Renaissance had to take the form of translation of the auditory into visual terms, of the plastic into retinal form.

161 Typography tended to alter language from a means of perception and exploration to a portable commodity.

164 Typography is not only a technology but is in itself a natural resource or staple, like cotton or timber or radio; and, like any staple, it shapes not only private sense ratios but also patterns of communal interdependence.

166 The passion for exact measurement began to dominate the Renaissance.

170 The print-made split between head and heart is the trauma which affects Europe from Machiavelli till the present.

174 The Machiavellian mind and the merchant mind are at one in their simple faith in the power of segmental division to rule all—in the dichotomy of power and morals and of money and morals.

176 Dantzig explains why the language of number had to be increased to meet the needs created by the new technology of letters.

178 How the Greeks encountered the confusion of tongues when numbers invaded Euclidean space.

180 The great sixteenth century divorce between art and science came with accelerated calculators.

183 Francis Bacon, PR voice for the *moderni*, had both his feet in the Middle Ages.

186 A strange wedding of the medieval Book of Nature and the new book from movable types was conducted by Francis Bacon.

188 Bacon's Adam is a medieval mystic and Milton's a trade union organizer.

191 How far did the mass-produced page of print become a substitute for auricular confession.

194 Aretino, like Rabelais and Cervantes, proclaimed the meaning of Typography as Gargantuan, Fantastic, Supra-human.

196 Marlowe anticipated Whitman's barbaric yawp by setting up a national PA system of blank verse—a rising iambic system of sound to suit the new success story.

199 Print, in turning the vernaculars into mass media, or closed systems, created the uniform, centralizing forces of modern nationalism.

200 The divorce of poetry and music was first reflected by the printed page.

201 The oral polyphony of the prose of Nashe offends against lineal and literary decorum.

202 The printing press was at first mistaken for an engine of immortality by everybody except Shakespeare.

206 The portability of the book, like that of the easel-painting, added much to the new cult of individualism.

208 The uniformity and repeatability of print created the "political arithmetic" of the seventeenth century and the "hedonistic calculus" of the eighteenth.

212 The typographic logic created "the outsider," the alienated man, as the type of integral, that is, intuitive and *irrational*, man.

213 Cervantes confronted typographic man in the figure of Don Quixote.

216 Typographic man can express but is helpless to read the configurations of print technology.

218 The historians, although aware that nationalism originated in the sixteenth century, have yet no explanation of this passion that preceded theory.

220 Nationalism insists on equal rights among individuals and among nations alike.

222 The citizen armies of Cromwell and Napoleon were the ideal manifestations of the new technology.

225 The Spaniards had been immunized against typography by their age-old quarrel with the Moors.

228 Print had the effect of purifying Latin out of existence.

229 Typography extended its character to the regulation and fixation of languages.

231 Print altered not only the spelling and grammar but the accentuation and inflection of languages, and made "bad grammar" possible.

233 The levelling of inflexion and of wordplay became part of the program of applied knowledge in the seventeenth century.

235 Print created national uniformity and government centralism, but also individualism and opposition to government as such.

239 Nobody ever made a grammatical error in a non-literate society.

240 The reduction of the tactile qualities of life and language constitute the refinement sought in the Renaissance and repudiated now in the electronic age.

241 The new time sense of typographic man is cinematic and sequential and pictorial.

244 The denuding of conscious life and its reduction to a single level created the new world of the "unconscious" in the seventeenth century. The stage has been cleared of the archetypes or postures of individual mind, and is ready for the archetypes of the collective unconscious.

246 Philosophy was as naive as science in its unconscious acceptance of the assumptions or dynamic of typography.

248 Heidegger surf-boards along on the electronic wave as triumphantly as Descartes rode the mechanical wave.

251 Typography cracked the voices of silence.

253 The Gutenberg galaxy was theoretically dissolved in 1905 with the discovery of curved space, but in practice it had been invaded by the telegraph two generations before that.

255 Pope's *Dunciad* indicts the printed book as the agent of a primitivistic and Romantic revival. Sheer visual quantity evokes the magical resonance of the tribal horde. The box office looms as a return to the echo chamber of bardic incantation.

259 The new collective unconscious Pope saw as the accumulating backwash of private self-expression.

261 The last book of *The Dunciad* proclaims the metamorphic power of mechanically applied knowledge as a stupendous parody of the Eucharist.

MARSHALL MCLUHAN is an Honours graduate in English and Philosophy from the University of Manitoba, where he also received his M.A. in English. He went on to take a B.A. degree at Cambridge University, and then a Ph.D. He has taught at the University of Wisconsin, the University of St. Louis, Assumption University, and the University of Toronto; he has been a professor of English in St. Michael's College of the latter university since 1950. A noted authority on communications, Professor McLuhan was Director of the "Understanding Media" project for the United States Office of Education, 1959–1960. He was co-editor of the influential *Explorations* magazine from 1954 to 1959, and his book-length publications include *The Mechanical Bride* (1951) and (with E. S. Carpenter) *Explorations in Communication* (1960).